A History of African-American Leadership

STUDIES IN MODERN HISTORY

General editors: John Morrill and David Cannadine

This series, intended primarily for students, tackles significant historical issues in concise volumes which are both stimulating and scholarly. The authors combine a broad approach, explaining the current state of our knowledge in the area, with their own research and judgements. The topics chosen range widely in subject, period and place.

Titles already published

A History of African-American Leadership

Third edition

Bruce J. Dierenfield and John White

PEARSON

Harlow, England • London • New York • Boston • San Francisco • Toronto • Sydney
Auckland • Singapore • Hong Kong • Tokyo • Seoul • Taipei • New Delhi
Cape Town • São Paulo • Mexico City • Madrid • Amsterdam • Munich • Paris • Milan

PEARSON EDUCATION LIMITED

Edinburgh Gate
Harlow CM20 2JE
United Kingdom
Tel: +44 (0)1279 623623
Fax: +44 (0)1279 431059
Website: www.pearson.com/uk

First edition published in Great Britain in 1985 as *Black Leadership in America*
Second edition 1990
Third edition published in 2012 as *A History of African-American Leadership*

Pearson Education is not responsible for the content of third-party internet sites.

ISBN: 978-1-4058-1156-9

British Library Cataloguing in Publication Data
A CIP catalogue record for this book can be obtained from the British Library

Library of Congress Cataloging in Publication Data
Dierenfield, Bruce J., 1951-
    A history of African-American leadership / Bruce J. Dierenfield and John White. -- 3rd ed.
      p. cm.
    Previous ed.: Black leadership in America : from Booker T. Washington to Jesse Jackson /
John White. London ; New York : Longman, 1990.
    Includes bibliographical references and index.
    ISBN 978-1-4058-1156-9 (pbk.)
    1. African American leadership--History.   2. African Americans--Politics and government.
3. African Americans--Biography.   4. Black nationalism--United States--History.   5. United
States-Race relations.   I. White, John, 1939-   II. White, John, 1939- Black leadership in
America.   III. Title.
    E185.D54 2012
    920.009296073--dc23
    [B]

                                                                                        2011049050

10 9 8 7 6 5 4 3 2 1
16 15 14 13 12

Set in 10/13.5pt Sabon by 35
Printed and bound in Malaysia (CTP-PPSB)

Contents

Preface to Third Edition

Since the appearance of the second edition of this book (*Black Leadership in America: From Booker T. Washington to Jesse Jackson*) in 1990, the political landscape has shifted dramatically with the improbable election of Barack Obama, the first African-American president. In the jubilation that followed Obama's triumph, there was talk of a "post-racial America," where race is no longer an impediment to someone of color. Although it is clear that the United States has not yet become the color-blind society that Martin Luther King, Jr., dreamed of in his memorable speech on the steps of the Lincoln Memorial in Washington, D.C., it also seems that in some important ways race is less of a barrier than it was when King gave that speech nearly four decades ago.

Interest in African-American history remains as great as, if not greater than, it was when the first and second editions of this book appeared. A virtual tidal wave of books, articles, and encyclopedias have appeared on black leaders, black radicals, black women, black organizations, and the like, especially on the civil rights movement, variously defined. This third edition incorporates some of this new scholarship throughout the text. The introduction, conclusion, and all of the chapters have been revised, especially those on Martin Luther King, Jr., and Malcolm X, and Jesse Jackson, and there are new chapters on Barack Obama and African-American women. This edition remains interested in the themes of continuity and change, conflict and competition, race and class, theory and ideology, as exemplified by the thirteen major leaders selected, and the movements which they inspired or led. In sum, this book gives attention to the goals of successive black protest movements as perceived by their "leaders," participants, and critics, as well as the interactions between the racial philosophies of the leaders themselves.

According to historian H. Viscount "Berky" Nelson, there have been multiple paths to black leadership, with some leaders arising from the humblest of origins, including enslavement, and others from middle-class professions, especially the ministry, journalism, education, government service, the law, and the media. Institutions and organizations, such as the Tuskegee Institute, the National Association for the Advancement of Colored People, the National Council of Negro Women, and the Southern Christian Leadership Conference, often provided the platform for African Americans to become visible, to announce an agenda for change, and to draw upon considerable resources to promote that change. Regardless of their socioeconomic status, profession, or political ideology, all African-American leaders have had a threefold mission—"protect the dignity of their race, speak on behalf of the speechless black majority, and work relentlessly to enhance the fortunes of black Americans."[1]

As Nelson observed, different black leaders pursued different strategies to achieve these objectives, primarily as agents of change or responders to change, depending on the racial landscape at a given time and place. Some black leaders trusted in the democratic process and implored white politicians to protect African Americans. Others led by living exemplary personal lives. Still others demonstrated that African Americans are fully human beings with genuine emotions and talents equal to the demands of any field of endeavor. A large group believed that racial uplift was the key to success in American society, "exhorting their race to strive for social equality, economic development, and political prominence in the larger society." Still others led by adopting a militant posture, either by urging self-defense or racial separatism, if not the abandonment of American society altogether. As African Americans have moved into the mainstream of political life, the definition of black leadership is no longer always identical with race leadership, because most black politicians have at least some, even a majority, of constituents who are white. Furthermore, most black leaders have had to contend with white reactions to black demands, which sometimes affected their styles, tactics, and goals. Finally, the consequences of black leadership were often profound, because the actions taken by black leaders could, and often did, affect an entire race for generations.[2]

The figures selected here as great African-American leaders include men and women, those enslaved and their freed descendants, black nationalists and integrationists, charismatic figures and figures whose strength derived from their organizational bases, African Americans and West Indians, Christian ministers and ministers of the Nation of Islam, educators and the illiterate, journalists and media stars, and propagandists, diplomats, and presidents. Most were passionate speakers or eloquent writers who freely gave their energies to promote a more just society, sometimes at considerable cost, whether financial, social, imprisonment, or even death.

No African-American leader has been "simply followed." Rather, they articulated the feelings and the demands of their constituents. When they were notably in advance of or at variance with their "people," they became isolated, "leaders without followers," or faced criticisms from contending or aspiring "leaders."

After an introductory chapter which focuses on African-American problems and African-American leaders of the 19th century, including Frederick Douglass and Martin Delany, we present separate chapters on major African-American figures, including Booker T. Washington, whose self-help philosophy and apparent acquiescence in segregation cast a long shadow on the history of black leadership ever since; W.E.B. Du Bois; Marcus Garvey; Martin Luther King, Jr.; Malcolm X; Jesse Jackson; and Barack Obama. The chapter on African-American women examines the lives and leadership of Harriet Tubman, Ida B. Wells, Mary McLeod Bethune, Fannie Lou Hamer, Condoleezza Rice, and Oprah Winfrey. While additional black leaders are mentioned in passing, space limitations prevent consideration of still others who enriched the tapestry of black life. What follows is an overview of both African-American history and African-American leadership through a biographical approach. Particular attention is paid to each leader's origins and thoughts and to his or her critics.

Like its predecessors, this edition reflects our belief that an examination of preeminent African-American leaders will reveal one constant factor— reasoned black reactions to prevalent and frequently unremitting white racism. Primarily a work of synthesis and explication, this book will, we hope, encourage readers to consult the updated bibliography, which lists book-length treatments of black leaders, their critics, and the periods in which they lived. This edition draws on the more recent writings of American and British scholars; it is also informed by the constructive suggestions of students, colleagues, and critics in Europe and the United States.

Bruce J. Dierenfield
Department of History
Canisius College

John White
Altrincham
Cheshire
United Kingdom
November, 2011

References

1 H. Viscount "Berky" Nelson, *The Rise and Fall of Modern Black Leadership* (2003), p. xv.

2 Ibid., pp. xv–xvi.

Acknowledgements

Iam particularly grateful to my historian wife Kate, our daughter Elizabeth, my parents, my uncle Charles, and Bob Butler, my supportive colleague in African-American studies at Canisius College. I am also grateful for the friendship and encouragement of Jim Anderson, Mike Birkner, Ken Carter, Jim Giglio, Dean Kotlowski, and Martha & Margaret Swain, as well as my History department colleagues at Canisius. I gladly acknowledge the research help of Canisius students, especially Carrie Hadley and Kevin Valletta; the assistance of the Canisius interlibrary loan office; the tireless and accurate typing of Sylvia Bigler; and the editorial assistance of Brian Kantz, Tom Robb, and Dave Costello. Canisius College and the John R. Oishei Foundation underwrote a Distinguished Teaching Professorship in the African-American Experience, which allowed me to host many venerable leaders of the civil rights movement. At Pearson Education publishers, I thank acquisitions editor Mari Shullaw, publisher Christina Wipf Perry, senior editor Helen Savill, project manager Kathy Auger, and editorial assistants Josie O'Donoghue and Sarah Turpie for their extended patience in waiting for this new edition to be finished and for guiding it through to publication. For my part, this book is dedicated to my brother, David Dierenfield, an attorney and public defender, and his family in St. Paul, Minnesota.

Bruce J. Dierenfield

I am greatly indebted to Bruce J. Dierenfield for his contributions to this new edition—in refining, amplifying and updating much of the text, and for the excellent new chapters on African American Women and Barack Obama. Not least, he has greatly extended the Bibliography. The addition of photographs of major leaders is also welcome.

I would like to dedicate our book to the memory of my friend and mentor Professor John Hope Franklin (1915–2009), who illuminated African-American and Southern history for generations of his readers and students.

John White

Publisher's acknowledgements

We are grateful to the following for permission to reproduce copyright material:

Text

Extract on page 172 from *The Autobiography of Malcolm X, as told to Alex Haley*, Ballantine Books (X, Malcolm 1965) p. 7, From THE AUTOBIOGRAPHY OF MALCOLM X by Malcolm X and Alex Haley, copyright © 1964 by Alex Haley and Malcolm X. Copyright © 1965 by Alex Haley and Betty Shabazz. Used by permission of Random House, Inc. and also published by Hutchinson in the UK and Reprinted with the permission of The Random House Group Ltd.; Extract on page 176 from *The Autobiography of Malcolm X, as told to Alex Haley*, Ballantine Books (X, Malcolm 1965) pp. 294–298, From THE AUTOBIOGRAPHY OF MALCOLM X by Malcolm X and Alex Haley, copyright © 1964 by Alex Haley and Malcolm X. Copyright © 1965 by Alex Haley and Betty Shabazz. Used by permission of Random House, Inc. and also published by Hutchinson in the UK and Reprinted with the permission of The Random House Group Ltd.; Extract on page 177 from *The Autobiography of Malcolm X, as told to Alex Haley*, Ballantine Books (X, Malcolm 1965) p. 307, From THE AUTOBIOGRAPHY OF MALCOLM X by Malcolm X and Alex Haley, copyright © 1964 by Alex Haley and Malcolm X. Copyright © 1965 by Alex Haley and Betty Shabazz. Used by permission of Random House, Inc. and also published by Hutchinson in the UK and Reprinted with the permission of The Random House Group Ltd.; Extract on page 181 from *The Autobiography of Malcolm X, as told to Alex Haley*, Ballantine Books (X, Malcolm 1965) pp. 373–374, From THE AUTOBIOGRAPHY OF MALCOLM X by Malcolm X and Alex Haley, copyright © 1964 by Alex Haley and Malcolm X. Copyright © 1965 by Alex Haley and Betty Shabazz. Used by permission of Random House, Inc. and also published by Hutchinson in the UK and Reprinted with the permission of The Random House Group Ltd.; Extract on page 183 from *The Autobiography of Malcolm X, as told to Alex Haley*, Ballantine Books (X, Malcolm 1965) p. 59, From THE AUTOBIOGRAPHY OF MALCOLM X by Malcolm X and Alex Haley, copyright © 1964 by Alex Haley and Malcolm X. Copyright © 1965 by Alex Haley and Betty Shabazz. Used by permission of Random House, Inc. and also published by Hutchinson in the UK and Reprinted with the permission of The Random House Group

Ltd.; Extract on page 184 from *The Autobiography of Malcolm X, as told to Alex Haley*, Ballantine Books (X, Malcolm 1965) p. 54, From THE AUTOBIOGRAPHY OF MALCOLM X by Malcolm X and Alex Haley, copyright © 1964 by Alex Haley and Malcolm X. Copyright © 1965 by Alex Haley and Betty Shabazz. Used by permission of Random House, Inc. and also published by Hutchinson in the UK and Reprinted with the permission of The Random House Group Ltd.; Extract on page 184 from *The Autobiography of Malcolm X, as told to Alex Haley*, Ballantine Books (X, Malcolm 1965) pp. 215–216, From THE AUTOBIOGRAPHY OF MALCOLM X by Malcolm X and Alex Haley, copyright © 1964 by Alex Haley and Malcolm X. Copyright © 1965 by Alex Haley and Betty Shabazz. Used by permission of Random House, Inc. and also published by Hutchinson in the UK and Reprinted with the permission of The Random House Group Ltd.; Extract on page 184 from *The Autobiography of Malcolm X, as told to Alex Haley*, Ballantine Books (X, Malcolm 1965) pp. 372–373, From THE AUTOBIOGRAPHY OF MALCOLM X by Malcolm X and Alex Haley, copyright © 1964 by Alex Haley and Malcolm X. Copyright © 1965 by Alex Haley and Betty Shabazz. Used by permission of Random House, Inc. and also published by Hutchinson in the UK and Reprinted with the permission of The Random House Group Ltd.; Extract on page 185 from *The Autobiography of Malcolm X, as told to Alex Haley*, Ballantine Books (X, Malcolm 1965) p. 348, From THE AUTOBIOGRAPHY OF MALCOLM X by Malcolm X and Alex Haley, copyright © 1964 by Alex Haley and Malcolm X. Copyright © 1965 by Alex Haley and Betty Shabazz. Used by permission of Random House, Inc. and also published by Hutchinson in the UK and Reprinted with the permission of The Random House Group Ltd.; Extract on page 185 from *The Autobiography of Malcolm X, as told to Alex Haley*, Ballantine Books (X, Malcolm 1965) p. 351, From THE AUTOBIOGRAPHY OF MALCOLM X by Malcolm X and Alex Haley, copyright © 1964 by Alex Haley and Malcolm X. Copyright © 1965 by Alex Haley and Betty Shabazz. Used by permission of Random House, Inc. and also Reprinted with the permission of The Random House Group Ltd. and also published by Hutchinson in the UK and Reprinted with the permission of The Random House Group Ltd.; Extract on page 186 from *The Autobiography of Malcolm X, as told to Alex Haley*, Ballantine Books (X, Malcolm 1965) p. 350, From THE AUTOBIOGRAPHY OF MALCOLM X by Malcolm X and Alex Haley, copyright © 1964 by Alex Haley and Malcolm X. Copyright © 1965 by Alex Haley and Betty Shabazz. Used by permission of Random House, Inc. and also published by Hutchinson in the UK and

Reprinted with the permission of The Random House Group Ltd.; Extract on page 186 from *The Autobiography of Malcolm X, as told to Alex Haley*, Ballantine Books (X, Malcolm 1965) p. 385, p. 389, From THE AUTOBIOGRAPHY OF MALCOLM X by Malcolm X and Alex Haley, copyright © 1964 by Alex Haley and Malcolm X. Copyright © 1965 by Alex Haley and Betty Shabazz. Used by permission of Random House, Inc. and also published by Hutchinson in the UK and Reprinted with the permission of The Random House Group Ltd.; Extract on pages 182–3 from *The Autobiography of Malcolm X, as told to Alex Haley*, Ballantine Books (X, Malcolm 1965) pp. 54–58, From THE AUTOBIOGRAPHY OF MALCOLM X by Malcolm X and Alex Haley, copyright © 1964 by Alex Haley and Malcolm X. Copyright © 1965 by Alex Haley and Betty Shabazz. Used by permission of Random House, Inc. and also published by Hutchinson in the UK and Reprinted with the permission of The Random House Group Ltd.; Extract on pages 183–4 from *The Autobiography of Malcolm X, as told to Alex Haley*, Ballantine Books (X, Malcolm 1965) p. 43, From THE AUTOBIOGRAPHY OF MALCOLM X by Malcolm X and Alex Haley, copyright © 1964 by Alex Haley and Malcolm X. Copyright © 1965 by Alex Haley and Betty Shabazz. Used by permission of Random House, Inc. and also published by Hutchinson in the UK and Reprinted with the permission of The Random House Group Ltd.

The publisher would like to thank the following for their kind permission to reproduce their photographs:

Plate 1 Library of Congress: Harris & Ewing Collection; Plate 2 Library of Congress; Plate 3 Corbis; Plate 4 Alamy Images: CSU Archives / Everett Collection Inc; Plate 5 Corbis: Bettmann; Plate 6 Corbis: Gordon Parks; Plate 7 Corbis: Michael Brennan; Plate 8 Alamy Images: Alliance Images.

Every effort has been made to trace the copyright holders and we apologise in advance for any unintentional omissions. We would be pleased to insert the appropriate acknowledgement in any subsequent edition of this publication.

List of Plates

CHAPTER ONE

Introduction: African-American Leaders and Limited Options

American Negro history is basically a history of the conflict between integrationist and nationalist forces in politics, economics, and culture, no matter what leaders are involved and what slogans are used.[1]

[Harold Cruse]

In the long struggle for racial equality and economic opportunity, African Americans have responded to the rhetoric and proposals of leaders drawn from their ranks. But until the last few decades, African Americans have had only limited opportunities to select their own leaders. Before the American Civil War of the 1860s, enslaved black leaders in the South, such as Gabriel Prosser and Nat Turner, planned conspiracies or led revolts aimed at some form of freedom that was not dependent on white sponsorship or support. Other leaders, such as Frederick Douglass, an ex-slave and the most famous black abolitionist, were initially thrust into the public gaze by their white northern supporters. Booker T. Washington, also a former slave, owed his elevation as much to influential white patrons such as his teacher, Samuel Chapman Armstrong, president Theodore Roosevelt, and the industrialist-turned-philanthropist Andrew Carnegie, as to his own remarkable abilities. Similarly, W.E.B. Du Bois, the towering African-American intellect of the 20th century, became a key figure in the National Association for the Advancement of Colored People with the approval and financial support of white reformers of the Progressive era.

Of the male African-American leaders under consideration, Marcus Garvey, Martin Luther King, Jr., and Jesse Jackson, Sr., owed their rise to

the reception accorded to them by African Americans. Yet they were perceived, if not sanctioned, by whites as leaders of their respective movements.
Malcolm X gained his reputation as much from the distorted publicity he
received from the white-controlled media, as from the endorsement of his
black followers. Whatever their ideological or physiological complexion,
then, African-American leaders have historically depended on white, as
well as black, recognition of their claims to speak for their race. Like their
supporters, black leaders have faced a caste system based on racial discrimination. For long periods, they were effectively denied the franchise,
entry into the major political parties, or access to the centres of power. By
definition, African-American leaders occupied tenuous and vulnerable
positions in their own and surrounding white community. They were,
initially at least, self-styled exemplars of their race.

In *An American Dilemma* (1944), a monumental and influential
sociological study of race funded by the Carnegie Foundation, Swedish
economist Gunnar Myrdal concluded that the spectrum of positions taken
by black leaders ranged from accommodation to protest. In the southern
states, where the racial caste system was most rigid and strictly enforced,
whites sought alliances and tacit agreements with those "accommodating"
black leaders who could help them perpetuate the values and practices
of white supremacy. For their part, black southern leaders needed to
establish and maintain contact with influential whites, who, in turn,
provided them with influence and prestige within the black community.
As Myrdal noted, "The Negro leader in this setting serves a 'function'
to both castes and his influence in both groups is cumulative—prestige
in the Negro community being an effect as well as a cause of prestige
among whites." Similarly, in the northern states, government agencies,
political parties, and philanthropic organizations made "contact" with
the black community through white-appointed or white-approved black
"leaders."[2]

Much of the competitiveness, rivalry, and "opportunism" of black leadership in America has derived from this need to satisfy the demands of white
supporters, while remaining responsive to the desires of African-American
constituents. The black novelist James Baldwin, writing about Martin
Luther King, Jr., observed tartly that "the problem of Negro leadership . . .
has always been extremely delicate, dangerous, and complex. The term
itself becomes remarkably difficult to define, the moment one realizes that
the real role of the Negro leader, in the eyes of the American Republic,
was not to make the Negro a first-class citizen but to keep him content as
a second-class one."[3]

The goals and agitation of black radicals have often served to legitimize the claims of more moderate black leaders, especially Martin Luther King, Jr., in the eyes of white Americans. Thus personal, as well as ideological, rivalries have had positive, as well as dysfunctional, effects in the struggle for black freedom and racial equality. But as Myrdal noted, "Since power and prestige are scarce commodities in the Negro community, the struggle for leadership often becomes ruthless."[4]

Leadership among African Americans has not been confined or limited to a few individuals, however exceptional or charismatic. In the 20th century, the rise of national organizations such as the National Association for the Advancement of Colored People (NAACP), the National Urban League (NUL), the Southern Christian Leadership Conference (SCLC), the Student Nonviolent Coordinating Committee (SNCC), and the Black Panthers, as well as the powerful influence of the black church and the activities of grassroots movements at the state and local levels, have constituted a collective form of civil rights protest. The concerns, demands, and initiatives of black men and women at particular junctures and in specific places have not always been those recognized by the established black leadership class. In some instances, these leaders have, in effect, been led by their followers. Whatever their awareness of grassroots problems and demands, black leaders have necessarily operated within the constraints of what has been termed "a politics of limited options." Historically, these options often reflected significant differences between the limits of permissible activity in the states on either side of the Mason-Dixon line that separated North and South.[5]

The election of Barack Obama in 2008 as the nation's first black president signaled the ultimate triumph of African Americans within the political arena. In some ways, his triumph indicates that skin color is no longer the ultimate barrier to participation in American society that it has been since Africans first arrived in Virginia in 1619. Obama's victory was attributed to many factors, including his relative youth and handsome appearance, his Harvard pedigree and oratorical polish, his mastery of grassroots politics, his understanding of American democracy, and his ability to assuage white concerns about voting for a black man, while still appealing to African Americans who harbored doubts about his commitment to racial matters. Not least, the electorate as a whole was worried about the precipitous decline of the economy, disturbed by the continuing wars in Iraq and Afghanistan, and weary of the Republican administration of George W. Bush. For these reasons, the media—black and white—made Obama its darling newcomer, giving him a decided, perhaps decisive, boost. At the same time, the Obama administration chose to focus on problems facing American society as a whole, rather than address problems faced by poor African Americans.[6]

Perspectives: Black protest and accommodation, 1800–1877

The varied responses of African Americans to their inferior position date from the establishment of slavery in the colonial period. These responses multiplied during the American Revolution, which strengthened the institution of slavery and heightened black aspirations for freedom and equality. Enslaved and free blacks in the North and South resisted or made some kind of accommodation to enslavement and non-citizenship, supported or eschewed proposals for black repatriation or colonization overseas, adapted to or challenged emerging patterns of racial segregation, embraced or rejected notions of their African cultural heritage, favored or discounted alliances with whites, and, in the Negro Convention and abolitionist movements, attacked all forms of racial proscription. By the 1820s, northern and southern states were clearly distinguishable in their attitudes towards slavery, but not in their attitudes towards and treatment of blacks. Indeed, Alexis de Tocqueville, the perceptive French nobleman who visited America in the 1830s, believed that "race prejudice seems stronger in those states that have abolished slavery than in those where it still exists, and nowhere is it more intolerant than in those states where slavery was never known."[7]

Historical investigation has confirmed the accuracy of Tocqueville's impressions. Anti-black sentiment and legislation in the states of the Northeast and the territories of the West marked the period from the early 1800s to the Civil War. Believing that blacks were inferior in intellect and morality, nearly every northern state barred them from voting, serving in the militia, or receiving more than a rudimentary education. Racial segregation was evident in all forms of transportation and in hotels, restaurants, prisons, hospitals, and cemeteries. Several of the newly admitted states in the Midwest and West threatened to exterminate blacks who settled in them. Recalling what the Puritans did to the Wampanoag nation, one white man who lived in Indiana told a state constitutional convention, "It would be better to kill [blacks] off at once, if there is no other way to get rid of them." Some states compelled African Americans to post a $500 bond guaranteeing their good behavior and to produce a court certificate proving their freedom. Minstrel shows—the most popular kind of entertainment in 19th century America—conveyed romanticized images of plantation slavery and crude caricatures of the alleged stupidity, fecklessness, and gullibility of northern free blacks. As they faced increasing competition from white immigrants streaming in from Germany, Ireland, and Britain, free blacks in the North became frozen on the bottom rungs of the economic ladder.[8]

But in one respect at least, black northerners utilized an advantage not shared by their southern counterparts. The expansion of the North's white population through immigration and natural increase provided whites with a sense of security unknown to white southerners. Northern blacks were therefore allowed to retain certain basic liberties, including the right to petition for the redress of grievances, publish their own journals and newspapers, and engage in political protest and activities. In 1827, a group of New Yorkers founded *Freedom's Journal*, the first black newspaper, which was edited by John Russwurm and Samuel Cornish. Their paper attacked the thinly-veiled racism of the American Colonization Society, and asserted that the society's real aim was to strengthen slavery by removing free blacks from the United States and resettling them in West Africa.[9]

Similarly, Richard Allen, a Philadelphia-born slave who purchased his freedom in 1777—the year of his conversion to Methodism—experienced and rejected the church's discriminatory treatment of its black members. In the face of white hostility, Allen concluded that only a separate church, served by black clergy, could meet the spiritual and temporal needs of free blacks. He implemented a black version of Wesleyanism, became the first bishop of the African Methodist Episcopal (AME) Church, and encouraged Africans throughout the North to form their own congregations. While Allen preached a liberation theology that God sided with oppressed peoples, he also told African Americans to embrace Christian nonviolence as a powerful means to transform American society. "Love your enemies," Allen urged, "do good and lend, hoping for nothing again, and your reward will be great." Early in his career, Allen believed that American society could achieve racial reform because "we pray to the same God." As slavery expanded and northern racism intensified, Allen encouraged black emigration to the republic of Haiti, which had become the Western Hemisphere's first black-ruled nation. In 1830, he organized the initial meeting of the Negro Convention Movement, which sent aid to black expatriate communities in Canada. He also helped enslaved Africans in the United States by forming the Free African Society and operating a successful station on the Underground Railroad, both of which assisted freedom-seekers headed to the Promised Land. Allen's remarkable efforts to merge religion, racial politics, and republican citizenship made him one of America's "Black Founding Fathers."[10]

Allen's heroic and pioneering leadership inspired black clerics and other African Americans of the 19th century. In 1829, David Walker, the Boston agent for *Freedom's Journal*, issued his incendiary *Appeal*, which was, in essence, a Black Power manifesto, urging enslaved blacks to strike for their freedom. "To prove . . . that we are MEN and not *brutes*," Walker also called for educated black people to lift up the rest of the black community through literacy, religion, and political awareness. Smuggled copies of the *Appeal* surfaced in the South, leading to rumors of slave insurrection plots. Fearful white southerners enacted even more repressive racial controls, especially concerning "seditious" literature, manumission, and the movement of free blacks. A price tag was placed on Walker's head, and he died under mysterious circumstances the next year.[11]

Echoing Walker, Henry Highland Garnet, a Presbyterian minister of Mandingo descent, denounced human bondage as a system of "cold-blooded murder, blasphemy, and defiance of the laws of God." Having once been a slave on Maryland's Eastern Shore, Garnet's message against the "peculiar institution" was personal and powerful. Garnet declared to the 1843 National Convention of Colored Citizens in Buffalo, New York, that enslaved African Americans would be fully justified in using violence to gain their freedom. Garnet exhorted slaves to "Strike for your lives and liberties. Now is the day and the hour. . . . You cannot suffer greater cruelties than you have already. *Rather die freemen than live to be slaves.* Remember that you are *four millions!* . . . Let your motto be resistance! *resistance! resistance!*" Some in the audience wept, others clenched their fists, but after ex-slave Frederick Douglass refused to support Garnet's call for a slave rebellion, the convention failed to endorse Garnet's "war-like" proposal by a single vote. A disillusioned Garnet turned his attention to black emigration, urging African Americans to resettle in Mexico, Liberia, or the West Indies. In 1858, Garnet established the African Civilization Society to encourage blacks to immigrate to the Niger river valley in West Africa in order to civilize and Christianize indigenous peoples. He also hoped to end the African slave trade by forming cotton plantations in Africa, which would break the monopoly of the American South as the primary supplier to textile factories in the northern states and England. Near the end of his life, Garnet was appointed U.S. minister to Liberia, where he soon died and was buried, following a state funeral.[12]

Such uncompromising sentiments effectively separated black from white abolitionists. Most white abolitionists followed the lead of the unflinching radical William Lloyd Garrison in declaring themselves pacifists, and saw their call for emancipation as an appeal to reason and conscience. In the first issue of his provocative newspaper, the *Liberator*, Garrison set the tone for the radical wing of the anti-slavery movement: "I will be as harsh as truth, and uncompromising as justice. . . . I am in earnest, I will not equivocate, I will not excuse, I will not retreat a single inch, and I will be heard." Although African Americans, such as one-time Garrisonian Frederick Douglass, came to form separate and more militant abolitionist organizations, their earlier alliances with white reformers set precedents for interracial cooperation in the cause of civil rights, which were to be revived in the 20th century by the NAACP, the Urban League, and the Congress of Racial Equality.[13]

After 1830, black northerners increasingly denounced segregated schools as unequal and inferior, and demanded educational integration. The convention movement—confined to the northern states until after the Civil War—operated sporadically from 1830 to 1860. Early conventions, attended by African-American ministers, lawyers, business people, and physicians, lodged protests against slavery and the indignities faced by free blacks. With the support of white reformers, black delegates called for the creation of vocational schools for both blacks and whites. Just as the white-dominated abolitionist movement split between its moral suasionist and political activist wings, so, too, the convention movement became more militant, and endorsed independent black protest against disfranchisement and segregation. "If we act with our white friends," the *Colored American* wrote, "the words we utter will be considered theirs, or their echo." The convention movement failed to secure mass support for any one strategy—cooperation with whites, independent political action, emigrationism—or to achieve black political or social equality. But it did provide forums at the state and national levels for a developing black leadership class that would mature decades later.[14]

The outstanding black leader of the 19th century was undoubtedly Frederick Douglass. Born on Maryland's Eastern Shore in 1818, Douglass was a field hand and then a house slave in Baltimore, where he cleverly learned to read and write. When he could no longer tolerate his condition, Douglass escaped from slavery, married a free black named Anna Murray, and settled in New Bedford, Massachusetts. After seeing a copy of Garrison's abolitionist journal, Douglass became an avowed Garrisonian and a lecturer for the Massachusetts Anti-Slavery Society. An eloquent and impassioned orator, Douglass quickly became the leading spokesperson for abolitionism. When his eloquence raised doubts that he had ever been a slave, or even that he was black, Douglass stripped to his waist in front of white audiences to reveal the scars he had sustained from whippings. For larger audiences, he published his *Narrative of the Life of Frederick Douglass, An American Slave* (1845), a graphic and convincing description of his enslavement and a landmark in abolitionist and African-American literature. Fearful for his safety after the *Narrative* was published, Douglass's friends sent him on a two-year visit to Ireland and Britain, where he impressed audiences with his high intelligence and withering condemnations of slavery. After his British supporters purchased his freedom, Douglass returned to the United States, and moved to Rochester, New York, where he published his weekly newspaper, the *North Star*. The paper's motto was: "Right is of no Sex—Truth is of no Color—God is the Father of us all, and we are all brethren."[15]

As a journalist, essayist, and public speaker, Douglass inveighed against the twin evils of slavery and racial discrimination, but personal rivalries and ideological differences led to his split with the Garrisonians in 1851. Douglass rejected the Garrisonian slogan of "No Union with Slaveholders" as an abandonment of slaves to their often cruel owners. He also disagreed with Garrison's view that the U.S. Constitution was a pro-slavery document, and resented Garrison's intemperate attacks on northern churches, citing the existence of abolitionist sympathizers in some denominations. Douglass also disliked the patronizing attitudes of many white abolitionists, and believed that to be successful, abolitionists must endorse political activism. When John Brown told Douglass about his plan to incite an armed slave rebellion by raiding the federal arsenal at Harpers Ferry, Virginia, Douglass opposed it as fanciful. Virginia, thought Douglass, would "blow" Brown "sky-high." When Brown nonetheless attacked the armory in October, 1859, Douglass fled to Canada for a time, because U.S. marshals were hunting him as a co-conspirator. During the Civil War, Douglass pressed for the acceptance of African Americans into the Union's armed forces, believing that a northern victory would secure the permanent abolition of slavery and citizenship rights for freedpeople. Once president Abraham Lincoln authorized black troops, Douglass recruited African Americans for military service, and sent his son Lewis to fight with the famed 54th Massachusetts regiment. Even more welcome from Douglass's perspective, Abraham Lincoln issued the Emancipation Proclamation in 1863, which imbued the war with a moral imperative and declared the freedom of enslaved blacks in rebel-controlled areas of the South.[16]

In addition to supporting slave abolition, Douglass backed a variety of other reforms, including women's rights, temperance, and world peace, and opposed capital punishment, lynching, and the convict-lease system. He was also a notable advocate of industrial education for African Americans, and stressed the virtues of self-help, capital accumulation, and strict morality. Before the Civil War, Douglass saw formal education as a more pressing need for African Americans than suffrage. By espousing racial pride, protest against all forms of discrimination, and full integration of African Americans into society, Douglass anticipated Booker T. Washington's stress on vocational education and self-help, the concerns of 20th century black nationalists, and Martin Luther King, Jr.'s philosophy of non-violent direct action. During Reconstruction, Douglass stood behind Republican attempts to enforce civil rights for blacks in the defeated South, and pushed for enactment of civil rights legislation and the ratification of the 14th and 15th Amendments, with their guarantees of citizenship and voting rights for African Americans. As a loyal Republican, Douglass supported the corrupt administration of president Ulysses S. Grant, and the Compromise of 1877, despite the Union's abandonment of black southerners to local white rule. As a reward for faithful services to the Republican party, Douglass was appointed a U.S. marshal, a recorder of deeds for the District of Columbia, and the U.S. minister to Haiti.[17]

With the worsening of race relations in the post-Reconstruction South, Frederick Douglass protested vigorously against disfranchisement, lynching, and the spread of segregation, but also advised black southerners to make the best of their situation and to adjust to the reality of white supremacy. Anticipating Booker T. Washington, who delivered his "Atlanta Compromise" address in 1895—the year of Douglass's death—Douglass advocated the founding of an industrial college for blacks, and informed Harriet Beecher Stowe, the celebrated author of *Uncle Tom's Cabin*: "We need mechanics as well as ministers. We need workers in iron, clay, and leather. We have orators, authors, and other professional men, but these reach only certain classes, and get respect for our race in certain select circles. . . . We must not only be able to black boots but to make them."[18]

In 1877, Frederick Douglass moved to Cedar Hill, a fifteen-acre estate outside Washington, D.C., where he was a wealthy and respected elder statesman of the black protest movement. Following the death of his first wife, Douglass married Helen Pitts—a white feminist from a prominent Rochester family—which brought a storm of protest. Douglass's children regarded their father's second marriage as a formal repudiation of them and all black people. The *Weekly News*, a black paper, wrote, "Fred Douglass has married a red-head white girl. . . . Goodbye, black blood in that family. We have no further use for him. His picture hangs in our parlor, we will hang it in the stables." An unperturbed Douglass replied: "My first wife was the color of my mother, and the second, the color of my father." A European tour in the mid-1880s added to his already prodigious international reputation.[19]

Other 19th century African-American spokespersons viewed racial equality as an unrealizable dream and advocated the wholesale emigration of blacks to Africa or to Latin America as the only solution to implacable white racism. New England shipowner Paul Cuffe came from a Quaker background and devoted his fortune to black resettlement in British-ruled Sierra Leone on the coast of West Africa. Born a slave in Jamaica, pioneering newspaper publisher John Russwurm emigrated to Liberia, which borders Sierra Leone, where he edited the *Liberia Herald* and became superintendent of education in the capital of Monrovia. Another powerful advocate of black emigrationism was Martin Delany, who founded the *North Star* with Frederick Douglass and had been drummed out of Harvard's medical school by racist classmates. In his best-known work, *The Condition, Elevation, Emigration, and Destiny of the Colored People of the United States* (1852), Delany declared that African Americans were "a nation within a nation" just "as the Poles in Russia, the Hungarians in Austria, the Welsh, Irish and Scotch in the British dominions." Opposed to black repatriation to Liberia, as Cuffe and the American Colonization Society proposed, and criticizing "those who love to live among whites better than blacks," Delany advocated the establishment of an independent "Black Israel" on Africa's east coast to which African Americans could emigrate. Still later, he thought the West Indies or Latin America offered better prospects. But when the Civil War erupted, Delany abandoned emigrationism in favor of working for racial equality in America. He became the first African-American to become a major in the U.S. army and was later transferred to the Freedmen's Bureau, the one federal agency created to protect the rights of formerly enslaved blacks liberated by the Emancipation Proclamation and Confederate defeat.[20]

In the antebellum period, few blacks responded to calls for mass emigration, since they lacked sufficient funds and, more significantly, regarded themselves as more American than African. But in articulating concepts of black separatism, voluntary repatriation, and identification with Africa, mid-19th century emigrationists made very apparent their conviction that racial equality within America was a chimera.[21]

Within the slave-holding states of the South, black resistance to servitude was pervasive and took many forms, which provided some protection against the power and authority of the master class. These forms ranged from malingering, feigned illness, sabotage, open rebellion, and escape, to the more metaphysical forms of resistance offered by a distinctive African-American religion, with its selective reading of the scriptures, and African-American culture, which was characterized by trickster folktales, songs, dances, jokes, rituals, and family and kinship bonds. Many of the slave songs borrowed the Bible's freedom motif. One spiritual observed, "O my Lord delivered Daniel. O why not deliver me, too? He delivered Daniel from de lion's den, Jonah from de belly ob de whale, And de Hebrew children from de fiery furnace, And why not every man?" Other spirituals had a double meaning: "Run to Jesus, shun the danger, I don't expect to stay much longer here." To survive this hostile environment, the slave community relied on the leadership provided by preachers, conjurers, musicians, and family elders. Despite attempts by some historians to celebrate, if not romanticize, the autonomy of the slave community in the antebellum South, enslaved African Americans, by definition, had severely limited options and room for maneuver, and signally—but understandably —failed to develop traditions of protest or revolutionary leadership. In several dramatic instances, however, black leaders in the slave South of the early 19th century demonstrated their resolve and capacity to plan uprisings against a system designed for their perpetual subjugation.[22]

In 1800, Gabriel, an unusually large and intelligent 24-year-old slave of Thomas Prosser in Henrico County, Virginia, organized a conspiracy aimed at overthrowing slavery and setting up a black state with himself as king. Several hundred men carrying clubs, crudely-made scythes and bayonets, and a few guns were to enter Richmond, capture additional weapons, overcome the white population, and seize governor James Monroe as a hostage to negotiate an end to slavery. The guerrillas were to spare women and children, as well as antislavery Methodists, Quakers, and Frenchmen, and to forge an interracial alliance with white laborers and Catawba Indians. Gabriel, a skilled and literate blacksmith who had been hired out in Richmond foundries, was inspired by the Hebrews' break from Egyptian slavery, the success enjoyed by free urban blacks, the egalitarian philosophy trumpeted during the American and French Revolutions, and the successful Haitian revolt led by Toussaint L'Ouverture, a black general.[23]

Gabriel's meticulous plan involved the systematic allocation of tasks to various individuals, the calculation of how many slaves were likely to support the coup, and clandestine meetings to formulate strategy and tactics. Gabriel hoped that his coup would lead Virginia's 300,000 enslaved Africans to throw off their chains. The far-reaching conspiracy was sabotaged by torrential rains that washed out roads and bridges, and then betrayed to Virginia authorities by two of Gabriel's followers. The incipient slave revolt was crushed, and Gabriel, together with two dozen of his followers, was executed. Despite its failure, Gabriel's conspiracy riveted the fear of slave revolt—and black power—on the mind of the white South. In the aftermath of this close call, Virginia ordered free blacks to leave the state or face re-enslavement. Enslaved Africans found new restrictions, if not outright prohibitions, on their movement, education, and hiring out, especially in cities.[24]

America's largest slave revolt occurred in Louisiana in January, 1811. Five hundred angry slaves wielding cane knives, hoes, axes, and guns left their sugar plantations near Lake Pontchartrain and headed to New Orleans, twenty-five miles away. The rebels were led by Charles Deslondes, a slave driver whose father was a white plantation owner. Shouting "Freedom or Death," the rebels wore militia uniforms they had seized, and marched behind flying flags to the rhythm of the African drums they knew so well, stopping along the way to burn homes, sugarhouses, and crops. Drawing from their Akan, Kongolese, and Creole traditions of armed resistance, the Louisiana rebels intended to capture the city of New Orleans and exercise state power throughout the region. As was typical for slave insurrections, the revolt was crushed quickly, in this case by federal troops and the local militia. Ultimately, more than a hundred rebels were killed, executed, or decapitated, with severed heads put on pikes as a grim reminder to other slaves who might contemplate rebellion. As for Deslondes, his hands were chopped off, his thigh bones broken, and his body roasted on a bed of straw before dying as a martyr to his cause.[25]

A third major slave revolt was organized by Denmark Vesey, a 55-year-old carpenter and former slave from the Caribbean, who was a leading member of the AME Church in Charleston, South Carolina. He had purchased his freedom after winning a lottery, but was unable to buy freedom for his wife or children, which produced an abiding anger against the institution of slavery. Inspired by Old Testament accounts of Jewish enslavement and liberation, Vesey saw himself as a black Moses, destined to lead his people—the new Israelites—out of bondage. He organized small cells of free black and slave insurrectionists, all operating independently from one another. In this way, the detection of a single cell would not doom the entire complex conspiracy. Vesey's audacious plan, which was scheduled for the anniversary of the start of the French Revolution, was to seize the arsenal and block bridges at midnight, kill the governor, set fire to the downtown, and kill every white person the rebels came upon. Vesey also hoped to secure external aid from the West Indies and Africa in order to maintain an independent black state. Like Gabriel's conspiracy, this scheme was betrayed. Vesey had burned all lists of names, but too many people knew who the leaders were. Over 130 of the alleged participants were arrested, and three dozen, including Vesey, were hanged. Although Vesey was nebulous as to the form and structure of the state he wished to establish after the overthrow of slavery, his conspiracy, like that of Gabriel, demonstrated that enslaved Africans and free blacks possessed the capacity for militant leadership and the ability to attract many followers.[26]

The immensity and ingenuity of Vesey's plot greatly frightened slaveholders, who razed the local AME Church, exiled church leaders, and stepped up efforts to preach a more compliant Christianity to their slaves. The state assembly forbade free blacks from entering South Carolina's ports, and the city of Charleston greatly beefed up the municipal guard at an arsenal called the Citadel. The memory of Vesey's conspiracy—whatever it was in fact—lived on, despite efforts to suppress it, and Vesey became a symbol in the struggle for freedom and an inspiration for later abolitionists, including John Brown. When the Civil War erupted, the first black regiment gave this battle cry: "Remember Denmark Vesey of Charleston!"[27]

The most memorable slave rebellion in American history was organized by Nat Turner in Southampton County, Virginia, in August, 1831. The son of an African-born mother, Turner was moved to violence by the mystical experiences of his youth. Like Vesey, Turner drew upon an apocalyptic version of Christian doctrine, together with revelations and prophetic dreams and visions to inspire—and later, to justify—his actions. Notwithstanding the fact that he had been kindly treated by his latest master, Joseph Travis, Turner and seventy of his followers—slave and free—hacked, stabbed, or bludgeoned to death about sixty whites, including the Travis family. At least ten children were decapitated by the "banditti," as newspapers described the assailants. The state militia put down the insurrection within two days, and the state banished or executed several dozen blacks. After eluding capture for several weeks, Turner was discovered, tried, and hung. His revolt terrified the white South, prompted the Virginia state legislature to consider ending slavery, and provided later generations of black militants with an authentic hero.[28]

The small, free black caste in the South led few slave rebellions, but it gained a strong sense of collective worth and individual identity through the founding of religious, fraternal, and educational institutions. This anomalous caste was largely created during the American Revolutionary era of the late 18th century, when the British and the colonists who sought independence offered freedom to slaves who joined their respective armies. Increasingly restrictive laws made manumission more difficult the deeper one moved in the South, but individual blacks joined this caste as they managed to buy their freedom or were otherwise manumitted by their owners. There remained the danger that free blacks could be kidnapped and sold as slaves. Never united as a group because of class, color, and denominational divisions, free blacks faced increasing discrimination and repression in the decades before the Civil War. As the South established institutions and facilities, such as schools, poorhouses, libraries, and steamboats, blacks were either barred from or segregated within them. In 1846, Virginia governor William Smith declared, "The will of God has declared the separation of the negro and the white man, and our laws and feelings approve it." When black convicts could not be readily segregated in Virginia's prisons, state officials leased them to canal and railroad companies, a lucrative arrangement for all but the laborers. Attempting to keep free blacks in line, southern cities required them to register their status, raided free black haunts, whipped those who had not registered, and shipped them beyond city limits. The New Orleans city council required blacks "to wear different clothes than do the whites." Generally more skilled, better-educated, and lighter-skinned than the mass of enslaved Africans, free blacks also faced economic competition from both slaves and whites.[29]

Although free blacks and enslaved blacks had much in common, including ancestry, family ties, work experiences, and church membership, there were also conflicting pressures which effectively weakened any strong sense of racial unity and precluded a slave/free black alliance to overthrow the slaveholding class. Some states barred free blacks from marrying slaves and from gambling, trading, or entertaining bondspeople. The *Richmond Daily Dispatch* conceded, "The whole purpose of the police laws is to prevent the association of free negroes and slaves." However degraded or uncertain their position, free blacks in the South were aware that their prospects for survival, as well as for any economic advancement, depended on their ability to distinguish themselves, in the eyes of whites, from the mass of slaves. Accordingly, wealthy and light-skinned free blacks shunned African churches and benevolent and fraternal organizations favored by darker and poorer free blacks, and formed their own exclusive clubs and organizations. As historian Ira Berlin observed, free blacks of the slave South deferred to whites, and in doing so "satisfied the paternalistic pretensions of upper-class whites," while implicitly renouncing "their objections to the Southern caste system."[30]

To a remarkable degree, these strategies continued into the post-Civil War period. Black southern leaders continued to favor the cautious and conciliatory racial policies that they had practiced and perfected during slavery, and displayed conservative, rather than radical, tendencies. Militant proposals for effecting racial change came out of the northern states with their traditions of free speech and political agitation; more cautious, conciliatory, and diplomatic proposals for racial improvement continued to impress black southerners, aware of the dangers posed by virulent white racism and the continued existence of various forms of coerced labor. During and after Reconstruction, African-American leaders in the former Confederate states were drawn disproportionately from the ranks of antebellum free people of color, or were former slaves who had occupied relatively privileged positions. Collectively, they were moderates, aware of the necessity for compromise or dissimulation, if they were to gain the white patronage necessary to advance themselves and their communities.[31]

The successful African-American leader, Gunnar Myrdal believed, became "a consummate manipulator," cajoling the white man into doing what the black leader desired. Inevitably, the black leader came to derive satisfaction in his manipulative skills in "flattering, beguiling, and outwitting the white man." But there was also the real danger that the southern black leader, who survived by his wits, might become simply a self-seeker, "having constantly to compromise with his pride and dignity." In contrast, black northern leaders were the beneficiaries of a long tradition of sanctioned protest, and were therefore expected to produce displays of "actual opposition" to white racism; in exercising such leadership, northern blacks faced less danger of retaliation from offended whites. But whether they functioned in a more or less relaxed racial environment, black leaders, Myrdal noted, have historically been engaged in a similar "keen and destructive personal rivalry." He was quick to add that "national Negro leadership is no more corrupt nor more ridden with personal envy and rivalry than any other national leadership."[32]

From Booker T. Washington to Barack Obama

Since 1900, six African-American men have gained recognition as outstanding advocates of racial advancement; a seventh African American eschewed race as a category, but he represented the triumph of racial advancement. After the death of Frederick Douglass in 1895, Booker T. Washington (1856–1915), as even his most vociferous critics conceded, was the acknowledged leader of African Americans. The most powerful and influential black man of his day, Washington remains a complex and ambiguous figure. Born a slave, Washington embraced the Protestant ethic of work, godliness, and personal hygiene, and urged the building of black character and business enterprise. Well-versed in the racial mores and etiquette of the South, Washington turned white paternalism and patronage to his advantage, if not to that of his race. As founder and principal of the Tuskegee Institute, a vocational school for African Americans in Alabama, Washington demonstrated his gifts as an administrator, educator, and leader. He also made Tuskegee into a power base—"the Tuskegee Machine"—and extended its influence into the towns and cities of the United States. Any assessment of the black experience after slavery must reckon with this controversial educator, reformer, and interracial diplomat.[33]

At the height of his influence, Washington encountered in William Edward Burghardt Du Bois (1868–1963), his most articulate and distinguished black critic. A New Englander by birth, Du Bois earned a doctorate from Harvard University and became the self-appointed spokesperson for the "talented tenth"—the intellectual black elite which, he believed, would provide the vanguard leadership for the race as a whole. Dedicated to the acquisition of civil and political rights for African Americans, and initially espousing racial integration, Du Bois joined with northern black militants, such as William Monroe Trotter, and with liberal whites, to challenge Washington's influence and power. A poet, novelist, sociologist, historian, and a founding member of the NAACP, Du Bois castigated Washington as the witting or unwitting supporter of white supremacy and permanent black inferiority. Battle lines were drawn, and by the early years of the 20th century, the black protest movement appeared to be polarized between its "accommodationist/conservative" and "radical/ activist" wings. Du Bois spent his long life searching for a way out of the box in which African Americans found themselves, moving successively from political reform, institutional activism, education, propaganda, Communism, and, finally, emigrationism to his beloved Africa. Harvard professor Henry Louis Gates, Jr. observed that Du Bois "spent his intellectual life coming to grips with the past, addressing the present, envisioning a future for American race relations."[34]

While neither Washington nor Du Bois ever commanded a mass following among African Americans, the Jamaican-born Marcus Garvey (1880–1940) achieved that distinction in the course of his short, but spectacular, American career. A declared disciple of Booker T. Washington, Garvey became the leading black nationalist in the United States during and immediately after the First World War. Pledged to the eventual liberation of Africa from white colonial rule, the inculcation of racial pride in African Americans, and the separation of races in America, Garvey's philosophy and his organizational blunders attracted the scorn of Du Bois to an extent that made his earlier differences with Washington appear comparatively innocuous. Garvey returned Du Bois' enmity—and that of other established black leaders—with interest. Where Washington had spoken primarily for a poverty-stricken black peasantry, only recently "up from slavery," and Du Bois for a growing northern black middle class, Garvey capitalized on the depressed condition of the growing urban black population, confined within the physical and psychological constraints of the ghetto. Although Garvey's American career was short-lived, it reflected the rise and significance of Harlem—the black ghetto in New York City—as the most important concentration of African Americans in the United States. Garvey's influence persisted into the 1960s and 1970s, with the re-emergence of a militant black nationalism expressed in the emotive slogan "Black Power," with its connotations of racial assertiveness, separatism, and pride in African-American culture.[35]

When Marcus Garvey was deported for fraud, his star plummeted, leaving room for other leaders to fill, especially as the nation endured the Great Depression and World War II. In the 1930s, Adam Clayton Powell, Jr., pastor of the nation's largest Protestant church, pioneered the use of the black church for social justice ends. A handsome, spellbinding speaker who was inspired by Garvey, Powell organized mass meetings and rent strikes, and pressured Harlem stores, the transit authority, and utility companies to hire black workers, one of the early instances of affirmative action. "Mass action," he remarked, "is the most powerful force on earth." Powell was later elected as the first black U.S. congressman from New York, and helped shepherd major reform legislation through the U.S. House of Representatives. A contemporary of Powell's, black socialist A. Philip Randolph, also embraced the power of mass action. As the United States mobilized for World War II, Randolph threatened U.S.

president Franklin D. Roosevelt with a potentially embarrassing march to the nation's capital to guarantee jobs for African Americans in segregated defense industries. The gambit worked, resulting in a million jobs for African Americans. This March on Washington Movement signaled a shift in black strategy for economic and civil rights.[36]

These innovations by Powell and Randolph notwithstanding, it was not until the appearance of the young black clergyman, Martin Luther King, Jr. (1929–1968), during the momentous Montgomery, Alabama, bus boycott of the mid-1950s, that another African-American spokesperson commanded national—even international—attention. A practitioner of "non-violent" confrontation and direct action to achieve racial integration, King became the personification of the civil rights movement, which had as its ultimate goal the realization of a biracial "beloved community" in America. The climax of King's remarkable career came in his "I Have a Dream" speech in the March on Washington for Jobs and Freedom demonstration of 1963, just as Du Bois died in self-imposed exile in Ghana. It was the passing of the guard. Towards the end of his life, King envisioned a coalition of the underprivileged, black and white, in America. He also became increasingly critical of the American capitalist system and its military involvement in Vietnam.[37]

King's vision for a biracial society did not go unchallenged. Malcolm X (1925–1965), born Malcolm Little, was a preacher and activist like Martin Luther King and, for a significant period, the leading spokesperson for the separatist Nation of Islam, known colloquially as the Black Muslims. Besides being a disciple of the Nation's Elijah Muhammad, Malcolm was an admirer of Marcus Garvey. Following his break with the Nation on doctrinal and personal grounds, Malcolm X became the best-known ideologue for black militancy and racial separatism; he specialized in indicting white America for crimes against humanity. Where Martin Luther King insisted on a gospel of non-violent protest and the redemptive value of love and suffering, Malcolm X urged blacks to defend themselves by "whatever means necessary" and appeared to condone, if not actively promote, racial warfare. The "Black Power" slogan and the subsequent rise of extremist groups, such as the Black Panther party, were, in part, offshoots of Malcolm's black nationalism. Like Garvey, Malcolm X struck a responsive chord among the black underclass of the nation's ghettos; like Martin Luther King, he was to die a violent death, with his attitudes undergoing significant change.[38]

African-American women have always borne a double burden, with their race and gender too often subjecting them to discrimination or scorn.

Even within the black community, women have long been relegated to supporting roles, while their male counterparts took the lead in various fields, especially in religion, business, politics, and civil rights agitation. The list of African-American women who have been leaders in the black community is, of course, a very long one, and these women have represented many fields, ideas, and tactics. While surely not an exhaustive list, certain names come to mind when thinking of extraordinary black women, including businesswomen Madam C.J. Walker and Maggie Lena Walker; entertainers Bessie Smith and Josephine Baker; novelists Zora Neale Hurston and Toni Morrison; athlete Althea Gibson; organizer Dorothy Height; protesters Pauli Murray, Daisy Bates, and Gloria Richardson; philosopher Angela Davis; and children's rights advocate Marian Wright Edelman. Regrettably, limited space in this volume prevents treatment of them. This book does refer to Ella Baker, Carol Moseley Braun, Mary Ann Shadd Cary, Shirley Chisholm, Septima Clark, Barbara Jordan, Diane Nash, Sarah Parker Remond, Jo Ann Robinson, Rosa Parks, Sojourner Truth, and other women as they appear in the historical narrative. An entire chapter looks at the lives and leadership of freedom fighter Harriet Tubman (1820–1913), journalist Ida B. Wells (1862–1931), educator Mary McLeod Bethune (1875–1955), civil rights activist Fannie Lou Hamer (1917–1977), diplomat Condoleezza Rice (b. 1954), and media mogul Oprah Winfrey (b. 1954).[39]

Immediately following the deaths of Martin Luther King and Malcolm X, no African-American leader approached their stature or influence. *Black Enterprise* reported the results of a poll of 5,000 readers which showed that in the 1970s "the absence of clear-cut leadership has been the single most noticeable handicap of the black struggle for equality." The death in 1981 of Roy Wilkins, who had served as the NAACP's executive director for twenty-two years, and the resignation of Vernon Jordan, president of the National Urban League for the previous ten years, came at a time of increasing demoralization and frustration within an already fragmented civil rights movement. After campaigning successfully to outlaw segregation in public accommodations and transportation, and to obtain legislation guaranteeing civil and voting rights, the civil rights coalition became increasingly concerned with economic issues. The average black family income was less than two-thirds that of whites, and the unemployment rate for African Americans was three times greater than that for whites. Accompanying the economic and educational advances made by some African Americans, there was a marked decline in the life-styles and the prospects of millions of other blacks who lived in decaying inner cities. The election of Ronald Reagan to the U.S. presidency in 1980 signaled the onset of a conservative reaction against the "affirmative action" programs instituted by his predecessor, Lyndon Johnson. One poll examining Reagan's election revealed that many whites voted Republican for the first time because—among other reasons—they believed that the Democrats had been too concerned with issues of race relations, poverty, and civil rights.[40]

In the next two election cycles, a serious black contender for the Democratic party's nomination emerged for the first time, and African Americans voted for him in droves. This candidate, Jesse Jackson, Sr. (b. 1941), was a disciple of Martin Luther King, Jr. and had been a prominent member of the Southern Christian Leadership Conference. Jackson failed to gain the party's nomination in 1984 and again in 1988, but he gained enormous popular support among blacks and whites for his projected "Rainbow Coalition"—a modern populist movement of racial minorities, working families, women's rights groups, environmentalists, farmers, labor unions, and peace activists, especially on college campuses. Having been denied elective office, Jackson leveraged black economic power to persuade large corporations to hire and promote African Americans and to award lucrative contracts to black businesses.[41]

After twice failing to win the Democratic party's presidential nomination, Jesse Jackson's political appeal ran dry, and for a generation, no other African-American leader mounted a serious bid for the White House. That changed when president George W. Bush, a Republican, led the United States into two simultaneous wars and drove the economy into the ground. Americans hungered for change in 2008, and found it in the person of U.S. senator Barack Obama (b. 1961) of Illinois, a Harvard-educated lawyer who ran a skillful grassroots campaign that transcended racial boundaries. Obama had a white mother from Kansas and a black father from Kenya, but in the racial understanding of American society, he is "black." And so, Obama is America's first black president, and as such, represents the culmination of the political ambitions of African Americans. But Obama accomplished little for the black masses because he had little inclination to do so and because of the severe constraints of the economic meltdown represented by the collapse of Wall Street.[42]

The following chapters summarize and evaluate the contributions of Booker T. Washington, W.E.B. Du Bois, Marcus Garvey, Martin Luther King, Jr., Malcolm X, prominent African-American women, Jesse Jackson, and Barack Obama in assisting the African-American community and Americans generally to resolve the Gordian knot of race. Particular attention is paid to the words of these African-American leaders, perceptions of them by contemporaries, and subsequent evaluations of them by later commentators. By placing their philosophies and leadership strategies in historical context, we hope to illustrate the themes of change and continuity in black leadership agendas and demands from the late 19th century to the present. Essentially, continuity will be seen to lie in persistent black protest against the inequities of a caste system in a democratic society pledged to the principles enshrined in the Declaration of Independence and the U.S. Constitution. Change will be evident in the varying connotations of such concepts as "integration," "separatism," "accommodation," "conservatism," "radicalism," and "equality" at significant junctures in the African-American experience. In short, our intention is to provide, within short compass, both individual and interrelated biographies of major African-American leaders—and the responses of those whom they professed to lead.

References

1 Harold Cruse, *The Crisis of the Negro Intellectual: From its Origins to the Present* (1967), p. 564.

2 Gunnar Myrdal, *An American Dilemma: The Negro Problem and Modern Democracy* (1944), pp. 722–723.

3 James Baldwin, "The most dangerous road before Martin Luther King," in C. Eric Lincoln, ed., *Martin Luther King Jr.: A Profile* (1970), pp. 106–107.

4 Myrdal, *An American Dilemma*, p. 775.

5 David A. Gerber, "A Politics of Limited Options: Northern Black Politics and the Problem of Change and Continuity in Race Relations Historiography," *Journal of Social History* 14 (1980): 235–355.

6 For thorough accounts of the 2008 presidential election, see David Plouffe, *The Audacity to Win: The Inside Story and Lessons of Barack Obama's Historic Victory* (2009); Dan Balz and Haynes Johnson, *The Battle for America 2008: The Story of an Extraordinary Election* (2009); John Heilemann and Mark Halperin, *Game Change: Obama and the Clintons, McCain and Palin, and the Race of a Lifetime* (2010); Evan Thomas, *"A Long Time Coming": The Inspiring, Combative 2008 Campaign and the Historic Election of Barack Obama* (2009).

7 Howard Holman Bell, *A Survey of the Negro Convention Movement, 1830–1861* (1969); Alexis de Tocqueville, *Democracy in America*, ed. J.P. Mayer & Max Lerner (1966), vol. 1, p. 426.

8 Leon F. Litwack, *North of Slavery: The Free Negro in the Free States, 1790–1860* (1961), pp. 64–186; Robert C. Toll, *Blacking Up: The Minstrel Show in Nineteenth-Century America* (1974), pp. 25–103.

9 Jacqueline Bacon, *Freedom's Journal: The First African-American Newspaper* (2007), pp. 71–280.

10 Richard S. Newman, *Freedom's Prophet: Bishop Richard Allen, the AME Church, and the Founding Fathers* (2008), pp. 9, 20–23, 158–253.

11 Peter P. Hinks, *To Awaken My Afflicted Brethren: David Walker and the Problem of Antebellum Slave Resistance* (1997), pp. 91–115.

12 Martin B. Pasternak, *Rise Now and Fly to Arms: The Life of Henry Highland Garnet* (1995), pp. 3, 45–48; Earl Ofari, *"Let Your Motto Be Resistance": The Life and Thought of Henry Highland Garnet* (1972), pp. 1–2, 30–44, 79–102, 122–123, 144–153.

13 Henry Mayer, *All on Fire: William Lloyd Garrison and the Abolition of Slavery* (2000), pp. 112, 127–150, 327–328, 357, 366–371.

14 Bell, *A Survey of the Negro Convention Movement*, pp. 38–68.

15 William S. McFeely, *Frederick Douglass* (1991), pp. 3–153; Frederick Douglass, *Narrative of the Life of Frederick Douglass, An American Slave* (1845).

16 McFeely, *Frederick Douglass*, pp. 95, 146–149, 192–201, 215–218, 224–226.

17 Ibid., pp. 83, 189, 205, 249–250, 255–256, 265–269, 285, 299, 314–315, 318, 334–356, 361, 363–364, 378–379.

18 Ibid., pp. 231, 235, 241, 245–247, 250–258, 361, 364, 378–379; Frederick Douglass, letter to Harriet Beecher Stowe, 8 March 1863, in Frederick Douglass, *Life and Times of Frederick Douglass* (1884), p. 251.

19 McFeely, *Frederick Douglass*, pp. 296–297, 320.

20 James Oliver Horton and Lois E. Horton, *In Hope of Liberty: Culture, Community, and Protest Among Northern Free Blacks, 1700–1860* (1997), pp. 177–200; Dorothy Sterling, *The Making of an Afro-American: Martin Robison Delany, 1812–1885* (1971), pp. 96–97, 122–135, 140–158, 252–277; Martin Robison Delany, *The Condition, Elevation, Emigration, and Destiny of the Colored People of the United States* (1852), p. 177; P.J. Staudenraus, *The African Colonization Movement, 1816–1865* (1961).

21 Horton and Horton, *In Hope of Liberty*, pp. 200–202.

22 John Hope Franklin and Loren Schweninger, *Runaway Slaves: Rebels on the Plantation* (2000); Lawrence Levine, *Black Culture and Black Consciousness: Afro-American Folk Thought from Slavery to Freedom* (1977), pp. 3–135.

For slave rebellions in New York, see Jill Lepore, *New York Burning: Liberty, Slavery, and Conspiracy in Eighteenth-Century Manhattan* (2005), and Peter Charles Hoffer, *The Great New York Conspiracy of 1741* (2003).

23 Douglas R. Egerton, *Gabriel's Rebellion: The Virginia Conspiracies of 1800 and 1802* (1993), pp. 18–49.

24 Ibid., pp. 50–115.

25 Daniel Rasmussen, *American Uprising: The Untold Story of America's Largest Slave Revolt* (2011).

26 Douglas R. Egerton, *He Shall Go Out Free: The Lives of Denmark Vesey* (2004), pp. 72–202.

27 Ibid., pp. 203–228.

28 Herbert Aptheker, "The Event," in Kenneth S. Greenberg, ed., *Nat Turner: A Slave Rebellion in History and Memory* (2004), pp. 45–57.

29 Ira Berlin, *Slaves without Masters: The Free Negro in the Antebellum South* (1974), pp. 284–340; Leonard P. Curry, *The Free Black in Urban America, 1800–1850* (1981), pp. 1–95.

30 Berlin, *Slaves without Masters*, pp. 326–327, 340.

31 Eric Foner, *Reconstruction: America's Unfinished Revolution, 1863–1877* (1988), pp. 346–411.

32 Myrdal, *An American Dilemma* (1944), pp. 773, 778–779.

33 Robert J. Norrell, *Up from History: Booker T. Washington* (2009).

34 Henry Louis Gates, Jr., and Cornel West, eds., *The African-American Century: How Black Americans Have Shaped Our Country* (2000), pp. 1–7.

35 Colin Grant, *Negro with a Hat: The Rise and Fall of Marcus Garvey* (2008).

36 Charles V. Hamilton, *Adam Clayton Powell, Jr.: The Political Biography of an American Dilemma* (2002); Paula Pfeffer, *A. Philip Randolph: Pioneer of the Civil Rights Movement* (1990), pp. 45–88; Herbert Garfinkel, *The March on Washington Movement in the Organizational Politics for FEPC* (1969).

37 Peter Ling, *Martin Luther King, Jr.* (2002); Marshall Frady, *Martin Luther King, Jr.* (2002); Harvard Sitkoff, *King: Pilgrimage to the Mountaintop* (2008).

38 Peter Goldman, *The Death and Life of Malcolm X* (1979); Bruce Perry, *Malcolm: The Life of the Man Who Changed Black America* (1992).

39 Darlene Clark Hine, ed., *Black Women in America* (2005); Jessie Carney Smith, ed., *Notable Black American Women* (1992).

40 Isaiah J. Poole, "Leadership," *Black Enterprise* 11 (August 1980), pp. 53–56; Andrew E. Busch, *Reagan's Victory: The Presidential Election of 1980 and the Rise of the Right* (2005), pp. 16–17, 98–144.

41 Marshall Frady, *Jesse: The Life and Pilgrimage of Jesse Jackson* (1996).

42 David Remnick, *The Bridge: The Life and Rise of Barack Obama* (2010).

CHAPTER TWO

Booker T. Washington: The Wizard of Tuskegee

I have learned that success is to be measured not so much by the position that one has reached in life as by the obstacles which he has overcome while trying to succeed.[1]

[Booker T. Washington]

I wanna tell yuh young people ef yuh take de mind and de heart uv Booker Washington, a real race leader, yuh will nevah think yo'self above nobody else. . . . Booker Washington wuz a great man come down frum Heaven wid a great cane in his han en laid hold de ol' dragon. . . . Dat dragon . . . wuz prejudice. . . . One reason I luv Booker Washington wuz dat he wuz no 'spector uv pussons. He loved evahbody. Do' Booker Washington wuz a mulatto he wuz not color struck. He wuz sich a great man.[2]

[Henry Baker]

They gived that man piles of money to run this school business here in the state of Alabama. But I wouldn't boost Booker Washington today up to everything that was industrious and right. . . . He didn't feel for and respect his race of people to go rock bottom with 'em. He leaned too much to the white people that controlled the money . . . he had a political pull any way he turned and he was pullin' for Booker Washington.[3]

[Nate Shaw]

Booker T. Washington was not an easy person to know. He was wary and silent. He never expressed himself frankly or clearly until he knew exactly to whom he was talking and just what their wishes and desires were.[4]

[W.E.B. Du Bois]

Perspectives: Separate and unequal: southern race relations, 1865–1895

In 1865, the Confederate States of America finally lost its bloody bid for independence. Although the South was defeated on the battlefields, it fought a successful campaign after the war against "Yankee" occupation and the imposition of direct rule from Washington, D.C. Slavery had been eradicated by the war, but the white South was determined that its pattern of race relations would not undergo fundamental change. The withdrawal of the last remaining Union troops from the South in 1877 marked the formal end of Reconstruction—the attempt by northern Republicans to secure legal and political equality for freedpeople in the former Confederacy. The 13th, 14th, and 15th Amendments to the U.S. Constitution, wide-ranging reforms embodied in the new southern state constitutions, the establishment of black schools, and attempts to suppress white supremacist organizations, such as the Ku Klux Klan, had been notable achievements of Reconstruction. In large measure, such progress had been possible because black southerners voted in state and local elections, held political offices, moved into urban areas, and attempted to exercise their economic rights in a free labor system. In short, black southerners exercised a wide range of choices that had been effectively closed under slavery.[5]

These gains were distinctly limited once the Reconstruction experiment ended. By the terms of the Compromise of 1877, the Republican Rutherford B. Hayes of Ohio gained the presidency over his Democratic opponent, Samuel Tilden of New York. As part of the bargain, northern Republicans abandoned the freedpeople to the "Redeemers"—Democrats who regained control of southern state governments. Unable to resurrect the slave system in name, white southerners soon devised legal and extra-legal measures that deprived African Americans of the franchise, the right to hold public office, or to engage in political activities. The "Black Codes," adopted during president Andrew Johnson's control of the Reconstruction process, were designed to keep African Americans as a landless and closely controlled labor force. Although they were voided by Congressional Reconstruction, the Black Codes reappeared in the form of labor laws enacted by southern state legislatures in the 1870s and 1880s. Vagrancy laws, enticement acts, contract enforcement statutes, and the criminal surety system were all designed to replace slavery by forms of involuntary servitude for blacks. Staple crop production was resumed on southern farms and plantations under the sharecropping system, whereby planters and merchants kept black farmers in a state of peonage, unable to clear themselves of debt, and required by law to work indefinitely for their employers. In the urban labor market, freedpeople found employment in tobacco factories and flour mills and in the extractive industries, but throughout the South, cotton mills were reserved for whites only.[6]

During and after Reconstruction, southern race relations were marked by increasing separation—in public accommodations, hospitals, prisons, schools, and places of entertainment. Historians disagree as to when racial segregation first appeared in the post-war South—whether it was before, during, or after Reconstruction—but point to its full-blown operation in both law and custom in towns and cities throughout the South by the 1890s, with a rigidly separated caste system as the substitute for slavery. Whenever it occurred, segregation marked a decisive change from the South's earlier and almost total exclusion of blacks from medical, welfare, educational, and other facilities.[7]

Thus, one of the achievements of Congressional or Radical Reconstruction was to secure segregated facilities for African Americans where they had previously faced exclusion. Moreover, the Republican state governments in the South, while effecting some progressive reforms, never pushed for racial integration as either a desirable or even a possible goal. With the piecemeal ending of Reconstruction, the Redeemer governments simply continued and extended segregationist practices. The best that African Americans and idealistic northern Republicans could hope for was separate accommodations and facilities identical to those provided for whites, but Redeemer Democrats had no such expectations or intentions. Black southern resistance to increasing racial discrimination may have prompted whites to take the final step in adopting *de jure* segregation.[8]

One response to the restoration of white supremacy in the South was a renewed call for black emigration. Henry McNeal Turner, a preacher in the African Methodist Episcopal (AME) Church and a Republican party leader, had been expelled from the Georgia state legislature after the Democrats returned to power. President Ulysses S. Grant then appointed Turner as postmaster of Macon, Georgia, but he had to resign when he was smeared with rumors of immorality and passing counterfeit money. A fiery black nationalist, Turner condemned the failings of American society, and tried to get the federal government to pay reparations to African Americans for their long period of enslavement. "We were born here," Turner wrote in explaining why one's American citizenship mattered, "raised here, fought, bled and died here, and have a thousand times more right here than hundreds of thousands of those who help to snub, proscribe and persecute us, and that is one of the reasons I almost despise the land of my birth." It was Turner's conviction that "whoever the white race does not consort with, it will crush out." Turner roundly denounced both major political parties for their betrayal of freedpeople and called for a select group of talented and resourceful blacks to emigrate to Africa and build a new state. In 1891, Turner visited West Africa for the first time, sent back enthusiastic reports, and returned to the United States determined to launch an intensive campaign to promote black emigration.[9]

With the aid of white entrepreneurs, Henry McNeal Turner organized the International Migration Society (IMS), which recruited emigrants and sold passages on the Afro-American Steamship Company for transportation to Liberia. In March, 1895, twenty-two African Americans from various southern states sailed for the African continent. The following year, hundreds of more blacks left for Liberia. During his third visit to West Africa, Turner reported that the settlers were making steady progress. In fact, IMS officials had not provided the settlers with promised food and help, and many of the emigrants died from malaria, while those who survived begged to return to the United States. Not surprisingly, Turner's emigrationist campaign appealed only to a small, desperate segment of the southern black population. Most African Americans concluded that emigration was too great a price to pay for social equality. Undeterred, Turner advocated black emigration for the remainder of his life, and can be considered as the ideological forerunner of Marcus Garvey.[10]

Most black southerners of the late 19th century rejected emigration to Africa and favored securing better schools and welfare facilities in the United States over racial integration. The editor of the *Southern Appeal*, a black paper from Atlanta, Georgia, warned that Africa was no paradise: "Negroes must learn that there is no Eldorado nowadays. If there was the white man would have found it long ago. If he, with his energy, wealth, and progress, has not found Africa to be an Eldorado, why in the name of common sense can we expect to go there with a dollar, and find a country where bread grows on trees and syrup runs all over the country in rivers?" Aware of their precarious position in a society pledged to restore white supremacy, black delegates who attended the first freedpeople's conventions held in the post-Civil War South were careful not to offend white sensibilities by demanding political rights or social privileges. Instead, they stressed their southern identity and the common interests of blacks and whites. Disavowing the need for government protection of black agricultural workers, African Americans in the convention movement, like most black newspapers of the time, espoused the gospel of self-help, group advancement, and laissez-faire economic proposals.[11]

For a time, it appeared that agrarian discontent in the 1880s and 1890s might produce a biracial alliance of black and white southern farmers, both of whom battled falling cotton prices, greedy money lenders, and exorbitant railroad rates. The main vehicle for this discontent was the Populist movement, or People's party, which criticized Republicans and Democrats alike as the creatures of northern business interests. In the South, Populist leaders, such as the brilliant orator Tom Watson of Georgia, appealed for black support, arguing that economic distress transcended the color line. In 1892, the Arkansas Populist platform included a resolution submitted by a black delegate that the People's party sought to "elevate the downtrodden, irrespective of the race or color line." Across the South, Populist platforms denounced lynchings of blacks and endorsed black political rights. But these expressions of concern for African Americans were essentially rhetorical devices, rooted in expediency, rather than in idealism, and even this pretense at racial solidarity evaporated quickly, sometimes in a deadly hail of bullets.[12]

When southern planters and merchants used their influence to ensure that African-American tenant farmers voted the Democratic ticket, white southern Populists grew alarmed. If blacks voted Democratic, rather than Populist, entrenched white interests would prevail. As a result, white southern Populists abandoned their ostensibly pro-black pronouncements and joined with Democrats in espousing black disfranchisement and racial separation. In Georgia, white Populists resorted to Klan-like violence to discourage African Americans from voting. By the 1890s, then, white southerners of all political persuasions and socioeconomic classes united under the banner of white supremacy. The "Solid South" was not simply the South of Democratic dominance; it was increasingly a section in which African Americans were systematically reduced to positions of dependency, poverty, and severely restricted aspirations in a bifurcated social order. Growing up in Mississippi in the early 20th century, novelist Richard Wright, the son of a black sharecropper, learned quickly that:

Among the topics that Southern white men did not like to discuss with Negroes were the following: American white women; the Ku Klux Klan . . . [black boxing champion] Jack Johnson; the entire northern part of the United States; the Civil War; Abraham Lincoln; U.S. Grant; General Sherman; Catholics; the Pope; Jews; the Republican party;

slavery; social equality; Communism; Socialism; the 13th, 14th and 15th Amendments to the Constitution; or any topic calling for positive knowledge of manly self-assertion on the part of the Negro.[13]

In the North, the radical impulse that had initiated Congressional Reconstruction began to wane with the deaths or retirements from office of the old Radical Republican leadership. The election of president Ulysses S. Grant in 1868 and the subsequent rise of factionalism within the Republican party over military rule in the South, both pointed to the imminent abandonment of freedpeople in the cause of sectional harmony. By the early 1870s, northern business interests demanded an end to Reconstruction because it discouraged investment and commercial enterprise in the South. In a series of decisions, the U.S. Supreme Court aided white supremacy by finding that states could segregate public areas, despite the 14th Amendment, as long as the facilities were "separate but equal." Mississippi and South Carolina were the first former Confederate states to amend their constitutions with the purpose of disfranchising nearly all African Americans. Mississippi governor James Vardaman declared openly: "There is no use to equivocate. . . . Mississippi's constitutional convention of 1890 was held for no other purpose than to eliminate the nigger from politics." By 1915, all southern states had enacted legislation that permitted the Democratic party to exclude African Americans from primary elections that chose candidates for the *pro forma* general elections that followed.[14]

Once African Americans were politically impotent, the result was open season on them. During the 1880s and 1890s, a hundred and fifty blacks were lynched each year on average—an appalling index of racial tensions in the South. As historian Neil McMillen observed, "mob executions of blacks were so common that they excited interest only in the black community." Not surprisingly, black southerners, who retained their traditional loyalty to the Republican party, exercised little actual power or influence in the solidly Democratic South.[15]

Yet black protest was not entirely extinguished. From 1904 to 1908, black southerners organized a series of unsuccessful boycotts of segregated streetcars in cities such as Atlanta, Georgia; Houston, Texas; Mobile, Alabama; and New Orleans, Louisiana. More significantly, increasing numbers of African Americans "voted with their feet" by leaving the South for a new life in the industrialized states of the North, even before the mass exodus of the World War I era. Given the helplessness of black southerners in the face of white hostility and violence, there is a certain intended irony in historian C. Vann Woodward's observation, "It was an ex-slave who eventually framed the *modus vivendi* of race relations in the New South."[16]

Booker T. Washington: Early life

Booker Taliaferro Washington was born into slavery in 1856, on James Burroughs' small farm in Franklin County, Virginia, twenty-five miles from Roanoke. Booker was the son of an enslaved, illiterate cook named Jane and an unknown white father, perhaps his master or one of his sons, a neighbor who had fathered many children with enslaved women, or a hard-drinking blacksmith. Booker's older brother John was believed to have been the child of a Burroughs son. Washington later claimed that his unknown paternity did not especially trouble him. "I do not find especial fault with him," the invariably guarded Washington wrote. But he also wrote about his father, "Whoever he was, I never heard of his taking the least interest in me or providing in any way for my rearing." In a nearly incredible statement, Washington excused his white father as "simply another unfortunate victim of the institution which the Nation unhappily had engrafted upon it at that time."[17]

Once valued at $400, Washington spent nine years in slavery, living in a log cabin, fourteen by sixteen feet square. By his own account, he was poorly clothed, inadequately fed, and denied any opportunities for education, apart from tantalizing glimpses into the schoolroom attended by his young white "mistress." His plantation duties involved taking water to enslaved farmhands in the fields, carrying corn from grinding to the local mill, and operating a set of fans at the Burroughs' dinner table. Reflecting on this period of his life, Washington castigated slavery for having caused physical labor to be regarded "as a badge of degradation, of inferiority" by both whites and blacks. As for the "greatest injury" that slavery inflicted on African Americans, Washington later declared that it was "to deprive them of that executive power, that sense of self-dependence which are the glory and the distinction of the Anglo-Saxon race. For 250 years we were taught to depend on some one else for food, clothing, shelter and every move in life."[18]

In 1865, Washington went with his family to join his stepfather, Washington Ferguson, who had fled to Malden, West Virginia, during the Civil War. In Malden, the reunited family lived in a shantytown, and Washington worked for a time as a salt-packer and later as a coal miner, experiences that may partly explain his lifelong obsession with personal hygiene. "An intense longing to read" was among Washington's earliest memories, and he acquired the rudiments of literacy from a copy of Noah Webster's spelling book, a traditional text in American primary schools. He also attended a local school started by African-American parents, after completing a 4.00 a.m. to 9.00 a.m. shift at the salt works, with a further two-hour shift after the end of afternoon classes.[19]

At some point during his Malden years, Washington heard about the existence of a school for freedpeople—the Hampton Normal and Agricultural Institute in Virginia—where African Americans could receive academic training, while working for their room and board. He recalled, "I resolved at once to go to that school, although I had no idea where it was, or how many miles away, or how I was going to reach it. . . . I was on fire constantly with one ambition, and that was to go to Hampton."[20]

Hampton Institute had been founded in 1868 by Samuel Chapman Armstrong, the son of Hawaiian missionaries and a former brigadier general in the Union army. The view of European educators stressing the value of industrial schools had received a receptive hearing in America before the Civil War, and Frederick Douglass, the former slave and powerful race leader, was a vocal advocate of the idea. Armstrong was impressed with education for freedpeople as the best means of smoothing the transition from slavery to freedom. Armstrong also believed that such a program, in addition to elevating "dependent" and "backward" races, might also provide a strategic ground of compromise between white southerners, white northerners, and African Americans. He was convinced that former slaves should remain in the white South—among their "best friends," as he put it—engaged primarily in agriculture and programs of individual and collective self-help. Armstrong's conservative and moral educational philosophy appealed to southern planters and northern capitalists, who were united in their wish to have a tractable and trained labor force in the post-war South.[21]

Booker T. Washington's desire to attend Hampton was intensified during his eighteen-month service as a houseboy in the home of general Lewis Ruffner, owner of the Malden salt works and a coal mine. His stay with the Ruffner family marked the beginning of Washington's life-long association with—and affection for—upper-class whites. It was from Viola Ruffner, a strict New Englander, that he imbibed Puritan notions of thrift, cleanliness, and hard work, which formed the basis of his social thought. Ruffner encouraged Washington's persistent efforts to acquire an education, and allowed him to attend school for an hour a day during the winter.[22]

In 1872, Washington, aged sixteen, set out from Malden to cover the five hundred miles to Hampton, a journey that tested his mental, physical, and financial resources. At the first night's stagecoach stop, Washington, the only black passenger, was barred from "a common, unpainted house called a hotel," and refused a meal. When his meager funds ran out in northern Virginia, Washington walked and begged rides until he reached Richmond, eighty miles from Hampton, tired, hungry, and broke. Working at odd jobs in Richmond, he finally accumulated sufficient funds to undertake the last stage of his journey; he reached Hampton with fifty cents to spare. The head teacher at Hampton, Mary Mackie—like Viola Ruffner, a New Englander—was visibly unimpressed by the tramp-like figure who presented himself for admission. After some deliberation, she ordered him to sweep out the recitation room, a chore that Washington correctly surmised was his entrance examination. Thanks to Ruffner's training and his own unflagging enthusiasm, Washington passed the test. After a thorough inspection of the room, Mackie informed him: "I guess you will do to enter this institution."[23]

Booker T. Washington's three years in Hampton molded his life in a decisive manner. He later claimed that Hampton had given him a better education than he could have received at Harvard or Yale University. Working as a janitor for his room and board, and with his clothing and tuition provided by northern benefactors, Washington gained the rudiments of a liberal education, acquired trade skills, and was fully indoctrinated in Hampton's Christian work-and-cleanliness ethic. He also displayed promise as a student debater and orator. In general Armstrong, Washington found a mentor and surrogate father who shaped his attitudes and racial philosophy. Upon leaving Hampton, Washington spent a year at Wayland Seminary, a small Baptist theological school in Washington, D.C., but he disliked both the capital's atmosphere and the absence of moral and practical training in the Wayland curriculum. In particular, he criticized the frivolities and pretensions of the city's black population, and the insensitivity of Wayland's black graduates to the needs of black farmers. After briefly studying law, Washington gratefully accepted Armstrong's invitation to return to Hampton as a teacher in 1879. There, he administered the first night school class for preparatory students unable to afford part-time study during the day. Washington nicknamed his students "The Plucky Class," and under his driving force, the experiment was a success, confirming his belief that poverty was no excuse for ignorance.[24]

Tuskegee

In May, 1881, general Armstrong received a letter from the state commissioners of an African-American normal school in Tuskegee, Alabama, asking him to recommend its first principal. Their assumption was that Armstrong would recommend a white teacher for the post, which consisted of a dilapidated shack and an old church, but no teachers or pupils. Although obviously modest in the extreme, the school owed its origin to the persistence of the black vote in the Deep South in the period immediately after the end of Reconstruction. In the 1880 elections, colonel Wilbur Foster, a Confederate veteran and a former slaveholder, was a Democratic candidate for the Alabama state senate. Foster approached tinsmith Lewis Adams, a former slave and the leading citizen of Tuskegee, with a proposal: Foster promised that if Adams could deliver the black vote in the election—the county's population was 75 percent African American—he could expect to be rewarded. Adams, a Republican-turned-opportunist for the black community, secured Foster's promise to sponsor and aid passage of a bill for a black normal school in Tuskegee.[25]

Alabama Democrats won an overwhelming victory in 1880, and Foster fulfilled his part of the bargain. The state legislature approved the project, named a board of commissioners, and appropriated money for teacher salaries. Alabama's white conservatives, having regained political control, no longer felt fearful of blacks and, as historian Robert Norrell observed, "benevolent paternalism toward blacks made whites feel good about themselves." General Armstrong recommended 25-year-old Booker T. Washington for the Tuskegee position, characterizing him as "a very competent capable mulatto, clearheaded, modest, sensible, polite and a thorough teacher and superior man." The Tuskegee commissioners accepted the nomination, and Washington went to Tuskegee to put into practice the lessons he had learned and taught at Hampton. From the outset, Washington demonstrated his talents as an interracial diplomat.[26]

Cultivating Tuskegee's power brokers, Booker T. Washington cajoled the white community into supporting the new school. He traveled through the county, advertising the school to African Americans, and soliciting whatever financial or other help they could offer. On the symbolically chosen Fourth of July, 1881, Washington formally opened the school, with an intake of thirty students and one teacher—himself. Within a year, he had moved the school to an abandoned slave plantation, which he purchased for $500, half of which was borrowed from general James Marshall, Hampton's treasurer, with a promise to repay the other half within a year. Both debts were repaid within five months.[27]

With the help of student labor and Booker T. Washington's assistant, Olivia Davidson, who became Washington's second wife, Tuskegee followed the "head-hand-heart" model of education, and thereby grew in size and scope. The student body built classrooms, barns, and furniture, and, in the process, learned skilled trades. After several failures, Tuskegee produced its own bricks; in short order, cabinet and mattress making shops, blacksmith operations, wagon-making, and wheelwright work were added to the school catalogue. In particular, Washington concentrated the school's efforts on retaining an all-black faculty, teaching modern agricultural techniques, training skilled artisans, and preparing female students to be good housekeepers. New appointments to the Tuskegee staff included George Washington Carver—like Washington, a former slave—who was a horticulturalist best known for developing hundreds of products from sweet potatoes and peanut butter.[28]

Tuskegee's main goal was not to produce farmers and tradesmen, but teachers of farming and trade for new high schools and colleges across the South. Washington theorized that, as African Americans pro-vided needed social skills and proved to be responsible, reliable citizens, white southerners would accept them as full-fledged members of society. Talented and industrious African Americans would provide proof to white America that they were not " 'naturally' stupid and incompetent." For Washington, then, the potential contributions of Tuskegee Institute to black welfare were enormous.[29]

The regime at Tuskegee, modeled on that of Hampton, was even stricter and more spartan. As principal, Booker T. Washington ruled as a not-so-benevolent despot, alert to any infraction of the school rules by either staff or students. Although Tuskegee was a nonsectarian school—and Washington always displayed a low regard for the moral and educa-tional standards of black ministers—religious training, in the form of daily attendance at chapel and weekly Sunday evening talks by the principal himself, ensured that Tuskegee graduates would equate education with Christian precepts. Washington also steadily increased the influence of Tuskegee into the surrounding community, with extension courses and annual conferences for farmers that emphasized not only innovative agricultural techniques, but also the personal and moral qualities neces-sary for success. Even before he emerged as a national black leader, Washington, in speeches and letters to the northern and southern press, constantly stressed that great benefits would come to the South and the entire nation if the Tuskegee experiment proved successful.[30]

Conservative white southerners could only be reassured by Washington's pronouncements on race relations in the 1880s. He informed a meeting of the National Education Association in Wisconsin that "Any movement for the elevation of the Southern Negro in order to be successful, must have to a certain extent the cooperation of the Southern whites. They control the government and own the property— whatever benefits the black man benefits the white man. . . . In spite of all talk of exodus, the Negro's home is permanently in the South: for coming to the bread-and-meat side of the question, the white man needs the Negro, and the Negro needs the white man." Booker T. Washington informed the editor of the *Tuskegee Macon Mail* that "the race will grow in proportion as we learn to help ourselves in matters of education." In an address to the Alabama State Teachers' Association, Washington made an artful plea for the industrial education of blacks, one calculated to reassure and impress his white audience:

Two hundred years of forced labor taught the colored man that there was no dignity in labor but rather a disgrace. . . . The child of the ex-slave, naturally influenced by his parents' example, grows up believing that he sees what he thinks is a curse in work. To remove this idea is one of the great missions of the industrial school. The school teacher must be taught that it will not disgrace him to work with his hands when he cannot get a school.[31]

As Booker T. Washington's fame grew, he was frequently absent from Tuskegee, often on fund-raising drives in the northern states, where he impressed self-made, millionaire industrial-philanthropists, such as John D. Rockefeller, Henry Huttleston Rogers, and George Eastman, along with Sears Roebuck president Julius Rosenwald, with his own business-oriented and essentially conservative social philosophy. These donors helped swell the Tuskegee endowment to nearly $2 million by 1915, enabling the campus to become a showplace of industrial education with a hundred new buildings, two hundred black faculty, and a black student body from the world over. Washington not only needed the largesse of these men to support his institution, he admired them simply for their extraordinary success, the kind of success he hoped African Americans would begin to emulate in a small way. As the financial burdens of Tuskegee eased somewhat, Washington steered northern philanthropists to assist 5,000 other black schools and colleges in the South.[32]

Washington was, then, the outstanding black educator of his day, and Tuskegee was his great monument. It also became Washington's power base and the headquarters for the "Tuskegee Machine," an unflattering reference to his powerful and intricate network of organizations, spies, and informers. Washington's machine derived its power from his control of large sections of the black press and fraternal, business, and religious bodies, as well as to his disbursement of political patronage and philanthropic funds. An influential figure in the post-Reconstruction South, Washington was catapulted into national prominence after delivering an electrifying eight-minute speech.[33]

The Atlanta Compromise address

In 1895, Washington was invited to speak at the Cotton States and International Exposition held in Atlanta, Georgia. Replying to the invitation, Washington assured his white sponsors that he intended to use his remarks to "cement the friendship of the races and bring about hearty cooperation between them." Although there was nothing new in the address that Washington delivered on September 18th, the timing and circumstances of his speech ensured that it would reach and impress a national audience. Washington's purpose was to announce a pragmatic compromise that would resolve the antagonisms between white southerners, white northerners, and African Americans. In a period of worsening race relations and the largest number of lynchings in American history, Washington deprecated blacks for their performance as voters and legislators in Reconstruction, and urged them to remain in the South, work at "the common occupations of life," and accept the fact of white supremacy. Appealing to white self-interest, Washington stressed the loyalty and fidelity of black southerners—"the most patient, faithful, law-abiding and unresentful people the world has seen." He also stressed that blacks had absolutely no interest in securing social equality, and in an arresting metaphor declared: "In all things that are purely social we can be as separate as the five fingers, yet one as the hand in all things essential to human progress." Reduced to their most obvious terms, his proposals to the South were for economic cooperation and social separation. But Washington went further, assuring whites that they had nothing to fear and everything to gain from trusting African Americans, who comprised a third of the South's population: "As we have proved our loyalty to you in the past, in nursing your children, watching by the sick bed of your mothers and fathers, and often following them with tear-dimmed eyes to their graves, so in the future, in our humble way, we shall stand by you with a devotion that no foreigner can approach, ready to lay down our lives, if need be, in defense of yours." The Washington prescription of economic cooperation, he maintained, would produce a new and richer South for all.[34]

Turning to African Americans in the audience, Washington admonished them:

Our greatest danger is that in the great leap from slavery to freedom we may overlook the fact that . . . we shall prosper in proportion as we learn to dignify and glorify common labor. . . . No race can prosper till it learns that there is as much dignity in tilling a field as in writing a poem. It is at the bottom of life we must begin, and not at the top. . . . No race that has anything to contribute to the markets of the world is long in any degree ostracized. It is important and right that all the privileges of the law be ours, but it is vastly more important that we be prepared for the exercises of these privileges. The opportunity to earn a dollar in a factory just now is worth infinitely more than the opportunity to spend a dollar in an opera house.[35]

Washington assured white southerners that in their efforts to resolve the race problem "which God has laid at the doors of the South," they would "have at all times the patient, sympathetic help of my race." In effect, Washington's most famous speech was an adaptation of the optimistic late 19th century ideology of the "New South," as espoused by white southern publicists anxious to assure northern business interests and politicians, as well as themselves, that the trauma of Confederate defeat was over, that the section could readily transform itself into an agriculturally diversified and increasingly industrialized society. Prerequisites for this transformation were northern capital and the attraction of skilled white labor—possibly from Europe. But New South spokespersons, such as editor Henry W. Grady of the *Atlanta Constitution*, were resolved that in racial matters, the South would continue to practice self-determination. Grady, whose slaveholding father was killed by a Yankee bullet in the Civil War, was a convinced advocate of racial segregation, and contended that the two races had an instinctive desire for separation. Social equality, which African Americans did not enjoy anywhere in the United States, was out of the question. To New South ideologues, the concept offered more than industrial progress; it would also underwrite the new social order, with blacks as an integral part of the labor force. As Henry Watterson, another New South enthusiast, declared, "Under the old system we paid our debts and walloped our niggers. Under the new system we pay our niggers and wallop our debts."[36]

Washington would have rejected Watterson's derogatory terminology, but he implicitly endorsed his sentiments and those of Grady. Significantly, Washington contributed to the New South contention that the grosser forms of racial injustice were rapidly disappearing. Even before the Atlanta address, Washington had informed a northern audience that although "the practice of lynching colored people is one of the curses of the South . . . usually resorted to when there is a charge of rape," it was being criticized by the southern press and "we are sure that a healthy change in public sentiment is being wrought."[37]

Booker T. Washington's "Atlanta Compromise" address, as it came to be known, caused a sensation at the time and has been variously interpreted by commentators ever since. Not surprisingly, the southern press heartily endorsed the sentiments that it believed Washington had expressed. Grady's *Atlanta Constitution* termed the speech "the most remarkable address delivered by a colored man in America," and called Washington a "sensible and progressive Negro educator." A South Carolina newspaper acclaimed him as "one of the great men of the South," and added that "his skin may be colored, but his head is sound and his heart is in the right place." For the moment, a new era in race relations seemed to have dawned, and a euphoric Washington described the event as "the brightest, most hopeful day in the history of the negro race."[38]

With only a few dissenting black voices, northern opinion was equally enthusiastic. One headline read: "A Negro Moses Spoke for His Race." In an editorial widely reprinted in the South, a Chicago newspaper declared that Washington's remarks in Atlanta and his personal example as an educator had done "more for the improvement for the Negro in the South than has been accomplished by all the political agitators. The possession of a vote does not always ensure respect, but the possession of a good character, a good home, and a little money reserve always ensure respect. If every Southern state had such an institution as that at Tuskegee, Alabama, presided over by such a man as Professor Washington, the race question will settle itself in ten years." The correspondent of the *New York World* asserted that nothing since Henry Grady's address to the New England Society of New York had demonstrated so graphically "the spirit of the New South." On all counts—his own rise to eminence from slavery, his deprecation of political activity by blacks, his stress on economic advancement, his distrust of labor unions and "foreigners," and his generally conservative position on social issues—Washington stood revealed as the black defender of the New South creed.[39]

Most estimates of Washington's Atlanta Address have viewed it as an abject surrender of black civil and political rights to the forces of white racism. It is also possible to view it as a masterly exercise in dissimulation or, rather, in racial diplomacy. Writing from Wilberforce University in Ohio, the young black scholar, W.E.B. Du Bois, congratulated Washington on his "phenomenal success at Atlanta—it was a word fitly spoken" and thought the speech "might be the basis of a real settlement between whites and blacks in the South." A close reading of the text of the Atlanta Address reveals that it included nuances and goals that white southerners could not support. Reading between the lines, as historian August Meier perceptively noted, Washington, although he asserted that blacks must begin at the bottom, "surely . . . believed that eventually they would arrive at the top . . . his Negro supporters emphasized the future implication of his remarks . . . the dominant whites were impressed by his conciliatory phraseology, confused his means for his ends, and were satisfied with the immediate program he enunciated."[40]

Whatever the nuances, the Atlanta Address made Booker T. Washington an acclaimed African-American leader. James Weldon Johnson, executive secretary for the National Association for the Advancement of Colored People (NAACP), attributed Washington's fame to his "epochal" Atlanta speech, which had a profound consequence:

[Washington] had at a stroke gained the sanction and support of both the South and the North—the South, in general, construing the speech to imply the Negro's abdication of his claim to full and equal citizenship rights, and his acceptance of the status of a contented and industrious peasantry; the North feeling that the opportunity had arisen to rid its conscience of a disturbing question and shift it over to the South. The great body of Negroes, discouraged, bewildered, and leaderless, hailed Mr. Washington as a Moses. This was indeed a remarkable feat—his holding of the South in one hand, the North in the other, and at the same time carrying a major portion of his race along with him.[41]

For his part, Washington regarded himself as the successor to, if not the strict disciple of, Frederick Douglass. In his first autobiography, which was intended primarily for a black readership, Washington asserted, "Mr. Douglass had the same idea concerning the importance and value of industrial education that I have tried to emphasize. He also held the same ideas I do in regard to the emigration of the Negro to Africa, and was opposed to the diffusion and dissemination of the Negro throughout the North and Northwest, believing as I do that the Southern section of the country where the Negro now resides is the best place for him." But Washington also believed that the issues which Douglass had agitated were not relevant to the "New South." In his biography of Douglass, Washington noted that Douglass's career fell "almost wholly within the period of revolution and liberation." But "that period is now closed. We are at present in the period of construction and readjustment. Many of the animosities engendered by the conflicts and controversies of half a century ago still survive. . . . But changes are rapidly coming about that will remove, or at least greatly modify, these lingering animosities."[42]

It is unlikely that Frederick Douglass would have endorsed these Washingtonian sentiments and comparisons. In the last year of his life, when Douglass was asked by a student what advice he would give to the younger black generation, the great abolitionist reportedly replied, "Agitate! Agitate! Agitate!" When the same student posed the identical question to Booker T. Washington in 1899, he received the answer, "Work! Work! Work! Be patient and win by superior service."[43]

Up from Slavery

From 1895 until his death in 1915, Booker T. Washington's determination, power, and influence made him a force to be reckoned with. Washington continued to act as the autocratic and seemingly omnipotent principal of Tuskegee, but he also embarked on extensive fund-raising and lecturing tours. His message, with few exceptions, was a restatement of the Atlanta Address: blacks should eschew politics; cultivate habits of thrift, economy, sobriety, and honesty; and concentrate on acquiring Christian character, property, and industrial skills. Washington, in sum, linked behavior and socioeconomic condition, arguing that African Americans had the best chance of survival, if not success, in a racist and violent society if they earned an education, worked hard, lived frugally, and acted decently. Urged by his admirers to write an inspirational account of his remarkable career, Washington collaborated with a ghostwriter to publish *The Story of My Life and Work* (1900). Although sloppily produced and given luke-warm reviews in the press, the book sold 15,000 copies in its first year of publication.[44]

Washington's second autobiography, *Up from Slavery* (1901), which first appeared in serial form, was a more carefully planned and executed project. Max Bennett Thrasher, a white journalist and Tuskegee's public relations officer, ghostwrote the book, but the thoughts expressed were laid out in Washington's language. *Up from Slavery* presented Washington, the destitute former slave who rose to international prominence, as a black Horatio Alger, who succeeded because of his application of the Puritan work ethic instilled in him by successive white mentors. An immediate publishing success, the book appealed to a foreign readership as well, and was quickly translated into more foreign languages than any other American book of its time. Several of Tuskegee's most generous benefactors became converts to Washington's philosophy of race relations after reading his autobiography. Andrew Carnegie, who had earlier refused to meet Washington, felt that *Up from Slavery* exemplified his own brand of Social Darwinism, and donated a library building to Tuskegee, as well as $600,000 in U.S. Steel bonds, from which Washington benefited personally. White readers of the autobiography welcomed not only its retailing of familiar maxims of self-help and perseverance in the face of adversity, but also its sanguine portrayal of black life during and after the slave period. To this day, Washington's account remains one of the most widely read black autobiographies.[45]

In effect, *Up from Slavery* complemented the Atlanta Compromise address, which was included in the text. It presented the authorized view of race relations in the South during the period of Congressional Reconstruction that had been such an affront to white southerners. Black involvement in this phase of Reconstruction was also sternly criticized by Washington:

In many cases it seemed to me that the ignorance of my race was being used as a tool with which to help white men into office, and that there was an element in the North which wanted to punish the Southern white men. . . . Besides, the general political agitation drew the attention of our people away from the more fundamental matters of perfecting themselves in the industries at their doors and at securing properties. . . . I saw colored men who were members of the state legislatures, and county officers, who, in some cases, could not read or write, and whose morals were as weak as their education.

As Washington well understood, many white southerners believed that the alleged nightmare of Reconstruction—unqualified, often illiterate, voters and legislators—would sabotage the political process. Washington begged to differ: "I do not think that this will be true, because the Negro . . . is fast learning the lesson that he cannot afford to act in a manner that will alienate his Southern white neighbors from him."[46]

Most obviously, *Up from Slavery* was an extended song of praise—a series of "advertisements for myself"—to Booker T. Washington. As one literary critic has aptly remarked, the book "reads like a saint's life written by a saint." And "like [novelist Charles] Dickens" virtuous co-narrator in *Bleak House*, Washington is forced into the artless ruse of quoting everyone's praises of him so as not to be praising himself directly all the time. He does no wrong, has no enemies, suffers hardships willingly, is universally beloved, and is, for it all (as he confesses) quite humble." Mary Mackie, Washington's former teacher at Hampton, was inordinately proud of her pupil, and declared—without noting the irony—that the book "sets off more graphically than any article I have read, the transition from slavery to freedom. It reads like a romance."[47]

Race leader

In the last twenty years of his life, Booker T. Washington had a dual career as educator and race leader. During the U.S. presidential admin- istrations of Theodore Roosevelt and William Howard Taft, Washington dispensed the limited federal patronage for African Americans, streng- thened the intricate network of the "Tuskegee Machine," and, with the help of his devoted secretary, Emmett Scott, monitored the activities of his black critics. In 1900, putting one of his favorite precepts into practice, Washington founded the National Negro Business League, a kind of black chamber of commerce intended to promote black entrepreneurship and advertise the economic success that African Americans had achieved. The league not only reflected Washington's belief that black advancement lay in economic progress, but also provided him with a cadre of loyal supporters in the major cities of the North. In the South, Washington was keenly aware of the precarious position of African Americans, and so ingratiated himself with successive governors of Alabama, recommended health measures for blacks, and promoted economic ventures, such as black owned and operated cotton mills and land purchase schemes.[48]

By 1901, Washington was at the height of his fame, and received the presidential seal of approval when the new president, Theodore Roosevelt, invited him to dinner to discuss education, politics, and patronage. Roosevelt had known Washington for some time, and had opened his Long Island home to Washington for an overnight stay. Washington appealed to Roosevelt because the Wizard of Tuskegee sought evolution- ary racial change through self-help, rather than agitation or violence, and because Washington was a good judge of character, a useful quality in making presidential appointments. Washington knew that Roosevelt liked individual African Americans, but regarded the "darkey" race as plainly "inferior" until it overcame the slave experience and fully adopted the supposedly superior traits of white civilization. At the same time, Washington had heard Roosevelt condemn lynching, racial demagoguery, and white southern hypocrisy on interracial sex. After a day of mulling over the implications of accepting the invitation—the first time a black person would dine with a president in the White House—Washington agreed to come. Roosevelt hoped that Washington could deliver black votes in big cities and the border states to him at Republican presidential nominating conventions; Washington hoped that Roosevelt could derail the rising, but still indeterminate, effort to fully reestablish white supremacy in the United States. Given their mutual interests, it was not surprising that Roosevelt flattered Washington by calling him "the most useful, as well as the most distinguished, member of his race in the world."[49]

The interracial dinner meeting, which was discovered by an enterprising reporter, unsettled Washington and plunged the flabbergasted Roosevelt into the first controversy of his presidency. The White House and Tuskegee Institute were inundated with hate mail and death threats over this "damnable outrage" of permitting a black man to eat with the president's wife and 17-year-old daughter. The episode infuriated white southerners who felt Washington had breached the unwritten rules of racial etiquette. "Every Southern man of intelligence honors Booker T. Washington," one white letter-writer from Dixie wrote to a Chicago newspaper, "but no Southern gentleman would sit at table with him under any consideration whatever. We are willing to pay him homage for his good works, but we cannot admit him to social equality, because that involves a principle which is vital to the preservation of the Southern white race from the evils of intermarriage with blacks." For James Vardaman, the firebrand former governor and U.S. senator from Mississippi, the White House was now "so saturated with odor of the nigger that the rats have taken refuge in the stable." U.S. senator Ben Tillman of South Carolina warned ominously of wholesale murder that would inevitably result from president Roosevelt "entertaining that nigger." The dinner would, Tillman declared, "necessitate our killing a thousand niggers in the South before they will learn their place again." But, as even his critics reluctantly conceded, the White House episode greatly enhanced Washington's national reputation. Emigrationist Henry McNeal Turner informed Washington: "You are about to be the great representative and hero of the Negro race, notwithstanding you have been very conservative." As for Roosevelt, he insisted the invitation was morally right, and he continued to consult Washington, but never again over a meal at the White House.[50]

Although Booker T. Washington had the ear of presidents and philanthropists, he could not by himself halt—let alone improve—the deteriorating racial situation of the Progressive era. In 1896, the U.S. Supreme Court's decision in *Plessy v. Ferguson* gave judicial sanction to the "separate but equal" doctrine, apparently already endorsed by Washington at Atlanta. Although Washington helped to deliver black votes to the Republicans in state and national elections, Roosevelt ignored Washington's plea to reconsider his summary and unjustified dismissal of three companies of black troops in Brownsville, Texas, after they had forcibly resisted a white mob. Similarly, Taft's policy of removing black southern officeholders indicated the very real limits of Washington's political influence.[51]

On numerous occasions, Washington himself was made painfully aware of the virulence of white racism. When a white chambermaid in an Indiana hotel reportedly refused to make up Washington's bed and was fired as a consequence, a Texas newspaper solicited funds "For a Self-Respecting Girl." Washington also discovered that segregation, imposed by whites on African Americans, had produced accommodations that were certainly separate but decidedly unequal. He once confessed: "The mere thought of a trip on a railroad brings me to a feeling of intense dread and I never enter a railroad coach unless compelled to do so."[52]

At the same time, Washington worked to end the more blatant forms of racial discrimination. Wearing a mask of amiability that implied acceptance, Washington surreptitiously challenged white supremacy by submitting pseudonymous letters to anti-segregation newspapers; secretly funding lawsuits against all-white juries, black disfranchisement, and peonage; alerting friendly editors to civil rights violations; and mobilizing political allies to undermine legislation aimed at blacks. In his last years—possibly because of his failures to prevent presidents Roosevelt, Taft and Woodrow Wilson from sanctioning racial segregation—Washington became more outspoken against Jim Crow. He criticized economic discrimination, disparities in educational funding, conditions in the cars and waiting rooms of southern railroads, the persistence of lynching, a Congressional proposal to block African immigrants to the United States, and the blatant racism of D.W. Griffith's epic motion picture, *The Birth of a Nation*, with its romantic portrayal of the Ku Klux Klan. In sum, as historian Robert Norrell concluded, Booker T. Washington anticipated much of the NAACP's agenda, though he chose to do so "carefully and indirectly," not "aggressively and defiantly."[53]

Washington's strongest protest against discrimination was published posthumously in "My View of the Segregation Laws." Racial segregation,

Washington asserted, was "ill-advised" in that it was both unjust and pro-ductive of further injustices. It was also "unnecessary" and "inconsistent" since "the Negro is separated from his white neighbor, but the white businessmen are not prevented from doing business in Negro neighbor-hoods." Finally, Washington declared, segregation was harmful to both its victims and its sponsors: "Wherever a form of segregation exists, it will be found that it has been administered in such a way as to embitter the Negro and harms more or less the moral fibre of the white man." That African Americans did not openly express their detestation of the system was no proof that they did not resent it.[54]

In the early 20th century, Washington traveled extensively at home and abroad, and had a world-wide following, though not uniform approval. His fame radiated from his educational laboratory—the Tuskegee Institute—which was visited regularly by Africans, West Indians, Asians, European missionaries, and white colonialists. On his three trips to Europe, Washington had tea with Queen Victoria and met the Danish royal family. He stayed with and impressed British science fiction writer H.G. Wells, who compared Washington favorably to W.E.B. Du Bois, co-founder of the NAACP. Du Bois, Wells concluded, was more of an "artist" than a statesman, who "conceals his passionate resentment all too thinly," whereas Washington was a "statesman" who possessed "a mind that can grasp the situation and destinies of people." For his part, Washington concluded that despite handicaps, African Americans were better off than "the man farthest down" in Europe, because American blacks enjoyed a better standard of living and more educational, eco-nomic, and political opportunities. Du Bois dissented vigorously. When Washington told a meeting of the London Anti-Slavery Society that American race relations were improving, Du Bois accused Washington of relating only selected racial facts to European audiences because Washington depended on white support. Du Bois stressed instead wide-spread discrimination, lynching, and the failure of the courts to protect African Americans as the less sanguine sides of American life.[55]

Despite his foreign travels, Booker T. Washington did not alter his fundamental outlook, which was essentially that of a provincial southerner. He never visited Africa, Asia, or the West Indies, and before he sailed to Europe, he resolved not to enter a single art gallery, museum, or palace. Washington also had little awareness of or interest in the African heritage of African Americans. He was, however, quite prepared to advise European colonial powers to adopt industrial education programs among African people in the Belgian Congo, Liberia, Nigeria, South Africa, and

Togo. He also urged that Africans be taught English in order to give them a *lingua franca*, and to promote their Western acculturation. Although he endorsed German colonialism in Africa, Washington criticized white imperialist oppression in the Congo and South Africa, not because of any pan-Africanist sentiments, but rather to highlight the impracticality of black emigration to Africa as a solution to the American race problem. Some years earlier, Washington had forcefully opposed Henry McNeal Turner's promotion of African emigration: "This talk of any appreciable number of our people going to Africa is the merest response. . . . It does no good, but . . . does a great deal of harm among the ignorant of our people, especially in the far South."[56]

In 1915, while on a speaking engagement in New York, the 59-year-old Washington collapsed from nervous exhaustion, arteriosclerosis, and kidney failure, which elevated his blood pressure to twice that of normal. An initial diagnosis of syphilis was withdrawn after protests from Washington's personal physician. Informed that he had only a short time to live, Washington asked to be taken to Tuskegee: "I was born in the South, I have lived and labored in the South, and I expect to be buried in the South." He died at Tuskegee on November 14th. Washington's statue on the Tuskegee campus expresses his life in the form of a parable. He is depicted lifting "the veil of ignorance" from the kneeling figure of a young black man, holding on his knees an open book and agricultural and industrial tools. Washington's critics, in his lifetime and after, suggested another reading of the tableau: rather than lifting, Washington was lowering a "veil of ignorance" over the eyes of his people.[57]

A black Benedict Arnold?

Opposition to Booker T. Washington's ideas and to his white-sanctioned position as race leader, came mainly from a relatively small group of black northerners—journalists, lawyers, clergymen, and educators. Initially united by their dislike of various elements of Washington's program, his critics accused him of a range of offenses, miscalculations, and misdemeanors. He was faulted for denigrating political action on the part of African Americans, while at the same time functioning as a "boss"; condemned for attempting to impose a partisan and regional strategy for racial advancement on the country as a whole; and castigated for his control of the black press and his friendships with white editors, which suppressed criticism of him. Washington's policies of industrial education were pronounced anachronistic and his portrayals of harmonious race relations as travesties of the truth. In a letter published in an Atlanta journal after the Atlanta Address, a black correspondent expressed alarm at Washington's overnight elevation to the position of race leader, and rejected as unseemly any comparisons between Washington and Frederick Douglass:

Every race must make its own heroes. . . . If another race selects our heroes, puts them upon pedestals, and tells us to bow down to them and serve them, woe be unto us. It is supreme folly to speak of Mr. Washington as the Moses of the race. If we are where Mr. Washington's Atlanta speech placed us, what need have we of a Moses? Who brought us out from Egypt, through the wilderness to these happy conditions? Let us pray that the race will never have a leader, but leaders. Who is the leader of the white race in America? It has no leader, but leaders. So with us.

The *Atlanta Advocate*, a black journal, lampooned Booker T. Washington as "Prof. B.T. or Bad Taste Wash has made a speech. . . . The white press style Prof. Bad Taste the new Negro, but if there is anything in him except the most servile type of the old Negro, we fail to find it in any of his last acts . . . let the race labor and pray that no more new Negroes such as Prof. Bad Taste will bob up."[58]

As black migration to the North continued, along with the growth of a professional black elite, attacks on Washington became sharper and more concerted. Julius Taylor, the black editor of the *Chicago Broad Ax*, was an ardent Democrat who resented Washington's involvement in Republican patronage politics. Taylor typified Washington as "the Great Beggar of Tuskegee" and "the greatest white man's nigger in the world," and warned: "The time is not far distant when Booker T. Washington will be repudiated as the leader of our race, for he believes that only mealy-mouthed Negroes like himself should be involved in politics."[59]

William Monroe Trotter, the Harvard-educated editor of the *Boston Guardian*, was an early and bitter critic of Washington. When Andrew Carnegie donated large sums to Tuskegee, Trotter expressed the hope that Washington would no longer need to engage in fund-raising tours, asserting, "This man, whatever good he may do, has injured and is injuring the race more than he can aid it by his school. Let us hope that Booker Washington will remain mouth-closed at Tuskegee. If he will do this, all his former sins will be forgiven." Taking issue with Washington's statement that the revised constitutions of the southern states placed "a premium on intelligence, ownership of property, thrift and character," Trotter accused him of self-deception and asked rhetorically, "what man is a worse enemy to the race than a leader who looks with equanimity on the disfranchisement of his race in a country where other races have universal suffrage by constitutions that make one rule for his race and another for the dominant race?" Trotter deplored Washington's rise to fame, and charged him with being the "Benedict Arnold" of the black race. He appealed for a "black Patrick Henry" who would save his people from the dangers into which Washington had led them, one who would inspire them with the immortal words, "Give Me Liberty or Give Me Death."[60]

The most influential critique of Washington's precepts and policies was produced by W.E.B. Du Bois, in his seminal essay, "Of Mr. Booker T. Washington and Others," a chapter of *The Souls of Black Folk* (1903). Du Bois lived a long life, and during it, he continually revised his estimates of Washington, presenting him in a more sympathetic light, and stressing the significant differences in their background and education. But it was his well-reasoned, thoughtful, and unequivocal essay "Of Mr. Booker T. Washington" that propelled Du Bois into the position of a rival black leader. Although he conceded that "the most striking thing in the history of the American Negro since 1876 is the ascendancy of Mr. Booker T. Washington," Du Bois charged that Washington's leadership had resulted in black disfranchisement, the creation of an inferior civil status for blacks, and the withdrawal of funds from institutions of higher training for African Americans. Washington, Du Bois suggested, faced a "triple paradox" in that:

1 He is striving to make Negroes artisans, businessmen and property owners; but it is utterly impossible, under modern competitive methods, for workingmen and property-owners to defend their rights and exist without the right of suffrage.

2 He insists on thrift and self-respect, but at the same time counsels a silent submission to civic inferiority such as is bound to sap the manhood of any race in the long-run.

3 He advocates common-school and industrial training, and deprecates institutions of higher learning; but neither the Negro common-schools, nor Tuskegee itself, could remain open a day were it not for teachers trained in Negro colleges, or trained by their graduates.[61]

Although he paid tribute to Washington's achievements in placating the white South and in shrewdly appealing to the North's commercial spirit, Du Bois pronounced Washington's vision narrow, crass, and pessimistic.

Washington, he concluded, was a "Great Accommodator" who represented "in Negro thought the old attitude of adjustment and submission." James Weldon Johnson recalled that Du Bois' critique provided a rallying point for African Americans opposed to Washington "and made them articulate, thereby creating a split of the race into two contending camps." The Niagara Movement and its successor, the NAACP, were to institutionalize opposition to Washington.[62]

Booker T. Washington's responses to his critics consisted of a few half-hearted attempts at reconciliation and cooperation, together with unremitting efforts to influence, infiltrate, or sabotage their organizations. In 1904, he persuaded the Du Bois-led faction—though not Du Bois himself—to attend a secret meeting in New York City with the ostensible purpose of ironing out their differences. This conference, which was held in Carnegie Hall, was marked by mutual suspicions and failure to achieve a truce or agreement between the Washington and Du Bois forces. With the support of benefactors such as Andrew Carnegie, Washington controlled the proceedings, outmaneuvered his opponents, and secured the election of loyal followers to a Committee of Twelve for the Advancement of the Negro Race, a purely advisory body which, during its brief existence, reported directly to Tuskegee.[63]

Washington keenly resented challenges to his leadership. As Du Bois later confirmed, their conflict was essentially a power struggle, couched in terms of differences in educational and political ideology. With some justification, Washington argued that his black critics in the North had no real appreciation of racial conditions in the South. In a revealing letter, Washington summarized what he regarded as the outstanding differences between him and Du Bois: "I believe that the Negro race is making progress . . . that it is better for the race to emphasize its opportunities than to lay over-much stress on its disadvantages. He believes the Negro race is making little progress. I believe that we should cultivate an ever manly, straightforward manner and friendly relations between white people and black people. Dr. Du Bois pursues the policy of stirring up strife between white people and black people. . . . [H]e fails to recognize the fact that it is a work of construction that is before us now and not a work of destruction."[64]

Assessment

In the circumstances of his time and place, Booker T. Washington evolved a program and strategy designed to secure the acquiescence of southern and northern whites in the educational and economic elevation of African-

American farmers and an aspiring black urban middle class. Aware that slavery had brought physical labor into disrepute, Washington—in tune with his age—preached a gospel of hard work, self-help, and self-reliance. His advocacy of industrial education reflected this belief, as it also reconciled southern whites to the idea of *any* form of education for blacks. The Tuskegee Institute, the Tuskegee Machine, and the carefully-crafted phrase of the "Atlanta Compromise" made Washington's position as the most visible black leader of his day virtually impregnable. Above all, Washington was a master tactician, interracial diplomat, and archetypal "trickster" who relied on manipulation to carve out a better world for blacks. He appeared to be a public appeaser on race, while he pursued a comprehensive, though covert, program to elevate African-Americans.

In many respects, the unctuous and egotistical Washington bears an unfortunate, but intentional, resemblance to Dr. A. Herbert Bledsoe, the black college principal in Ralph Ellison's powerful novel, *Invisible Man* (1952). Describing his methods and rise to power in the South to the ingenuous narrator, Bledsoe could well have been retailing Washington's personal success formula:

Negroes don't control this school or much of anything else. . . . True they *support* it, but *I* control it. I's big and black and I say "Yes, suh" as loudly as any burrhead, when it's convenient. . . . The only ones I even pretend to please are *big* white folk, and even those I control more than they control me. . . . I tell *them*; that's my life, telling white folks how to think about the things I know about. . . . It's a nasty deal and I don't always like it myself. But . . . I didn't make it, and I know that I can't change it. . . . I had to be strong and purposeful to get where I am. I had to wait and plan and lick around. . . . Yes, I had to act the nigger! . . . I don't even insist that it was worth it, but now I'm here and I mean to stay—after you win the game, you take the prize and you keep it, protect it; there's nothing else to do.[65]

Despite repeated invitations to move North, Washington realized that his work lay in the South, although the growing criticism from nor-thern critics forced him later on to sharpen his portrayals of persisting racial inequalities. In a period of deteriorating race relations, the canny Washington built up resources for other black southern schools and colleges. Unable to prevent the erosion of black voting rights, escalating racial violence, and economic exploitation, Washington attempted to hold the line publicly and privately. As sociologist Gunnar Myrdal noted, Washington was misunderstood by his critics, and was never a totally "accommodating" race leader; Washington looked to complete equality as the "ultimate goal" of black leadership. Dependent on the support of northern sympathizers and white southern paternalists, Washington balanced on a precarious tight-rope. Myrdal concluded, "For his time, and for the region where he worked and where the nine-tenths of all Negroes lived, his policy of abstaining from talks of rights and of 'casting down your buckets where you are' was entirely realistic."[66]

Booker T. Washington's faults were glaring. His shortcomings included his astigmatism on the intensity and prevalence of white racial prejudice, his unquestioning acceptance of the values of white middle-class America, his unabashed materialism and philistinism, his tendency to blame African Americans for their condition, and his paranoid jealousy of other black spokespersons. Yet, he also promoted public health measures for African Americans, such as the establishment of the National Negro Health Week, and supported black enterprises, notably, the National Negro Business League, which anticipated later forms of economic black nationalism. Moreover, the National Urban League (NUL) grew out of organizations that subscribed to Washington's advice to rural black southerners. In its emphasis on training, the NUL echoed and amplified one of Washington's favorite themes, while his obsession with the tooth-brush foreshadowed the league's efforts to instruct black migrants in the rudimentary practices of urban life.

Most importantly, during the years of Washington's ascendancy, which coincided with increasing hardships, proscriptions, and dangers for African Americans, militant black protest in the South was not simply unrealistic, but might have proved a warrant for genocide. Washington lived dangerously, forced, in writer Langston Hughes' phrase, to spend most of his life with his head "in the lion's mouth." Addressing the Peace Jubilee in Chicago that celebrated the end of the Spanish-American War, Washington unguardedly declared that racial hatred, especially in the South, was a "cancer" that would one day destroy the nation. White southerners were displeased, but Washington's assertion that the victims of lynching in the South "are invariably vagrants, men without property and standing," more than made amends for such slips of the tongue. Some white observers were not fooled. Thomas Dixon, Jr., author of *The Clansman: An Historical Romance of the Ku Klux Klan*, alleged that Washington, precisely because of his skill in disguising his real aims, was quietly preparing the way for the amalgamation of the races, or the building of a separate black nation. Even Washington's endorsement of industrial training for blacks was subversive, Dixon wrote, since "if there is one thing a southern white man cannot endure it is an educated Negro." By the same token, Washington's efforts to make African Americans into potential competitors in the marketplace with white men seemed to portend bloodshed.[67]

Booker T. Washington, one of his biographers contends, has not been accorded a fair evaluation "partly because his methods were too compromising and un-heroic to win him a place in the black pantheon, but also because he was too complex and enigmatic for historians to know what to make of him." Yet, as historian J.R. Pole suggested, Washington's role-playing, which certainly exacted a price in nervous tensions and exhaustion, although devious, was not unique: "In many ways he emerges as a type remarkable for its familiarity among the operators of American interest groups—that familiarity being disguised by skin pigmentation. He worked assiduously within the system, to whose economic and political conventions he faithfully subscribed; he took conservative views of larger social causes while showing great tactical skill in maintaining his own personal power base."[68]

Throughout the South of the Jim Crow era, local African-American leaders mainly followed policies of racial conservatism, stressing economic opportunity over social equality and espousing a Washingtonian gospel of black progress through thrift, material accumulation, and industrial training. And, as historian Neil McMillen stated of black Mississippi leaders of the late 19th and early 20th centuries, they and their counterparts else-where "conceded nothing to whites that had not already been taken by force." Although there is no scholarly consensus on Booker T. Washington's achievements or limitations as a black leader, he certainly should not be blamed for the failure of African Americans to secure racial equality, however defined, in his own lifetime or afterwards. Nor should he be seen as a power-hungry politician who bartered away his people's rights for his own self-interest. As Martin Luther King, Jr. judiciously observed, Washington should not be dismissed simply as "an Uncle Tom who com-promised for the sake of keeping the peace." His sincerely held belief was that "if the South was not pushed too hard . . . it would voluntarily rally to the Negro's cause." But his faith was misplaced and reviled, King maintained: "Washington's error was that he underestimated the structures of evil; as a consequence his philosophy of pressureless per-suasion only served as a springboard for racist Southerners to dive into deeper and more ruthless oppression of the Negro." In historian Robert J. Norrell's estimation, the Booker T. Washington who believed that black economic progress would gradually lead to civil rights was "a heroic failure," because it would take a civil rights revolution that relied on the very methods he eschewed—agitation and confrontation—to transform the plight of African Americans.[69]

References

1 Booker T. Washington, *Up from Slavery: An Autobiography* (1901), p. 39.

2 Henry Baker, in John W. Blassingame, ed., *Slave Testimony: Two Centuries of Letters, Speeches, Interviews, and Autobiographies* (1977), p. 675.

3 Theodore Rosengarten, *All God's Dangers: The Life of Nate Shaw* (1974), pp. 568–569.

4 W.E.B. Du Bois, *Dusk of Dawn: An Essay toward an Autobiography of a Race Concept* (1940), pp. 78–79.

5 John Hope Franklin and Alfred A. Moss, Jr., *From Slavery to Freedom: A History of African Americans* (2000), pp. 246–271.

6 Ibid., pp. 273–291.

7 Howard N. Rabinowitz, *Race Relations in the Urban South, 1865–1890* (1978), pp. 128–140.

8 Ibid., pp. 127, 151.

9 Edwin S. Redkey, *Black Exodus: Black Nationalist and Back-to-Africa Movements, 1890–1910* (1969), pp. 24–46.

10 Ibid., pp. 170–251.

11 Rabinowitz, *Race Relations in the Urban South*, pp. 252–253.

12 Robert C. McMath, *Populism: A Social History, 1877–1898* (1993), pp. 171–175; Gerald H. Gaither, *Blacks and the Populist Revolt: Ballots and Bigotry in the New South* (1977).

13 McMath, *Populism*, p. 174; Richard Wright, *Black Boy* (1947), pp. 253–254.

14 Jerrold M. Packard, *American Nightmare: The History of Jim Crow* (2002), p. 69.

15 Neil R. McMillen, *Dark Journey: Black Mississippians in the Age of Jim Crow* (1989), p. 228.

16 Leon F. Litwack, *Trouble in Mind: Black Southerners in the Age of Jim Crow* (1998), pp. 242–243; August Meier and Elliott Rudwick, "The Boycott Movement against Jim Crow Streetcars in the South, 1900–1906," *Journal of American History* 55 (March, 1969): 756–775; C. Vann Woodward, *Origins of the New South* (1951), p. 356.

17 Louis R. Harlan, et al., eds., *The Booker T. Washington Papers*, vol. 1 (1972), p. 215 (cited hereafter as *Washington Papers*); Robert J. Norrell, *Up from History: The Life of Booker T. Washington* (2009), pp. 18–19.

18 *Washington Papers*, vol. 4 (1975), p. 92.

19 Norrell, *Up from History*, pp. 21–24.

20 *Washington Papers*, vol. 1, p. 236.

21 Robert Francis Engs, *Educating the Disfranchised and Disinherited: Samuel Chapman Armstrong and Hampton Institute, 1839–1893* (1899), pp. 80–114.

22 *Washington Papers*, vol. 1, pp. 237–238; Louis R. Harlan, *Booker T. Washington: The Making of a Black Leader* (1972), pp. 40–44.

23 *Washington Papers*, vol. 1, pp. 241, 245; Washington, *Up from Slavery*, p. 53.

24 Norrell, *Up from History*, pp. 32–42.

25 *Washington Papers*, vol. 2 (1972), p. 127; Robert J. Norrell, *Reaping the Whirlwind: The Civil Rights Movement in Tuskegee* (1985), pp. 12–13, 15; Norrell, *Up from History*, pp. 40, 43–51.

26 Norrell, *Reaping the Whirlwind*, p. 14; Harlan, *Booker T. Washington: The Making of a Black Leader*, p. 110.

27 *Washington Papers*, vol. 2, p. 135.

28 *Washington Papers*, vol. 1, pp. 34, 294; Harlan, *Booker T. Washington: The Making of a Black Leader*, p. 126; Norrell, *Up from History*, pp. 61–70; Booker T. Washington, *Working with the Hands: Being a Sequel to "Up from Slavery"* (1904), p. 63; Linda O. McMurry, *George Washington Carver: Scientist and Symbol* (1981), pp. 41–47, 85–87, 171–178, 219–241.

29 Norrell, *Up from History*, p. 73; Stanley Crouch, *The Artificial White Man: Essays on Authenticity* (2005), p. 96.

30 *Washington Papers*, vol. 1, pp. 281–285, 308–309; Norrell, *Up from History*, pp. 66–67.

31 *Washington Papers*, vol. 2, pp. 194, 256, 258.

32 Norrell, *Up from History*, pp. 153–156, 311–312, 362; *Washington Papers*, vol. 4 (1975), pp. 409–410.

33 Norrell, *Up from History*, pp. 288–310.

34 Ibid., pp. 122–126.

35 Washington, *Up from Slavery*, pp. 220–224.

36 Paul M. Gaston, *The New South Creed: A Study in Southern Mythmaking* (1970), p. 147; Henry Watterson, *The Compromises of Life, and Other Lectures and Addresses, Including Some Observations on Certain Downward Tendencies of Modern Society* (1903), p. 290.

37 *Washington Papers*, vol. 3 (1974), p. 29.

38 Norrell, *Up from History*, pp. 127–128; Raymond W. Smock, *Booker T. Washington: Black Leadership in the Age of Jim Crow* (2010), pp. 97–98.

39 Smock, *Booker T. Washington*, p. 98; Rayford W. Logan, *The Betrayal of the Negro: From Rutherford B. Hayes to Woodrow Wilson* (1965), p. 285.

40 August Meier, *Negro Thought in America, 1880–1915* (1963), p. 101.

41 James Weldon Johnson, *Black Manhattan* (1930), pp. 131–132.

42 *Washington Papers*, vol. 1, p. 56; Booker T. Washington, *Frederick Douglass* (1906), pp. 3–4.

43 Philip S. Foner, ed., *The Life and Writings of Frederick Douglass*, vol. 4 (1950), pp. 149–150.

44 Booker T. Washington, *The Story of My Life and Work* (1900); Norrell, *Up from History*, pp. 216–217.

45 Washington, *Up from Slavery*; Norrell, *Up from History*, pp. 216–224.

46 Washington, *Up from Slavery*, pp. 84–86; David Littlejohn, *Black on White: A Critical Survey of Writing by American Negroes* (1966), p. 30.

47 Harlan, *Booker T. Washington: The Making of a Black Leader*, p. 248.

48 Norrell, *Up from History*, p. 229; W. Fitzhugh Brundage, ed., *Up from Slavery by Booker T. Washington with Related Documents* (2003), pp. 26–29.

49 Norrell, *Up from History*, pp. 238–244; Kathleen Dalton, *Theodore Roosevelt: A Strenuous Life* (2002), p. 215; Nathan Miller, *Theodore Roosevelt: A Life* (1992), pp. 361–364; H.W. Brands, *TR: The Last Romantic* (1997), pp. 421–422; Edmund Morris, *Theodore Rex* (2001), pp. 52–54.

50 Norrell, *Up from History*, pp. 244–252; Brundage, ed., *Up from Slavery*, p. 3; Emma Lou Thornbrough, "Booker T. Washington As Seen By His White Contemporaries," *Journal of Negro History* 53 (1968): 172; Louis R. Harlan, *Booker T. Washington: The Wizard of Tuskegee, 1901–1915* (1983), p. 5; Morris, *Theodore Rex*, pp. 54–58.

51 Norrell, *Up from History*, pp. 143, 345–353, 383–386; Harlan, *Booker T. Washington: The Wizard of Tuskegee*, pp. 323–337; *Washington Papers*, vol. 9 (1980), p. 590.

52 *Washington Papers*, vol. 2, p. 271.

53 Norrell, *Up from History*, p. 392.

54 Booker T. Washington, "My View of Segregation Laws," *New Republic* 5 (4 December 1915): 113–114.

55 Harlan, *Booker T. Washington: The Wizard of Tuskegee*, p. 284.

56 *Washington Papers*, vol. 3, p. 377.

57 Harlan, *Booker T. Washington: The Wizard of Tuskegee*, p. 424.

58 Philip S. Foner, "Is Booker T. Washington's Idea Correct?" *Journal of Negro History* 55 (1970): 344; Harlan, *Booker T. Washington; The Making of a Black Leader*, p. 226.

59 David G. Nielson, *Black Ethos: Northern Urban Negro Life and Thought, 1890–1930* (1977), pp. 199–200.

60 August Meier, et al., eds., *Black Protest Thought in the Twentieth Century* (1971), pp. 32–35.

61 W.E.B. Du Bois, *The Souls of Black Folk* (1903), pp. 30–42.

62 Ibid., p. 36; Johnson, *Black Manhattan*, p. 134.

63 Harlan, *Booker T. Washington: The Wizard of Tuskegee*, p. 70; *Washington Papers*, vol. 7 (1977), pp. 384–387; David Levering Lewis, *W.E.B. Du Bois: Biography of a Race, 1868–1919* (1993), p. 308.

64 *Washington Papers*, vol. 10 (1981), pp. 608–609.

65 Ralph Ellison, *Invisible Man* (1952), pp. 142–143.

66 Gunnar Myrdal, *An American Dilemma: The Negro Problem and Modern Democracy* (1944), p. 741.

67 Thornbrough, "Booker T. Washington As Seen By His White Contemporaries," p. 180.

68 Harlan, *Booker T. Washington: The Making of a Black Leader*, p. vii; J.R. Pole, "Of Mr. Booker T. Washington and Others," in *Paths to the American Past* (1979), pp. 184–185.

69 McMillen, *Dark Journey*, p. 300; Martin Luther King, Jr., *Where Do We Go From Here? Chaos or Community?* (1968), p. 137; Norrell, *Up from History*, p. 440.

CHAPTER THREE

W.E.B. Du Bois: Talented Propagandist

The problem of the twentieth century is the problem of the color-line,—the relation of the darker to the lighter races of men in Asia and Africa, in America and the islands of the sea.[1]

[W.E.B. Du Bois]

My first clear memory of Dr. Du Bois was my pride in his recognized scholarship and authority in his many fields of work and writing. . . . We Negro students joined the NAACP which Dr. Du Bois helped to organize and build; we read religiously The Crisis *of which he was editor for so many years, and in which he wrote clearly, constructively and militantly on the complex problems of the American scene, on the Negro question, on Africa, and on world affairs.*[2]

[Paul Robeson]

I first read Du Bois' The Souls of Black Folk *in my home and his novel* The Quest of the Silver Fleece. *He writes, my father would say, but he doesn't lead anybody.*[3]

[unknown African American]

Perspectives: Northern blacks organize for protest, 1890–1910

The late 19th century saw several attempts to protest racial discrimination and Washingtonian accommodationism. In 1887, T. Thomas Fortune, editor of the *New York Age* and the most able black journalist of his day, appealed to African Americans to organize a

National Afro-American League which would agitate for the removal of six principal grievances: (1) the suppression of voting rights in the South, which denied blacks political participation in the states where they were most numerous, (2) the prevalence of mob rule and lynching in the South, (3) the inequitable distribution of government funds between black and white schools, (4) the degrading prison system in the South, (5) the racial segregation on southern railroads, and (6) the denial of accommodations to African Americans in public places. Writing from his Tuskegee Institute, Booker T. Washington supported these proposals, which led to a convention in 1890 in Chicago, Illinois. The delegates endorsed Fortune's recommendation that the desired goals be secured by appealing to public opinion, pursuing litigation, and organizing non-violent demonstrations.[4]

Just three years later, Fortune announced that the Afro-American League was defunct because of inadequate support. In 1898, at a meeting in Rochester, New York, the league was revived as the National Afro-American Council, with a statement of objectives similar to the league's original platform. Conceived as a comprehensive civil rights organization, the council was rent by factionalism and was largely ineffectual during its ten-year existence. At first, Washington did not hold any office in the council, but through his friendship with Fortune, he became a dominant influence in its activities. To a large extent, black responses to the council reflected approval of or opposition to Washington's policies. When W.E.B. Du Bois, a young professor at Atlanta University, was made director of a business bureau promoted by the council, Washington sensed a challenge to his leadership and formed the National Negro Business League, with the help of a list of African-American entrepreneurs provided to him by Du Bois. It was also true that Washington believed that the council would concentrate on protest, rather than on economic approaches to uplifting the race.[5]

Because the Afro-American Council continued to be dominated by Washingtonians, Du Bois insisted that something more be done. He issued an appeal to twenty-nine African-American "radicals" to meet on the Canadian side of Niagara Falls in July, 1905, to form an organization opposed to Washington's Tuskegee Machine. The Niagara Movement, which resulted from this meeting, placed responsibility for the racial problem squarely on whites. Its list of demands included the end to discrimination in voting and jury selection, equal economic and education opportunity, livable housing, and an end to the convict-lease system. The reformers refused to apologize for complaining "loudly" about these injustices and called for "persistent manly agitation," an oblique reference to the Tuskegee Machine. The statement was sharply critical of employers, labor unions, the Christian Church, and American public opinion. In many respects, the Niagara Movement reflected the aspirations of the college-educated black elite and its determination to effect profound changes in American race relations through direct action. Journalist Ray Stannard Baker described this effort as "a party of protest which endeavors to prevent Negro separation and discrimination against Negroes by political agitation and political influence."[6]

Predictably, Booker T. Washington opposed the Niagara Movement from its inception. His obstructionist tactics and ubiquitous influence undermined the organization, which was never able to gain white support. It was also unable to gain an appreciable following among the black masses, and went down to short-term defeat as a protest movement. But the Niagara Movement was further evidence of the growing dissatisfaction of black northerners with Washington's southern-style leadership and claim to speak for the black race. Baker characterized Washington as "an opportunist and optimist" who "teaches that if the Negro wins by real worth a strong economic position in this country, other rights and privileges will come to him naturally." And, Baker added, "many highly educated Negroes, especially in the North, dislike and oppose" Washington. To Gunnar Myrdal, who spearheaded an important study of the black condition, the Niagara Movement signified "the first organized attempt to raise the Negro protest against the great reaction after the Reconstruction. Its main importance was that it brought to open conflict and wide public debate two types of Negro strategy—one stressing accommodation and the other raising the Negro protest. Booker T. Washington and W.E.B. Du Bois became national symbols for these two main streams of Negro thought."[7]

The short-lived Niagara Movement was never effective because of serious organizational flaws, including insufficient funding and inadequate leadership, as well as Booker T. Washington's determined opposition. But the movement laid the foundation for the National Association for the Advancement of Colored People (NAACP), a biracial coalition of black radicals and white liberals, pledged to advance civil and political rights for African Americans. The NAACP would represent a more serious challenge to Washington's dominance and would become the most important civil rights organization in American history.[8]

The origins of the NAACP grew out of a shocking 1908 race riot in Springfield, Illinois, home of Abraham Lincoln, the Great Emancipator.

The riot resulted in the deaths of eight blacks, fifty injured people, and a mass exodus of African Americans from the city. William English Walling, a white Kentuckian, socialist, and social worker, reported the appalling incident in an article entitled, "The Race War in the North." He appealed for a revival of the abolitionist spirit, and urged the formation of a national organization of whites and blacks to work for social justice. Among those responding to Walling's appeal were Henry Moskowitz, a Jewish social worker, and Mary White Ovington, a wealthy northerner from an abolitionist background who had just completed a study of African Americans in New York City. At their suggestion, Oswald Garrison Villard, the editor of the *New York Evening Post*, an early supporter of Booker T. Washington, and the grandson of the famed abolitionist William Lloyd Garrison, issued a "call" on the centennial of Lincoln's birth, for a national conference to debate "the renewal of the struggle for civil and political liberty." Those responding to the call included leading white Progressive reformers, such as settlement house organizer Jane Addams, philosopher John Dewey, Rabbi Stephen Wise, and the "muckraking" journalists Ray Stannard Baker and Lincoln Steffens. Black respondents included Du Bois; journalist Mary Church Terrell, a leader in the women's club movement; Ida B. Wells-Barnett, renowned for her anti-lynching campaign and co-founder of the first national organization for black women; and Bishop Alexander Walters, who had served in the Afro-American League and its successor, the Afro-American Council.[9]

The civil rights meeting called by Garrison was held in the spring of 1909, and was known as the National Negro Committee Conference. Booker T. Washington declined to attend to avoid jeopardizing his work in the South. He said he was interested only in "progressive, constructive" work for the race, and not in "agitation and criticism," but he dispatched a loyal lieutenant to watch the proceedings. In his address to the conference, W.E.B. Du Bois emphasized the interrelatedness of politics and economics, but avoided attacking Washington directly. Resolutions were adopted condemning the repression of African Americans, appealing to the federal government to compel southern states to honor the 14th and 15th Amendments, and demanding that African-American children receive a proportional share of educational appropriations. Although the conference organizers were anxious not to alienate Washington, black delegates rejected a proposal inviting him to join the steering committee, and forced through a resolution critical of his policies: "We fully agree with the prevailing opinion that the transformation of the unskilled colored laborers in industry and agriculture into skilled workers is of vital importance to that race and to the nation, but we demand for the Negroes, as for all others, a free and complete education . . . a grammar school and industrial training for all, and technical, professional, and academic education for the most gifted." Although Villard attempted to prevent the Committee from taking an anti-Washington stance, Washington declared that he would have no association with the body unless guarantees were given that neither Du Bois nor William Monroe Trotter of the *Boston Guardian* would formulate its policies.[10]

In 1910, the National Negro Committee changed its name to the National Association for the Advancement of Colored People, with the patrician white lawyer and Progressive reformer Moorfield Storey, as president. The new organization's announced aim was "to make 11,000,000 Americans physically free from peonage, mentally free from ignorance, politically free from disfranchisement, and socially free from insult." From its inception, the NAACP promoted change by lobbying for corrective legislation, educating public opinion, and securing favorable court decisions. Its first judicial victory came in 1915, when it won a U.S. Supreme Court ruling that Oklahoma's "grandfather clause"—designed to withhold the ballot from blacks—was unconstitutional. By then, the NAACP had 6,000 members in fifty branches and a circulation of over 31,000 for its magazine, the *Crisis*. Washington declared his opposition to the NAACP, and expressed concern that white delegates to the 1910 meeting had duped African Americans into believing that they could achieve progress "by merely making demands, passing resolutions and cursing somebody." When Du Bois resigned his professorship at Atlanta University and accepted an invitation to become the NAACP's director of publications and research, any hope of a rapprochement between the association and the Tuskegee Machine was lost. Already perceived as Washington's most formidable critic, Du Bois, as editor of the *Crisis*, cemented his reputation as the most gifted propagandist of the black protest impulse.[11]

W.E.B. Du Bois: Biography

William Edward Burghardt Du Bois was born to a working-class family in Great Barrington, Massachusetts, in 1868, the year of president Andrew Johnson's impeachment; he died in self-imposed exile in the West African nation of Ghana in 1963, at the time of the civil rights March on Washington. A poet, novelist, historian, sociologist, and essayist, Du Bois occupies a towering position in African-American letters, with twenty-two books, including three autobiographies and five novels, and several thousand articles and essays to his credit. An outstanding scholar and teacher, Du Bois also became a political activist, a founding member of the NAACP, and the editor of its journal. In all of these roles, he was consistently the champion of racial justice. At various points of his long career, Du Bois was the declared opponent of Booker T. Washington and Marcus Garvey; yet, he had more in common with them than he cared to admit. Du Bois was also a socialist and communist, an integrationist and advocate of a form of voluntary segregation, a black nationalist and a pioneering pan-Africanist. A supporter of African-American participation in World War I, he became a pacifist and a Soviet Union/Chinese sympathizer during the Cold War of the 1950s. An elitist who singularly lacked the common touch and championed the cause of the "talented tenth," Du Bois was aloof, arrogant, and visionary. During the 1930s he alienated the black bourgeoisie and intelligentsia who had earlier supported his integrationist "radicalism."[12]

Despite claims by admirers to the contrary, Du Bois' intellectual biography is marked by fluctuation and inconsistency in his thinking, if not outright contradiction. An ardent supporter of Western cultural values and achievements, he also stressed racial pride and consciousness as the prerequisites for black advancement. Du Bois expressed his fundamental ambivalence concerning racial and national identity in his essay, "Of Our Spiritual Strivings," in *The Souls of Black Folk* (1903):

One ever feels his two-ness—an American, a Negro; two souls, two thoughts, two unreconciled strivings; two warring ideals in one dark body, whose dogged strength alone keeps it from being torn asunder. The history of the American Negro is the history of this strife,—this longing to attain self-conscious manhood, to merge his double self into a better and truer self. In this merging he wishes neither of the older selves to be lost. He would not Africanize America, for America has too much to teach the world and Africa. He would not bleach his Negro soul in a flood of white Americanism, for he knows that Negro blood has a message for the world.[13]

To no African American is this statement of twin souls warring in each black body more applicable than to Du Bois himself. Of French Huguenot, Dutch, and African ancestry, Du Bois described his racial background as consisting of "a flood of Negro blood, a strain of French, a bit of Dutch, but, thank God! no 'Anglo-Saxon.'" Because his father Alfred deserted the family and his puritanical mother Mary suffered an incapacitating stroke, Du Bois had to rely on handouts from his extended family and after-school jobs. By his own account, Du Bois grew up in a bucolic New England town of 5,000 inhabitants with only a few African Americans, and racism was largely hidden from his view until an incident opened his eyes. When a white girl who was new in school refused to accept one of Du Bois' "calling cards" during a game, Du Bois became more conscious of his darker complexion and more alert to racial innuendo and vindictiveness. He now felt a "vast veil" shut him off from his white companions. The result, he wrote, was that he developed "a great bitterness" early in his life that transformed his good-natured personality to one that was sullen and introspective. Still, Du Bois absorbed ideas and values from local white schools and the Congregational church that left him "quite thoroughly New England."[14]

An exceptional student, the 15-year-old Du Bois contributed literary, political, and social essays to the *New York Globe* and the *New York Freeman*. In these early pieces, he urged African Americans to join the temperance movement, form literary societies, and take a greater interest in politics. After graduating as high school valedictorian in 1885, Du Bois won a scholarship to attend Fisk University, a black college in Nashville, Tennessee, where he encountered extreme racism and, simultaneously, began to cultivate his identity as an African American: "No one but a Negro going into the South without previous experience of color caste can have any conception of its barbarism. . . . I was thrilled to be for the first time among so many people of my own color or rather of such extraordinary colors, which I had only glimpsed before, but who it seemed were bound to me by new and exciting eternal ties. . . . Into this world I leapt with enthusiasm: henceforward I was a Negro."[15]

At Fisk, Du Bois also encountered rural poverty and ignorance first hand, when for two summers, he taught in rural schools in the hill country. His students came from poor black families who believed rote learning and minimal literacy were sufficient in a subsistence farming economy. The experience confirmed his growing belief in the power of education and reason to resolve racial conflict and secure black advancement. Simultaneously, it increased his awareness of the enormous intellectual gulf between himself and the generality of black people. For those who remained uneducated, for whatever reason, Du Bois optimistically concluded that he and other educated African Americans, such as his Fisk classmates, would necessarily lift up the black masses, whom he dubbed "enslaved Israelites," "out of [their] still enduring bondage in short order."[16]

Graduating from Fisk in 1888, Du Bois entered Harvard University, where he was greatly influenced by the philosophers William James,

Josiah Royce, and George Santayana. He never felt at home at Harvard, but he still earned two degrees there. In 1892, Du Bois left for Europe to study on a graduate scholarship from the Slater Fund. Intent on earning a doctorate in social science, he enrolled in history, economics, and sociology courses at the University of Berlin, where he studied under the economist Gustav Schmoller and the historian Heinrich von Treitschke. A declared admirer of Otto von Bismarck, who had created the German state through the force of his will and personality, Du Bois' later pan-Africanism was undoubtedly influenced by his exposure to the rise of German national consciousness. His stay in Germany also acquainted him with socialist theory and practice.[17]

On his return to the United States, Du Bois had arrived at his basic intellectual and ideological convictions. The black race, he believed, could only advance through its own self-help and the assistance of whites of good will. Black leadership, he reasoned, must be provided by the race's intellectuals—the talented tenth—who would inspire their own people, while seeking aid and stimulation from whites. At Harvard, he claimed to have "conceived the idea of applying philosophy to an historical inter-pretation of race relations," and saw the discipline of sociology "as the science of human action." In his doctoral dissertation, *The Suppression of the African Slave Trade to the United States of America, 1638–1870*, Du Bois argued that moral cowardice, encouraged by greed, had sustained slave trafficking after it had been prohibited by law; its suppression had resulted from a mixture of humanitarian, economic, and political pressures. He concluded that the slave trade had been indispensable in the develop-ment of the American economy and capitalism generally. His original and provocative thesis was published in 1896 as the first volume of the Harvard Historical Series.[18]

As the first African American with a Harvard Ph.D., Du Bois seemed destined for a distinguished academic career. From 1894–1896, he was a professor of Latin and Greek at Wilberforce University, a black college in Ohio, having rejected an offer from Booker T. Washington to teach mathematics at Tuskegee. In his autobiography, Du Bois noted wryly, "It would be interesting to speculate just what would have happened if I had received the offer of Tuskegee first, instead of that at Wilberforce." Repelled by the religious fervor that erupted frequently at Wilberforce in the form of spiritual revivals, Du Bois gratefully accepted an invitation from the University of Pennsylvania to study the black population of Philadelphia. *The Philadelphia Negro* (1899) was a sociological work that criticized the city's African Americans for their alleged immorality and

criminality, neglect of education, and failure to organize for social better-
ment, as well as the inattention of the black middle class to its leadership
potential. White Philadelphians were judged guilty of racist attitudes, and
were urged to cooperate with "better" African Americans by recognizing
class and status distinctions within the black community. Widely regarded
as a model study of an urban black community, *The Philadelphia Negro*
established Du Bois' academic reputation. Research for the book also
broadened his racial outlook, and he later confessed: "I became painfully
aware that merely being born in a group, does not necessarily make
one possessed of complete knowledge concerning it. I had learned far
more from Philadelphia Negroes than I had taught them concerning the
Negro Problem."[19]

From 1897 to 1910, Du Bois taught sociology and history at Atlanta
University in Georgia, where he published a series of studies about segregation in every area of American life, including labor unions, prisons,
business, and industry. But significantly, in view of his controversial proposal for "voluntary segregation" in the 1930s, the Atlanta Studies also
acknowledged segregation as a unifying force in black life. In this period
also, Du Bois refined and amplified his conception of blackness and the
meaning of the African-American experience. "The Conservation of Races
and the Negro," an address delivered to the newly-formed American Negro
Academy in 1897, was Du Bois' most detailed statement on the nature of
racial prejudice and discrimination, and called on the black community
to maintain a separate racial identity. Du Bois claimed that "spiritual,
psychical, differences" between the races transcended physical differences
as they coalesced into separate nations. Where the English had bestowed
on the world ideas of "constitutional liberty and commercial freedom,"
and the Germans, discoveries in science and philosophy, black people still
had to reveal their gifts and qualities. These gifts, celebrated by Du Bois
in *The Souls of Black Folk*, were those of "pathos and humor," folktales,
and artistic and musical abilities. He advised the American Negro Academy
to seek "to comprise something of the best thought, the most unselfish
striving and the highest ideals."[20]

During the early 1900s, then, Du Bois had been deeply engaged in
scholarship about African-American history and society, but he became
increasingly convinced that the worsening racial situation required more
direct confrontation on his part. The lynching of Sam Hose, a black farm-
hand, by a blood-thirsty, sadistic mob southwest of Atlanta prodded Du
Bois to put service to his people ahead of his academic ambitions. Du Bois
had been horrified to learn that Hose's knuckles were for sale in a grocery

store jar, and concluded that the scientific study of racism was of small import compared to immediate agitation for full civil rights. Du Bois' publication of *The Souls of Black Folk*, with its devastating critique of Booker T. Washington, his instigation of the Niagara Movement, and his response to the call that saw the founding of the NAACP completed Du Bois' transition from academician to propagandist. In addition to condemning Washington's accommodationism, Du Bois opposed the allegiance of most African Americans to the Republican party that had freed them and the complete assimilation of blacks into white society. Du Bois used his position as editor of the *Crisis* to offer his alternative visions of the present condition and future prospects of African Americans.[21]

The *Crisis* editor

The first issue of the *Crisis* appeared in November, 1910, with a monthly circulation of 1,000 copies. Within a year, it sold 16,000 copies; within ten years, its circulation soared to 100,000. As editor of the magazine from its inception to 1934, W.E.B. Du Bois acknowledged that during this period he dedicated his life to making the NAACP's house journal an "organ of propaganda and defense" through which he mounted "one of the most effective assaults of liberalism upon reaction that the modern world has seen." Never modest about his considerable abilities and accomplishments, Du Bois observed that "if . . . the *Crisis* had not been in a sense a personal organ and the expression of myself, it could not possibly have attained its popularity and effectiveness."[22]

Certainly, some of Du Bois' finest and most polemical prose appeared in his monthly editorials. Determined from the outset that the journal would reflect his own ideas, even when they ran counter to those of the (white) NAACP leadership, Du Bois aimed his editorial shafts at the literate, middle-class black public. He regularly criticized the South for its inhuman treatment of African Americans, as evidenced by segregation, white primaries, the convict-lease system, and especially lynching. Early issues also featured editorials and articles on "Colored High Schools," "The Colored College Athlete," and "Women's Clubs," as well as assertions that African Americans possessed a superior spiritual sense and beauty that made them a chosen people. Du Bois called for resistance to segregated schools outside the South, attacked black churches for their racial conservatism, lambasted scientific racism and eugenics, and defended the rights of women, including their right to vote. In the event that he was attacked verbally or otherwise, Du Bois issued this avowal in an early issue of the

Crisis: "I am resolved to be quiet and law abiding, but to refuse to cringe in body or in soul, to resent deliberate insult, and to assert my just rights in the face of wanton aggression." He recommended black self-defense against white vigilante mobs.[23]

Anticipating later theorists, Du Bois linked the struggles of African Americans and women: "Every argument for Negro suffrage is an argument for women's suffrage; every argument for women's suffrage is an argument for Negro suffrage; both are great movements in democracy." At the same time, Du Bois was concerned about the racism in the white women's suffrage movement, and predicted that "the women's vote, particularly in the South, will be cast almost unanimously, at first, for every reactionary Negro-hating piece of legislation." Aware of the double oppression—racial and sexual—suffered by African-American women, Du Bois wrote in *Darkwater: Voices From Within the Veil* (1920) that although he could forgive the South for slavery and its attempt to destroy the American Union, he could not forgive "its wanton and continued and persistent insulting of the black womanhood it sought and seeks to prostitute to its lust."[24]

Employing an array of techniques and literary devices, Du Bois wrote in a clear, direct style, and used savage invective and sardonic humor to depict racial indignities and atrocities. Du Bois often made hate crimes a prime focus of his editorials. In 1911, he dramatically described a lynching in Pennsylvania: "Ah, the splendor of that Sunday night dance. The flames beat and curled against the moonlight sky. The church bells chimed. The scorched and crooked thing, self-wounded and chained to his cot, crawled to the edge of the ash with a stifled groan, but the brave and sturdy farmers pricked him back with the bloody pitchforks until the deed was done. Let the eagle scream! Civilization is again safe!" In 1914, Du Bois published a letter of an anonymous witness to the lynching of Samuel Petty, accused of having killed a deputy sheriff in Leland, Mississippi:

The man who had killed the officer submitted to arrest by the mob, which . . . numbered about 400. Placing a rope around his neck he was led to the center of the town and in the presence of women and children they proceeded to hold a conference as to the kind of death that should be meted out to him. Some yelled to hang him; some to burn him alive. It was decided in a few minutes. Willing hands brought a large dry-goods box, placed it in the center of the street; in it was straw on which was poured a tub of oil; then the man was lifted with a rope around his neck and placed in this box head down, and then another tub of oil was poured over him. A man from the crowd deliberately lit a match and set fire to the living man. . . . [T]he poor creature managed to lift himself out of the box, a mass of flames, and . . . attempted to run. The crowd allowed him to run to the length of the rope . . . until he reached a distance of about twenty feet; then a yell went up . . . to shoot. In an instant there were several hundred shots and the creature fell in his tracks. . . . Not a voice was heard in the defense of the man. . . . I looked into the faces of men whom I knew to be officers in the town lending a willing hand in the burning of this man.[25]

After an intensive investigation, the NAACP published *Thirty Years of Lynching in the United States, 1889–1918*, which reported that 3,224 black men and women had been lynched during this period. In only 19 percent of these cases had rape or other forms of sexual assault been alleged, despite the South's repeated contention that lynching was "necessary" to protect white women from black ravishment. Shocking examples of lynch law appeared on the pages of the *Crisis*, most dramatically the seizure and lynching of Jesse Washington, a mentally-impaired adolescent, sentenced to death in 1916 for the murder of a white woman in Waco, Texas. "The Waco Horror," an eight-page report of the episode, complete with photographic evidence, was used as the opening move in an NAACP campaign for an anti-lynching fund. Distributed to 42,000 subscribers of the *Crisis*, 52 black weeklies, and 700 white newspapers, it was also sent to all members of Congress and to a long list of "moneyed men" in New York, who were asked to subscribe to the appeal. "The Waco Horror" included the information that "Washington . . . was dragged through the streets, stabbed, mutilated and finally burned to death in the presence of a crowd of 10,000. After the death, what was left of his body was dragged through the streets and parts of it sold as souvenirs. His teeth brought $5 a piece and the chain that bound him 25 cents a link."[26]

Du Bois attributed the increase in lynching during this period partly to the influence of the modern motion picture, *The Birth of a Nation*, which glorified the Ku Klux Klan in defense of white southern society after the Civil War. Du Bois asserted that the film "fed to the youth of the nation and to the unthinking masses . . . a story which twisted the emancipation and enfranchisement of the slave in a great effort toward universal democracy, into an orgy of theft and degradation and wide rape of white women."[27]

Du Bois' editorship of the *Crisis* was marked by almost constant friction between himself and the NAACP board. At issue was usually disagreement over the relationship between the journal and the association. Without consulting the board, Du Bois attacked large sections of the black press, asserting that they did not publish the truth about the dismal racial situation or consistently support the imperative of civil rights. Irritated black editors responded sharply to such attacks, and in 1914, at its annual convention, the NAACP passed a resolution praising the black press and, indirectly, rebuking Du Bois. In response, Du Bois charged that some of his white critics within the association were racists, and argued that the "Negro problem" could not be separated from other humanitarian and social concerns of the day. In these, as in other views, his editorial statements often diverged from agreed NAACP policy.[28]

On Booker T. Washington's death in 1915, Du Bois paid him a critical tribute in the *Crisis*. Washington was, he conceded, "the greatest Negro leader since Frederick Douglass, and the most distinguished man, white or black, who has come out of the South since the Civil War." Washington had correctly directed the attention of African Americans to economic development and stressed the desirability of "technical education," and the securing of property, Du Bois wrote. Although Washington had induced white southerners to "at least think of the Negro as a possible man," Du Bois concluded that Washington must also bear "a heavy responsibility for the consummation of Negro disfranchisement, the decline of the Negro college and public school, and the firmer establishment of color caste in this land."[29]

Even after Booker T. Washington died, his influence compelled the NAACP to extend an olive branch to his followers. In 1916, Du Bois, with other leading African Americans, attended a meeting called by Joel Spingarn, a white member of the NAACP, at his home in Amenia, New York. In a series of conciliatory resolutions, the Amenia Conference attempted to bridge the differences between the Washingtonians and their opponents. All forms of education were declared desirable for blacks; political rights were to be secured through the cooperation of all black leaders, and "antiquated subjects of controversy . . . and factional alignments" were to be discarded. Du Bois later recalled that the Amenia Conference "not only marked the end of the old things and the old thoughts . . . and ways of attacking the race problem . . . in addition to this it was the beginning of new things." Yet it was Du Bois himself who soon violated the Amenia principle of cooperative and concerted black protest. As editor of the *Crisis*, he continued to attack the idea of industrial education, advised blacks to leave the South, and castigated black southern leaders for their timidity.[30]

The outbreak of World War I proved particularly problematic for Du Bois, although he saw tremendous opportunity in the conflict. On the one hand, Du Bois thought that the war resulted from a spasm of imperial self-interest as European rivals quarreled over Africa; on the other hand, Du Bois expected that if African Americans fought in the war and if the Allies (England and France) defeated the Central Powers (Germany and Austria-Hungary), a lessening of racism in American society would occur. President Woodrow Wilson, after all, had combined his call to war with a call for the world to "be made safe for democracy." Du Bois also hoped that the yoke of European colonialism in Africa—particularly Germany's—would finally be broken. In the expectation that African Americans would benefit from the war, Du Bois penned "Close Ranks," the most controversial editorial ever published in the *Crisis*. "Let us, while this war lasts," Du Bois implored in July, 1918, "forget our special grievances and close our ranks shoulder to shoulder with our white fellow citizens and the allied nations that are fighting for democracy. We make no ordinary sacrifice, but we make it gladly and willingly, with our eyes lifted to the hills."[31]

Radicals denounced W.E.B. Du Bois for preferring war over the struggle for justice. A. Philip Randolph, a leading black socialist, asserted that "Close Ranks" was as shameful as Washington's Atlanta Compromise, and castigated Du Bois as a sycophant. When Du Bois was offered a commission in the Intelligence branch of the United States Army, his critics accused him of having been bribed to support the Wilson administration's policies. Du Bois had earlier supported Wilson under the mistaken impression that the president would support black civil rights. The army eventually withdrew the offer, but Du Bois' behavior in the affair, which included the demand that he should receive $1,000 a year from the NAACP to supplement his army pay, called into question his judgment and commitment to black protest.[32]

If, as his critics maintained, Du Bois had been an accommodationist in time of war, his optimism about black advances was short-lived. He was angered by continued racial discrimination by the American Federation of Labor (AF of L), and appalled by the race riots during the war and in the "Red Summer" of 1919 that greeted returning black veterans. The reemergence of the Ku Klux Klan and its rapid growth in American cities exacerbated an already volatile racial situation. Du Bois' response to these events was a powerful editorial, "Returning Soldiers," of May, 1919, which advised blacks to "return fighting" in the struggle at home against racism. America, victorious over German imperialism, was still a "shameful land":

It *lynches*. And lynching is barbarism of a degree of contemptible nastiness unparalleled in human history. Yet for fifty years we have lynched two Negroes a week. It *disfranchises* its own citizens. . . . It encourages *ignorance*. . . . It *steals* from us. . . . It *insults* us. . . . This is the country to which we soldiers of Democracy return. . . . By the God of Heaven, we are cowards and jackasses if now that the war is over we do not marshal every ounce of our brain and brawn to conquer a sterner, longer, more unbending battle against the forces of hell in our own land. We *return*. We *return from fighting*. We *return fighting*. Make way for Democracy! We saved it in France, and by the Great Jehovah, we will save it in the United States of America, or know the reason why.

"Returning Soldiers" prompted the U.S. Justice Department to investigate the *Crisis* and other black journals. It published a condemnatory report, "Radicalism and Sedition Among Negroes As Reflected in Their Publications," but did not prosecute any editor or publisher.[33]

After World War I ended, Du Bois visited France, England, Belgium, Switzerland, Portugal, Germany, Russia, and Africa. These journeys, he wrote, "gave me a depth of knowledge and a breadth of view which was of incalculable value for realizing and judging modern conditions and, above all, the problem of race in America and the world." While America's racial problems continued to engage most of his attention, Du Bois came to believe that they had to be set in the context of the universal problem of the "color line."[34]

During the 1920s, Du Bois used the *Crisis* to hammer away at various racial inequities. He directed a campaign against black colleges and universities that did not have representative numbers of African Americans on their faculties or in administrative positions. This campaign was particularly close to Du Bois because he had attended Fisk University, an all-black institution with a mostly white faculty. In a second campaign, Du Bois suggested that the NAACP, the AF of L, and the railroad brotherhoods organize an interracial commission to create integrated labor unions. But the NAACP's leadership, which was primarily concerned with political and civil rights, did not consider the promotion of unionism among blacks as a cause it could endorse. Du Bois himself soon abandoned his earlier tolerant attitude toward organized labor in the face of increasing discrimination within the union movement, and his growing conviction that African Americans could not expect white support or good will. He did not empathize with bloody textile strikes because "I knew that factory strikers like these would not let a Negro work beside them or live in the same town."[35]

It was also in the Jazz Age that Du Bois used the pages of the *Crisis* to promote new directions in African American literature. The magazine played a major role in fomenting the Harlem Renaissance, a burst of creativity by black writers and artists in the 1920s. Du Bois published early pieces by Langston Hughes, Countee Cullen, Jean Toomer, and Aaron Douglas. Eventually, Du Bois concluded that some writers were politically irresponsible. In his essay, "Criteria of Negro Art," Du Bois argued that all art is essentially propaganda and should therefore be used to promote racial advancement. Such progress could be accomplished by deploying "Truth" to promote "universal understanding" and "Goodness" to engender "sympathy and human interest."[36]

The Great Depression of the 1930s pushed W.E.B. Du Bois to adopt a new line of thought. Although he agreed with other militants that economic considerations were of paramount importance to the black masses, Du Bois no longer considered a black/white alliance of the disadvantaged to be a possibility, given the intensity of American racism. Accordingly, he proposed the formation of black economic cooperative enterprises based on socialist principles and the notions of self-help and cultural nationalism. His assumption was that the black church and black businesses created the possibility of a self-sufficient economy, which African-American consumers already supported in some areas, such as Farmville, Virginia, and Durham, North Carolina. There, black-owned businesses flourished, including banking, grocery stores, barbershops, funeral homes, brick-making, steam laundry, and drugstores. Du Bois proposed that African Americans should develop this separate economy, and to the consternation of the NAACP and many black radicals, he advocated racial "self-segregation" as the road to ultimate black political and economic power. While he welcomed the expansion of government activities under president Franklin D. Roosevelt's New Deal, Du Bois did not expect the administration's policies to effect any sea change in black-white relations. Although he conceded that African Americans had undoubtedly gained from New Deal welfare and public works programs, Du Bois did not want them to remain dependent on a supposedly benevolent president. Rather, they should accept the persistence of racial prejudice, including the reality of enforced segregation, and develop their own institutions.[37]

In presenting the case for black economic separatism, Du Bois attempted to reassure readers of the *Crisis* that his ideas did not conflict with NAACP objectives and policies. The association's traditional opposition to segregation, he argued, had been opposition to discrimination, and the two were not necessarily synonymous. Since the NAACP had long supported "segregated" institutions, such as churches, schools and newspapers, a self-segregated black economy was simply another step in the formation of institutions that would bolster black pride and morale. In essence, Du Bois urged African Americans—and the NAACP—to face the fact of enforced segregation and turn it to their advantage. Members of the talented tenth should become planners of producer and consumer cooperatives that would form "a Negro nation within a nation." Unless African Americans patronized black-owned stores and used the services of the black professional classes, "there is no hope for the Negro in America."[38]

Other black leaders were appalled by Du Bois' new thinking. To Du Bois' critics, "a Negro nation within a nation" smacked of petty capitalism and, worse, Booker T. Washington's accommodationism. NAACP executive secretary Walter White claimed that Du Bois' editorial on "voluntary segregation" had been used by federal agencies to freeze relief projects for African Americans, and reasserted the association's position that "to accept the status of separateness means inferior accommodations . . . and spiritual atrophy for the group segregated." When the NAACP passed a resolution condemning "enforced segregation," Du Bois launched an unsuccessful campaign to reorganize the association along more "progressive" lines. In advocating black economic self-sufficiency and in appearing to condone—if not actively encourage—racial segregation, Du Bois was running against the tide of dominant black thought of the day. Francis Grimké, a black minister who had helped create the NAACP, asserted that Du Bois' apparent acceptance of Jim Crow signaled the end of his role as a race leader. A black Chicago newspaper mourned the passing of a "race champion" by turning conventional wisdom about two great black leaders upside down: Over a picture of Booker T. Washington, it placed the caption, "Was He Right After All?"; above Du Bois' picture, it asked, "Is He A Quitter?" Du Bois heatedly denied that his proposals for economic cooperatives bore any resemblance to Washington's National Negro Business League, which sought to develop a black economy on the basis of free competition and private profit.[39]

The relationship between Du Bois and the NAACP had reached a critical point. The NAACP tried to rein in Du Bois by forbidding criticism of the association in the *Crisis* without prior approval, but Du Bois ignored the resolution and continued to regard the journal as his own personal medium. Black newspaper editors now expressed concern over the rift in the NAACP, and sided with the association against Du Bois. Walter White charged Du Bois with accepting Jim Crow and undermining the association's integrationist ideals. With no possibility of compromise, Du Bois resigned from the NAACP that he had helped found and returned to Atlanta University in June, 1934. Accepting his resignation, while rejecting Du Bois' criticism of the association, the NAACP leadership paid Du Bois a generous and deserved tribute. Through the *Crisis*, Du Bois had created "what never existed before, a Negro intelligentsia, and many who have never read a word of his writings are his spiritual disciples and descendants. . . . We shall be the poorer for his loss, in intellectual stimulus, and in searching analysis of the vital problems of the American Negro; no one in the Association can fill his place with the same intellectual grasp." If Du Bois' call for a separate black community failed to win either elite or majority support, his pan-African enthusiasms also failed to resonate with most NAACP members and readers of the *Crisis*.[40]

Pan-Africanism

As a young child, W.E.B. Du Bois heard his grandmother singing a "heathen melody" to her children, and instinctively felt that the strange-sounding words spoke to his African "roots": "Do ba-na co-ba, ge-ne me, ge-ne me! Ben d' nu-li, nu-li, nu-li, ben d' le." These lines were handed down orally in the Du Bois family, and "we sing it to our children, knowing as little as our fathers what its words may mean, but knowing well the meaning of its music. This was African music . . . the voice of exile." After his rejection as a youngster by white children in Great Barrington, Massachusetts, and his experiences as a student at Fisk University, Du Bois discovered his "African racial feeling" and felt himself to be both African by "race" and "an integral member of the group of dark Americans who are called Negroes."[41]

Concern with Africa, the ancestry and culture of African Americans, and the deliverance of the African continent from European colonizing powers became central themes of Du Bois' thoughts and writings. He came to the conclusion that before Africans, including African Americans, could be free anywhere, they had to be free everywhere. And so, he called for African peoples worldwide "to bring about at the earliest possible time the industrial and spiritual emancipation of the Negro peoples." Yet whether as a scholar, propagandist, or the organizer of four Pan-African Congresses between 1919 and 1927, Du Bois' conception of Africa was that of a romantic racialist. He ignored cultural differences and conflicts between Africans themselves, and gave African Americans an inspirational role which they—and most Africans—found faintly ludicrous. Reporting on his first experiences of Africa in 1923, when he attended the inauguration of the president of Liberia, Du Bois apprised *Crisis* readers: "The spell of Africa is upon me. The ancient witchery of her medicine is burning my drowsy, dreary blood. This is not a country, it is a world—a universe of itself and for itself, a thing Different, Immense, Menacing, Alluring. It is a great black bosom where the Spirit longs to die. . . . Things move— black shiny bodies, bodies of sleek and unearthly poise and beauty." Idyllic pictures of African village and tribal life, with "well-bred and courteous children, playing happily and never sniffing or whining" were intended to awaken in African Americans pride in Africa and, by implication, pride in themselves. Although he was to ridicule Marcus Garvey's glorification of blackness, Du Bois was himself a racial chauvinist, holding for all of his life a near-obsession with color.[42]

Du Bois' active interest in Africa began in 1900, when he went to the first Pan-African Congress, which was held in London, England, and attended by delegates from Ethiopia, the Gold Coast, Liberia, Sierra Leone, the Caribbean, and the United States. As chairman of the Committee of the Address to the Nations of the World, Du Bois issued a call to action:

Let the Nations of the World respect the integrity and independence of the free Negro States of Abyssinia, Liberia, Hayti, etc. and let the inhabitants of these States, the independent tribes of Africa, the Negroes of the West Indies and America, and the black subjects of all nations take courage, strive ceaselessly, and fight bravely, that they may prove to the world their incontestable right to be counted among the great brotherhood of mankind.[43]

Du Bois found himself at the center of pan-Africanism for four decades, until it dissolved at the end of World War II. The Second Pan-African Congress, organized by Du Bois and held in Paris, France, in 1919, was attended by delegates from fifteen countries. They resolved that Germany's African colonies should be turned over to an international organization, and that a code of laws be drawn up for the protection of Africans. At the Third Pan-African Congress, which was held in 1921 in London, Paris, and Brussels, Belgium, a committee headed by Du Bois petitioned the League of Nations on behalf of the African colonies. At the Fourth Pan-African Congress, which met in Paris and Lisbon, Portugal, in 1923, the delegates issued a set of eight demands seeking equality for black people around the world. At the Fifth Congress, held in New York City in 1927, the major resolutions demanded "the development of Africa for the Africans and not merely for the profit of the Europeans," and asked for independence for India, China, and Egypt. Du Bois either organized or played a leading role in each of these Congresses; yet, as he was to admit, African Americans—not to mention European powers—were not inspired by his pan-African visions. A Du Bois biographer suggested that in many respects, the Pan-African Congresses echoed the Niagara Movement: "a handful of self-appointed spokesmen challenged a staggering problem by passing resolutions. Even the principal techniques were familiar: the periodic conferences to recodify the platform, refresh personal contacts, and exchange enthusiasm and information, and the manifestos designed to rally colored support and to convert white opinion. In the end, the congresses accomplished, if anything, less than Niagara."[44]

Such a judgment is not entirely fair. Just as the Niagara Movement was a forerunner of organized black protest in 20th-century America, the Pan-African Congresses pointed to the later course of political independence in Africa and the Third World. African nationalists, such as Ghana's Kwame Nkrumah and Kenya's Jomo Kenyatta, were to acknowledge Du Bois as a founding father of pan-Africanism. In the United States, such ideologically divergent leaders as Martin Luther King, Jr., and Malcolm X were also to pay tribute to Du Bois' African dream. And for all his romanticization of Africa, Du Bois never advocated the "return" of African Americans to their ancestral homeland, but rather equated pan-Africanism with Zionism, while his celebration of African primitivism and the sensuousness of its arts, was in tune with the dominant mood of the Harlem Renaissance, the remarkable flowering of African-American culture in the period after World War I. At the height of the Garvey Movement in America, Du Bois cautioned, "Africa belongs to these Africans. They have not the slightest intention of giving it up to foreigners, white or black. . . . They resent that attitude that other folk of any color are coming in to take and rule their land."[45]

In the short term, Du Bois blamed the failure of pan-Africanism on the opposition of the European colonial powers, the patronizing and selfish attitudes of whites toward Africa, and the indifference of African Americans to the plight of their African contemporaries. Ironically, Marcus Garvey's fantastic notion of uniting all blacks of the world into one great organization was to eclipse Du Bois' pan-Africanism, just as it also underlined Du Bois' inability to reach a mass audience.[46]

A leader without followers, 1934–1963

The most prolific and gifted of all African-American scholars and intellectuals, W.E.B. Du Bois was never a successful leader or organizer. After his resignation from NAACP in 1934, at the age of sixty-six, he became increasingly isolated and bitter—in historian Francis Broderick's phrase, "a leader without followers." Du Bois' romantic faith in Africa, contempt for capitalist values, and attraction to world socialism left him remote from the everyday concerns of the majority of African Americans. From the time of his return to Atlanta University until his death in Ghana in 1963, Du Bois remained estranged from the talented tenth because of their opposition to socialism and voluntary segregation, and their support of integration and increased opportunity within the capitalist system. His rejection of interracial cooperation, insistence that racial prejudice was on the increase, and calls for racial separation were also out of step with the liberal reformism of the New Deal.[47]

Shortly after his return to Atlanta, Du Bois published two major works. *Black Reconstruction in America: An Essay toward a History of the Part which Black Folk Played in the Attempt to Reconstruct Democracy in America, 1860–1880* (1935) offered a Marxist interpretation of the role played by African Americans in securing the Confederacy's defeat in the Civil War. Enslaved African Americans, Du Bois argued, had engaged in a "general strike" when they fled from the plantations to join the invading Union armies. More realistically, *Black Reconstruction* stressed the problems faced by and the substantial achievements of African Americans during the Reconstruction era, and anticipated 1960s "revisionism" of the subject. *Dusk of Dawn*, which appeared in 1940, was subtitled "An Autobiography of a Race Concept" and presented Du Bois' account and defense of his dual careers as an African American and pan-African propagandist. "My life," he declared, had "its only deep significance because it was part of a Problem; but the Problem was . . . the central problem of the world's democracies and so the Problem of the future world . . . of which the concept of race is today one of the most unyielding and threatening."[48]

The central theme of *Dusk of Dawn* is Du Bois' search for meaning and harmony in a troubled and racially-divided world. He reiterated his belief in voluntary self-segregation as the only means of ensuring black progress in the United States, expressed a favorable view of the Marxist interpretation of history—although Du Bois denied that he was a communist—and reviewed the famous controversy with Booker T.

Washington. There had, Du Bois conceded, been significant differences between him and Washington. Where Washington had placed his faith in industrial education and "common labor," "I believed in the higher education of a Talented Tenth who through their knowledge of modern culture could guide the American Negro into a higher civilization." These theories, Du Bois later maintained, were not necessarily opposites, and indeed could have been complementary. But the striking feature of Washington's leadership was that "whatever he . . . believed in or wanted must be subordinated to common public opinion and that opinion deferred to and cajoled until it allowed a deviation toward better ways." The roots of the controversy lay in the "discrepancies and paradoxes" of Washington's influence and leadership: "It did not seem fair . . . that on the one hand Mr. Washington should decry political activities among Negroes, and on the other hand dictate Negro political objectives from Tuskegee. At a time when Negro civil rights called for organized and aggressive defense, he broke down that defense by advising acquiescence or at least no open agitation." Above all, Du Bois argued, the Tuskegee Machine, which bribed the black press and stifled "even mild and reasonable opposition" to Washington had to be resisted.[49]

At the end of his life, Du Bois allowed for a greater respect for—if not approval of—Booker T. Washington's leadership. At a dinner party, someone implied that Washington had been "a stooge for the bosses." Du Bois, who had grown up in a New England home, strongly disagreed with this assessment, noting that his aunts had firmly reprimanded him for criticizing anyone who had survived the brutality of slavery. Besides, Du Bois recognized that Washington's accommodationist approach to the plight of African Americans was understandable, given the unrelenting hostility of whites to black advancement. In sum, the differences between Washington and Du Bois owed much to the place and socioeconomic status that each matured in. Whatever their differences, Du Bois thought that Washington had achieved some noteworthy gains. Du Bois' dinner companions were impressed by the empathy shown to the "Wizard of Tuskegee," whom he had so often excoriated publicly.[50]

At the same time, Du Bois expressed his increasingly radical orientation in many different ways. When Atlanta University forced Du Bois to retire in 1944 because he was 76-years-old, he returned to the NAACP, this time to address international issues, particularly the question of decolonization of Africa. After World War II erupted, Du Bois criticized European colonial powers more than Hitler, but came to regard the war as another opportunity for the self-determination of oppressed peoples.

He wrote a bristling polemic, *Color and Democracy: Colonies and Peace* (1945), which linked the future of Africa to that of the rest of the world, aligned African nationalism with socialist thought, and condemned international organizations for their tacit approval of colonialism. Du Bois' thinking in this regard was deepened by his service as a consultant to the American delegation at the founding session of the United Nations in San Francisco, California. This new forum seemed to be an ideal venue to lay bare America's sorry record of racism, and so Du Bois presented the UN's Commission on Civil Rights with a controversial pamphlet, "An Appeal to the World." In the 1948 race for the White House, Du Bois broke ranks with the NAACP in preferring Henry Wallace's third-party candidacy over the reelection bid of Democrat Harry Truman, whose uncompromising Cold War mentality saw the world in terms of West versus East, effectively preserving colonial rule of less developed areas, including Africa. The break was irrevocable. Never again did Du Bois work for the association he helped found and lead.[51]

As the U.S. and USSR competed for world domination, Du Bois was firmly identified with international peace movements against the Cold War, with socialism, and with representation of African colonial peoples in the United Nations. His expressed sympathies for the Soviet Union, his condemnation of the Korean conflict as a capitalist war, an abortive attempt in 1950, at age 82, to become U.S. senator for New York on the American Labor party ticket, and his chairmanship of the Peace Information Center which circulated a Soviet-inspired nuclear disarmament proposal, were all indications of Du Bois' radical stances and activities. He accused the United States of being "drunk with power . . . leading the world to hell in a new colonialism with the same old human slavery, which once ruined us, to a third world war, which will ruin the world."[52]

As the witch-hunting era known as McCarthyism unfolded, the U.S. Justice Department went after "that old man," suspecting Du Bois of communism and insisting he register as an agent of a "foreign principal." When he refused, a federal grand jury indicted him, but sufficient evidence was lacking, resulting in his acquittal. Even so, his passport was revoked for seven years. He did not endear himself to the government when he defended Julius and Ethel Rosenberg against charges of atomic espionage for the Soviet Union. When Du Bois' passport was finally returned, he was fêted in the Communist world on visits to China and Russia, where he received the Lenin Peace Prize. On his 91st birthday in Peking, Du Bois informed a large and responsive audience that "in my own country for nearly a century I have been nothing but a 'nigger.' "[53]

In 1946, Du Bois, sensing the heightened aspirations of the post-war generation of African Americans, informed an audience in Columbia, South Carolina, that "The future of the American Negro is in the South. . . . This is the firing line not simply for the emancipation of the American Negro but for the emancipation of the African Negro and the Negroes of the West Indies; for the emancipation of the colored races; and for the emancipation of the white slaves of modern capitalistic monopoly." He was initially elated by the U.S. Supreme Court's 1954 *Brown* school desegregation decision, but soon concluded that the decision did not go nearly far enough. In like manner, Du Bois applauded "black workers" for boycotting segregated buses in Montgomery, Alabama, but he was disappointed in Martin Luther King, Jr., the young leader who seemed unlikely to transfigure southern racists by moral suasion and who, unlike Gandhi, lacked an ambitious economic agenda. "I myself long stressed Negro private business enterprise," Du Bois admitted, but he now comprehended that "the one hope of American Negroes is socialism." Du Bois therefore remained aloof from the biracial civil rights coalition.[54]

Reviewing Samuel Spencer's biography *Booker T. Washington and the Negro's Place in American Life* (1955), Du Bois strongly dissented from Spencer's view that Washington anticipated the modern civil rights movement, but in his own day "did what was possible, given the time and place in which he lived, and did it to the utmost." Noting that Spencer, a white southerner, was bound to reach a favorable verdict on Washington, Du Bois repeated his contention that if African Americans, contrary to Washington's advice and example, had not struggled to retain voting and civil rights and struggled "for the education of his gifted children, for a place among modern men, their situation today would have been disastrous." White southerners had dishonored the terms of the compromise offered by Washington at Atlanta, yet he had been "treated with extraordinary respect by his fellow Negroes, even when they believed he was bartering their rights for a mess of pottage." Here, Du Bois was not simply restating his differences with Washington but was also, by implication, linking the militant protest of the NAACP in the early years and his own editorship of the *Crisis* in particular, with the post-World War II civil rights coalition. On a more personal note, Du Bois could hardly approve of a book in which he was accused of having had "delusions of grandeur" when he dared to challenge the Tuskegee Machine, or of the description of himself as "imperious, egocentric, aloof."[55]

At the end of his long and extraordinarily productive life, Du Bois made his rupture with American society complete. In 1961, Du Bois successfully applied for membership in the American Communist party, having come to the conclusion that "Capitalism cannot reform itself; it is doomed to self-destruction. No universal selfishness can bring social good to all. Communism—the effort to give all men what they need and to ask for each the best they can contribute—this is the only way of human life." Before the announcement of his application was made public, Du Bois went to Ghana at the urging of its president, Kwame Nkrumah. There, Du Bois resumed work on an *Encyclopedia Africana*, a monumental project he had already attempted as early as 1909, and became a Ghanaian citizen. If he had lived three more years, Du Bois would have seen Nkrumah ousted by a military coup, and a new regime that suppressed socialism, the doctrine of pan-Africanism, and publication plans for his encyclopedia. The *Encyclopedia Africana* was not completed until 1999.[56]

Despite his self-exile and disappointments, Du Bois, as one of his last letters revealed, preserved an optimistic view of his life and labor: "I have loved my work. I have loved people and my play, but always I have been uplifted by the thought that what I have done will live long and justify my life; that what I have done ill or never finished can now be handed on to others for endless days to be finished, perhaps better than I could have done."[57]

Assessment

"In the course of his long, turbulent career," Pulitzer prize-winning author David Levering Lewis wrote, "W.E.B. Du Bois attempted virtually every possible solution to the problem of twentieth-century racism— scholarship, propaganda, integration, national self-determination, human rights, cultural and economic separatism, politics, international communism, expatriation, third world solidarity." Through all his ideological shifts and turns, Du Bois attempted to resolve what he experienced and regarded as being the fundamental dilemma of the African American— "one ever feels his two-ness." Unlike Booker T. Washington, Du Bois always felt himself apart from the black masses and, for significant periods of his life was decidedly out of step with mainstream black responses to such ideologies as socialism, Marxism, and pan-Africanism. Nevertheless, Du Bois, as editor of the *Crisis*, was the outstanding agitator and propagandist of the protest movement that arose partly as a reaction against Washington's power and policies. Essentially a man of letters, Du Bois, more than any other African-American leader, influenced the black intelligentsia and contributed to the formation of that black consciousness which had its flowering in the Harlem Renaissance. Du Bois himself admired but was rejected by white society, and partly out of this rejection came his reasoned, but impassioned, hatred of racial discrimination and injustice.[58]

From the formation of the Niagara Movement until his resignation from the NAACP in the 1930s, Du Bois put aside his preference for historical and sociological research to advance African-American life in order to become the singularly gifted spokesperson for black economic and political rights. With Booker T. Washington's death, the continuing black exodus from the South, and the rising expectations of an educated black middle class, Du Bois achieved leadership of the talented tenth. Simultaneously, he waged a bitter internal campaign against what he regarded as the elitism, conservatism, and narrowness of the organization that had chosen him as its major propagandist. The NAACP rejected Du Bois' call for voluntary segregation and did not share his collectivist or pan-African enthusiasms. Yet, on the eve of his departure from the NAACP, Du Bois was opposed to enforced segregation and any deprivation of any political, civil, or social rights. As one of his biographers suggested, Du Bois made the *Crisis* "a record of Negro achievement" and "in this context, even Du Bois' aloofness became an asset; it removed him in Negro eyes from everyday life and, by giving him a transcendent quality, it raised the goal of aspiration."[59]

Throughout his long and eventful life, Du Bois was inspired by a vision of reasoned, ordered, and dynamic social change. This vision was perhaps best expressed in the "Postlude" to his second autobiography, subtitled, "A Soliloquy on Viewing My Life from the Last Decade of Its First Century" (1968): "This is a beautiful world. This is a wonderful America, which the founding fathers dreamed until their sons drowned it in the blood of slavery and devoured it in greed. Our children must rebuild it. Let then the Dreams of the Dead rebuke the Blind who think that what is will be forever and teach them what is worth living for must live again."[60]

Du Bois' vision was sometimes flawed. His call to "Close Ranks" during World War I, although implicitly recognizing that African Americans *were* pressing for equality, too readily assumed that they would be prepared to suspend their agitation. His plan for segregated cooperatives of consumers and producers was unrealistic. He viewed Africa through a haze of romanticism, yet also inspired African nationalists. His politics alternated between a radical optimism and a gloomy conservatism, and, at the end of his life, he embraced the tenets of totalitarian regimes. But through all his ideological searchings, Du Bois was the keeper of America's moral conscience on the question of race and racial inequality. In a real sense, Du Bois was the father of the modern civil rights era. Martin Luther King, Jr., in the last major address before his assassination, delivered a fitting tribute to Du Bois, marking the centennial of his birth:

Dr. Du Bois was a tireless explorer and a gifted discoverer of social truths. His singular greatness lay in his quest for the truth about his own people. . . . Whatever else he was, with his multitude of careers and professional titles, he was first and always a black man. . . . Some people would like to ignore the fact that he was a communist in his later years. . . . It is time to cease muting the fact that Dr. Du Bois was a genius and chose to be a communist. Our irrational obsessive anticommunism has led us into too many quagmires to be retained as if it were a mode of scientific thinking. . . . Dr. Du Bois's greatest virtue was his committed empathy with all the oppressed and his divine dissatisfaction with all forms of injustice.[61]

References

1 W.E.B. Du Bois, *The Souls of Black Folk* (1903), p. 13.

2 Paul Robeson, "The Legacy of W.E.B. Du Bois," in Philip S. Foner, ed., *Paul Robeson Speaks: Writings, Speeches, and Interviews, 1918–1974* (1978), pp. 474–475.

3 Harold R. Isaacs, *The New World of Negro Americans* (1963), p. 195.

4 Emma Lou Thornbrough, "The National Afro-American League, 1887–1908," *Journal of Southern History* 27 (November, 1961): 494–512.

5 Cyrus Field Adams, *The National Afro-American Council, Organized 1898, A History* (1902); Alexander Walters, *My Life and Work* (1917), pp. 98–102; Robert J. Norrell, *Up from History: The Life of Booker T. Washington* (2009), p. 229.

6 David Levering Lewis, *W.E.B. Du Bois: Biography of a Race, 1868–1919* (1993), pp. 297–330; Ray Stannard Baker, *Following the Color Line: American Negro Citizenship in the Progressive Era* (1908), p. 224.

7 Norrell, *Up from History*, pp. 321–322; Baker, *Following the Color Line*, p. 220; Gunnar Myrdal, *An American Dilemma: The Negro Problem and Modern Democracy* (1944), p. 743.

8 Patricia Sullivan, *Lift Every Voice: The NAACP and the Making of the Civil Rights Movement* (2009), pp. 1–4.

9 Ibid., pp. 5–6.

10 Ibid., pp. 7–13; Elliott M. Rudwick, *W.E.B. Du Bois: Propagandist of the Negro Protest* (1969), p. 216.

11 Louis R. Harlan, *Booker T. Washington: The Wizard of Tuskegee, 1901–1915* (1983), p. 367.

12 Henry Louis Gates, Jr. and Cornel West, eds., *The African-American Century: How Black Americans Have Shaped Our Country* (2000), pp. 1–7.

13 Du Bois, *The Souls of Black Folk*, pp. 3–4.

14 W.E.B. Du Bois, *Darkwater: Voices from Within the Veil* (1920), p. 9; Reiland Rabaka, *Du Bois's Dialectics: Black Radical Politics and the Reconstruction of Critical Social Theory* (2008), p. 122.

15 W.E.B. Du Bois, *The Autobiography of W.E.B. Du Bois: A Soliloquy on Viewing My Life from the Last Decade of Its First Century* (1968), pp. 107–108, 133.

16 Lewis, *Du Bois: Biography of a Race*, pp. 67–70; Derrick P. Alridge, *The Educational Thought of W.E.B. Du Bois: An Intellectual History* (2008), pp. 19–20.

17 Lewis, *Du Bois: Biography of a Race*, pp. 86–89, 99, 130–145.

18 Du Bois, *Autobiography*, pp. 148, 168.

19 Ibid., pp. 185–199; Manning Marable, *W.E.B. Du Bois: Black Radical Democrat* (1986), p. 27.

20 W.E.B. Du Bois, "The Conservation of Races," *American Negro Academy, Occasional Papers 2* (1897), p. 13.

21 Lewis, *Du Bois: Biography of a Race*, p. 226.

22 Du Bois, *Autobiography*, pp. 258–261.

23 Jacob U. Gordon, *The Black Male in White America* (2002), p. 113; Sondra K. Wilson, ed., *The Crisis Reader: Stories, Poetry, and Essays from the N.A.A.C.P.'s Crisis Magazine* (1999); W.E.B. Du Bois, "I Am Resolved," *Crisis* 3 (January, 1912): 113.

24 Lewis, *Du Bois: Biography of a Race*, p. 419; Marable, *W.E.B. Du Bois*, pp. 85–86; Du Bois, *Darkwater*, p. 100.

25 *Crisis* (September, 1911, May, 1914); Gordon, *The Black Male in White America*, p. 114.

26 Langston Hughes, *Fight for Freedom: The Story of the NAACP* (1962), p. 34; Patricia Bernstein, *The First Waco Horror: The Lynching of Jesse Washington and the Rise of the NAACP* (2006).

27 Du Bois, *Dusk of Dawn: An Essay toward an Autobiography of a Race Concept* (1940), p. 240.

28 Lewis, *Du Bois: Biography of a Race*, pp. 466–483.

29 Ibid., pp. 414, 501–503.

30 Rudwick, *W.E.B. Du Bois*, p. 186.

31 Lewis, *Du Bois: Biography of a Race*, p. 556.

32 Jervis Anderson, *A. Philip Randolph: A Biographical Portrait* (1986), pp. 99–101; Lewis, *Du Bois: Biography of a Race*, pp. 555–557.

33 W.E.B. Du Bois, "Returning Soldiers," *Crisis* 18 (May, 1919): 13–14.

34 Du Bois, *Dusk of Dawn*, p. 267.

35 David Levering Lewis, *W.E.B. Du Bois: The Fight for Equality and the American Century, 1919–1963* (2000). pp. 432–448; Lewis, *Du Bois: Biography of a Race*, pp. 419–420.

36 Wilson, *The Crisis Reader*, pp. 317–325; Lewis, *Du Bois: The Fight for Equality and the American Century*, pp. 176–177, 181.

37 Lewis, *Du Bois: The Fight for Equality and the American Century*, pp. 325–330; Alridge, *The Educational Thought of W.E.B. Du Bois*, pp. 76–79.

38 Julius Lester, ed., *The Seventh Son: The Thought and Writings of W.E.B. Du Bois*, vol. 2 (1971), p. 405.

39 Marable, *W.E.B. Du Bois*, p. 140.

40 Du Bois, *Dusk of Dawn*, pp. 314–315; Raymond Wolters, *Du Bois and His Rivals* (2002), p. 238.

41 Du Bois, *Souls of Black Folk*, p. 184; Du Bois, *Dusk of Dawn*, pp. 114–115.

42 W.E.B. Du Bois, "Little Portraits of Africa," *Crisis* 27 (April, 1924): 273–274; W.E.B. Du Bois, "Pan-Africa and the New Racial Philosophy," *Crisis* 40 (November, 1933): 247; Lewis, *Du Bois: The Fight for Equality and the American Century*, pp. 118–119.

43 David Levering Lewis, ed., *W.E.B. Du Bois: A Reader* (1995), p. 640.

44 Francis L. Broderick, *W.E.B. Du Bois: Negro Leader in a Time of Crisis* (1959), p. 130.

45 Lewis, *Du Bois: The Fight for Equality and the American Century*, pp. 512–515; W.E.B. Du Bois, "Helping Africa," *Crisis* 28 (July, 1924): 106.

46 W.E.B. Du Bois, *The World and Africa* (1947); Harold R. Isaacs, "Pan-Africanism as 'Romantic Racism,'" in Rayford W. Logan, ed., *W.E.B. Du Bois: A Profile* (1971), pp. 210–248.

47 Broderick, *W.E.B. Du Bois*, p. 175.

48 Du Bois, *Dusk of Dawn*, p. vii.

49 Ibid., pp. 69–77.

50 Eugene D. Genovese, *In Red and Black: Marxian Explorations in Southern and Afro-American History* (1971), p. 154.

51 Lewis, *Du Bois: The Fight for Equality and the American Century*, pp. 493, 502–510, 521–523, 528–538.

52 Ibid., pp. 545–549, 551–553, 555, 557; Lewis, *W.E.B. Du Bois: A Reader*, p. 9.

53 Rudwick, *W.E.B. Du Bois*, p. 293.

54 Marable, *W.E.B. Du Bois*, pp. 200–201; Sterling Stuckey, *Slave Culture: Nationalist Theory and the Foundations of Black America* (1987), p. 301; Lewis, *Du Bois: The Fight for Equality and the American Century*, pp. 557–558.

55 W.E.B. Du Bois, "Booker T. Washington and the Negro's Place in American Life," *Science & Society* 20 (Spring, 1956): 183–185.

56 Marable, *W.E.B. Du Bois*, p. 212.

57 William M. Brewer, "Some Memories of Dr. W.E.B. Du Bois," *Journal of Negro History* 53 (1968): 348.

58 Lewis, *Du Bois: The Fight for Equality and the American Century*, p. 571.

59 Broderick, *W.E.B. Du Bois*, pp. 230–231.

60 Du Bois, *Autobiography*, pp. 422–423.

61 Philip S. Foner, ed., *W.E.B. Du Bois Speaks: Speeches and Addresses, 1890–1919* (1970), pp. 13–19.

CHAPTER FOUR

Marcus Garvey: Black Moses

I am only the forerunner of an awakened Africa that shall never go back to sleep.[1]

[Marcus Garvey]

Garvey is giving my people backbones where they [only] had wish-bones.[2]

[A black southerner]

Garvey, Garvey is a big man, To take his folks to monkey-land. If he does, I'm sure I can Stay right here with Uncle Sam.[3]

[Harlem jingle]

Perspectives: The northern black ghetto, 1900–1920

Even before the end of the Civil War, black southerners began leaving rural areas for the cities of the South, and, increasingly, cities of the North. They were driven from the land by a series of natural disasters, including the ravages of the boll weevil and catastrophic floods; the mechanization of southern agriculture; the spread of Jim Crow laws; and the adoption of disfranchisement techniques. In 1879, thousands of black tenant farmers—victimized by a vicious credit system that kept them in unending poverty and "Redeemer" governments that stripped them of their rights gained during Reconstruction—fled the states of Louisiana, Mississippi, Tennessee, and Texas, without waiting for a black messiah, and headed for the plains of Kansas. Kansas, often

termed the "Negro Canaan," had a special place in the memory of formerly enslaved African Americans, because it was there that the abolitionist John Brown had massacred several slaveholders. One migrant with
Kansas Fever drew a parallel between blacks who fled the "young hell"
of the post-war South and the enslaved Hebrews of pharoah's Egypt:
"We's like de chilun ob Israel when dey was led from out o' bondage by
Moses." Nothing white southerners tried could dissuade many blacks
from fleeing.[4]

These "Exodusters" were the advance wave of the "Great Migration"
of black southerners, attracted by the prospect of greater opportunities in
the cities of the Northeast, Midwest, and the Pacific coast. Between 1890
and 1910, the black population of Chicago, Illinois, increased from 1.3
to 2.00 percent; in Philadelphia, Pennsylvania, from 3.8 to 5.5 percent;
in Pittsburgh, Pennsylvania, from 3.3 to 4.8 percent; and in Los Angeles,
California, the African-American population was 2.5 percent of the total
population in 1890. In New York City, between 1890 and 1920, the black
population more than doubled to over 150,000, the majority southern-
born, with a significant influx from the West Indies. In this same period, one
area of New York City—Harlem—was transformed from a fashionable,
all-white section into a congested, working-class black neighborhood.
In every northern city, African Americans were more segregated than were
white immigrant groups—a residential pattern that had been true since
the mid-19th century.[5]

Although there were important differences in the urban experiences
of African Americans, reflecting the nature of race relations, the origins
and composition of the black population, economic opportunities, and the
structure of the black leadership class, there was also a marked similarity
in the forces that produced all-black residential areas in the major cities.
The black ghetto was the product of white racism, which confined African
Americans to less desirable areas of settlement, as well as the result of
black entrepreneurship, adaptability, and community spirit.[6]

In Harlem, this entrepreneurial spirit was evident in 1904 with the
formation of the Afro-American Realty Company, which was organized
by Philip Payton to exploit the area's depressed property market. The
Afro-American Realty Company specialized in acquiring five-year leases
on property owned by whites and then renting to blacks. Charles
Anderson, the leading New York Republican, and T. Thomas Fortune,
editor of the *New York Age*, supported Payton's enterprises. All were
protégés of Booker T. Washington and members of his National Negro
Business League. Ironically, Washington, despite his anti-urban bias,

helped found the black ghetto that by the 1920s had become, in the words of writer James Weldon Johnson, "the intellectual and artistic capital of the Negro world."[7]

A variety of African-American institutions and businesses proliferated in Harlem. By 1918, black churches were the area's largest property-owners, investing heavily in real estate and building new places of worship. St. Mark's Methodist Episcopal Church purchased an apartment house on Lenox Avenue, while the high-society St. Philip's Protestant Episcopal Church owned or controlled twenty large buildings on West 135th Street. Many other black institutions, including fraternal orders, the National Association for the Advancement of Colored People (NAACP), social service agencies, missionary societies, and the *New York News* and *Amsterdam News*, also established themselves in Harlem, contributing to its fame and growing population. An astounding 200,000 African Americans and West Indians inhabited 1,100 different houses within a twenty-three block area of Harlem. At one time, Harlem had been an elegant, tree-lined neighborhood, but it was becoming a gigantic slum, as housing and welfare facilities deteriorated under the sheer weight of numbers.[8]

The National Urban League (NUL) was one organization that sought better accommodations for African Americans who flocked to the cities. Founded in 1910, the league grew out of two organizations, the National League for the Protection of Colored Women, and the Committee for Improving the Industrial Conditions of Negroes in New York. The league, which was a biracial coalition of progressive whites and professional blacks, offered recently-arrived blacks the kinds of welfare and employment services already available to native and foreign-born whites through settlement houses, charities, and immigrant-aid societies. More conservative than the NAACP, the league reflected Washingtonian priorities of de-emphasizing civil and political rights in favor of moral and economic progress, especially through vocational training. It attempted to secure employment and homes for migrants, and offered advice on the etiquette and sanitary standards of city life. The league also conducted surveys among urban blacks, issued reports, and (unsuccessfully) lobbied the American Federation of Labor (AF of L) to outlaw "lily-white" union practices. Echoing Booker T. Washington, the league urged African Americans to adopt standard middle-class expectations of cleanliness, especially bathing regularly with soap, combing one's hair, and brushing one's teeth. The NUL and the NAACP agreed to follow their own strategies of racial advancement, but neither organization could avoid the charges of black militants, such as labor activist A. Philip Randolph, that they were middle-class agencies, heavily dependent on white philanthropic support and pledged to the perpetuation of the capitalist system.[9]

The entry of the United States into World War I encouraged further black migration from the South. The war placed greater demands on northern industries, because the English and French allies depended on American assistance at the very time that European immigration to the States was cut off. But when African Americans arrived in the Promised Land north of Dixie, they found an imperfect paradise. A prime problem was suitable housing. After the U.S. Supreme Court declared municipal segregation ordinances unconstitutional in 1917, white improvement associations devised ways to keep certain neighborhoods lily white. These racist agreements—called "restrictive covenants"—prohibited white home-owners from selling their property to blacks. As a result, African Americans were confined to overcrowded, deteriorating housing stock, which led to significant health and crime problems. As urban conditions worsened, earlier black migrants blamed newcomers for the increasing discrimination with which all northern blacks had to contend.[10]

West Indian immigration to Harlem added another layer of problems to the area. Many African Americans resented the growing community of West Indians for their business acumen and differing social mores. West Indians were accused of being too clannish, arrogant, and overly-ambitious—always willing to work for lower wages than native-born blacks. West Indians, it was said, disregarded the norms of American racial customs, while also standing aloof from black protest organizations. In particular, African Americans were disturbed by the reluctance of West Indian immigrants to become naturalized citizens, their failure to assimilate within the black host community, and their formation of exclusive fraternal and benevolent associations. A common saying claimed that West Indians came to Harlem "to teach, open a church, or start trouble." West Indians were ridiculed, subjected to rock-throwing, and taunted with epithets, such as "monkey-chaser," "ring-tale," and "cockney." "If you West Indians don't like how we do things in this country," an African American remarked, "you should go back where you came from."[11]

On top of these interracial tensions, the general racial climate in America worsened after World War I, producing an intensified militancy among African Americans. A. Philip Randolph and NAACP co-founder W.E.B. Du Bois advocated black resistance to white mobs and the united action of black and white workers against predatory capitalists.

In literature, the arts, and music, the Harlem Renaissance signified the advent of the "New Negro," who was assertive, racially proud, and in search of a positive African-American identity. Into this climate, a West Indian agitator and visionary injected a compelling appeal to urban blacks, who were, for all practical purposes, already living in a social environment that resembled an all-black and separatist nation. As his fellow West Indian, the poet and novelist Claude McKay, observed, Marcus Garvey came to the United States "as a humble disciple of the late Booker T. Washington, founder of Tuskegee Institute."[12]

Marcus Garvey: Black Jamaican

Marcus Mosiah Garvey was born in St. Ann's Bay, Jamaica, the youngest of eleven children. His parents were of unmixed African stock and descended from Maroons—enslaved Africans who had successfully defied the Jamaican slave regime and formed virtually independent black communities in the island's mountains in the 17th and 18th centuries. Because of his heritage, Garvey was fiercely proud of his blackness, and came to display an almost pathological distrust of light-skinned blacks. In his autobiography, Garvey recalled, "My parents were black Negroes. My father was a man of brilliant intellect and dashing courage. He once had a fortune; he died poor." Garvey's father, a skilled stone-mason, was literate, possessed a private library, and acted as a local lawyer. Garvey remembered that his mother was "a sober and conscientious Christian, too soft and good for the time in which she lived."[13]

As a child, Garvey, like W.E.B. Du Bois, was friendly with white children. In Garvey's case, he played with the children of a white Wesleyan minister whose church the Garvey family attended, and was especially attached to one of the minister's daughters. But when the daughter became a teenager, her parents separated her from Garvey, and the shock was traumatic: "They sent her and another sister to Edinburgh, Scotland, and told her that she was never to write or try to get in touch with me, for I was a 'nigger.' It was then that I found that there was some difference in humanity, and that there were different races, each having its own separate and distinct social life. . . . After my first lesson in race distinction, I never thought of playing with white girls anymore."[14]

After a few years of elementary education, Garvey left school at the age of fourteen to work as a printer's apprentice. Moving to Kingston, where he hoped to continue his education, Garvey was forced instead to work in a printing shop owned by his godfather. By the age of twenty, he became the city's youngest foreman printer, at a time when British and Canadian immigrants were generally taking such jobs. When the printer's union went on strike for higher wages, Garvey was elected its leader. The strike failed when the printer imported new machinery and immigrant labor, and the treasurer absconded with the union's funds. Garvey was fired and blacklisted. He became skeptical of the value of the labor movement and of socialism, and went to work for the government's printing office. Increasingly conscious of the related issues of race and politics, Garvey also began to oppose British colonial rule in Jamaica. "I started to take an interest in the politics of my country," Garvey recalled, "and then I saw the injustice done to my race because it was black."[15]

As a young man, Garvey toured Latin America and became increasingly aware of the mistreatment of his fellow Jamaicans. In Costa Rica, Garvey worked as a timekeeper on a United Fruit Company banana plantation. He observed the exploitation of West Indian immigrant workers, and founded a newspaper called *La Nacion*, in which he attacked the British consul for indifference to the situation. Garvey then moved to Panama and was appalled by the depressed condition of Jamaican laborers on the Panama Canal, and produced another newspaper, *La Prensa*. Moving on through Ecuador, Nicaragua, Honduras, Colombia, and Venezuela, he discovered essentially similar conditions, and in each case attempted to organize black laborers. Then, according to his wife, Garvey, already ill with fever and "sick at heart over appeals from his people to help on their behalf," returned to Jamaica in 1911, determined to arouse the government and the people of Jamaica to the plight of their expatriate countrymen.[16]

Unable to interest government officials in the terrible conditions faced by Jamaican workers in other lands, Garvey traveled through Europe, and settled for a time in London, England, where he met and worked with Egyptian nationalist Dusé Mohamed Ali, an admirer of Booker T. Washington and the publisher of the *African Times and Orient Review*. From Ali, Garvey increased his knowledge of African cultures and learned of the subjugation of blacks throughout Africa. Garvey also read Washington's *Up from Slavery*, and later remembered: "I read of conditions in America . . . and then my doom—if I may so call it—of being a race leader dawned upon me." "Where is the black man's Government?" Garvey asked himself. "Where is his King and his kingdom? Where is his President, his country, and his ambassador, his army, his navy, his men of big affairs? I could not find them, and then I declared, 'I will help to make them.' "[17]

The Universal Negro Improvement Association

In 1914, Garvey returned again to Jamaica with the plan of forming an international black organization that would set up an independent state. That August, he established the Universal Negro Improvement and Conservation Association and African Communities League (UNIA). As defined by Garvey, the UNIA's grandiose objectives were:

To establish a Universal Confraternity among the race; to promote the spirit of race pride and love; to reclaim the fallen of the race; to administer to and assist the needy; to assist in civilizing the backward tribes of Africa; to strengthen the Imperialism of independent African states; to establish Commissaries or Agencies in the principal countries and cities of the world for the protection of all Negroes, irrespective of Nationality; to promote a conscientious Christian worship among the native tribes of Africa; to establish Universities, Colleges and Secondary Schools for the further education and culture of the boys and girls of the race; to conduct a worldwide commercial and industrial intercourse.[18]

The motto of the new organization was "One God! One Aim! One Destiny!"—similar to the phrase, "One God, one law, one element," in Alfred Lord Tennyson's poem, "In Memoriam," which Garvey admired. Garvey later said of the UNIA's motto that, "Like the great Church of Rome, Negroes the world over MUST PRACTISE ONE FAITH, that of Confidence in themselves, with One God! One Aim! One Destiny!" In a pamphlet published that same year, Garvey styled himself as "President" of the new movement, and addressed the issue of "The Negro Race and Its Problems." He argued that "Representative and educated negroes have made the mistake of drawing and keeping themselves away from the race, thinking it is degrading and ignominious to identify themselves with the masses of people who are still ignorant and backward; but who are crying out for true and conscientious leadership." Echoing Booker T. Washington, Garvey declared that although the Negro was "handicapped by circum-stances . . . no one is keeping him back. He is keeping back himself, and because of this, the other races refuse to notice or raise him."[19]

Washington's example was also evident in Garvey's plan to establish educational and industrial colleges for black Jamaicans. As it happened, West Indian students and staff at Tuskegee Institute had already asked a visiting Jamaican delegation to set up a school similar to Tuskegee in the British West Indies. When Washington invited Garvey to visit Tuskegee as part of the Jamaican's fund-raising tour in 1915, Garvey solicited

Washington's support for a plan to uplift Negroes of all stripes: "I need not reacquaint you of the horrible conditions prevailing among our people in the West Indies as you are so well informed of happenings all over Negrodom." Garvey also enclosed a copy of the UNIA's manifesto, which included among its objectives the establishment of industrial schools. Washington wished Garvey every success, but failed to appreciate the heroic aims of the UNIA and his Jamaican admirer. Washington said, dismissively, that he was "sorry," but he had no time "to give more careful study to your plans so outlined."[20]

Booker T. Washington died before Garvey reached the United States. At a UNIA memorial for Washington held in Jamaica, Garvey eulogized his mentor: "Since the Negro has no national or set ideal of himself . . . we can only acclaim him as the greatest hero sprung from the stock of scattered Ethiopia. Washington has raised the dignity and manhood of his race to midway, and it is now left to those with fine ideals who have felt his influence to lead the race on to the highest height in the adopted civilization of the age. He was the man for America. Without the presence of such a man the dominant race would have long ago obliterated the existence of the American Negro as a living force even as the Indians were outdone. . . . Every true negro mourns the loss of Dr. Booker T. Washington, scholar, orator, educator, race leader and philanthropist."[21]

Throughout his life, Garvey expressed admiration—although often qualified—for Washington. After a visit to Tuskegee, Garvey wrote that "language fails to express my high appreciation for the service Dr. Washington has rendered to us as a people"; he was "an originator and builder who, out of nothing, constructed the greatest educational and industrial institution of the race in modern times." Garvey also expressed his enthusiasm for Washington's emphasis on self-help and race pride, along with his hostility to social equality. But in a later appraisal of Washington's leadership, Garvey voiced a reservation: "The world held up the great Sage of Tuskegee . . . as the only leader for the race. They looked forward to him and his teachings as the leadership for all times, not calculating that the industrially educated Negro would himself evolve a new ideal." Reiterating one of W.E.B. Du Bois' criticisms of Washington, Garvey asserted, "If Washington had lived he would have had to change his program. No leader can successfully lead this race of ours without giving an interpretation of the awakened spirit of the New Negro, who does not seek industrial opportunity alone, but a political voice."[22]

At the height of his power in the United States, Garvey could argue that whereas Booker T. Washington had looked for concessions from whites, the true race leader must be more aggressive and demanding. Revising an earlier estimate, Garvey concluded that Washington was "not a leader of the Negro race. We did not look to Tuskegee. The world has recognized him as a leader, but we do not. We are going to make demands." When Washington's successor at Tuskegee, Robert Moton, failed to provide the kind of leadership that Garvey believed necessary, Garvey denounced him as the captive of "white philanthropists" and therefore unfit to speak for the black race.[23]

In Jamaica, the UNIA failed to attract the mulatto group of islanders, while the use of the term "Negro" in its title was resented by many native Jamaicans who preferred the term "colored." One Jamaican critic wrote of Garvey's new "Society with the long name and its big aims." After a year, the movement had only a hundred members in his native land. Reflecting bitterly on this period, Garvey declared:

I really never knew there was so much color prejudice in Jamaica until I started the work of the Universal Negro Improvement Association. . . . I had just returned from a successful trip to Europe, which was an exceptional achievement for a black man. The daily papers wrote me up with big headlines and told of my movement. But nobody wanted to be a negro. "Garvey is crazy; he has lost his head" . . . such were the criticisms passed upon me. Men and women as black as I, and even more so, had believed themselves white under the West Indian order of society . . . yet every one beneath his breath was calling the black man a negro. I had to decide whether to please my friends and be one of the "black-whites" of Jamaica, and be reasonably prosperous, or come out openly and defend and help improve and protect the integrity of the black millions and suffer. I decided to do the latter, hence my offense against the "colored-black-white" society in the colonies and America.[24]

Garvey in America

When Marcus Garvey arrived in New York in March, 1916, on a fund-raising tour for an industrial school in Jamaica, he intended to stay for five months. He visited Tuskegee and "paid my respects to the dead hero, Booker T. Washington," toured thirty-eight states, and, at the end of the year, returned to New York City to establish a base in Harlem. Scornful of existing African-American leadership, with its neglect of the masses and dependence on white support, Garvey set up a division of the UNIA in the United States, and turned to the West Indian element in Harlem for assistance. Faced with opposition from Harlem's established black leadership, Garvey cut his ties with the chapter in Jamaica in order to recruit members in America. Within three weeks, Garvey claimed to have recruited 2,000 members in Harlem; by 1919, he reported branches in twenty-five states and additional divisions in the West Indies, Central America, and West Africa, with a total of 2 million members, a figure likely exaggerated. A defensive Du Bois maintained in 1923 that the UNIA had fewer than 20,000 members. But Garvey could have reasonably claimed that within the United States at that point the UNIA had twenty times the membership and support of all the other black organizations combined, including Du Bois' NAACP.[25]

In 1919, Garvey began publication of a weekly newspaper, the *Negro World*, the UNIA's official organ. As its masthead proclaimed, it was "A Newspaper Devoted Solely to the Interests of the Negro Race." With a weekly circulation of 200,000, the *Negro World* was Garvey's greatest propaganda device and his most successful publishing venture. It appeared in English, French, and Spanish editions and lasted until 1933. Every issue carried a front-page polemic by Garvey and articles on black history and culture, racial news, and UNIA activities. The UNIA's program was stated in an eight-point platform in the *Negro World*:

1   To champion Negro nationhood by redemption of Africa.

2   To make the Negro Race conscious.

3   To breathe ideals of manhood and womanhood in every Negro.

4   To advocate self-determination.

5   To make the Negro world-conscious.

6   To print all the news that will be interesting and instructive to the Negro.

7   To instill Racial self-help.

8   To inspire Racial love and self-respect.

To underline the last point, the *Negro World* refused to print advertising copy for skin-whitening and hair-straightening compounds—staple revenue sources for much of the black press.[26]

Garvey's ideological statements in the *Negro World* spread the UNIA's gospel not only throughout the United States, but also in Latin America, the Caribbean, and Africa, much to the consternation of the colonial powers. Kenyan nationalist Jomo Kenyatta recalled that illiterate Kenyans "would gather around a reader of Garvey's newspaper and listen to an article two or three times." They would then run into surrounding areas "carefully to repeat the whole, which they had memorized, to Africans hungry for some doctrine which lifted them from the servile consciousness in which Africans lived."[27]

Garvey repeatedly called for international black solidarity, denounced lynching, and supported the Irish, Indian, and Egyptian independence movements. Wherever he spoke in North America, his message was essentially the same: "The white man of the world has been accustomed to deal with the Uncle Tom cringing negro. Up to 1918, he knew no other negro than the negro represented through Booker Washington. Today he will find a new negro is on the stage. Every American negro and every West Indian negro must understand that there is but one fatherland for the negro, and that is Africa. And as the Germans fought and struggled for the fatherland of Germany; as the Irish man is fighting for the fatherhood of Ireland, so must the new negro of the world fight for the fatherland of Africa." Anticipating the rhetoric of Malcolm X and the Black Power advocates of the 1960s, Garvey informed a UNIA meeting at New York City's Carnegie Hall: "The first dying that is to be done by the black man in the future will be done to make himself free."[28]

Such thoughts seemed revolutionary. First seen as a charlatan, Garvey was quickly perceived as a threat to the established international order. His activities were carefully monitored by American and British intelligence agencies, whose agents accused Garvey of fomenting racial strife. In Washington, D.C., a young J. Edgar Hoover, then second in command of the Bureau of Investigation, showed a marked interest in deporting Garvey as an undesirable alien. Government agents infiltrated street and church-hall meetings, and reported that Garvey's recipe for racial self-defense included this chilling exhortation: "For every negro lynched by whites in the south, negroes ought to lynch a white in the north."[29]

Unaware of the growing hostility of government authorities, Garvey pushed onward, building the largest black mass movement in American history. In July, 1919, he purchased a large auditorium in Harlem—"Liberty Hall"—for UNIA meetings, and Liberty Halls were also opened by hundreds of other UNIA branches. By 1926, the UNIA had sixteen divisions and chapters in California alone. Amy Jacques Garvey, Garvey's second wife, described the multiple functions of these halls, designed to serve "the needs of the people": "Sunday morning worship, afternoon Sunday schools, Public meetings at nights, concerts and dances were held. . . . Notice boards were put up where one could look for a room, a job, or a lost article. In localities where there were many members out of work there were 'Soup Kitchens' to give them a warm meal daily. . . . In the freezing winter days stoves had to be kept going to accommodate the cold and homeless until they 'got on their feet again.' "[30]

The Negro Factories Corporation was also established in 1919, and, according to the *Negro World*, was designed "to build and operate factories in the big industrial centers of the United States, Central America, the West Indies and Africa to manufacture every marketable commodity." The corporation developed a chain of grocery stores, a restaurant, a tailoring establishment, a hotel, printing presses, a black doll factory, and a steam laundry in Harlem. Garvey's advertising skills were revealed in the promise of the Negro Factories Corporation Laundry Service: "We Return Everything But The Dirt." By 1920, the UNIA and its allied enterprises put into practice Booker T. Washington's precept of economic self-help and employed 300 people.[31]

The Black Star Line

Garvey's most spectacular undertaking was the organization of an all-black steamship company that would link the world's people of color in commercial and industrial intercourse. The Black Star Steamship Line, incorporated in Delaware in June, 1919, was capitalized at $500,000, with 100,000 shares of stock at $5 a share. The Black Star Line (BSL) also stemmed from Booker T. Washington's axiom that blacks must seek to become independent of white capital. Stock circulars for the projected company appealed directly to racial pride: "The Black Star Line Corporation presents to every black man, woman, and child the opportunity to climb the great ladder of industrial and commercial progress. If you have $10, $100 or $5,000 to invest for profit, then take out shares in the Black Star Line, Inc. . . . The Black Star Line will turn over large profits and dividends to stockholders, and operate to their interest even whilst they will be asleep." The sale of stock in the Black Star Line was limited to blacks, with a maximum of 200 shares per person. The money poured in. Within months, the Black Star Line was recapitalized at $10 million.[32]

Garvey never intended that his shipping company would be the agency for the mass transportation of blacks back to Africa; rather, it was conceived as a commercial operation, a source of justifiable racial pride, and a demonstration of black entrepreneurial and nautical skills. Amy Jacques Garvey recalled that "The main purpose of the formation and promotion of the Black Star Line was to acquire ships to trade between the units of the Race—in Africa, the USA, the West Indies, and Central America, thereby building up an independent economy of business, industry, and commerce, and to transport our people on business and pleasure, without being given inferior accommodation or refusal of any sort of accommodation." Unfortunately, the BSL's operations and administration were marked by financial failure, as well as by elements of farce and ineptitude.[33]

The Black Star Line was economically unsound, and its operations were less than seaworthy. For example, the BSL's first ship, a small freighter called the *SS Yarmouth*, cost $165,000 and was in constant operational and legal trouble. Other ships purchased by the company, the aptly-named *Shadyside*, an old Hudson river excursion boat, and the steam-powered yacht *Kanawha*, never realized a fraction of their purchase prices. The *Yarmouth*—later named *SS Frederick Douglass*—sailed for Cuba with a cargo of whiskey, narrowly escaped sinking, and arrived at its destination with a good part of the cargo having been consumed by the crew. The Pan Union Company, the importers of the whiskey, was awarded $6,000 by a court for its losses. The *Yarmouth* was finally sold as scrap metal. In less than five months of active service, the *Shadyside* cost the BSL $11,000 in operating losses. The Black Star Line as a whole was an unmitigated disaster.[34]

In August, 1920, Garvey and the Harlem branch of the UNIA staged the First International Convention of the Negro Peoples of the World. Delegates representing twenty-five countries attended the proceedings in New York. An agent for the federal government's Bureau of Investigation reported that many of the "so-called foreign delegates" had, in fact, been "living in the United States for years." Consequently, "the majority of his followers and especially the general public are under the impression that *all* these delegates had just arrived here especially for Garvey's convention."[35]

The 1920 convention was certainly a splendid and glamorous affair. Parades through Harlem of the UNIA's various elements—the African Legion in blue and red uniforms, the Black Cross Nurses, dressed in dazzling white, the Black Flying Eagles, and the Universal African Motor Corps—attracted and delighted the black community. Garvey also took the opportunity to advertise the UNIA at the expense of his rivals. One of the slogans carried in the convention parade read: "NAACP: Nothing Accomplished After Considerable Pretence/UNIA: United Nothing Can Impede Your Aspirations." The UNIA's flag—red for black blood, green for black hopes, and black for black skin—was prominently displayed, and the convention speeches stressed the themes of African nationalism and the meaning of Garvey's movement. The Rev. James David Brooks, the UNIA's secretary-general, defined the spirit of Garveyism as "the spirit to help God work out the destiny of the black race. The spirit of Garveyism is the spirit to contend for that which belongs to you. Garveyism is the spirit of self-reliance. Garveyism is the freedom for Africa. You have to get the spirit of Garvey and let it touch your heart until it becomes part of your life ... until at night you dream Garveyism." Two years later, Brooks had grown disillusioned with Garveyism, and unsuccessfully sued Marcus Garvey for an unpaid loan and unpaid wages.[36]

Roi Ottley, a journalist and social worker, remembered that as a child he had witnessed the UNIA's historic convention: "During the whole month of August, 1920, delegates from all the states, the West Indies, South America and Africa assembled in Liberty Hall, in a demonstration that proved to be a series of rousing 'bravos' and 'hallelujahs' to the black leader. People were fascinated by all the bustle and animation in the streets. There were loud speeches, stock-selling from the curbstones, and indeed fisticuffs as men clashed. 'Is Garvey greater than Jesus Christ?' people asked. 'Give he a chance' shot back his devoted West Indian followers in their quaint English dialect. 'He's a young mon yet!' "[37]

At the 1920 convention, Garvey was elected Provisional President of the African Republic, and informed the delegates: "We are here to celebrate the greatest event in the history of the Negro people for the last 500 years. We are in sympathy with the great Irish people who have been overrun for the last 700 years by the tyrants of Great Britain; we are in sympathy with the people of India ... who are also dominated by Great Britain. We are in sympathy with the Chinese, with the Egyptians but one and all are in sympathy with ourselves ... to find ourselves a free people and a great people, too." Sociologist Charles S. Johnson, writing in *Opportunity*, the Urban League's magazine, detected a possible inspiration for Garvey's exalted title: "Just prior to the first International Convention of the UNIA, [Eamon] De Valera was elected Provisional President of Ireland. Garvey then became Provisional President of Africa." The UNIA convention also created a nobility—Knights of the Nile—and honors—the Distinguished Service Order of Ethiopia. Delegates drafted a "Declaration of the Rights of the Negro Peoples of the World," which included the demand that "Negro" be spelled with a capital "N," as well as condemnations of European imperialism in Africa and lynchings in the United States.[38]

Above all, the UNIA's appeal rested on Garvey's charisma and drive, rather than on his limited administrative or organizational abilities. He undertook a series of energetic promotional tours to Jamaica, Cuba, Costa Rica, Panama, and British Honduras to sell Black Star Line stock and memberships in the UNIA. But a series of misfortunes, miscalculations, and tactical blunders hastened his eventual downfall. In 1921, president Warren G. Harding, speaking in Alabama, asserted his belief in the Washingtonian ideal of the separation of the races. Garvey endorsed the speech, and was roundly condemned by other African-American leaders. The following year, Garvey went to Georgia for a meeting with Edward Young Clarke, imperial kleagle of the racist and terroristic Ku Klux Klan, in an improbable attempt to elicit Klan support for the UNIA's African program. From their opposing perspectives, Clarke and Garvey shared a common belief in racial purity and racial separation. As Garvey later announced, "Whilst the Ku Klux Klan desires to make America absolutely a white man's country, the UNIA wants to make Africa absolutely a black man's country."[39]

Garvey's critics were astounded and outraged by the Klan episode. A disgusted NAACP field secretary William Pickens informed Garvey: "I gather you are now endorsing the Ku Klux Klan, or at least conceding the justice of its aim to crush and repress colored Americans and incidently other racial and religious groups in the United States. You compare the aim of the Ku Klux Klan in America with your aims in Africa—and if that be true, no civilized man can endorse either one of you. . . . I would rather be a plain black American fighting in the ranks AGAINST the Klan and all its brood than to be the Imperial Wizard of the Ku Klux Klan or the allied Imperial Blizzard of the UNIA." An editorial by Chandler Owen in the *Messenger*, the black socialist paper, was headlined: "Marcus Garvey! The Black Imperial Wizard Becomes Messenger Boy Of The White Ku Klux Kleagle," and concluded: "The issue is joined, and we shall spare no pains to inform the American, West Indian, African, South American and Canal Zone Negroes of the emptiness of all this Garvey flapdoodle, bombast and lying about impossible and conscienceless schemes calculated not to redeem but to enslave Africa and the Negro everywhere. . . . [T]he *Messenger* is firing the opening gun in a campaign to drive Garvey and Garveyism in all its sinister viciousness from the American soil." An NAACP organizer called Garvey "a cowardly, whining adventurer, an individual of doubtful honesty and a demagogic charlatan."[40]

In turn, Garvey stigmatized his black critics as proponents of "racial equality" as distinct from his own philosophy of "racial purity." His continuing support of white segregationists, and his contacts with U.S. senator Theodore Bilbo of Mississippi, who adamantly opposed racial intermixing and espoused black repatriation to West Africa, indicated that in his quest and zeal for black separatism, Garvey disregarded the sensibilities of most African Americans. Garvey recognized that Bilbo's motives in proposing legislation to send blacks back to Africa might "not be as idealistic as Negroes may want," but "independent nationality is the greatest guarantee of the ability of any people to stand up in our present civilization."[41]

By 1922, Garveyism was in serious trouble. At that year's UNIA convention, Garvey attacked his critics within the movement, and removed them from office after a series of acrimonious show trials. At the same time, he modified his demands for the expulsion of the European powers from Africa, disavowed his connection with radicalism, but continued to denounce his enemies—real and imagined—within the NAACP. Such actions could not forestall a precipitous decline in Garvey's movement. Garvey and three of his associates were arrested and charged with using the U.S. mail to defraud. These arrests had been made possible by information unwittingly supplied to the Bureau of Investigation by Cyril Briggs, leader of the African Blood Brotherhood, a radical, black self-defense group with ties to the Communist party. Garvey had attacked Briggs, who was of light complexion, as a "white man" trying to pass as black. Briggs was an ardent supporter of the Russian Revolution, leading Garvey to condemn him as a "dangerous Bolshevik."[42]

At his trial, the prosecution declared that Garvey had promoted the sale of BSL stock, although he knew that the company was in serious financial trouble. Garvey conducted his own defense in a melodramatic fashion and blamed his colleagues, white competitors, the NAACP, and other enemies for the shipping company's collapse. He was convicted, fined $1,000 and sentenced to five years in prison. He blamed the Jewish judge, Jewish prosecutor, and Jewish jurors for his conviction. Released on bond, he returned to UNIA activity and attempted to obtain permission from the Liberian government to establish a UNIA base in that country. The Liberians informed the U.S. government that they were "irrevocably opposed, both in principle and fact, to the incendiary policy of the Universal Negro Improvement Association headed by Marcus Garvey." In addition, Garvey faced the opposition of the European imperialist powers, as well as that of W.E.B. Du Bois and J. Edgar Hoover, to his Liberian scheme. In 1925, Garvey's appeal against his mail fraud conviction was rejected by the U.S. Circuit Court of Appeals, and he was sent to the penitentiary in Atlanta, Georgia. After two years, president Calvin Coolidge, whom Garvey had supported for reelection, commuted his sentence; but as an alien convicted of a felony, Garvey was deported to Jamaica.[43]

For the rest of his life, Garvey worked to rebuild the UNIA, and branches were opened in London, and Paris, France. In 1929, the Sixth International Convention of Negro Peoples of the World met in Jamaica, but Garvey quarreled with the American delegates, whom he accused of financial malpractice. He also refused to accept their demand that the headquarters of the organization remain in New York. With the defection of his remaining American followers, Garvey's influence in the United States declined even further, although UNIA offshoots reappeared from time to time in the 1930s and 1940s. Garvey himself remained active. He denounced Italy's rapacious attack on Ethiopia in 1935, castigated Harlem spiritual leader George Baker (Father Divine) for claiming divinity, and continued to envision a world-wide organization of black people dedicated to African liberation. None of his causes aroused the mass support that he had commanded in America. In 1940, Garvey died of a stroke at age 52 in London, impoverished and without ever having set foot in Africa.[44]

Garveyism

The ideology of Marcus Garvey and his UNIA combined the various elements of black nationalism—religious, cultural, economic, and geographic—into a distinctive philosophy. Basic to this worldview was the emotive power of *blackness*. Garvey was essentially a racial Zionist who offered an eschatology of color, in which black was good and white was evil. Garveyism advocated black economic self-determination and African redemption. It preached the power of the black race and the revitalization of people of color throughout the world. Garvey was also well aware of the importance of religion in black culture and consciousness. The religious component of Garveyism was the African Orthodox Church, established in 1921, with the West Indian George Alexander McGuire as the UNIA's chaplain-general. Garvey believed that as God was made in the image of humankind, black people ought to visualize and worship a black God and a black Christ. As he expressed it, "Since the white people have seen their God through white spectacles, we have only now started out to see our God through our own spectacles. . . . We Negroes believe in the God of Ethiopia, the everlasting God . . . but we shall worship Him through the spectacles of Ethiopia."[45]

To many of its followers, the UNIA was a surrogate or civil religion, with Garvey a "Black Moses," blacks the Chosen People, and Africa the Promised Land. At the same time, the rituals, symbols, and beliefs of the UNIA's civil religion were sufficiently generalized to permit members to remain in their own particular religious denominations. Benjamin Mays, the black theologian and teacher—and Martin Luther King, Jr.'s mentor—observed that Garvey used the idea of a black God "to arouse the Negro to a sense of deep appreciation for his race . . . to stimulate [him] to work to improve his social and economic conditions." Culturally, Garveyism extolled and intensified the race consciousness that already existed among African Americans, only too painfully aware of their ethnic identity in a racist society. It was Garvey's considerable achievement to give his awareness a more positive and international focus. As a statement of economic nationalism, Garveyism derived many of its principal tenets from Booker T. Washington, including black economic independence and self-sufficiency, but it avoided endorsing either capitalism or socialism. The Black Star Line and the Negro Factories Corporation were, in fact, more cooperative than corporate forms of business enterprise. The UNIA's proposed Liberian colony would have comprised family units together with larger cooperative farms administered by the association.[46]

The most important element in Garveyism was its emphasis on a return to Africa (whether in a physical or a spiritual sense), the expulsion of European powers from the African continent, and the belief that once a strong and independent "African nation" was established, blacks would gain automatically in power and prestige. Although Garvey hardly expected all African Americans to "return" to Africa, he viewed the UNIA as representing the vanguard in the struggle for African liberation. As he once informed an audience in New York City's Madison Square Garden: "The thoughtful and industrious of our race want to go back to Africa, because we realize it will be our only hope of permanent existence. We do not want all the Negroes in Africa. Some are no good here, and naturally will be no good there. The no-good Negro will naturally die in fifty years. The Negro who is wrangling about and fighting for social equality will naturally pass away in fifty years, and yield his place to the progressive Negro who wants a society and country of his own."[47]

Failing the peaceful resettlement of a black elite in colonized Africa, Garvey advocated the use of force. To that end, the UNIA included such paramilitary units as the African Legion, the Black Eagle Flying Corps, and the Universal African Motor Corps. Garvey informed delegates to the 1920 convention and the European colonist powers in Africa: "We are striking homewards towards Africa to make her the big black republic . . . and we say to the white man who now dominates Africa that it is to his interests to clear out of Africa now, because we are coming, not as in the time of Father Abraham [Lincoln], 200,000 strong, but we are coming 400,000,000 strong; and we mean to retake every square inch of the 12,000,000 square miles of African territory belonging to us by right divine."[48]

The liberation of Africa from European colonial rule, and the repatriation there of the "best" blacks—mulattoes, by definition, were excluded—appear as constant, although not always clearly expressed, themes in Garvey's writings and speeches. But the mass appeal asserted in Garveyism transcended the impracticality and fantasy of its "Back-to-Africa" ideology. For most Garveyites, the *idea* of an African homeland was more appealing than any actual desire or ability to leave the United States.[49]

Recalling his encounters with Garveyites in Chicago in the 1920s, novelist Richard Wright felt that they "had embraced a totally racialistic outlook that endowed them with a dignity I have never seen before in Negroes. Those Garveyites I knew could never understand why I liked them but would never follow them, and I pitied them too much to tell them that they would never achieve their goal, that Africa was owned by the imperial powers of Europe, that their lives were alien to the mores of the natives of Africa, that they were people of the West. . . . It was when the Garveyites spoke fervently of building their own country, of someday living within the boundaries of a culture of their own making, that I sensed the passionate hunger of their lives."[50]

Alain Locke, editor of an influential anthology on the Harlem Renaissance, observed in his essay, "The New Negro," that "When the racial leaders of twenty years ago spoke of developing race-pride and stimulating race-consciousness, and of the desirability of race solidarity, they could not in any accurate degree have anticipated the abrupt feeling that has surged up and now pervades the awakened centers. . . . With the American Negro, his new internationalism is primarily an effort to recapture contact with the scattered peoples of African derivation." Locke viewed Garveyism as constituting perhaps "a transient" but certainly a "spectacular phenomenon" animated by "the sense of a mission of rehabilitating the race in world esteem from the loss of prestige for which the fate and conditions of slavery have so largely been responsible."[51]

Garvey and his black critics

Even more than Booker T. Washington, Marcus Garvey aroused critical responses from many of his African-American contemporaries. From the time of his arrival in Harlem until his deportation, Garvey faced the often bitter opposition of established and aspiring black leaders of differing ideological persuasions. To the middle-class, integrationist members of the NAACP and the Urban League, as well as to black socialists and radicals, Garvey was viewed as a visionary, a charlatan, a demagogue, and a madman. He was accused of advocating racial segregation and of pandering to the prejudice of white southerners, of injecting a divisive consciousness of color among African Americans, and of duping his gullible followers.[52]

Despite Garvey's expressed admiration for Booker T. Washington, members of the Urban League were unenthusiastic about his agenda, which was not altogether surprising, given the league's goal of racial integration. Charles S. Johnson, writing for the league's journal *Opportunity* in 1923, characterized Garvey as a "dynamic, blundering, temerarious visionary, and a trickster." Not only were his ideas unrealistic, his "financial exploits were ridiculously unsound, his plans for the redemption of Africa absurdly visionary, and the grand result, the fleecing of hundreds of thousands of poor and ignorant Negroes." By league standards, Garveyism was "a gigantic swindle," providing a "dream-world escape for the 'illiterati' from the eternal curse of their racial status in this country." All that Garvey offered the urban poor was "an opiate for their hopelessness—a fantastic world beyond the grasp of the logic and reason in which they might slake cravings never in this social order to be realized." Urban Leaguers, like most of Garvey's black opponents, saw him as an outsider, undereducated, and bombastic. League board members were light-skinned, and this fact alone ensured animosity between the league and the UNIA. On all counts, then, Garvey and the Urban League were antithetical. But leaguers were not insensible to Garvey's mass appeal, based on the twin pillars of racial pride and the right of self-determination. Johnson conceded that Garvey's personal characteristics were precisely those which made him a charismatic figure: "His extravagant self-esteem could be taken for dignity, his hard-headedness as self-reliance, his ignorance of law as transcendency, his blunders as persecution, his stupidity as silent deliberation, his churlishness and irascibility as the eccentricity of genius."[53]

On the left wing of the black protest movement, Garvey earned the enmity of socialists A. Philip Randolph and Chandler Owen, joint editors of the *Messenger*. Randolph, the most notable black labor organizer of the early 20th century, had helped to form the Brotherhood of Sleeping Car Porters. Despite profound differences in their racial and political attitudes, Randolph and Garvey enjoyed cordial relations for a time, and Randolph claimed to have given Garvey his first opportunity of addressing a Harlem street audience. In 1919, Randolph addressed a UNIA meeting that considered sending a black delegate to the Paris Peace Conference which concluded World War I. Earlier, Garvey had attended a conference organized by Randolph that led to the formation of the short-lived International League of Darker Peoples, which aimed to secure African liberation by an interracial alliance of radical, liberal, and labor movements.[54]

As the UNIA grew, relations between Randolph and Garvey became increasingly strained. A *Messenger* editorial typified Garvey as "A Supreme Jamaican Jackass." Garvey's glorification of black capitalism ran counter to Randolph's belief in democratic socialism, and other aspects of Garveyism also earned their disapproval. In a series of articles in the *Messenger*, Randolph and Owen attacked Garvey's African schemes as being based on simplistic reasoning, since the oppression of the masses, worldwide, was color-blind. Garvey was also accused of stirring white prejudice against blacks and of fostering tensions between West Indians and African Americans. In fact, the *Messenger*'s critiques of Garvey had a pronounced anti-West Indian tone. In a slashing article that appeared in the *Messenger*, Robert Bagnall, director of the NAACP's branches, depicted Garvey as:

A Jamaican Negro of unmixed stock, squat, fat and sleek, with protruding jaws and heavy jowls, small bright pig-like eyes and rather bull-dog-like face. Boastful, egotistical, tyrannical, intolerant, cunning, shifty, smooth and suave, avaricious . . . gifted at self-advertisement, without shame in self-laudation, promising ever, but never fulfilling . . . a lover of pomp and tawdry finery and garish display, a bully with his own folk but servile in the presence of the Klan, a sheer opportunist. . . . If he is not insane, he is a demagogic charlatan, but the probability is that the man is insane. Certainly the movement is insane, whether Garvey is or not.

Following Garvey's overtures to the Ku Klux Klan, Chandler and Randolph served notice that they would campaign for his expulsion from the United States. The *Messenger* now adopted the slogan "Garvey Must Go."[55]

In 1923, eight leaders of the "Garvey Must Go" campaign, with Chandler Owen as secretary, wrote to the U.S. attorney general, urging the federal government to speed up its prosecution case against Garvey for mail fraud. The signatories against Garvey included Owen, Harry Pace of the Urban League, and William Pickens, field secretary of the NAACP. A. Philip Randolph, despite his major role in the campaign, did not sign the letter. For his part, Garvey countered by charging the committee with offenses against race solidarity. Later, during Garvey's imprisonment, the *Messenger* advocated the total destruction of the UNIA, and commended W.E.B. Du Bois' critique of Garvey as either a "Lunatic or Traitor." Randolph and Owen rejected Garvey's intense black nationalism and resented his achievement in leading a movement composed almost entirely of the black working class. Above all, they resented his challenge to the talented tenth's monopoly of race leadership. Garvey observed with some accuracy that "my success as an organizer was more than rival Negro leaders could tolerate." Nowhere was this jealousy and resentment more apparent than in the responses of Du Bois to the rise and fall of Garvey in America.[56]

Du Bois and Garvey

In his autobiography, W.E.B. Du Bois recalled that he had first heard of Garvey in 1915, when he was warmly received by Garvey and his associates on a visit to Jamaica. Du Bois reported Garvey's arrival in America in the *Crisis*, noting that Garvey was on a visit to raise funds for the establishment of an industrial school for blacks in Jamaica. Four years later, Du Bois conceded that Garvey had "with singular success capitalized and made vocal the great and long suffering grievances and spirit of protest among the West Indian peasantry," and commended his eloquence as an orator. Garvey, as Du Bois noted, "has become to thousands of people a sort of religion."[57]

But Du Bois' subsequent references to Garvey, open or veiled, became increasingly bitter and occasionally shrill. In one cryptic *Crisis* editorial, Du Bois obviously referred to Garvey when he predicted, "We must expect the Demagogue among Negroes more and more. He will come to lead, inflame, lie, and steal. He will gather large followings and then burst and disappear." Garvey did not let such oblique references pass unchallenged, and regularly blamed Du Bois and the NAACP for most of his problems, including the thwarting of his Liberian plans, the collapse of the Black Star Line, and his trial and imprisonment. Du Bois, in turn, was angered because Garvey's African schemes were competing—and often confused—with his own pan-African philosophy and activities.[58]

From 1920 onwards, Du Bois aimed *Crisis* editorials directly at Garvey and the UNIA. Among other misdemeanors, Garvey was charged with having attempted to introduce the black-mulatto schism in the United States, where, Du Bois claimed unconvincingly, "it has never had any substantial footing and where today it is absolutely repudiated by every thinking Negro." In accentuating this division, Garvey had "aroused more bitter color enmity inside the race than has ever before existed." Two weeks before the UNIA's 1920 convention, Garvey wrote to Du Bois, inviting him to stand for election as "the accredited spokesman for the Negro people." Du Bois icily refused the provocative invitation, and sent several requests to Garvey for information on the UNIA's membership, finances, and activities, for a "critical estimate" to be published in the *Crisis*.[59]

At the UNIA's convention, Du Bois told an interviewer: "I do not believe that Marcus Garvey is sincere. I think that he is a demagogue, and that his movement will collapse in a short time. His followers are the lowest type of negroes, mostly from the West Indies. It cannot be considered an American movement. . . . Most of his following are in Jamaica and other islands of the West and East Indies. They are allied with the Bolsheviks and the Sinn Feiners [from Ireland] in their world revolution." In retaliation, Garvey castigated Du Bois as "the associate of an alien race" and accused him of being "more of a white man than a Negro [and] only a professional Negro at that." Warming to this theme, Garvey ridiculed Du Bois' "aristocratic pretensions" and his professed African, French, and Dutch ancestry: "I have but the ancient glories of Ethiopia to imitate. . . . Anyone you hear always talking about the kind of blood he has in him other than the blood you can see, he is dissatisfied with something, and I feel sure that many of the Negroes of the United States of America know that if there is a man who is most dissatisfied with himself, it is Dr. Du Bois." With relations between the two men worsening rapidly, Du Bois denied that he envied Garvey's success, rather that he feared Garvey's failure: "He can have all the power and money that he can efficiently and honestly use, and if in addition he wants to prance down Broadway in a green shirt—let him—but do not let him foolishly overwhelm with bankruptcy and disaster one of the most interesting spiritual movements of the modern Negro world."[60]

Du Bois intensified his campaign against Garvey and again attempted —unsuccessfully—to secure details of the Black Star Line's finances. In a long article published in *Century* in 1923, Du Bois linked Booker T. Washington with Garvey and deplored the influence of both master and his disciple: "The present generation of negroes has survived two grave temptations, the greater one, fathered by Booker T. Washington, which said, 'Let politics alone, keep your place, work hard, and do not complain,' and which meant perpetual color caste status for colored folk by their own cooperation and consent, and the consequent inevitable debauchery of the white world; and the lesser, fathered by Marcus Garvey, which said, 'Give up! Surrender! The struggle is useless; back to Africa and fight the white world.'" In the same article, Du Bois ridiculed the Jamaican as "a little, fat black man, ugly, but with intelligent eyes and big head . . . seated on a plank platform beside a 'throne,' dressed in a military uniform of the gayest mid-Victorian type."[61]

Garvey's response was immediate and savage. The *Negro World* carried the banner headline: "W.E.B. Du Bois As A Hater of Dark People," subtitled "Calls His Own Race 'Black and Ugly,' Judging From the White Man's Standard of Beauty." On the sensitive issue of physical and personal appearance, Garvey claimed that to Du Bois, anything black was repellent, and that was why "he had but the lightest colored people in his [NAACP] office, when one could hardly tell whether it was a white show or a colored vaudeville he was running at 5th Avenue." Du Bois, Garvey charged, sought out the company of whites, danced, and even slept with them. Comparing their respective backgrounds to his own advantage in terms of self-reliance and achievements, Garvey conceded that Du Bois was highly educated, but if that education "fits him for no better service than being a lackey for good white people, then it were better that Negroes were not educated." Du Bois, Garvey claimed, was the avowed enemy and known saboteur of the UNIA, an all-black organization grounded in the common people. But for the support of white patrons, the fastidious and mannered Du Bois "would be eating his pork chops from the counter of the cheapest restaurant in Harlem like so many other Negro graduates of Harvard and Fisk." Garvey concluded his indictment by pointing up the fundamental ideological differences which separated him from Du Bois and the NAACP: "Du Bois cares not for an Empire for Negroes, but contents himself with being a secondary part of white civilization. We of the Universal Negro Improvement Association feel that the greatest service that the Negro can render to the world and himself . . . is to make his independent contribution to civilization." Garvey ignored Du Bois' charge that he was a Jamaican agitator uninterested in the African-American struggle for civil rights.[62]

Following Marcus Garvey's trial and conviction, Du Bois published his most bitter attack on Garvey in a *Crisis* editorial headed, "A Lunatic or A Traitor." It revealed to Du Bois that the basic principles in conflict were those of racial integration as opposed to separation, and the interracial antagonisms fostered by Garvey's racial chauvinism. The "half-concealed" planks in the UNIA's platform were seen as meaning "That no person of Negro descent can ever hope to become an American citizen. That forcible separation of the races and the banishment of Negroes to Africa is the only solution of the Negro problem. That race war is sure to follow any attempt to realize the program of the NAACP." Garvey, Du Bois insisted, far from attacking white prejudice, was attacking fellow blacks, for whom he only had contempt. Du Bois refused to accept that Garvey was the victim of white prejudice because "no Negro in America ever had a fairer and more patient trial." In Du Bois' view, Garvey had "convicted himself by his own admissions [and] his swaggering monkey-shines in court": "The American Negroes have endured this wretch all too long and with fine restraint and every effort at cooperation and understanding. But the end has come. Every man who apologizes for or defends Marcus Garvey from this day forth writes himself down as unworthy of the countenance of decent Americans. As for Garvey himself, this open ally of the Ku Klux Klan should be locked up or sent home." In a dramatic climax to his piece, Du Bois claimed that he had been advised not to publish this editorial, "lest I be assassinated," and concluded with a heroic flourish: "I have been exposing white traitors for a quarter century. If the day has come when I cannot tell the truth about black traitors it is high time that I died."[63]

Garvey did not let Du Bois' editorial assault go unchallenged. He described Du Bois as "purely and simply a white man's nigger" who is "a little Dutch, a little French, a little Negro . . . a mulatto . . . a monstrosity." At the end of the 1924 UNIA convention, a resolution was passed which declared: "In view of the fact that W.E.B. Du Bois has continually attempted to obstruct the progress of the UNIA to the loss and detriment of the Negro race and that he has . . . gone out of his way to try to defeat the cause of Africa's redemption, that he be proclaimed as ostracized from the Negro race as far as the UNIA is concerned, and from henceforward he be regarded as an enemy of the black people of the world." Garvey suspected Du Bois of sabotaging the Black Star Line and other UNIA businesses. From his prison cell in Atlanta, Garvey continued to lambast Du Bois and the NAACP as deadly adversaries.[64]

After Garvey's release and deportation, Du Bois adopted a different pose concerning the Jamaican. Du Bois denied that the NAACP had opposed the UNIA, and claimed that the *Crisis* had published only five articles on Garvey; Du Bois ignored the editorials that had attacked Garvey indirectly. In later years, Du Bois was more magnanimous toward Garvey, and in *The World And Africa* (1947) characterized Garveyism as "a poorly conceived but intensely earnest determination to unite the Negroes of the world, especially in commercial enterprise." The UNIA's strength "lay in its backing by the masses of West Indians" and by substantial numbers of African Americans. Its weakness and shortcomings "lay in its demagogic leadership, intemperate propaganda, and the natural fear which it threw into the colonial powers." In his autobiography, Du Bois denied any "enmity or jealousy" in his feud with Garvey and cited that part of his *Crisis* editorial—published after Garvey's deportation—which credited Garvey with "a great and worthy dream. We wish him well. He is free; he has a following; he still has a chance to carry on his work in his own home and among his own people and to accomplish some of his ideas. . . . We will be the first to applaud any success he might have." The message was clear: with Garvey's spectacular American career at an end, Du Bois could consign him thankfully to the West Indies, and oblivion.[65]

For his part, Garvey refused to come even to partial peace terms with his most influential African-American protagonist. In the 1930s, when Du Bois espoused the idea of a nonprofit, cooperative racial economy, Garvey roundly accused him of stealing the UNIA's clothes and preaching latter-day Garveyism. The *Negro World* carried the headline: "Dr. Du Bois agrees with UNIA leader—Takes Program Over Finally—But Does Not Openly Confess It." In a short essay, published in 1934, Garvey repeated his contention that Du Bois was "exceptional" only in his admiration for and imitation of white culture: "To us he was never a leader . . . just a vain opportunist who held on to the glory and honor showered on him because he was one of the first experiments of Negro higher education. He was never a born leader. He is too selfish to be anything but Du Bois." Writing from England about that time, Garvey delivered a final verdict on Du Bois as a man with "no racial self-respect, no independent ideas, nothing of self-reliance," and was prepared to compose, decades before it was required, Du Bois' obituary notice: "When Du Bois dies he will . . . be remembered as the man who sabotaged the Liberian colonization scheme of the Negro, the man who opposed the American Negro launching steamships to the seas . . . the man who tried to wreck the industrial education system of Tuskegee, the man who never had a good word to say for any other Negro leader, but who tried to down every one of them."[66]

Assessment

Where W.E.B. Du Bois and the NAACP failed to reach a mass black constituency, Marcus Garvey, through the Universal Negro Improvement Association, succeeded in building a popular movement for his program of racial uplift and the "redemption" of Africa. Garvey's greatest achievement was to arouse in lower-class African Americans, unaffected by or unaware of the Harlem Renaissance and the "New Negro," a fierce pride in their color and racial identity. Like all leaders, Garvey was a visionary. That his prophetic vision of an African continent free of European colonialism had no chance of being realized in the short term never occurred to him, though it would come to pass in two generations. In effect, Garvey wanted to create a "United States of Africa," where African Americans and black people throughout the world could live, or least exist, psychologically speaking.

Garveyism struck a responsive chord among the black underclass of the 1920s partly because it exalted all things black and inverted white standards, while largely retaining the practices of the surrounding white society. For every white institution and belief, Garveyism offered a black counterpart—the Black Star Line, the Black Cross Nurses, the *Negro World*, the Black Legion and the Black Flying Corps, a black God, and a black Christ. Although none of these institutions survived—unlike Booker T. Washington's Tuskegee Institute or W.E.B. Du Bois' NAACP and the *Crisis*—Garvey did leave behind a powerful and enduring legacy, namely, black cultural nationalism.

Both a religious and secular impulse, Garveyism linked its constituent elements in the concept of blackness. It was Marcus Garvey, rather than the Black Power theorists of the 1960s, who deserves credit for the slogan, "Black is Beautiful." His tri-color flag of red, black, and green was a call to black cultural nationalism, an ubiqitous symbol it has retained to the present day. The UNIA's program, with its stress on economic nationalism and African liberation, encouraged African Americans to identify with "primitive" Africans from a position of technological and material supe-riority. But the bulk of Garvey's followers, in common with most African Americans during the 1920s, were never seriously attracted by the prospect of going "Back-to-Africa."

The nationwide interest that the UNIA and its flamboyant leader aroused reflected the disillusionment of blacks for whom the promised land of the American city had turned into the harsh reality of the squalid ghetto. With the anti-black climate of the post-World War I era, Garvey's rhetoric, together with the UNIA's pomp and ceremony, drew a con-siderable following. But, as in the 19th century, few African Americans were prepared to leave the United States and undertake the uncertain and thankless task of "redeeming" Africa. Garvey's larger significance as a leader lies in the fact that he articulated the grievances of those blacks for whom the civil rights goals of desegregation and political rights were largely meaningless. He made the established black leadership class and its white allies painfully aware of their distance from the rank-and-file of the urban underclass. After Garvey's deportation, and particularly during the Depression and New Deal, black protest organizations tried more strenuously than before to close the gap between the elitist concerns of the talented tenth and the day-to-day problems of the majority of African Americans.

The less attractive face of Garveyism was its authoritarianism, para-militarism, and racial chauvinism. Garvey himself has been portrayed as a charismatic leader and a shameless demagogue, a revolutionary, and a reactionary, the father of the heightened black consciousness of the 1960s, and the purveyor of a falsified and incomplete version of the African past and the African-American experience. From his published *Papers*, he sometimes emerges as an artful dodger, hypersensitive to real or imagined criticism, and constantly, but not always convincingly, protesting his fiscal integrity. There is no doubt that Garvey, more than any previous leader, stimulated racial pride and confidence among African Americans. As sociologist E. Franklin Frazier observed perceptively in the 1920s, part of Garvey's success as the leader of a mass movement was due to the regalia, pomp, and circumstances that the UNIA offered to its adherents: "A uniformed member of a Negro lodge paled in significance beside a soldier of the Army of Africa. A Negro might be a porter during the day, taking his orders from white men, but he was an officer in the black army when it assembled at night in Liberty Hall."[67]

To the Rev. Adam Clayton Powell, Sr., pastor of Harlem's influential Abyssinian Baptist Church and a harsh critic of the UNIA, Garvey's arrival in 1916 "was more significant to the Negro than the World War, the Southern exodus and the fluctuation of property values. . . . During the reign of Garvey there were two places in America—the federation of 48 states, and Harlem, and two million Negroes thought that Harlem was both of them. . . . it is recording the truth . . . to say that [Garvey] is the only man that ever made Negroes who are not black ashamed of their color."[68]

Novelist and fellow Jamaican Claude McKay applauded Garvey's propagandistic skills, and the sheer audacity of the Black Star Line, which "had an electrifying effect upon all the Negro peoples of the world." Unfortunately, Garvey's revolutionary fervor had not been accompanied by a true revolutionary's consciousness. His ignorance of Africa was profound, taking no account of its tribal, geographic, linguistic, and geographical divisions. His schemes of black capitalism had foundered with the collapse of the Black Star Line. But, McKay conceded, Garvey's

"five years of stupendous vaudeville" had made him "the biggest popular-
izer of the Negro problem, especially among Negroes, since *Uncle Tom's
Cabin*" had been published before the Civil War.[69]

NAACP executive director James Weldon Johnson found little to
praise in Garvey or the movement he led. A "supreme egotist" who had
surrounded himself with "cringing sycophants" and "cunning knaves,"
Garvey, in advocating the repatriation of African Americans, was simply
plagiarizing ideas put forward by the American Colonization Society a
century earlier, and rejected by the majority of African Americans then and
in the 1920s: "The central idea of Garvey's scheme was absolute abdication
and the recognition as facts of the assertions that this is a white man's
country . . . in which the Negro has no place, no right, no chance, no future."
To that idea, the "overwhelming majority of thoughtful American Negroes
will not subscribe."[70]

Garvey's feuds with his American detractors drained the energies of
all the participants, inhibited the development of the unified black community he claimed to want, and polarized the black protest movement
during a period of "white backlash." Garvey's movement and its adherents
aroused only scorn and derision from the emerging black middle class.
An affluent black physician in Chicago informed E. Franklin Frazier that
the letters "UNIA" really stood for "Ugliest Negroes in America." Verdicts
on Garvey's leadership inevitably reflect attitudes toward the subsequent
trends in American race relations. Certainly, Marcus Garvey relished conflict and competition, and this was both a source of his appeal and a factor
in his defeat. As sociologist Gunnar Myrdal observed, this Jamaican
"outsider" "denounced practically the whole Negro leadership. They were
all bent upon cultural assimilation; they were all looking for support . . . ;
and they were making a compromise between accommodation and protest.
Within a short time he succeeded in making bitter enemies of practically
all Negro intellectuals. Against him were mobilized most leaders in the
Negro schools, in the Negro churches, the Negro organizations and the Negro
press. He heartily responded by naming them opportunists, liars, thieves,
traitors and bastards."[71]

On a visit to Jamaica in 1965, a notable African American placed
a wreath on Garvey's memorial, and informed his audience: "Marcus
Garvey was the first man of color in the history of the United States to
lead and develop a mass movement. He was the first man on a mass scale
and level to give millions of Negroes a sense of dignity and destiny, and
make the Negro feel he is somebody. You gave Marcus Garvey to the
United States of America, and gave to millions of Negroes . . . a sense

of personhood, a sense of manhood, and a sense of somebodiness." The speaker on that occasion was Martin Luther King, Jr.[72]

References

1 Robert A. Hill, ed., *The Marcus Garvey and Universal Negro Improvement Association Papers*, vol. 1, (1983), p. xc. (Cited hereafter as *Garvey Papers*.)

2 Amy Jacques Garvey, *Garvey and Garveyism* (1963), p. 27.

3 E. David Cronon, *Black Moses: The Story of Marcus Garvey and the Universal Negro Improvement Association* (1962), p. 73.

4 Nell Irvin Painter, *Exodusters: Black Migration to Kansas after Reconstruction* (1976), pp. 184–201.

5 Eric Arnesen, *Black Protest and the Great Migration: A Brief History with Documents* (2002); James R. Grossman, *Land of Hope: Chicago, Black Southerners, and the Great Migration* (1991); Steven Hahn, *A Nation under Our Feet: Black Political Struggles in the Rural South from Slavery to the Great Migration* (2003), p. 465; Nicholas Lemann, *The Promised Land: The Great Black Migration and How It Changed America* (1991).

6 Arnesen, *Black Protest and the Great Migration*, pp. 1–37.

7 Gilbert Osofsky, *Harlem: The Making of a Ghetto* (1963), pp. 92–104; James Weldon Johnson, *Black Manhattan* (1930), p. 147.

8 Osofsky, *Harlem*, pp. 105–123.

9 Nancy J. Weiss, *The National Urban League, 1910–1940* (1974), pp. 15–70.

10 Stephen Grant Meyer, *As Long As They Don't Move Next Door: Segregation and Racial Conflict in American Neighborhoods* (2000), pp. 7, 9–10; Clement E. Vose, *Caucasians Only: The Supreme Court, the NAACP, and the Restrictive Covenant Cases* (1959), pp. 5–13, 58–59, 77.

11 Osofsky, *Harlem*, pp. 131–135.

12 Claude McKay, *Harlem: Negro Metropolis* (1940), p. 143.

13 Amy Jacques Garvey, ed., *Philosophy and Opinions of Marcus Garvey* (1969), p. 124.

14 Ibid., p. 125.

15 *Garvey Papers*, vol. 1, p. 5.

16 Garvey, *Garvey and Garveyism*, p. 8.

17 Garvey, *Philosophy and Opinions of Marcus Garvey*, p. 126; *Garvey Papers*, vol. 1, p. 5.

18 Garvey, *Garvey and Garveyism*, p. 11.

19 *Garvey Papers*, vol. 1, pp. 54–55, 61.

20 Ibid., p. 116; Louis R. Harlan, *Booker T. Washington: The Wizard of Tuskegee, 1901–1915* (1983), p. 281.

21 *Garvey Papers*, vol. 1, p. 166.

22 Tony Martin, *Race First: The Ideological and Organizational Struggles of Marcus Garvey and the Universal Negro Improvement Association* (1976), pp. 281–283; Garvey, *Philosophy and Opinions of Marcus Garvey*, p. 56.

23 Theodore G. Vincent, *Black Power and the Garvey Movement* (1972), p. 26; *Garvey Papers*, vol. 5 (1987), p. 52.

24 *Garvey Papers*, vol. 1, p. 146; Garvey, *Philosophy and Opinions of Marcus Garvey*, pp. 127–128.

25 Colin Grant, *Negro with a Hat: The Rise and Fall of Marcus Garvey* (2008), pp. 73–82, 117, 164, 174, 482.

26 Garvey, *Garvey and Garveyism*, pp. 28, 31–32.

27 C.L.R. James, *The Black Jacobins: Toussaint L'Ouverture and the San Domingo Revolution* (1980), p. 396.

28 *Garvey Papers*, vol. 1, pp. 503, 505.

29 Grant, *Negro with a Hat*, p. 104.

30 Garvey, *Garvey and Garveyism*, p. 91.

31 Cronon, *Black Moses*, p. 60.

32 Ibid., p. 52.

33 Garvey, *Garvey and Garveyism*, p. 86.

34 Grant, *Negro with a Hat*, pp. 204–205, 233, 321.

35 *Garvey Papers*, vol. 2 (1983), p. 566.

36 Ibid., pp. 442–443, 647.

37 Roi Ottley, *New World A-Coming: Inside Black America* (1968), p. 75.

38 *Garvey Papers*, vol. 2, p. 482; Charles S. Johnson, "After Garvey—What?", *Opportunity* 1 (August, 1923): 231–233; Cronon, *Black Moses*, pp. 66–67.

39 *Garvey Papers*, vol. 4 (1985), p. 309.

40 Ibid., pp. 748–749, 758, 933.

41 Cronon, *Black Moses*, pp. 166, 186–187.

42 Richard B. Moore, "Critics and Opponents of Marcus Garvey" in John Henrik Clarke, ed., *Marcus Garvey and the Vision of Africa* (1974), p. 224.

43 Cronon, *Black Moses*, p. 129.

44 Ibid., pp. 150–155, 162, 166–168; Elton C. Fax, *Garvey: The Story of a Pioneer Black Nationalist* (1972), pp. 269–270; Grant, *Negro with a Hat*, pp. 439–440, 450.

45 Garvey, *Philosophy and Opinions of Marcus Garvey*, p. 44.

46 Benjamin E. Mays, *The Negro's God as Reflected in His Literature* (1938), pp. 184–185.

47 Garvey, *Philosophy and Opinions of Marcus Garvey*, p. 122.

48 Johnson, *Black Manhattan*, p. 97; Cronon, *Black Moses*, p. 66; *Garvey Papers*, vol. 10 (2005), p. 502.

49 Cronon, *Marcus Garvey*, pp. 221–222.

50 Richard Wright, *American Hunger* (1977), pp. 28–29.

51 Alain Locke, ed., *The New Negro* (1980), pp. 7–15.

52 Moore, "The Critics and Opponents of Marcus Garvey," pp. 210–235.

53 Weiss, *The National Urban League*, pp. 148–149; Johnson, "After Garvey—What?", p. 232.

54 Grant, *Negro with a Hat*, pp. 128, 174.

55 Ibid., pp. 336–337, 355; Theodore Kornweibel, Jr., *No Crystal Stair: Black Life and the Messenger, 1917–1928* (1975), p. 148.

56 *Garvey Papers*, vol. 1, p. 83.

57 W.E.B. Du Bois, *Dusk of Dawn: An Essay toward an Autobiography of a Race Concept* (1940), p. 277.

58 Arnold Rampersad, *The Art and Imagination of W.E.B. Du Bois* (1976), p. 149.

59 Julius Lester, ed., *The Seventh Son: The Thought and Writings of W.E.B. Du Bois*, vol. 2 (1971), p. 183.

60 *Garvey Papers*, vol. 2, p. 620; Elliott M. Rudwick, *W.E.B. Du Bois: Propagandist of the Negro Protest* (1969), p. 219; Lester, *Seventh Son*, p. 183; Cary Wintz, ed., *African American Political Thought, 1890–1930: Washington, Du Bois, Garvey, and Randolph* (1996), p. 129.

61 Martin, *Race First*, pp. 297–299.

62 Garvey, *Philosophy and Opinions of Marcus Garvey*, pp. 310–320.

63 Lester, *Seventh Son*, pp. 184–186.

64 Martin, *Race First*, pp. 306–307.

65 W.E.B. Du Bois, *The World and Africa* (1947), p. 236; David Levering Lewis, ed., *W.E.B. Du Bois: A Reader* (1995), p. 345.

66 E.U. Essien-Udom and Amy Jacques Garvey, eds., *More Philosophy and Opinions of Marcus Garvey* (1977), p. 124; Martin, *Race First*, p. 311.

67 E. Franklin Frazier, "Garvey: A Mass Leader," *Nation* 123 (18 August 1926): 147–148.

68 Adam Clayton Powell, Sr., *Against the Tide: An Autobiography* (1938), pp. 70–71; Randall K. Burkett, *Garveyism as a Religious Movement: The Institutionalization of a Black Religion* (1978), p. 3.

69 Claude McKay, "Garvey as a Negro Moses" in Wayne F. Cooper, ed., *The Passion of Claude McKay: Selected Poetry and Prose, 1912–1948* (1973), pp. 65–69.

70 Johnson, *Black Manhattan*, pp. 256–257.

71 E. Franklin Frazier, *Black Bourgeoisie: The Rise of a New Middle Class* (1965), p. 250; Gunnar Myrdal, *An American Dilemma: The Negro Problem and Modern Democracy* (1944), p. 746.

72 Leonard E. Barrett, *Soul-Force: African Heritage in Afro-American Religion* (1974), p. 151.

CHAPTER FIVE

Martin Luther King, Jr.: Apostle of Nonviolence

I refuse to accept the view that mankind is so tragically bound to the starless midnight of racism and war that the bright daybreak of peace and brotherhood can never become a reality. . . . I believe that unarmed truth and unconditional love will have the final word.[1]

[Martin Luther King, Jr.]

In 1960, my mother bought a television set. . . . [O]ne day, there appeared the face of Dr. Martin Luther King, Jr. At the moment I first saw him, he was being handcuffed and shoved into a police truck. He had dared to claim his rights as a native son, and had been arrested. He displayed no fear, but seemed calm, serene, unaware of his own extraordinary courage. . . . He Was The One, The Hero, The One Fearless Person for whom we had waited.[2]

[Alice Walker]

Redemptive suffering has always been the part of Martin's argument which I found difficult to accept. I had seen distress fester souls and bend people's bodies out of shape, but I had yet to see anyone redeemed from pain, by pain.[3]

[Maya Angelou]

Perspectives: A New Deal for African Americans? Civil rights and black protest, 1932–1954

For most African Americans, the collapse of the economy after 1929 simply aggravated an already desperate situation. Black unemployment figures were vastly out of proportion to their percentage of the population. In 1933, a National Urban League (NUL) report indicated that over 17 percent of the black population was on public relief, compared to 10 percent of whites. Conditions were equally bad in the North and the South, but in the southern states, black tenant farmers and share-croppers slipped ever deeper into debt, and charitable organizations often refused to aid them. Those organizations traditionally concerned with black welfare—the Urban League and the National Association for the Advancement of Colored People (NAACP)—were unable to cope with the economic emergency produced by the Great Depression. Beginning in the South Side of Chicago, Illinois, "Jobs-for-Negroes" campaigns organized boycotts of businesses that did not hire African Americans. Such boycotts soon spread across the country, but encountered difficulties as white merchants obtained court injunctions prohibiting black organizations from picketing their establishments. The Urban League offered its services to Herbert Hoover, the Republican president; successfully petitioned for the inclusion of an African American on the President's Emergency Committee for Unemployment; and sought a fair share of jobs and relief measures for African Americans. But with whites now willing to take even the most menial positions, the league's emphasis shifted from expanding opportunities to retaining those low-level jobs blacks already held. Although the Urban League became more reliant than ever on white philanthropic foundations, it could do little to improve either the employment status or the prospects of African Americans during the Depression.[4]

For some, but hardly most, African Americans, the American Communist party proposed the most enlightened platform on race. When the Communist party publicized racial injustices and attacked civil rights groups and black middle-class organizations, several black intellectuals, including John P. Davis, Ralph Bunche, and E. Franklin Frazier, joined with the party to form the National Negro Congress (NNC) in 1936, with labor leader A. Philip Randolph as its first president. Randolph was supposed to deliver organized labor to a broad coalition of black groups addressing the challenging economic, political, and social problems of that time. From the beginning, however, the NNC was plagued by concerns over group autonomy and by the Communist party's involvement. The NNC foundered after the stunning Nazi-Soviet non-aggression pact of 1939, when Randolph and other black leaders withdrew their support. Randolph asserted that "Negroes cannot afford to add to the handicap of being *black* the handicap of being *Red*."[5]

The election of Franklin D. Roosevelt (FDR) as president in 1932, with his promise of a "New Deal" for the American people at the height of the Great Depression, raised black hopes and marked a turning point in the nation's race relations. Out of gratitude, African Americans began shedding their traditional loyalty to the Republican party of slave emancipation in favor of FDR's Democratic party of economic recovery. In 1936, three-fourths of northern blacks voted for Roosevelt's re-election. Although New Deal reform policies and governmental agencies were not free of racial discrimination—and no major piece of civil rights legislation was adopted during Roosevelt's long tenure—African Americans shared in New Deal relief measures, and the administration eventually appointed black advisers in the major departments. Mary McLeod Bethune was made director of the Division of Negro Affairs of the National Youth Administration; William Hastie served in various capacities, including that of civilian aide to the secretary of war during World War II; and Robert Weaver was adviser to the Interior Department. Although these appointments were largely symbolic, they were also the highest positions held by African Americans in the federal government since the Taft administration. Despite being the most attractive president to African Americans since Abraham Lincoln, FDR was a consummate politician. He was keenly aware that he could not offend white southern sensibilities on race issues, because he depended on southern Democratic votes in Congress to win passage of New Deal legislation.[6]

Yet precisely because African Americans did benefit from New Deal reforms, the established black protest organizations increased pressure on the government to make government programs in housing, education, health, and labor even more responsive to black needs. In 1933, following an NAACP initiative, various race advancement organizations established the Joint Committee on National Recovery to fight discriminatory practices in federal relief agencies. The emergence of the Congress of Industrial Organizations (CIO) saw an attempt by the American Federation of Labor (AF of L) to organize black skilled and unskilled workers into industrial unions. In response, the NAACP reversed its critical stance toward organized labor and worked to build an alliance with the CIO. There was also a significant increase in the size of the black electorate in the North during the Great Depresssion, and the mobilization of organizations in the South to promote black voter registration. FDR's judicial appointments to the U.S. Supreme Court resulted in the gradual ending of discriminatory practices, such as segregation in interstate transportation and inequalities in the pay of black and white school teachers.[7]

Eleanor Roosevelt, the president's wife, also promoted civil rights causes. In 1938, at the opening session of the Southern Conference for Human Welfare in Birmingham, Alabama, Mrs. Roosevelt defied a local segregation ordinance by taking a seat on the "colored" side of the auditorium. The following year, when the snobbish Daughters of the American Revolution (DAR) refused to let Marian Anderson, the famed black contralto, perform at Constitutional Hall in Washington, D.C., Mrs. Roosevelt resigned from the DAR, and she and Interior secretary Harold Ickes arranged for Anderson to give her recital from the steps of the Lincoln Memorial, which was on federal government land. The hour-long event attracted 75,000 people—though the Roosevelts were not among them—and was a resounding success. NAACP leader Walter White described what happened when the concert ended: "As the last notes of 'Nobody Knows the Trouble I've Seen' faded away the spell was broken by the rush of the [enthralled] audience toward Mrs. Anderson, which almost threatened tragedy." To explain why U.S. senators, U.S. Supreme Court justices, cabinet secretaries, military commanders, ambassadors, and ordinary Americans attended this historic event, historian Raymond Arsenault wrote: "They had come to see Eleanor Roosevelt's friend and fellow American, a forty-five-year-old woman . . . who had seemingly done the impossible, reawakening a nation's sense of fair play and tolerance with the sound of her voice and the force of her character."[8]

Although the New Deal raised black hopes, it failed to satisfy them fully. A conference sponsored by the National Youth Administration concluded that the majority of African Americans still faced a high rate of unemployment, inadequate educational and recreational facilities, poor health and housing, and the threat of mob violence. A subsequent conference concluded that certain measures were imperative if there was to be any meaningful improvement in the status of African Americans. These steps included federal legislation to outlaw lynching, an end to disfranchisement, the elimination of discrimination in the federal civil service, the expansion of low-rent housing, the extension of social security coverage to domestic and agricultural workers, additional black appointments to federal policy-making bodies, and the expansion of federally-funded work-relief programs. In a *Crisis* editorial, the NAACP commended president Roosevelt for having included African Americans in New Deal programs, but condemned his failure to support a federal anti-lynching bill and his unwillingness to address persistent racial discrimination in civilian life and the armed forces. In March, 1935, the continuing frustrations over unemployment and police brutality led thousands of African Americans organized by the Young Communist League to riot in Harlem, New York.[9]

On the eve of American involvement in World War II, black protest organizations were united in demanding full and equal participation in the military and an end to discriminatory practices in the defense industries. More than a quarter million jobs were completely closed to African Americans, regardless of their qualifications. In the aircraft industry, only 240 of 107,000 workers were black. According to the U.S. Employment Service, more than half of the war industries refused point-blank to hire African Americans. The construction industry was desperate for workers, but adamantly opposed calling any of the 75,000 experienced black carpenters, electricians, painters, bricklayers, and plasterers. When African Americans demanded the removal of the color barrier at Boeing Aircraft in Seattle, Washington, an official for the International Association of Machinists turned aside the request, commenting, "Labor has been asked to make many sacrifices in the war and has made them gladly, but this sacrifice is too great." After the Japanese attack on Pearl Harbor, some black newspapers adopted a more conciliatory tone, arguing that the national crisis demanded that civil rights agitation should be suspended—or at least muted—for the duration of the war. More radical leaders disagreed.[10]

The March on Washington Movement (MOWM) was the most striking demonstration of more aggressive trends in black protest thought and action. The idea of exerting mass pressure on the federal government to end discrimination in the defense industries did not originate with A. Philip Randolph's call for a march on Washington, D.C., in early 1941. Agitation for mass pressure of some kind had grown since the failure of black leaders to gain any major concessions from Roosevelt, with protest meetings around the country sponsored by the NAACP and the Committee for the Participation of Negroes in National Defense. Randolph suggested that 10,000—later raised to 100,000—African Americans march on the nation's capital with the slogan: "We loyal Americans demand the right to work and fight for our country."[11]

The MOWM, which was conceived as an all-black action by and for African Americans, anticipated the forms of black protest of the 1950s and 1960s. As it happened, Randolph's threatened March on Washington never occurred because black pressure forced the federal government's hand at the last minute. In June, 1941, president Roosevelt issued Executive Order 8802, which stipulated that defense industries should end discrimination based on "race, creed, or national origin." The number of African Americans working in shipyards, aircraft factories, government service, and iron and steel industries doubled or tripled. Other parts of the MOWM agenda were ignored. MOWM had sought an executive order forbidding the awarding of government contracts to firms practicing racial discrimination in their hiring practices, and a similar order ending segregation and discrimination in the armed forces and all departments of the federal government, as well as a request for legislation forbidding the benefits of the National Labor Relations Act to unions denying black membership. In 1943, A. Philip Randolph planned a strategy of civil disobedience, based on the Gandhian example in India, to attack segregation and discrimination in the northern states.[12]

Mohandas (Mahatma) Gandhi's philosophy and techniques were also reflected in the formation of the Congress of Racial Equality (CORE) in 1942. Founded by James Farmer, Jr. and other members of the Fellowship of Reconciliation (FOR), a Christian pacifist organization, CORE was chiefly responsible for pioneering the use of nonviolent protest as a civil rights strategy. CORE engaged in its first "sit-in" later that year, when Farmer and an interracial group of members employed the tactic against a Chicago restaurant that had refused to serve African Americans. In 1947, CORE sponsored a "Journey of Reconciliation"—a forerunner of the 1961 "Freedom Rides"—through the Upper South to test compliance with a recent U.S. Supreme Court decision banning segregation in interstate transportation. CORE was to remain active in the direct-action protests of the 1950s and 1960s, concentrating its efforts on voter-registration drives in the southern states.[13]

World War II had created a climate in which African Americans and some whites perceived possibilities for decisive changes in race relations. Black membership in labor unions and employment in white-collar and semi-skilled jobs increased, and the NAACP's membership rose tenfold. African Americans who fought in the war demanded more rights at home and were less willing to put up with second-rate citizenship. These heightened expectations, the growing importance of the black vote, and continuing migration out of the South combined to produce improvements in several areas. In recognition of these demographic, economic, and politic shifts, the federal government took steps towards racial equality. In addition to his executive order forbidding job discrimination in defense industries, Roosevelt

strengthened the enforcement capability of the Committee on Fair Employment Practice (FEPC), increasing its budget, hiring a full-time staff, and
enlarging its powers. By war's end, almost 8 percent of defense industry jobs
were held by African-Americans. At the same time, these blacks still suffered
from job segregation, lower pay than whites, and restrictions on union
involvement. In 1944, the U.S. Supreme Court outlawed the Texas white
primary law, meaning that states could not use election laws to disfranchise
African-American voters. In the South, the number of African Americans
registered to vote increased six-fold to 12 percent between 1940 and 1947.[14]

Roosevelt's successor, Harry Truman, had forebears who fought for
the Confederacy, but he was the first president to address the NAACP,
and urged a variety of far-reaching civil rights measures on a Congress
controlled by conservative southern Democrats and northern Republicans.
In *To Secure These Rights*, Truman backed recognition of lynching as a
federal crime, the abolition of poll taxes and discrimination in interstate
travel, and the establishment of a federal civil rights commission and a
civil rights division in the Justice Department. He also issued Executive
Order 9981, which called for "equality for all persons in the armed forces,
without regard to race, color, or national origin." Although sections of
the military were slow to implement the policy, there was a substantial
measure of racial integration in the armed forces by the time of the Korean
War. In addition, Truman ordered the military to purchase supplies from
private companies with policies on equal treatment of minorities. He also
appointed the first African-American to the federal judiciary and ended
racial discrimination in the federal civil service. In the 1948 presidential
election, Truman's bold espousal of civil rights reforms provoked southern
Democrats to bolt for the new States' Rights ("Dixiecrat") party, which
carried four states for its candidate, governor Strom Thurmond of South
Carolina. In the end, the populist campaign run by Truman gave him the
greatest election upset in American history, helped in no small measure by
large black majorities in northern and midwestern states.[15]

During the same period, NAACP attorneys Charles Houston and his
protégé, Thurgood Marshall, filed lawsuit after lawsuit to destroy the
edifice of Jim Crow. The legal initiative against segregation depended on
local plaintiffs who risked their homes, jobs, and lives to challenge the
unjust status quo in court. In 1938, the U.S. Supreme Court made an initial
move against the "separate but equal" doctrine in *Missouri ex rel. Gaines
v. Canada*, when it ruled that the state of Missouri violated the 14th
Amendment because it failed to provide a law school for blacks. In a 1950
ruling, *Sweatt v. Painter*, the Court ordered the state of Texas to admit
African Americans to the law school of the University of Texas. Spurred by

these successes, the NAACP legal team, together with social psychologists Kenneth and Mamie Clark and sympathetic black and white historians, including John Hope Franklin and C. Vann Woodward, repeatedly pushed the Court to abandon the "separate but equal" principle altogether. In 1954, chief justice Earl Warren handed down the historic *Brown v. Board of Education* decision, which unanimously held that separate educational facilities were "inherently unequal." The following year, the Court ordered school desegregation to proceed with "all deliberate speed," provoking massive and well-organized opposition among whites in the Deep South. The Court's ruling in *Brown* marked the triumphant conclusion of the NAACP's long campaign against segregated schools, and overturned the despised *Plessy v. Ferguson* decision of 1896. The *Brown* decision was recognized immediately by its supporters and opponents as a landmark step in American race relations, since it appeared to remove constitutional sanction for the whole system of racial segregation.[16]

Although he completed Truman's directive to desegregate the military, president Dwight Eisenhower compiled a mixed record on black civil rights—the defining moral issue of his time. To civil rights supporters, Eisenhower seemed apathetic or even hostile to racial questions. To his credit, he appointed Earl Warren and several federal judges whose decisions on race were progressive. But he interfered with the Court's consideration of the *Brown* school desegregation case, and he refused to endorse the decision, which encouraged southern segregationists to stand their ground. Consistent with his understanding of the presidency, however, Eisenhower did order desegregation of federal facilities. He also used executive authority to implement the *Brown* decision in September, 1957, when Arkansas governor Orval Faubus ordered state militia to halt token integration of Central High School in Little Rock. Faubus withdrew the troops on court order, but when hysterical white mobs accosted nine African-American children, Eisenhower promptly directed federal troops to enforce the law by accompanying them into the school building. The victory proved temporary, because Little Rock schools were closed the following year. Other southern state governors employed less violent, but more effective, methods to circumvent the *Brown* decision. Two such methods provided state money to enable any white student "threatened" with integration to attend a private school and allowed any school district to close its schools if desegregation offended the local white community.[17]

With two branches of the federal government now enforcing racial desegregation, black southerners became increasingly active in demanding a more just society. As a younger, more educated and affluent generation of black activists challenged racial discrimination and segregation in the South, they faced not only the opposition of a majority of whites, but also that of black "conservatives," the older and entrenched leadership class that had long practiced Booker T. Washington's politics of conciliation, caution, and restraint in their dealings with the white power structure.[18]

In Montgomery, Alabama, "the cradle of the Confederacy," Jo Ann Robinson, an English instructor at Alabama State College, decided to challenge segregation head on. Robinson was a member of the influential Dexter Avenue Baptist Church and the president of the Women's Political Council (WPC), a local black organization founded in 1946 by one of her colleagues, Mary Fair Burks, when the local League of Women Voters had refused to integrate. In 1953, the WPC complained to city officials about the treatment of black passengers on the city's buses, a principal source of friction being the bus company's loosely defined seating policy which varied from route to route and driver to driver. African Americans were frequently required to shift their seats when peremptorily commanded to do so by drivers, all of whom were white. They were also compelled to get on at the front door of buses to pay their fare, and then get off and re-enter at the back door, instead of simply being allowed to walk down the aisle. Drivers sometimes drove off before black passengers had time to re-board. In 1954, Claudette Colvin, a 15-year-old black girl, refused to vacate her bus seat when ordered to do so by a driver and was placed on probation for assault and battery against the policeman who removed her. In May of that year, the WPC wrote to the Montgomery mayor, threatening a boycott if significant improvements were not forthcoming.[19]

On December 1, 1955, a week after the federal government's Interstate Commerce Commission banned segregation on vehicles and in facilities engaged in interstate travel, Rosa Parks, a 42-year-old black seamstress in a downtown Montgomery store, violated the city ordinance that required African Americans to surrender their seats to whites. Parks, a high school graduate with an unblemished personal life and an unthreatening demeanor, had been training for this moment all her life. Her grandfather had stood up to the Ku Klux Klan, and she had married a civil rights activist, served as an officer in the local NAACP, investigated brutal white-on-black rape cases, trained black youngsters to demand equality, recruited a young black attorney to represent activists, worked for a liberal white couple who encouraged her integrationist impulse, and attended an activist workshop in the hill country of Tennessee. For years, Parks had avoided riding in segregated elevators, and she had been ejected from Montgomery buses on several occasions for refusing to accept segregated seating. On this occasion, she was arrested, convicted, and fined. "Why," she asked the arresting officer, "do you push us around?"[20]

Following Parks' arrest, Jo Ann Robinson drafted, furtively mimeo-graphed, and, with the help of her students, distributed a leaflet calling for a boycott of the bus company. As Robinson recalled, "We had planned the protest long before Parks was arrested. There had been so many things that happened, that black women had been embarrassed over, and they were ready to explode." The leaflet read in part:

Another Negro woman has been arrested and thrown in jail because she refused to get up out of her seat on the bus for a white person to sit down. . . . If we do not do something to stop these arrests, they will continue. The next time it may be you, or your daughter, or mother. . . . We are, therefore, asking every Negro to stay off the buses Monday in protest of the arrest and trial. Don't ride the buses to work, to school or to anywhere on Monday. . . .[21]

Edgar D. Nixon, president of the local chapter of the International Brotherhood of Sleeping Car Porters, and a dominant figure in Montgomery's NAACP, remembered calling on Rosa Parks after her arrest and telling her: "We can break this situation on the bus with your case." After talking to her fearful husband and mother, the fearless Parks replied: "You know, Mr. Nixon, if you say so, I'll go along with it." Following Nixon's initiative, a group of black ministers formed the Montgomery Improvement Associa-tion (MIA) to direct and coordinate what became a 381-day boycott of the City Lines bus company. Nixon shrewdly recognized that African Americans could be more effectively organized for a mass protest through the indigenous black church, which bridged social classes and political factions, than through a secular movement. The facilities of the black churches, which provided meeting places and fund-raising machinery, were particularly important in a community without a black-owned radio station or newspaper. The vast majority of bus passengers were African Americans, and the company stood to lose $3,000 a day in revenues, the city of Montgomery part of its $20,000 a year in taxes on the bus line, and Montgomery department stores over $1 million in lost sales, if the proposed boycott worked.[22]

The MIA's original demands were modest, and had been accepted by other southern municipalities. Two years earlier, African Americans in Baton Rouge, Louisiana, had boycotted the city's buses and forced an agreement that passengers would be given "first come, first served" segre-gated seating. The MIA asked for greater courtesy from bus drivers, the hiring of African-American drivers on predominantly black routes, and the seating of African Americans from the back toward the front of buses and whites from the front to the back, without a section reserved exclusively for each race. Essentially, then, the initial thrust of the Montgomery bus boycott was for a modification of segregationist practices, but whites were unwilling to compromise. By charging Rosa Parks with violating the segregated transportation statute, the Montgomery authorities inadvertently made possible an appeal to a federal court and, ultimately, to the U.S. Supreme Court, challenging the constitutionality of segregated transportation.[23]

Martin Luther King, Jr., a 26-year-old African-American minister who had arrived in Montgomery only a year before, was unanimously elected to preside over the MIA. E.D. Nixon agreed to serve as treasurer, but refused to run for the presidency of the new organization because he would be away from Montgomery for long periods on railroad business. By all accounts, King was surprised to gain leadership of the MIA. During his first year in Montgomery, he had concentrated his energies on his pastorate of the Dexter Avenue Baptist Church, serving a middle-class black congregation that included college faculty, and on completing his doctoral dissertation. King recalled that his election as MIA president "caught me unawares. It happened so quickly I did not even have time to think it through. It is probable that if I had, I would have declined the nomination." Before leading the MIA, King had refused the presidency of the city's NAACP chapter, had not engaged in any organized civil rights protest, and had not met Rosa Parks.[24]

On several counts, King was an ideal choice for the MIA presidency. As a relative newcomer, he was not involved in the factionalism of local black politics, and had not been compromised by his dealings with the white community. His selection also reflected hostility within the MIA to the Rev. L. Roy Bennett, president of the Interdenominational Ministerial Alliance. In addition, as E.D. Nixon recognized, King possessed the personal and educational qualities necessary in a leader who could conduct negotiations at a high level. In other respects, Martin Luther King, Jr. was an unknown quantity. The Montgomery bus boycott was to transform him into a national and even international figure. In his first speech as MIA leader, King issued a ringing call to action, coupled with a plea for an orderly protest:

We are here this evening to say to those who have mistreated us for so long that we are tired—tired of being segregated and humiliated; tired of being kicked about by the brutal feet of oppression. . . . For many years we have shown amazing patience. We have sometimes given our white brothers the feeling that we like the way we were being treated. But we come here tonight to be saved from that patience that makes us patient with anything less than freedom and justice . . . if you will protest courageously and yet with dignity and Christian love, when the history books are written in future generations the historians will pause and say: "There lived a great people—a black people—who injected new meaning and dignity into the veins of civilization."[25]

Martin Luther King, Jr.: The making of a leader

Martin (born "Michael") Luther King, Jr., was born in 1929 to a well-respected family which lived on "Sweet Auburn" Avenue in Atlanta, Georgia. His remarkable maternal grandfather, the Rev. Adam Daniel Williams, was a preacher of unusual power and successfully built up the Ebenezer Baptist Church. A pioneer in the development of a distinctive black social gospel, Williams combined elements of Booker T. Washington's emphasis on black business development with W.E.B. Du Bois' call for civil rights. Williams helped found the Georgia Equal Rights League to protest the white primary, and headed the Atlanta chapter of the NAACP to fight segregation, establish black schools, and encourage African Americans to vote. Upon Williams' death, his son-in-law, the Rev. Martin Luther King, Sr., took over Ebenezer's pulpit, and was also a determined foe of Jim Crow, heading Atlanta's NAACP and Civic and Political League, fighting for equalized teacher salaries and refusing to ride the city's segregated buses.[26]

Martin Luther King, Jr., thus inherited the struggle against segregation, and grew up in a close-knit, middle-class, and deeply religious family. He seemed destined for the ministry like his father and grandfather. At the age of fifteen, he entered the all-black male Morehouse College in Atlanta, where he was influenced by its president, Benjamin Mays, a leading African-American theologian and church historian. Mays' attacks on racial injustice, and his beliefs in Christian social responsibility and political engagement greatly impressed King, who had considered law or medicine despite his mediocre academic record. He elected, after all, to follow the family tradition and become a Southern Baptist minister. In his philosophy course, King was intrigued by Hegelian dialecticism, which finds truth emerging from conflict, and Henry David Thoreau's classic essay *Civil Disobedience*, which asserts that oppressed peoples are entitled to disobey unjust laws and should refuse to cooperate with evil systems.[27]

In 1948, King graduated from Morehouse with a degree in sociology, and enrolled at Crozer Theological Seminary in Chester, Pennsylvania, to study for the ministry. At Crozer, he was introduced to the writings of the Social Gospel theologian Walter Rauschenbusch, and endorsed his contention that the church should concern itself with social conditions, as well as with the salvation of souls. In his first book, *Stride Toward Freedom* (1958), an account of the Montgomery bus boycott, King revealed, "It has been my conviction ever since reading Rauschenbusch, that any religion which professes to be concerned about the souls of men and is not concerned about the social and economic conditions that scar that soul, is a spiritually moribund religion." King was also introduced to American theologian Reinhold Niebuhr's concept and reality of "collective evil." Although King rejected Marxism as atheistic and materialistic, he endorsed Marxism's social concerns, and believed that "communism grew as a protest against the hardships of the underprivileged." With respect to Christianity, King, the seminarian, scorned fundamentalism and rejected several core orthodox beliefs, including the full divinity of Jesus of Nazareth (the Trinity) and the Virgin Birth, Resurrection, and Second Coming.[28]

While in seminary, King became interested in Gandhi's teachings, after hearing a lecture by Howard University president Mordecai Johnson, who had recently returned from a trip to India. Already a declared pacifist, King added Gandhi's philosophy of coercive nonviolent resistance to injustice to his intellectual system, and later celebrated the redemptive power of love and suffering as forces for social change. King acknowledged his debt to the Indian philosopher and nationalist: "Gandhi was probably the first person in history to lift the love ethic of Jesus above mere interaction between individuals to a powerful and effective force on a large scale. It was in this Gandhian emphasis on love and nonviolence that I discovered the method of social reform for which I had been seeking. I came to feel that this was the only morally and practically sound method open to oppressed people in their struggle for freedom. . . . Gandhi convinced me that true pacifism is not nonresistance to evil, but nonviolent resistance to evil."[29]

Upon graduating as valedictorian at Crozer, King entered the doctoral program in theology at Boston University, after Yale rejected his application. There, he met and married Coretta Scott, from Alabama, then a voice student at the New England Conservatory of Music. Before completing his thesis on the opposing theological views of Paul Tillich and Henry Nelson Wieman, King accepted a pastorate in Montgomery. In addition to his academic credentials, King brought to his first ministerial appointment a love of the South, a supportive wife, and a social philosophy based on a belief in Christian activism. As the boycott unfolded, King quickly displayed considerable powers as an orator and public performer— qualities that would distinguish his career as the prophet and practitioner of nonviolent resistance to denials of civil and human rights.[30]

As president of the MIA, King understood that its initial demands fell short of demanding an end to desegregation, but he, more than anyone else, united and inspired the boycott movement. When Montgomery blacks followed the call not to ride the city's buses, the MIA created and maintained a complicated and expensive car pool, which gave more affluent African Americans an opportunity to participate in the protest by giving rides to the walkers. After white Montgomerians pressured insurance companies to cancel the policies of motorists offering their services to the MIA, the boycotters turned to Lloyd's of London for coverage. When an attempt to divide the black community into its traditional factions failed, the mayor and city fathers resorted to other tactics. King was arrested and jailed briefly for allegedly driving too fast, and in January, 1956, his house was bombed with his wife and infant daughter Yolanda inside. The next month, a grand jury indicted 115 blacks for allegedly breaking an old anti-labor law that forbade injury to a legitimate business enterprise without "just cause or legal excuse." Faced with such provocations, King continued to preach a message of nonviolent resistance, and the boycott attracted national support and financial donations from various sources including the NAACP, the United Auto Workers, and overseas.[31]

Following the attack on his home, King was visited and coached by Bayard Rustin and Glenn Smiley, members of the Fellowship of Reconciliation, admirers of Gandhi, and followers of A.J. Muste, an American pacifist clergyman. During this period, King also developed a close working relationship with the Rev. Ralph David Abernathy, the activist preacher of Montgomery's First Baptist Church. But according to King's account, it was Juliette Morgan whose letter in the *Montgomery Advertiser* alerted him to the parallels between the bus boycott and Gandhi's strategy in India. Morgan was a genteel, church-going white woman with New Deal sympathies, who had spent sixteen years confronting segregation prior to the bus boycott. Her latest letter infuriated whites, and Morgan saw a cross burning on her lawn, answered obscene telephone calls, and was fired from her job as a city librarian. Severely depressed, Morgan swallowed a fatal dose of sleeping pills. Morgan's letter set King to thinking, and he defined "non-violent resistance . . . as the technique of the movement, while love stood as the regulating ideal. Christ furnished the spirit and motivation, while Gandhi furnished the method."[32]

Despite a U.S. Supreme Court ruling against segregation on interstate buses in South Carolina, the Montgomery city government obtained a local court injunction ordering the continuance of segregated buses. The NAACP then sued Montgomery to compel integrated buses. In June, 1956, a federal district court ruled that the city ordinance violated the U.S. Constitution, but the city appealed, and the boycott continued. As King and his associates awaited a determination as to the legality of the car pool, news came of the Supreme Court's decision striking down Alabama's state and local laws upholding bus segregation as unconstitutional. King and the MIA now worked to prepare the black community for the arrival of the desegregation order, and urged African Americans to behave courteously when they went back on the buses. They were instructed to "read, study and memorize" a list of "Integrated Bus Suggestions" which included the following: "Pray for guidance and commit yourself to *complete* non-violence as you enter the bus. . . . Be quiet but friendly; proud, but not arrogant; joyous, but not boisterous. . . . If cursed, do not curse back. If pushed, do not push back. If struck, do not strike back, but evidence love and goodwill at all times."[33]

As Montgomery's buses desegregated, angry whites attacked African Americans and firebombed black churches. King was not discouraged by such retaliation, for he viewed the boycott as a demonstration and vindication of the efficacy of nonviolent direct action. While the boycott was still in progress, he declared, "We now know that the Southern Negro has become of age, politically and morally. Montgomery has demonstrated that we will not run from the struggle, and will support the battle for equality. . . . This is a protest—a *non-violent* protest against injustice . . . and the great instrument is the instrument of love. . . . [N]o matter what sacrifices we have to make, we will not let anybody drag us so low as to hate them."[34]

Rufus Lewis, a former football coach at Alabama State College, a successful businessman, and chair of the Citizens' Steering Committee for improved treatment of Montgomery's blacks, believed that King's "greatest contribution" to the boycott "was interpreting the situation to the mass of the people. He could speak better than any man I've ever heard in expressing to the people their problem and making them see clearly what the situation was and inspiring them to work at it." Yet there is also evidence to suggest that the mass of Montgomery blacks, although supporting the boycott, were confused by or indifferent to the Gandhian gloss that King put on the movement. In retrospect, it is clear that the Montgomery boycott was a seminal event, but it did not touch off a national revolt among African Americans. In one way, refusing to ride the buses was a conservative protest—the withdrawal of patronage—which was an act of omission, rather than commission. It involved participants in considerable hardship and inconvenience, but, for most, little actual physical danger. As for the origins of the boycott, it had been initiated by the WPC and not by the black ministers of Montgomery. In effect, they were presented with a *fait accompli*, and as Jo Ann Robinson wryly observed after her circular was made public: "It was then that the ministers decided that it was time for them, the leaders, to catch up with the masses. . . . Had they not done so, they might have alienated themselves from their congregations."[35]

The Southern Christian Leadership Conference

In 1957, Martin Luther King, Jr. and other black clergymen formed the Southern Christian Leadership Conference (SCLC) to spread and coordinate the strategy of nonviolent civil rights protest across the South. The new organization benefited considerably from advice given by Bayard Rustin of the Fellowship of Reconciliation and the War Resisters League and Stanley Levison, a Jewish attorney and businessman from New York, who championed leftwing causes and formerly served as a fundraiser and paymaster for the American Communist party. Levison and his brother built a business empire that included an automobile dealership, which funneled $10,000 a year to the communists. Levison became one of King's closest confidants, writing speeches and filing tax returns for King, and raising money, organizing events, and arranging publicity for SCLC, all *gratis*. Levison continued to contribute large sums of money to the Communist party into the early 1960s, when he concluded that the party was lukewarm about or "inept" concerning the civil rights movement. Most of King's advisers and associates had no communist connections whatsoever.[36]

SCLC's statement of purpose declared that "the American dilemma in race relations can best and most quickly be resolved through the action of thousands of people, committed to the philosophy of nonviolence, who will physically identify themselves in a just and moral struggle. . . . The true nonviolent resister presents his physical body as an instrument to defeat the system. SCLC is firmly opposed to segregation in any form . . . and pledges itself to work unrelentingly to rid every vestige of its scars from our nation through nonviolent means. . . . Our ultimate goal is genuine intergroup and interpersonal living—*integration*." In a nutshell, SCLC envisioned what it described as an interracial "beloved community."[37]

An unstructured and unorthodox organization, SCLC did not offer individual memberships in order to avoid direct competition with the mammoth NAACP, to which many SCLC founders belonged. Southern Baptist ministers were heavily represented in SCLC affiliates and provided leadership of the organization, but they were atypical of most black clergy who had a vested interest in the racial status quo that maintained their own positions. For the remainder of his life, King was to be identified with SCLC, while the organization itself capitalized on King's growing fame and prestige.[38]

Bayard Rustin and Stanley Levison urged King to remain nonpartisan, because they saw little difference between the Republicans and Democrats on civil rights issues. In stressing nonviolence and Christian principles, Rustin and Levison believed that SCLC would appeal to a wide liberal constituency. As part of SCLC's strategy to present King as a national figure, King attended a "Prayer Pilgrimage" to Washington, D.C., in May, 1957, in the company of NAACP executive secretary Roy Wilkins and labor leader A. Philip Randolph, who had orchestrated the March on Washington Movement during World War II. The event attracted little media attention, but King received the greatest ovation after a speech in which he demanded that African Americans be given the ballot forthwith to enforce their constitutional rights.[39]

SCLC's original aim of spreading the Montgomery example by supporting similar boycotts in other cities had met with little success, and in Montgomery, the MIA did little to challenge directly other forms of segregation. Believing that white southerners were less opposed to black voting rights than to desegregation, SCLC engaged in an unsuccessful effort during its first three years to double the number of black voters in the South. Ella Baker, SCLC's interim executive director and the only woman on the board, initiated this "Crusade for Citizenship," but with inadequate financial resources and a lack of effective organization at the local levels, little was achieved. Baker, an experienced protest organizer, became increasingly critical of King's "leader-centered" approach to effecting change, regarding him as pompous and condescending toward women. While King believed that "leadership never ascends from the pew to the pulpit, but . . . descends from the pulpit to the pew," Baker believed that "the Negro must quit looking for a savior, and work to save himself." As far as Baker was concerned, King's chief weakness was that he championed a civil rights strategy that seemed ineffective, if not counter-productive. For their part, the ministers of SCLC thought Baker was temperamentally unsuited for her role in their organization. Certainly before 1960, SCLC was inadequately staffed and, without a clearly-defined purpose, undecided as to whether to instigate its own protests or simply to assist in local actions.[40]

After barely surviving a stabbing by a deranged black woman in Harlem in 1959, King made a spiritual pilgrimage to India and went to Gandhi's shrine. The Indian visit was a significant event in King's intellectual and political growth. In particular, he was impressed by prime minister Jawaharlal Nehru's explanation that under the Indian con-stitution, caste discrimination was punishable by imprisonment; King concluded that India had made greater progress against the iniquitous caste system than had the United States against racial discrimination. He returned to America with the renewed conviction that nonviolent resistance was "the most potent weapon available to the oppressed people in their struggle for freedom."[41]

In November, 1959, King resigned his pastorate in Montgomery and moved to metropolitan Atlanta—"the city too busy to hate"—where he would co-pastor his father's Ebenezer Baptist Church. "Daddy" King reassured Atlanta's leaders in the black and white communities that his son was not "coming to cause trouble" because "he's chosen the pulpit." King had several reasons to make this move, including a desire to escape the weekly grind of preparing sermons, live in a more cosmopolitan city, take advantage of easier airline travel, stroke his growing ego on a national stage, and nurture his fledgling SCLC, which was to continue its voter-registration drive and pursue direct-action protests against segrega-tion. In explaining his departure, King told his Dexter Avenue flock that his dual responsibilities of ministering to them and leading the bus boycott had left him a "physical and psychological wreck." With many of Atlanta's established black leaders hostile to civil rights agitation, King diplomatically agreed that SCLC would not undertake any protests there. He kept his word even when an Episcopal school denied his children admission based on their race.[42]

It was the "sit-in" movement of 1960 that inaugurated a new and more aggressive phase of the civil rights struggle. On February 1st, four black students from the North Carolina Agricultural and Technical

College in Greensboro demanded service at a Woolworth's lunch counter, and the ensuing denial of food and drink inspired a whole generation to demand simple justice. Various forms of nonviolent action protests soon utilized the Greensboro strategy—"wade-ins" at municipal swimming pools and segregated beaches, "stand-ins" at theaters refusing to sell tickets to blacks, and "pray-ins" at segregated churches. Many of the student activists had been inspired by the Montgomery boycott and had read King's account of it. In turn, King realized that a new element had been injected into the black freedom movement, and was concerned to retain SCLC's influence in the face of growing rivalry among civil rights organizations.[43]

When Ella Baker arranged a meeting of student leaders at her alma mater, Shaw University in Raleigh, North Carolina, in April, 1960, King attempted to mold the resulting Student Nonviolent Coordinating Committee (SNCC) in SCLC's image. SNCC (pronounced "Snick") initially adopted King's nonviolent philosophy, and King advised the student leaders to recruit volunteers willing to go to jail rather than pay fines for alleged infractions of the law, to adhere to the doctrine of nonviolence, and, by direct-action protests, to compel the federal government to intervene in the civil rights struggle. Although it soon moved beyond what it came to regard as King's cautious, conciliatory, and unrealistic approach, SNCC initially embraced SCLC principles: "We affirm the philosophical or religious ideal of non-violence as the foundation of our purpose, the pre-supposition of our faith, and the manner of our action. Non-violence as it grows from Judaic-Christian traditions seeks a social order of justice permeated by love. . . . Love is the central motif of non-violence. . . . It matches the capacity of evil to inflict suffering with an even more enduring capacity to absorb evil, all the while persisting in love."[44]

Yet Ella Baker was aware of growing student dissatisfaction with the established civil rights leadership, and urged SNCC to maintain a separate identity. Diane Nash, a student at Fisk University in Nashville, Tennessee, and a leader of the student sit-in movement, recalled that Baker was "very important in giving direction to the student movement . . . in terms of seeing how important it was that the students should set the goals and directions and maintain control of the student movement." After the founding of SNCC, Baker noted that the conference had made it very apparent that the "current sit-ins and other demonstrations are concerned with something much bigger than a hamburger or even a giant-sized Coke. . . . [T]he Negro and white students, North and South, are seeking to rid America of the scourge of racial segregation and discrimination—not only at lunch counters but in every aspect of life."[45]

MLK and JFK

Whereas Martin Luther King, Jr. had been unhappy with president Dwight Eisenhower's overall record on civil rights, he entertained greater hopes for U.S. senator John F. Kennedy of Massachusetts, the Democratic challenger in the 1960 presidential election. When King was given a four-month prison sentence for driving with an out-of-state driver's license in Georgia, he was released following Kennedy's intervention. Although Martin King did not officially support Kennedy, Daddy King, in gratitude, reversed his Republican loyalties and urged African Americans to vote for the Democratic candidate despite Kennedy's Roman Catholic faith. Then, weeks before the election, the younger King criticized both political parties as "hypocritical" on race: "Each of them has been willing to follow the long pattern of using the Negro as a political football." He called for the election of a president "who not only rises up with righteous indignation when a Negro is lynched in Mississippi, but will be equally incensed when a Negro is denied the right to live in his neighborhood, or join his professional association, or secure a top position in his business. This is no day to pay mere lip service to integration; we must pay life service to it." Black support was crucial in Kennedy's razor-thin victory over Republican candidate Richard Nixon, because Kennedy captured 68 percent of the black vote. Once in office, Kennedy ignored his campaign promise to prohibit discrimination in federally-funded housing projects by executive order, and elevated three segregationists to federal judgeships in the South. The political realities of that time convinced Democratic presidents to appease southern Democrats who held most of the power in Congress.[46]

Shortly before Kennedy's inauguration, civil rights activists gained a legal victory when the U.S. Supreme Court ruled that bus terminals serving interstate travellers must be integrated. In 1961, the Congress of Racial Equality sponsored a series of "Freedom rides" into the South to test compliance with that decision. When the Freedom Riders were met by violence in Alabama, the Kennedy administration was forced to intervene to protect the riders, but began to promote voter registration projects as a less provocative form of civil rights activity. King did not participate in the dangerous Freedom Rides, but quickly realized that the intensive press coverage of southern attacks on the riders should be utilized by SCLC and its allies. As a result, King became involved in several forms of direct-action protest, with varying degrees of success. SCLC, under Wyatt T. Walker, an imperious Baptist minister who replaced Ella Baker as executive director, was determined to capitalize on King's image, and regain leadership of the civil rights coalition.[47]

Albany, Birmingham, and the March on Washington

From December, 1961, to the summer of 1962, King and the SCLC belatedly joined a direct-action campaign in Albany, Georgia, demanding not only integrated facilities, but employment for African Americans in the city's police force and other municipal jobs. In the short-run, the Albany campaign failed for many reasons, not least because King was wholly unprepared for the campaign and because of the divided energies and loyalties between SCLC, SNCC, and local blacks. SNCC's James Forman, suspicious of "charismatic" leadership, did not want King in Albany, believing that African Americans should rely on the grassroots organization that was already underway when King arrived. Police chief Laurie Pritchett did not employ open violence against the demonstrators, thus denying them media exposure and possible federal intervention. Pritchett had read King's writings on nonviolence and astutely arranged in advance for additional jail space, so that the demonstrators could not escape punishment. Attorneys for the city secured a federal injunction that halted demonstrations for ten days, effectively sapping their momentum. Although King and Abernathy were given jail sentences for marching without permits, they were quickly released after chief Pritchett quietly arranged for payment of their small fines. As a reaction to the demonstrations, the city closed its parks instead of integrating them, and the town's library was "integrated" only after all its chairs were removed. As King conceded, SCLC had gone into Albany inadequately briefed on and insufficiently prepared for the local situation. An Albany city official thought the movement collapsed because "we killed them with kindness."[48]

But the lessons of Albany were well-learned, and SCLC's next campaign—dubbed "Project Confrontation"—was carefully executed. King had come to realize that, in Bayard Rustin's words, "protest becomes an effective tactic to the degree that it elicits brutality and oppression from the power structure," and privately conceded that the success of "non-violent" resistance depended on the fostering of "creative tensions"— attacks by whites on demonstrators, coverage by the media, consequent national outrage, and subsequent federal intervention. A number of veterans from the voter registration campaigns provided strategic and logistical support for Project C and for key campaigns ahead, including James

Lawson, Jr., C.T. Vivian, James Bevel, Hosea Williams, and Andrew Young. All of these ingredients were to be present in the Birmingham, Alabama, campaign of 1963.[49]

The South's major industrial city, Birmingham was a stronghold of racial oppression, fully-fledged segregation, and an administration pledged to resist even minimal change. Martin Luther King called Birmingham the "most segregated city in America." The average income for blacks in the city was less than half that of whites, and unemployment for blacks was more than twice that of whites. Birmingham had no black police officers, firefighters, bank tellers, bus drivers, or department store clerks; blacks could either work in the steel mills or in black neighborhoods. T. Eugene "Bull" Connor, Birmingham's heavy-handed public safety commissioner and a Ku Klux Klansman, turned a blind eye to the wave of bombings of black churches and the homes of local civil rights leaders. To stop the violent attacks and breach the wall of segregation, the Rev. Fred Shuttlesworth formed the Alabama Christian Movement for Human Rights (ACMHR)—an SCLC affiliate—when the state's NAACP had been shut down. With the support of black college students, Shuttlesworth led a boycott of Birmingham stores to desegregate lunch counters and open up jobs for African Americans. To apply ever more pressure, Shuttlesworth invited King to direct a campaign against the business community, rather than wily politicians. King accepted and concentrated on three demands: (1) the integration of lunch counters, fitting rooms, restrooms, and drinking fountains in department stores; (2) the upgrading and hiring of African Americans in business and industry; and (3) the creation of a biracial committee to work out a time-table for desegregation in other areas of municipal life. Boycotts and sit-ins of downtown stores were to be combined with disruptive street demonstrations, and Wyatt T. Walker collected the names of hundreds of Birmingham residents prepared to go to jail. A.G. Gaston, a black millionaire entrepreneur, provided the campaign with rent-free headquarters at his hotel, while outside support was organized by Harry Belafonte, a black calypso singer.[50]

Demonstrations were twice postponed—once to allow for (abortive) negotiations with business leaders, and, a second time, to await the outcome of a disputed mayoralty election between commissioner Bull Connor, and Albert Boutwell, a racial moderate. When Connor obtained a court order temporarily enjoining all demonstrations, King defied a state, rather than a federal, court injunction. When King marched on city hall, he was arrested and held for two days without being allowed to contact his wife or his lawyers. Neither president Kennedy nor his brother

Robert, the U.S. attorney general, sympathized with SCLC's campaign, but they intervened so that King could communicate with his family and legal counsel.[51]

When King's activities in Birmingham were criticized by local white clergymen, who described him as an extremist and outside agitator, he responded with a classic statement on civil rights and nonviolence. In his "Letter from Birmingham Jail," King pointed out that he had been invited to the city by an SCLC affiliate, and declared that no one could be an "outsider" to injustice. He observed that direct action must always precede negotiation, and reiterated his belief in resistance to unjust laws. King expressed disappointment that his fellow clergymen confused nonviolence with extremism, and warned that black disaffection had already produced the Black Muslim sect "made up of people who have lost faith in America, who have absolutely repudiated Christianity, and who have concluded that the white man is an incurable 'devil.'" In contrast, King presented himself as a responsible moderate, as having "tried to stand between these two forces, insisting that we need not follow the 'do-nothingism' of the complacent or the hatred and despair of the black nationalist."[52]

Released on bail after eight days in prison, King left Birmingham, and, in his absence, James Bevel recruited hundreds of black schoolchildren to the faltering demonstration. This fateful step put youngsters into direct confrontation with white authorities. Bull Connor met the marchers with fire hoses, police dogs, and clubs, and 2,500 of them were arrested and jailed. Few serious injuries were inflicted on the marchers, but television and press coverage of the episode shocked the nation, with Connor as the villain of the piece. The federal government was forced to act, and with the arrival of Burke Marshall, head of the U.S. Justice Department's civil rights division, negotiations were opened between SCLC and the city government. The final agreement fell short of SCLC's original demands, but downtown stores agreed to desegregate their facilities and accepted the "gradual" hiring of black employees. It was the white business community, anxious to restore some measure of racial harmony and prosperity, which pushed for the limited settlement. The Birmingham agreement left untouched the issue of school desegregation, and Fred Shuttlesworth accused King of accepting only token gains, when total victory might have been achieved by further protests. Yet it was also probable, as King believed, that continuing demonstrations would have been counter-productive.[53]

Whatever its limitations, the Birmingham campaign provoked the Kennedy administration into introducing civil rights legislation. In a moving television address, Kennedy acknowledged as much when he stated that "the events in Birmingham and elsewhere have so increased the cries for equality that no city or state or legislative body can prudently choose to ignore them." Kennedy's successor, Lyndon Johnson, was finally to secure congressional cooperation resulting in the landmark Civil Rights Act of 1964, which not only included Kennedy's proposals but also gave the president powers to withdraw federal funds from state and local governments practicing discrimination. The Birmingham protest also atoned for the miscalculations of SCLC's Albany campaign, and propelled King into the leadership of the civil rights coalition. An opinion poll of African Americans indicated that 95 percent regarded King as their most successful spokesperson.[54]

Never was King more inspirational than on August 28, 1963, when he delivered his "I Have a Dream" oration—one of the great speeches of the 20th century—from the steps of the Lincoln Memorial in the nation's capital. The occasion was the March on Washington for Jobs and Freedom, during which 250,000 blacks and whites converged on the capital to press for passage of the civil rights bill. Some of the impact of King's speech derived essentially from its context rather than from its contents, but the cadences of King's oratory, and the repetition of his central theme had a cathartic effect on his audience:

I have a dream that one day on the red hills of Georgia the sons of former slaves and the sons of former slave holders will be able to sit down together at the table of brotherhood. I have a dream that one day even the state of Mississippi, a desert state sweltering with the heat of injustice and oppression, will be transformed into an oasis of freedom and justice. . . . I have a dream that one day the state of Alabama, whose governor's lips are presently dripping with the words of interposition and nullification, will be transformed into a situation where little black boys and black girls will be able to join hands with little white boys and white girls and walk together as sisters and brothers.

King borrowed his memorable closing passage—"from every mountainside, let freedom ring"—from Samuel Francis Smith's popular patriotic hymn, "America," and, evidently, a speech delivered to the 1952 Republican National Convention by his close friend, the Rev. Archibald Carey, Jr., of Chicago. Even as King spoke these unforgettable words, the speech had little immediate impact. *Newsweek* reported that most whites thought "Negroes smell different," "Negroes have less native intelligence," "Negroes have looser morals," and "Negroes tend to have less ambition." Ninety percent of whites said they would never let their daughter date an African American. Nor did Congress enact Kennedy's civil rights bill until Kennedy was assassinated, which created a groundswell to memorialize the dead president by approving this signature legislation.[55]

Not all of the marchers assembled at the Lincoln Memorial shared King's integrationist vision. SNCC chairman John Lewis had to be persuaded to modify his speech because some white supporters considered it too incendiary, especially against the Kennedy administration. The young black civil rights activist Anne Moody remembered, "I sat on the grass and listened to the speakers, to discover we had 'dreamers' instead of leaders leading us. Martin Luther King went on and on talking about his dream. I sat there thinking that in [Mississippi] we never had time to sleep, much less dream." Malcolm X dismissed the entire march as a "sellout" and the "Farce on Washington," and Black Muslims were forbidden to attend it.[56]

In 1964, Martin Luther King appeared on the cover of *Time*, in which he was credited with "an indescribable capacity for empathy that is the touchstone of leadership." In the same year, King was awarded the Nobel peace prize—its youngest recipient. King took the occasion to link the civil rights movement with the larger causes of world peace and human rights. Ironically, King was already under investigation by the Federal Bureau of Investigation (FBI), which, under J. Edgar Hoover's directive, kept SCLC under close surveillance. U.S. attorney general Robert Kennedy, convinced that King's close advisor, Stanley Levison, was still an active member of the Communist party, had authorized some FBI wiretaps on King. Hoover went far beyond the approved bugging plan and mounted a fanatical effort to "neutralize" Martin Luther King and the civil rights movement. Hoover loathed King for ignoring an FBI telephone call, consorting with suspected communists, and engaging in serial adultery. Nor could Hoover abide King's public criticism of FBI agents for ignoring plain evidence of police brutality during civil rights demonstrations. At one point, the FBI crafted an anonymous message designed to humiliate King as "a colossal fraud" and to prompt his suicide. The FBI went so far as to identify a possible successor—Samuel Pierce, a conservative New York attorney who later served as Housing secretary in the Reagan administration.[57]

St. Augustine and Selma

In the spring and summer of 1964, SCLC undertook a protest campaign in St. Augustine, Florida, to induce Congress to enact and president Lyndon Johnson to sign Kennedy's civil rights bill. A quarter of the city's population of 15,000 was African American. Wyatt T. Walker believed that SCLC could exploit the city's dependence on tourism and its expectation of federal funding for its 400th anniversary celebrations by launching an attack against racial discrimination. As in Birmingham, SCLC's strategy was to apply economic pressure on the business community that would compel the city to negotiate concessions or risk federal intervention. But Johnson, aware that civil rights would be a major issue in the upcoming presidential election and afraid that the conservative Republican, U.S. senator Barry Goldwater of Arizona, would appeal to white Democrats in the Deep South, was reluctant to act. SCLC protestors in St. Augustine were attacked by whites, including klansmen, and Florida governor Farris Bryant refused to use the National Guard to protect the demonstrators. The governor also reinstated a ban on night marches, despite a federal court order allowing such peaceful protest. The St. Augustine campaign ended in stalemate, with some of the city's hotels, motels, and restaurants desegregating their facilities, but no agreement was reached on other issues. Despite the impasse, SCLC believed that it had persuaded Johnson to press for congressional passage of the historic 1964 Civil Rights Act, which was signed in July with King in attendance.[58]

Black suffrage had always been a major goal of Martin Luther King and SCLC. Although the Civil Rights Act of 1964 had dealt a heavy blow to segregation, it had not guaranteed the constitutional right to vote as required by the 15th Amendment. In early 1965, SCLC joined with SNCC in a voter-registration drive in Selma, Alabama, to dramatize the need for additional legislation, once again by provoking confrontation with white authorities. SNCC workers had worked tirelessly and courageously for two years, but had achieved next to no progress, so Amelia Platts Boynton, a civil rights activist, persuaded King to make her hometown the target for their next voting rights project. SNCC field workers were at best ambivalent about cooperating with King. Although King's presence would bring valuable publicity to the campaign, SNCC disliked his excessive religiosity, his tendency to compromise at critical junctures, and SCLC's penchant for provoking crisis and then leaving the scene for other engagements.[59]

King's presence in Selma dramatized an already volatile situation. As expected, Dallas County sheriff Jim Clark, who had a hair-trigger temper like Bull Connor's in Birmingham, was provoked into violence against the demonstrators, notably on "Bloody Sunday" at the Edmund Pettus Bridge on the road out of Selma, where marchers were tear-gassed and beaten by mounted police. "Get those goddamned niggers!" Clark shouted. "And get those goddamned white niggers!" Television reporters captured the ugly episode on film and broadcast it across the land, igniting a storm of reaction.[60]

Two days later, King provided a stark example why younger activists distrusted him. King secretly negotiated a deal with local authorities to abort a protest march out of town. He led the unknowing marchers in prayer but then returned to Selma, even though the police barricade had stood aside to let the demonstrators through. Ironically, while his followers retreated, they sang, "Ain't Gonna Let Nobody Turn Me 'Round." Dumbfounded SNCC workers were openly contemptuous of King. King had, in fact, decided against confrontation with the Alabama police after discussions with the U.S. attorney general, but had not informed SNCC of his resolve.[61]

Clark's open assault of SCLC activists and the murder of Unitarian minister James Reeb of Boston, Massachusetts, by local white thugs produced a highly-charged atmosphere that moved Lyndon Johnson to call Congress into special session to enact new voting rights legislation. "It is wrong—deadly wrong—to deny any of your fellow Americans the right to vote," the president remarked in his Texas drawl, as he recalled the impediments that African Americans faced in seeking the vote. "We have already waited 100 years and more, and the time for waiting is gone. . . . What happened in Selma is part of a far larger movement . . . of American Negroes to secure for themselves the full blessings of American life." Johnson recognized that "their cause must be our cause," and he insisted that the nation finally "overcome the crippling legacy of bigotry and injustice. And we *shall* overcome." Congress erupted in wild applause, and Martin Luther King shed tears after hearing Johnson repeat the motto of the civil rights movement. It had taken the death of a white northern minister to prod the federal government to act. A month earlier, a state trooper had gunned down a young Alabama black man—Jimmie Lee Jackson—who tried to defend his family, but his death had not registered on the national consciousness.[62]

On March 17, 1965, a federal court approved the 54-mile, Selma-to-Montgomery march, and president Johnson mobilized Alabama state militia to protect the procession. As the marchers set out on their five-day trek, King gave an inspirational speech that was nearly drowned out by hovering helicopters: "Walk together, children. Don't you get weary, and it will lead us to the Promised Land, and Alabama will be a new Alabama, and America will be a new America." At the end of the march, King spoke to 25,000 people from the capitol steps in Montgomery, bringing the black protest movement back full circle to the scene of the bus boycott ten years earlier. He asked and answered the question that was on the minds of the marchers: "How long will it take?" to achieve justice. "How long? Not long, because no lie can live forever. How long? Not long, because you will reap what you sow. How long? Not long, because the arm of the moral universe is long but it bends toward justice." The Selma campaign marked the culmination of the civil rights movement in the South and, in retrospect, was King's finest hour. On August 6th, Lyndon Johnson signed the Voting Rights Act—a direct consequence of the Selma campaign— which would send federal registrars to the South in order to ensure that African Americans could vote in upcoming elections.[63]

Chicago, Black Power, and Vietnam

The urban race riots of the 1960s—euphemistically termed "civil disorders" —alerted Martin Luther King to the problems of poverty and social pathology, and the need for reaching the black underclass of the nation's inner city ghettos. Concurrently, he expressed concern over the cause and implications of the escalating American presence in Vietnam. These three issues—racism, poverty, and American imperialism—dominated King's thought and actions for the remainder of his life because he thought them interrelated. Together, they offer convincing evidence to support the contention that King became increasingly radical in his last years. Although King's position on Vietnam allied him with the younger elements of the civil rights coalition—SNCC and CORE—it alienated him from the established black leadership and earned him the enmity of Lyndon Johnson, as well as the renewed scrutiny of the FBI.[64]

In 1966, King moved to Chicago to lead a nonviolent demonstration against segregated slum housing, segregated schools, black unemployment, and job discrimination. James Bevel, SCLC's strategist in Chicago, noted that the black unemployment rate was twice that of whites and charged the city's Democratic party machine with allowing merchants to make minimal investments in black neighborhoods, thereby inflating prices and siphoning off profits to affluent white suburbs. SCLC's new campaign was strongly opposed by Bayard Rustin, who bluntly remarked that large northern cities were far different than southern towns like Albany and Selma, but King cut off the discussion by saying, "I have to pray now. I have to consult with the Lord and see what he wants me to do." Rustin was all too familiar—and furious—over King's penchant for invoking God's name to avoid disagreements.[65]

In going to Chicago, King was aware that he was taking on its formidable mayor, Richard Daley, Sr., a consummate politician and power broker in the national Democratic party. As the Rev. Arthur Brazier, who led the South Side's Woodlawn Association, observed: "King decided to come to Chicago because he thought Chicago was unique in that there was one man, one source of power, who you had to deal with. He knew this wasn't the case in New York or any other city. He thought if Daley could be persuaded on the rightness of open housing and integrated schools that things would be done." Although Daley treated King outwardly with respect, the city government's considerable resources were used to frustrate the campaign. When King moved into a rat-infested, urine-soaked apartment to highlight the housing crisis, the crafty Daley dispatched building inspectors with slum violation notices. When SCLC demonstrators marched through Chicago's blue collar suburbs, they encountered bitter and violent opposition from working-class whites, and King was nearly stoned to death, but Daley maintained that SCLC had encouraged the rioting.[66]

As events in Chicago were to prove, SCLC strategies did not transpose easily from the rural South to the urban North. Jesse Jackson, a King confidant and SCLC official, had used an organization called "Operation Breadbasket" to muster consumer boycotts against white employers practicing hiring discrimination. Despite Jackson's efforts, SCLC discovered that urban preachers lacked the prestige they enjoyed in the South, while the black church was also less efficient as an organizing institution for protest movements. Ill-prepared and inadequately briefed, SCLC workers did not even possess appropriate clothing for the severe Chicago winter. Moreover, the gathering protest against the Vietnam war depleted funds and sapped energy from the civil rights movement. Although SCLC claimed some success in working with Chicago street gangs—some of whom acted as King's bodyguards—they rejected King's philosophy of nonviolent protest. Even as King faced new challenges to his leadership, he was increasingly attracted to the kind of democratic socialism he had witnessed in Sweden, but his call for a drastic redistribution of wealth and political power in favor of the dispossessed got nowhere in Chicago. The Chicago Freedom Movement succeeded only in persuading Daley to concede an open housing agreement with the city's banking and real estate interests, which achieved little in practice. After Daley was re-elected, he simply disavowed the open housing policy. SCLC's first campaign outside the South had achieved little, while calling King's philosophy and strategies into question.[67]

The growing rift between SCLC and SNCC deepened during the continuation of James Meredith's one-man "March Against Fear" in June, 1966. Meredith had been the first African-American student to enroll at the University of Mississippi, but only after president Kennedy overwhelmed the state's segregationist governor, Ross Barnett, with the deployment of hundreds of U.S. marshals, and thousands of National Guardsmen and army troops. Meredith graduated from Ole Miss and subsequently earned a law degree at Columbia University in New York. When Meredith returned to Mississippi to challenge segregation once more, he was shot and wounded by a white sniper. As Meredith lay in a hospital bed, King joined Stokely Carmichael of SNCC and Floyd McKissick of CORE to complete Meredith's march. Carmichael's use of the emotional slogan "Black Power" became a source of tension, because it connoted racial separatism and apparent acceptance of violence. King threatened to withdraw from the march unless its leaders abandoned the Black Power slogan and made a commitment to nonviolence: "It was my contention that a leader has to be concerned about the problems of semantics. Each word, I said, has a denotative meaning—its explicit and recognized sense—and a connotative meaning—its suggestive sense. While the concept of Black Power might be denotatively sound, the slogan 'Black Power' carried the wrong connotations." While agreement was reached between King, Carmichael, and McKissick not to use the competing slogans of "Black Power" and "Freedom Now" for the remainder of the march, the dispute was indicative of the approaching split of the civil rights coalition along racial, as well as ideological and class, lines.[68]

Martin Luther King had questioned the morality of the Vietnam war early on. But he hesitated to join the anti-war lobby because of the Johnson administration's path-breaking civil rights legislation, because the NAACP and other venerable civil rights organizations reflexively supported the president, and because SCLC might not survive a probable backlash from angry contributors. Increasingly convinced that the war was deflecting the administration's attention and resources from civil rights, King crossed the Rubicon on the war after seeing a magazine photograph of a Vietnamese woman holding a baby who had been killed by U.S. troops. Soon thereafter, King broke with the president over the war and appeared in antiwar demonstrations with Benjamin Spock, the famed pediatrician. Coretta Scott King, an ardent pacifist, and a member of Women Strike for Peace, supported her husband's new stance. In a controversial address delivered at the Riverside Church in New York City in April, 1967, Martin Luther King demanded that the United States stop all bombing, announce a unilateral cease-fire, include the Vietnamese communists in peace talks, and establish a deadline to withdraw all U.S. troops. He called for all young American men who were drafted into the military to declare themselves conscientious objectors. As a gospel minister, King felt it incumbent upon him to denounce all violent actions, including those barbarisms committed by "the greatest purveyor of violence in the world today—my own government."[69]

As he protested the war, Martin Luther King aroused hostile press comment. *Newsweek* accused him of displaying "simplistic political judgment" and of being "in over his head" on issues about which he was singularly ill-informed. *Life* published an editorial on "Dr. King's Disservice to His Cause," which asserted that by linking the civil rights movement to the opposition to the American position in Vietnam, he had come "close to betraying the cause for which he has worked so long." It concluded: "Dr. King has claimed that the budgetary demands of the war in Vietnam are the key hindrance to progress in civil rights. Not so. If the drive for equal rights falters now, in the difficult time when life must be given to laws already on the books, Dr. King and his tactics must share the blame." Carl Rowan, a black journalist who had met King during the Montgomery boycott, published an article in *Reader's Digest*, in which he maintained that King's involvement in a conflict between the United States and communists would raise further suspicions concerning his loyalties and might endanger impending civil rights legislation.[70]

King's response to such attacks was to argue that there was an interrelationship between racism, poverty, and militarism—a conviction that deepened after shocking race riots in Newark, New Jersey, and Detroit, Michigan. King now asserted that it would be morally inconsistent for him to denounce the violence against blacks in the ghettos and to condone American violence in Vietnam. As winner of the Nobel peace prize, he felt an obligation to oppose war, particularly one that violated the right of self-determination by the Vietnamese. The FBI kept an apoplectic Lyndon Johnson informed of King's anti-war activities, and intensified its surveillance of SCLC. "What is that goddamned nigger preacher doing to me?" the president raged. "We gave him the Voting Rights Act of 1965; we gave him the War on Poverty. What more does he want?" King would never again be invited to the White House.[71]

The Poor People's Campaign and the Memphis strike

To bridge the divisions within the civil rights movement, Martin Luther King conceived of an interracial alliance that would reassert the principle of nonviolence and unite a coalition of the poor along class, rather than racial, lines. His aide, Stanley Levison, who recalled the 1932 "Bonus March" on Washington, D.C., suggested that a small "army" of demonstrators should erect a shanty town or tent city on government property in the capital. Within SCLC, Jesse Jackson and James Bevel opposed the idea, believing that priority should be given to ending American involvement in Vietnam. Longtime aide Bayard Rustin aired his opposition in public, and urged King to cancel the plan as quixotic. Desperate to reignite the spirit of protest and aware of his precarious position as a spokesperson for nonviolence, King explained the rationale behind what he called the Poor People's Campaign in an article published posthumously: "Our Washington demonstration will resemble Birmingham and Selma in duration. Just as we dealt with the social problem of segregation through massive demonstrations, and . . . with the political problem—the denial of the right to vote—through massive demonstrations, we are now trying to deal with economic problems—the right to live, to have a job and income —through massive protest."[72]

The planned march, which took place after his death, also revealed King's conviction that American society needed a fundamental redistribution of wealth and economic power. The immediate purpose of the march was to pressure Congress into enacting King's proposed Bill of Rights for the Disadvantaged—a huge federally-funded, anti-poverty program. He told an interviewer that "America is deeply racist and its democracy is flawed both economically and socially . . . the black revolution is much more than a struggle for the rights of Negroes. It is forcing America to face all its interrelated flaws—racism, poverty, militarism, and materialism. It is exposing evils that are deeply rooted in the whole structure of our society."[73]

Before the Poor People's Campaign reached the nation's capital, King was drawn into a labor dispute in Memphis, Tennessee. In February, 1968, black sanitation workers went on strike to stop job discrimination and to win union recognition, higher wages, and improved working conditions. King, who saw the strike as the beginning of the projected Poor People's Campaign, accepted an invitation from James Lawson, a leading civil rights theoretician and an old friend and ally, to lead a protest march in Memphis. The demonstration ended in disorder, when police shot a black youth during a pitched battle with protestors. King conceded that he had gone to Memphis inadequately briefed, and left abruptly. Sections of the press, taking their cues from FBI informants, predicted that the violence in Memphis would be repeated on a larger scale during the Washington march. The *Memphis Commercial Appeal* commented tartly, "Dr. King's pose as a leader of a non-violent movement has been shattered.

He now has the entire nation doubting his word when he insists that [the Poor People's Campaign] can be peaceful." King was deeply disturbed by events in Memphis and media commentary on his own culpability. But Lyndon Johnson's surprise announcement that he would not seek re-election in 1968, appeared to offer hope that the anti-war and anti-poverty movements might achieve a unified front if a new Democratic president were elected.[74]

King returned to Memphis in a more optimistic mood to lead a new march. On April 3rd King addressed a small, but enthusiastic, audience at Mason Temple, and referred to the increasing number of threats on his life. In a startling peroration, he declared that "it really doesn't matter with me now, because I've been to the mountaintop, and I don't mind. Like anybody, I would like to live a long life; longevity has its place. But I'm not concerned about that now. I just want to do God's will. And he's allowed me to go up to the mountain. And I've looked over. And I've seen the Promised Land. So I'm happy tonight. I'm not worried about anything. I'm not fearing any man. 'Mine eyes have seen the glory of the coming of the Lord. His truth is marching on.' "[75]

The very next day, a white sniper named James Earl Ray shot and killed Martin Luther King, Jr. as he stood on the balcony of the Lorraine Motel. When the news reached the FBI's Atlanta office, jubilant cries could be heard: "They finally got the SOB!" Ray was a habitual amphetamine drug user and criminal, who had served time for armed robbery, and he may have been motivated to kill King for money. Certainly, there were many groups who wanted King dead and were prepared to reward the assassin handsomely, including the Minutemen, the National Socialist White People's party, the American Nazi party, and Mississippi's White Knights of the Ku Klux Klan, which offered a $100,000 bounty for King's assassination. There were many African Americans who doubted that Ray acted alone, especially when he slipped through the grasp of law enforcement on his escape to Europe. The King family pointed their collective fingers at J. Edgar Hoover's FBI, which had so often targeted civil rights leaders, including King, for harassment and worse.[76]

King's death touched off a wave of violence across America, in which several dozen people died. *Newsweek*, in a memorial issue, commented: "King's martyrdom on a motel balcony did far more than rob Negroes of their most compelling spokesperson, and whites of their most effective bridge to black America. His murder, for too many blacks, could only be read as a judgment upon his non-violent philosophy—and a license for retaliatory violence." CORE's Floyd McKissick announced simply:

"Dr. Martin Luther King was the last prince of nonviolence. . . . Nonviolence is a dead philosophy, and it was not the Black people that killed it."[77]

In a testament to King's importance, his murder may have resulted in two developments that might otherwise have failed. Following his death, hundreds of black and white ministers marched to the Memphis city hall to demand recognition of the union, and Memphis businessmen also pressed for a settlement of the dispute. As a result, the strikers won an important victory, including union recognition, a guarantee of higher wages, and an automatic check-off for union dues from their paychecks. The passage of the 1968 Civil Rights Act, which incorporated fair housing proposals, may also have been facilitated by King's murder and the congressional sympathy it evoked.[78]

Assessment

From the time of the Montgomery bus boycott in 1955, until the Memphis sanitation workers" strike thirteen years later, Martin Luther King, Jr., was the principal advocate of nonviolence as both a method of protest and a way of life. To his admirers of both races, King was the outstanding African-American leader of the 20th century, whose unique contributions to the civil rights cause derived from his intense religious faith, expressed in the idioms and symbols of black Christianity. King's personal bravery and engagement with the forces of southern racism resembled, as they were intended, a medieval passion play in which the forces of good confronted those of evil. To his critics, King was the exponent of an unrealistic, if not pathological, doctrine that enjoined its adherents to love their oppressors and to abdicate the right of self-defense. King, his critics also charged, had not initiated the black protests of the 1950s and the 1960s, which began as local campaigns, had failed to gain mass support for either his reformist or radical ideas, and among his personal failings was pompous, sexist, and overbearing to subordinates. The divergent views of King's admirers and detractors deserve consideration and amplification.

During and after the Montgomery bus boycott, King served as a catalyst of increasing symbolic and charismatic significance, able to direct attention toward and support for protests started by others. It was King's ability to bring these local crises to the attention of the news media and, increasingly, to the federal government, that made him a pivotal figure. His expressed devotion to nonviolence and religious terminology, as well as his openness to compromise, made King appear "moderate," "respectable," and "reasonable" in the eyes of many whites.

Until the emergence of the Black Power slogan, King held together an obviously fragmenting civil rights coalition through his prestige and force of personality. In this respect, he served as the vital center of the movement, standing between the "conservatism" of the NAACP and Urban League, and the "radicalism" of SNCC and CORE. But King also recognized that "nonviolence" provoked violence, and SCLC came to deliberately precipitate assaults on black demonstrators in order to gain public sympathy for civil rights legislation. In this respect, also, King deserves credit for having inspired black southerners—and their white supporters—to gain a sense of individual and collective worth through political action. It is often not fully appreciated that to engage in civil rights activities in the southern states was to actively risk death or injury. As the acquittal of two white men accused of murdering Emmett Till, a Chicago teenager who had allegedly made "familiar" remarks to a white woman indicated, *any* infraction of the rigid standards of southern racial etiquette could lead to violent death for black "offenders" and the absolution of their murderers —should they even be brought to trial. As one cultural anthropologist observed, in their willingness to go to prison for their beliefs, the student activists who were initially inspired by the Montgomery boycott "undermined the traditional negative connotations of jail and turned it from a place of shame to one of political honor."[79]

It was also Martin Luther King's achievement to invest civil rights protest with universal significance, his declared purpose being "to redeem the soul of America" by appeals to its moral conscience and national values. Despite tangible victories over segregation and discrimination, King felt some empathy for Black Power and Marxist critiques of American society, and had moved perceptibly to the left in his social attitudes and awareness. King's latter-day radicalism can be traced to the Vietnam war, urban violence, and the realization that legal victories had to be followed by significant economic progress for all. That King even privately expressed admiration for Scandinavian-type democratic socialism is difficult for even his most ardent American admirers of either race to concede.

There can be no question that Martin Luther King was a courageous leader and a transformative figure in American history. At the same time, he exhibited serious shortcomings as a human being that should be acknowledged—shortcomings, his wife and close advisers agree, that made him "a guilt-ridden man." His 343-page doctoral dissertation at Boston University on systematic theology was substantially plagiarized. Decades later, scholars proved that King had lifted much of his writing from Jack Boozer's dissertation written three years earlier. Why King plagiarized is unclear, though there are several possible explanations, including pressure to begin a demanding new job while completing his graduate studies and a tradition among black clergy to freely expropriate the material of others as their own. Ultimately, these explanations are rationalizations—and nothing more. King plagiarized much of his academic work from the time he entered college. One interesting thought is that King's thesis adviser must share responsibility for King's dishonesty, because this professor had directed Boozer's dissertation from which King had plagiarized. As the argument goes, this adviser was either incompetent or a guilty white liberal who let King's plagiarism pass because King was a rare breed at that time—a promising, young black intellectual. When the dishonesty was uncovered, there was some brief debate as to whether King's doctorate should be revoked.[80]

In addition, King, like John F. Kennedy, had a large sexual appetite that he satisfied with frequent philandering. The evidence of King's adultery is indisputable because the FBI surreptitiously recorded the sounds made in his hotel rooms. Pulitzer prize-winning historian David Garrow suggested that King's compulsive sexual proclivities were simply "standard ministerial practice in a context where intimate pastor-parishioner relationships had long been winked at." King reportedly told an acquaintance: "I'm away from home twenty-five to twenty-seven days a month. Fucking's a form of anxiety reduction." On the night King died, his right-hand man reports that two mistresses were looking to have trysts with King.[81]

Primarily a strategist, negotiator, and charismatic speaker, King was not an organization man. He helped found SCLC after the Montgomery bus boycott, and presided over it until he died, but SCLC had serious limitations as an organization. Ralph Abernathy, SCLC's vice-president, called the organization simply "a faith operation." One of SCLC's principal shortcomings was that its social gospel orientation did not appeal to many black southern clergymen. SCLC executive director Wyatt T. Walker estimated that 90 percent of black ministers in Birmingham remained aloof from the campaign there. Poorly organized, SCLC was frequently inefficient and always male dominated. Septima Clark, active in the Highlander Folk School and a member of SCLC's executive staff, discovered that King and his male associates "didn't think too much of the way women could contribute" to the movement. Frequently patronized by King, Clark remembered that "in the black church men were always in charge. It was just the way things were." On the other hand, SCLC was also flexible, informal, and, because of its ministerial base, able to mobilize black southerners effectively. Andrew Young, who became SCLC's principal negotiator, observed that although King was in nominal charge of SCLC, it was more like "a jazz combo," in which each staff member had "a chance to solo." With King's death, SCLC lost an accomplished orchestrator/arranger, and was to engage in a leadership struggle between his appointed successor, Ralph Abernathy, and Jesse Jackson, until Jackson's resignation in 1971.[82]

If, as is now generally acknowledged, King's fame was created by the civil rights movement, rather than vice versa, it is also true that through his leadership and example, black protest in the southern states achieved its most significant victories. Judged only by his contribution to the "classic" phase of black protest, his influence in shaming Congress into enacting historic civil rights legislation, King will be remembered as the greatest black visionary leader of the 20th century, a fact attested to by a national holiday named in his honor and a massive stone monument erected to him in Washington, D.C., near the Lincoln Memorial, where he delivered his spine-tingling "Dream" speech. That the majority of Americans, black or white, were unable to endorse King's later critiques of capitalist society, suggests that he was also, at the end of his life, a leader in advance of most of his followers.[83]

Yet King never abandoned his fundamental belief that most African Americans wanted to end segregation and discrimination in order to achieve success in an integrated society. In a eulogy delivered at King's funeral service, former Morehouse College president Benjamin Mays declared, "No reasonable person would deny that the activities and personality of Martin Luther King, Jr., contributed largely to the success of the student sit-in movements in abolishing segregation in downtown establishments; and that his activities contributed mightily to the passage of the Civil Rights legislation of 1964 and 1965. . . . He had faith in his country. He died striving to desegregate and integrate America. . . . Nonviolence to King was total commitment not only to solving the problems of the race in the United States but in solving the problems of the world."[84]

At the same time, the integrationist movement of the 1950s and 1960s, of which King was the symbolic leader, gave rise to a revived sense of black nationalism, with demands for racial separatism and violent resistance against the forces of white oppression. As King himself became painfully aware, no one voiced these views more articulately than the son of another black minister—Malcolm X.

References

1 Clayborne Carson, ed., *The Autobiography of Martin Luther King, Jr.* (1998), p. 260.

2 Alice Walker, *In Search of Our Mother's Gardens: Womanist Prose* (1984), pp. 143–144.

3 Jeffrey M. Elliot, ed., *Conversations with Maya Angelou* (1989), p. 127.

4 Harvard Sitkoff, *A New Deal for Blacks: The Emergence of Civil Rights as a National Issue: The Depression Decade* (1978), pp. 34–57.

5 Paula E. Pfeffer, *A. Philip Randolph, Pioneer of the Civil Rights Movement* (1990), pp. 32–43.

6 Sitkoff, *A New Deal for Blacks*, pp. 58–101.

7 Risa Goluboff, *The Lost Promise of Civil Rights* (2007), pp. 16–34, 127.

8 Raymond Arsenault, *The Sound of Freedom: Marian Anderson, the Lincoln Memorial, and the Concert That Awakened America* (2009), pp. 145–187.

9 James Oliver Horton and Lois E. Horton, *Hard Road to Freedom: The Story of African America* (2001), pp. 256–260; Philip A. Klinkner, with Rogers M. Smith, *The Unsteady March: The Rise and Decline of Racial Equality in America* (1999), pp. 125–130; Cheryl Lynn Greenberg, *Or Does It Explode: Black Harlem in the Great Depression* (1991), pp. 198–224.

10 Pfeffer, *A. Philip Randolph*, pp. 46–47.

11 Ibid., pp. 47–49; Lucy G. Barber, *Marching on Washington: The Forging of an American Political Tradition* (2004), pp. 108–140.

12 Pfeffer, *A. Philip Randolph*, pp. 49–57; William H. Chafe, *The Unfinished Journey: America since World War II* (2003), pp. 17–18; Edward Ayers, et al., *American Passages: A History of the United States* (2009), p. 768.

13 August Meier & Elliott Rudwick, *CORE: A Study in the Civil Rights Movement, 1942–1968* (1973); James Farmer, *Lay Bare the Heart: An Autobiography of the Civil Rights Movement* (1985), pp. 101–116; Raymond Arsenault, *Freedom Riders: 1961 and the Struggle for Racial Justice* (2006), pp. 11–55.

14 Horton and Horton, *Hard Road to Freedom*, pp. 262–263; Adam Fairclough, *Better Day Coming: Blacks and Equality, 1890–2000* (2001), pp. 180–201.

15 Michael Gardner, *Harry Truman and Civil Rights: Moral Courage and Political Risks* (2002), pp. 14–146; David McCullough, *Truman* (1992), pp. 586–589, 629, 645, 653–719.

16 Howard Ball, *A Defiant Life: Thurgood Marshall and the Persistence of Racism in America* (2001), pp. 40–147; Richard Kluger, *Simple Justice* (1975), pp. 201–212, 259–283, 315–321, 545–584, 626–627, 703–750.

17 Robert Frederick Burk, *The Eisenhower Administration and Black Civil Rights, 1953–1961* (1984). For a vigorous defense of Eisenhower's record on race, see David A. Nichols, *A Matter of Justice: Eisenhower and the Beginnings of the Civil Rights Revolution* (2007).

18 Klinkner, *Unsteady March*, p. 205.

19 J. Mills Thornton, III, *Dividing Lines: Municipal Politics and the Struggle for Civil Rights in Montgomery, Birmingham, and Selma* (2002), pp. 20–55.

20 Ibid., pp. 57–61; Rosa Parks, with Jim Haskins, *My Story* (1992), pp. 108–124; Danielle L. McGuire, *At the Dark End of the Street: Black Women, Rape, and Resistance, A New History of the Civil Rights Movement from Rosa Parks to the Rise of Black Power* (2010), pp. 5–6, 12–13, 16, 26, 31, 47.

21 David J. Garrow, *Bearing the Cross: Martin Luther King, Jr., and the Southern Christian Leadership Conference* (1986), p. 16; David J. Garrow, ed., *The Montgomery Bus Boycott and the Women Who Started It: The Memoir of Jo Ann Gibson Robinson* (1987), pp. 45–46.

22 Howell Raines, *My Soul Is Rested: Movement Days in the Deep South Remembered* (1983), p. 43.

23 Thornton, *Dividing Lines*, pp. 61–88.

24 Martin Luther King, Jr., *Stride Toward Freedom: The Montgomery Story* (1958), p. 56.

25 Juan Williams, *Eyes on the Prize: America's Civil Rights Years, 1954–1965* (1988), p. 76.

26 Stephen B. Oates, *Let the Trumpet Sound: The Life of Martin Luther King, Jr.* (1982), pp. 5–8.

27 Henry Louis Gates, Jr. and Cornel West, eds., *The African-American Century: How Black Americans Have Shaped Our Country* (2000), pp. 256–257; Marshall Frady, *Martin Luther King, Jr.: A Life* (2002), pp. 11–19; Harvard Sitkoff, *King: Pilgrimage to the Mountaintop* (2008), pp. 3–13; David L. Lewis, *King: A Critical Biography* (1970), p. 20.

28 Lewis, *King*, pp. 27–38; King, *Stride Toward Freedom*, pp. 91–95; Clayborne Carson, ed., *The Autobiography of Martin Luther King, Jr.* (1996), p. 6; Martin Luther King, Jr., "The Humanity and Divinity of Jesus," *The Papers of Martin Luther King, Jr.*, vol. 1 (1992), p. 150; Martin Luther King, Jr., "What Experiences of Christians Living in the Early Christian Century Led to the Christian Doctrines of the Divine Sonship of Jesus, the

Virgin Birth, and the Bodily Resurrection," *The Papers of Martin Luther King, Jr.*, vol. 1, pp. 224, 229.

29 King, *Stride Toward Freedom*, pp. 96–97.

30 Sitkoff, *King*, pp. 16–17; Frady, *King*, pp. 22–28.

31 Stewart Burns, *To the Mountaintop: Martin Luther King Jr.'s Sacred Mission to Save America, 1955–1968* (2004), pp. 19–44.

32 John D'Emilio, *Lost Prophet: The Life and Times of Bayard Rustin* (2003), pp. 225–231; Daniel Levine, *Bayard Rustin and the Civil Rights Movement* (2000), pp. 78–87; King, *Stride Toward Freedom*, p. 85.

33 King, *Stride Toward Freedom*, pp. 160–169; Stewart Burns, ed., *Daybreak of Freedom: The Montgomery Bus Boycott* (1997), pp. 326–327.

34 August Meier and Francis L. Broderick, eds., *Black Protest Thought in the Twentieth Century* (1971), pp. 293–300.

35 Adam Fairclough, *To Redeem the Soul of America: The Southern Christian Leadership Conference and Martin Luther King, Jr.* (1987), p. 27; Troy Jackson, *Becoming King: Martin Luther King, Jr. and the Making of a National Leader* (2008), p. 87.

36 Fairclough, *To Redeem the Soul of America*, pp. 11–35; David J. Garrow, "The FBI and Martin Luther King," *Atlantic Monthly* 290 (July/August, 2002): 80–88; D'Emilio, *Lost Prophet*, pp. 245–248; Garrow, *The Montgomery Bus Boycott and the Women Who Started It*, pp. 53–54.

37 Manning Marable and Leith Mullings, eds., *Let Nobody Turn Us Around: Voices of Resistance, Reform, and Renewal, An African American Anthology* (2009), pp. 368–369.

38 Fairclough, *To Redeem the Soul of America*, p. 33.

39 Ibid., pp. 39–40; D'Emilo, *Lost Prophet*, p. 269.

40 Garrow, *Bearing the Cross*, pp. 97–104, 141; Barbara Ransby, *Ella Baker and the Black Freedom Movement: A Radical Democratic Vision* (2003), pp. 170–195.

41 Oates, *Let the Trumpet Sound*, pp. 137–145; James M. Washington, ed., *A Testament of Hope: The Essential Writings and Speeches of Martin Luther King, Jr.* (1986), p. 334; Lewis, *King*, pp. 85–111.

42 Sitkoff, *King*, pp. 67–68.

43 William H. Chafe, *Civilities and Civil Rights: Greensboro, North Carolina, and the Black Struggle for Freedom* (1981), pp. 98–141; Garrow, *Bearing the Cross*, pp. 127–129.

44 Marable and Mullings, eds., *Let Nobody Turn Us Around*, p. 371.

45 Williams, *Eyes on the Prize*, p. 137; Ransby, *Ella Baker and the Black Freedom Movement*, p. 246.

46 Oates, *Let the Trumpet Sound*, pp. 158–166, 179–180.

47 Arsenault, *Freedom Riders*, pp. 93–303; Oates, *Let the Trumpet Sound*, pp. 156–157, 174–178.

48 Lewis, *King*, pp. 140–170.

49 Robert Mann, *When Freedom Would Triumph: The Civil Rights Struggle in Congress, 1954–1968* (2007), p. 141.

50 Lewis, *King*, pp. 171–176.

51 Ibid., pp. 175–182.

52 Martin Luther King, Jr., *Why We Can't Wait*, pp. 86–87.

53 Fairclough, *To Redeem the Soul of America*, pp. 124–139.

54 Carl M. Brauer, *John F. Kennedy and the Second Reconstruction* (1977), pp. 193–194; Kai Wright, ed., *The African-American Experience: Black History and Culture through Speeches, Letters, Editorials, Poems, Songs, and Stories* (2009), p. 529; Garrow, *Bearing the Cross*, pp. 267–269, 337–340; Fairclough, *To Redeem the Soul of America*, pp. 134–135, 149–153, 188–189, 208–210.

55 Meier, et al., *Black Protest Thought in the Twentieth Century*, pp. 49–50; Drew D. Hansen, *The Dream: Martin Luther King, Jr. and the Speech that Inspired a Nation* (2003), pp. 25–165; Bruce Watson, *Freedom Summer: The Savage Season that Made Mississippi Burn and Made America a Democracy* (2010), p. 9.

56 John Lewis, with Michael D'Orso, *Walking with the Wind: A Memoir of the Movement* (1998), pp. 213–225; James Forman, *The Making of Black Revolutionaries* (1972), pp. 333–336; Anne Moody, *Coming of Age in Mississippi* (1968), p. 307; Taylor Branch, *Parting the Waters: America in the King Years, 1954–63* (1988), p. 874.

57 David J. Garrow, *The FBI and Martin Luther King, Jr.: From "Solo" to Memphis* (1983), pp. 21–213 *passim*; James Dickerson, *Dixie's Dirty Secret: The True Story of How the Government, the Media, and the Mob Conspired to Combat Integration and the Vietnam Antiwar Movement* (1998), p. 166.

58 Sitkoff, *King*, pp. 130–136.

59 Ibid., pp. 147–148.

60 David J. Garrow, *Protest at Selma: Martin Luther King, Jr. and the Voting Rights Act of 1965* (1978), pp. 73–77; Gene Roberts and Hank Klibanoff, *The Race Beat: The Press, the Civil Rights Struggle, and the Awakening of a Nation* (2007), p. 386; Oates, *Let the Trumpet Sound*, pp. 353–355.

61 Sitkoff, *King*, pp. 154–160.

62 Lewis, *King*, pp. 284–294.

63 Ibid., pp. 285–294.

64 Michael Eric Dyson, *"I May Not Get There with You": The True Martin Luther King, Jr.* (2000), pp. 51–100.

65 Garrow, *Bearing the Cross*, p. 455.

66 David Remnick, *The Bridge: The Life and Rise of Barack Obama* (2010), p. 151; Garrow, *Bearing the Cross*, pp. 431–474; Thomas F. Jackson, *From Civil Rights to Human Rights: Martin Luther King, Jr., and the Struggle for Economic Justice* (2007), pp. 276–307.

67 Garrow, *Bearing the Cross*, pp. 491–525.

68 Martin Luther King, Jr., *Where Do We Go From Here: Chaos or Community?* (1967), pp. 23–32.

69 Frady, *King*, pp. 184–186.

70 John J. Ansbro, *Martin Luther King, Jr.: The Making of a Mind* (1983), pp. 255–256.

71 Sitkoff, *King*, pp. 216–227.

72 Ibid., pp. 220–225; Gerald McKnight, *The Last Crusade: Martin Luther King, Jr., the FBI, and the Poor People's Campaign* (1998), p. 21; Washington, ed., *A Testament of Hope*, p. 65.

73 Garrow, *The FBI and Martin Luther King*, p. 214; Washington, ed., *A Testament of Hope*, pp. 314–315.

74 Fairclough, *To Redeem the Soul of America*, p. 377; Sitkoff, *King*, pp. 228–232.

75 Fairclough, *To Redeem the Soul of America*, pp. 380–381.

76 Hampton Sides, *Hellhound on His Trail: The Stalking of Martin Luther King, Jr. and the International Hunt for His Assassin* (2010), pp. 161–167; Gerald Posner, *Killing the Dream: James Earl Ray and the Assassination of Martin Luther King, Jr.* (1998), p. 137.

77 Oates, *Let the Trumpet Sound*, pp. 493–494; Robert V. Daniels, *Year of the Heroic Guerrilla: World Revolution and Counterrevolution in the Year 1968* (1989), p. 98.

78 Jackson, *From Civil Rights to Human Rights*, p. 353.

79 Richard H. King, "Citizenship and Self-Respect: The Experience of Politics in the Civil Rights Movement," *Journal of American Studies* 22 (1988): 12.

80 David J. Garrow, "King's Plagiarism: Imitation, Insecurity and Transformation," *Journal of American History* 78 (June, 1991): 87; Dyson, *"I May Not Get There with You,"* pp. 139–154.

81 David J. Garrow, *Bearing the Cross*, p. 375; Ralph David Abernathy, *And the Walls Came Tumbling Down* (1989), pp. 434–436; Dyson, *"I May Not Get There with You,"* pp. 155–174, 216; Frady, *King*, p. 62.

82 Fairclough, *To Redeem the Soul of America*, p. 1; Septima Clark, *Ready from Within: Septima Clark and the Civil Rights Movement*, ed. Cynthia Stokes Brown (1986), pp. 78–79.

83 James A. Colaiaco, *Martin Luther King, Jr.: Apostle of Militant Nonviolence* (1988), p. 53; "The Martin Luther King, Jr. Memorial," *Washington Post* (22 August 2011), http://www.washingtonpost.com/lifestyle/specialreports/MLKmemorial.

84 Benjamin A. Mays, " 'Eulogy of Dr. Martin' Luther King, Jr.," *Morehouse College Bulletin* 36 (Summer, 1968): 8–12.

CHAPTER SIX

Malcolm X: "The Angriest Negro in America"

Be peaceful, be courteous, obey the law, respect everyone; but if someone puts his hand on you, send him to the cemetery.[1]

[Malcolm X]

If Malcolm X were not a Negro, his autobiography would be little more than a journal of abnormal psychology, the story of a burglar, dope pusher, addict and jailbird—with a family history of insanity—who acquires messianic delusions and sets forth to preach an upside down religion of "brotherly" hatred.[2]

[*Saturday Evening Post*]

It does not promote the cause of responsible leadership to deny the import-ance of Malcolm X to the particular segment of people whose political and/or ideological leader he was, or sought to be. . . . Malcolm X made an impact on the minds of the black masses irrespective of his criminal past or his strong pro-black ideology.[3]

[C. Eric Lincoln]

Perspectives: Black nationalism after Garvey, the separatist impulse, 1930–1950

The separatist impulse of Marcus Garvey's crusade largely disappeared for a generation with his deportation in 1927 and the onset of the Great Depression. Black organizations and leaders, concerned with ensuring the sheer survival of African Americans, stressed interracial cooperation and the political and economic advancement of blacks within the United States. From the advent of the New Deal in 1933 to the climax of the civil rights movement in the mid-1960s, integration remained the dominant black ideology. The goals of integration and equal rights coincided with the aspirations of a growing black middle class which succeeded within a white-dominated society. During World War II, the number of NAACP branches tripled to over a thousand, and its total membership rose nine-fold to 450,000. The publication in 1944 of Gunnar Myrdal's monumental *An American Dilemma*, with its optimism, deprecation of separatist movements, and acceptance of racial integration as the proper goal of protest activity, also helped to set the ideological tone accepted by most civil rights activists.[4]

Not until the mid-1960s, with the emergence of the Black Power slogan, the growing disillusionment of many younger blacks with the "tokenism" of civil rights legislation, and their rejection of nonviolence as a strategy and a philosophy, did black nationalist theories and organizations enjoy the currency and publicity that had attended Garvey and the Universal Negro Improvement Association (UNIA). But even in the 1930s and 1940s, not all black leaders subscribed to the integrationist ethic. W.E.B. Du Bois, for one, clashed with the NAACP over his advocacy of a separate black economy.[5]

The American Communist party, founded in 1919, made some converts among black intellectuals with its Stalinist-derived call for "self-determination" for African Americans, including a proposal to create an all-black "49th State" out of the heart of the southern "black belt." Black activists, including Cyril Briggs, Hosea Hudson, and James W. Ford, attempted to address the "Negro question" in the United States through a variety of means, such as publishing the *Daily Worker* newspaper, infiltrating labor unions, organizing rent strikes, building a union of sharecroppers, forming groups such as the African Blood Brotherhood, and providing legal representation in the high-profile Scottsboro Boys rape case. But the Communist party attracted minimal interest among the black masses. By 1935, operating on the mistaken assumption that the proletarian revolution was at hand, American Communists reversed their nationalistic stance in favor of a policy of equal rights for blacks in the United States. The slogan, "Communism is twentieth century Americanism," encapsulated this new perspective.[6]

At the same time, the large-scale unemployment of the Depression saw the flowering of various mystic, black nationalist cults in northern ghettos. Noble Drew Ali's Moorish Science Temple of America, founded in Newark, New Jersey, in 1913, was built on the Muslim Qu'ran, the Christian Bible, and Garvey's Africanist ideology. Although Ali embraced a psychological, not a physical, return to Africa, a large influx of former Garveyites helped swell the membership rolls. Drew, a semi-literate train expressman who claimed a divine mission from Allah, required members to pray thrice daily as they faced Mecca, wear a black fez (men) or turban (women), add the "African heritage" suffix of "el" or "bey" to their last names, stick to a vegetarian diet, and refrain from smoking, drinking alcohol, using cosmetics, or straightening their hair. He insisted that African Americans would find salvation only when they rejected derogatory terms, such as "black," "colored," and "Negro," in favor of "Moorish Americans," or "Asiatics," whose true African homeland was Morocco. Ali's movement was strong in Detroit, Michigan; Philadelphia, Pennsylvania; and particularly Chicago, Illinois, which he expected to be the second Mecca.[7]

More well known was the Peace Mission Movement, which was established on Long Island, New York, in 1919, and functioned as much as a social as a religious movement. The Peace Mission was the unorthodox creation of George Baker, a short, ordinary looking, middle-aged preacher with a taste for the finer things in life. Although his speech was filled with malapropisms, manufactured words, such as "physicalating" and "tangiblated," and downright unintelligible sounds, Baker's followers regarded him as "Father Divine"—the very incarnation of God on earth— sent to institute a primitive communism patterned after Jesus of Nazareth's Last Supper of two millennia earlier. In the early 1930s, the Peace Mission grew to over a million followers or "angels," some of whom were ex-Garveyites. Converts were to remain celibate and to surrender hourly wages and any insurance policies to Baker in order to purchase additional missions and sex-segregated homes that were dubbed "Heavens," the largest of which was in Harlem. Through the collective efforts of his followers, Divine provided wholesome meals and accommodations at minimal prices, and employment in laundries, restaurants, gas stations, hotels, and farms for large numbers of African Americans in New York and New Jersey without resorting to the New Deal programs he despised. According to Nigerian social scientist E.U. Essien-Udom, the Peace Movement can be described as black nationalist because both Divine and black nationalists believed in "independence of white control, rejection of the traditional Christian concept of God, denial of the power of the dominant society, and differentiation of [their] followers from the Negro subculture and society." Divine had little interest in the civil rights protests of the period, other than organizing street demonstrations against Harlem department stores that practiced discrimination. He dressed ostentatiously and lived well, and published reports accused him of mishandling funds, sexual abuse, and homosexuality. He died in 1965 in his mansion on a large estate outside Philadelphia.[8]

During the Great Depression, emigrationist and repatriation ideas were confined to such miniscule organizations as the Ethiopian Pacific Movement. The movement was established in Harlem by street-orator Robert Jordan, a West Indian and former Garveyite, and Mittie Gordon, a former UNIA president in Chicago. In 1939, hundreds of members of the movement set out for Washington, D.C., to lobby the federal government in support of U.S. senator Theodore Bilbo's proposal to create an African homeland of 400,000 square miles for African Americans next to the American colony of Liberia. The new territory would come from England and France in part payment of their debts from World War I. Senator Bilbo, a Mississippi racist of the first rank, predicted that two-thirds of African Americans would eagerly accept a deal in order to escape racism at home and live off of the federal government's dole until they established their own farms and businesses. Most supporters of the Ethiopian movement never arrived in the capital, because their transportation broke down even before they had left Chicago's city limits, but they presented 1 million signatures to Congress in support of Bilbo's bill. The movement collapsed when Gordon was charged with inciting blacks to avoid conscription at the start of World War II.[9]

The most influential black nationalist group began in 1930, when a mysterious light-skinned man using several aliases, including Wallace D. Fard, founded the Lost-Found Nation of Islam in Detroit. Fard, a street peddler who claimed to have been born in Mecca, espoused black nationalism and once belonged to Marcus Garvey's UNIA. After being released from prison on a narcotics charge, Fard joined Noble Drew Ali's Moorish Science Temple, which declared that African Americans were descended from the Moors in north Africa and had originally been Muslims. Ali's brand of Islam combined elements of many religions and offered his followers a message of personal transformation and racial pride. As the movement attracted thousands of dues-paying members, Ali's appetite for women and a lavish lifestyle grew. When one of the inner circle demanded money to keep quiet about Ali's profligacy and polygamy, Ali evidently had him murdered. After Ali's arrest, he asked Fard to temporarily supervise the temple in Chicago. Ali himself died under suspicious circumstances a month later, and Fard claimed to be

Ali's reincarnation. The coroner ruled Ali had died of tuberculosis, but others pointed to police brutality or murder by rivals.[10]

Intrigue prevented Fard's accession, prompting him to form a new organizational vehicle altogether. Now presenting himself as a Muslim messiah (*Mahdi*) with the surname "Muhammad," Fard claimed that the black race had invented civilization and bequeathed it to the world. In Fard's cosmology, blacks were the first people to inhabit the earth— "Original Man"—and were members of the African tribe of Shabazz, the only people to have survived an explosion that split the moon from the earth 66 trillion years ago. Whites were castigated as "human devils," a degenerate mutation resulting from a centuries-long experiment carried out by a renegade black scientist named Yakub (Jacob). Allah had given whites 6,000 years of domination to test the capacity and strength of the Black Nation, but the Day of Judgment was at hand, when "Caucasians" and their Christian religion would be destroyed. In the interim, Fard called for the ritual slaying of whites, as well as African Americans whose loyalty to the U.S. government superceded that of Allah; those who carried out four such blood sacrifices were assured of salvation. Despite allegations of voodooism, Fard attracted a small following, founded the Temple of Islam and a school, taught young Muslim women the rudiments of domestic science, and organized a paramilitary organization called the Fruit of Islam which was prepared to use firearms to defend the membership. This fanciful Nation of Islam, Fard once allegedly confessed to authorities, was a "racket" intended to "get all the money out of it" he could.[11]

After one of his followers performed a blood sacrifice, Fard was interrogated by the police and then banished from Detroit in 1934. Questions arose as to his whereabouts. Did he go to the holy city of Mecca, his alleged homeland of New Zealand, or outer space in a flying saucer called the "Mother Plane"; or was he murdered like Noble Ali? Meanwhile, the Nation's leadership passed to another Garveyite named Elijah Poole, the unprepossessing son of a Georgia tenant farmer and Baptist minister. A persistent rumor was that Poole murdered Fard, and then recognized Fard as Allah's incarnation and predicted his eventual return to earth. Whatever happened with regard to Fard's disappearance, Poole took the name "Elijah Muhammad" and was called the "Messenger of Allah." During the 1930s and 1940s, the Nation of Islam grew slowly, drawing support mainly from the black lower class. Muhammad organized temples in Chicago; Milwaukee, Wisconsin; and Washington, D.C., and amplified the precepts of the faith.[12]

Under Elijah Muhammad, the Black Muslims accepted the notion that all of them were divine—with Allah being supreme—and advocated racial separatism, self-determination, and the establishment of an independent black republic within the borders of the United States. In part, this insistence on racial separatism could be traced to Muhammad's witnessing of three lynchings; he remarked that he had "seen enough of the white man's brutality to last him 26,000 years." Black Muslims also published their own history books that stressed the glories of their African past, and promoted a "return" to Africa. Angry over the continuing and debilitating effects of racism, Black Muslims were especially desirous to purge remnants of their slave past, substituting the suffix "X" for their own surnames and rejecting the derogatory term "Negro" in favor of "Afro-American." Muhammad renounced his citizenship and urged his followers to do likewise: "We [so-called Negroes] are not and cannot be American Citizens, since we are not Americans by nature or race." Converts to the Nation of Islam were enjoined to follow a strict code of personal conduct that prohibited the eating of pork, extra-marital sexual relations, and the use of tobacco, alcohol, or narcotics. Nor were Black Muslims allowed to engage in political activity, serve in the armed forces, or accept government welfare checks, even though Muhammad had received public assistance when he lost his job in an automobile factory during the Great Depression.[13]

At the beginning of World War II, Elijah Muhammad was convicted of draft evasion and sedition, and jailed for three years. It was in prison that Muhammad realized that the existing civil rights organizations had made no attempt to reach or recruit criminals, juvenile delinquents, or the black underclass. After the war, the Nation of Islam concentrated on just these elements, often with remarkable results. Drug addicts were rehabilitated and prostitutes reformed after they joined the Nation. Discipline within the organization was strict. Indolence was sternly reproved, and habits of thrift, personal cleanliness, and economic self-help were extolled as virtues. Until the federal government granted them a separate state, Muslims elected to avoid social, religious, or political contact with whites.[14]

In addition to being allowed to set up an independent state, Muslim demands, as formulated by Elijah Muhammad, included the following:

We want the government of the United States to exempt our people from ALL taxation as long as we are deprived of equal justice under the laws of the land.

We believe that intermarriage or race mixing should be prohibited.

We believe that the offer of integration is hypocritical and is made by those who are trying to deceive the Black peoples into believing that their 400-year-old open enemies of freedom, justice and equality are, all of a sudden, their "friends." Furthermore, we believe that such deception is intended to prevent Black people from realizing that the time in history has arrived for the separation from the whites of this nation.

We believe that Allah (God) appeared in the Person of Master W. Fard Muhammad, July, 1930—the long-awaited "Messiah" of the Christians and the "Mahdi" of the Muslims.[15]

In several respects, Black Muslims represented a latter-day version of Garveyism. The Muslims and the Garveyites both found their identity in racial separation. The group economy practiced by Muslims—dry cleaners, grocery stores, restaurants, dairy farms, and bakeries—duplicated that of the UNIA. In its commitment to racial uplift and redemption, the Nation of Islam retained fundamental tenets of Garveyism, which had itself drawn selectively on Booker T. Washington's economic nationalism. But where Washington was a "conservative" separationist in the racial climate of the early 1900s, Elijah Muhammad preached a more militant, assertive separatism grounded in his interpretation of Islam in the more integrationist atmosphere of the World War II era. Although it gained increasing attention, the Nation of Islam might have remained an obscure sect during the modern civil rights movement had it not attracted the attentions of its most notable convert, later to become its most famous apostate.[16]

Malcolm Little to Malcolm X

In 1925, Malcolm Little was born to a dysfunctional, abusive family in Omaha, Nebraska. His mother was a light-skinned West Indian named Louisa (Louise) Norton, and his physically imposing father was a jet-black construction worker and whoop-and-holler Baptist preacher from Georgia named Early (Earl) Little, who deserted his first wife and their three children. Malcolm suffered repeated beatings from his mother, which he attributed to her conflicted feelings about her Scottish father and illegitimate birth. Malcolm, the seventh of Earl's ten children, felt he was Louise's least favorite because of his skin color. When she wasn't beating Malcolm, Louise sometimes vigorously scrubbed her light-skinned son's face and neck. "I can make him look almost white if I bathe him enough," she told a white neighbor. At the same time, she ordered "Milky," as Malcolm was nicknamed, out of the house, so the sun would darken his skin. Malcolm's domineering father was a belligerent, sometimes brutal, man who beat his wife and children, and in a rage, once pulled off the head of a live rabbit with his bare hands and threw the carcass at his wife's feet. To scrape by, Earl Little drifted from city to city looking for steady carpentry work and donations from church-goers comforted by his promises of heavenly rewards.[17]

According to Malcolm, his father was a "dedicated organizer" for Marcus Garvey, who was then in Harlem "raising the banner of black-race purity and exhorting the Negro masses to return to their ancestral African homeland—a cause that made Garvey the most controversial man on earth." In fact, both parents were Garvey stalwarts who had met in Montreal, Canada, and volunteered to establish and lead a UNIA affiliate in the rural Midwest, where few African Americans lived. Racial trouble soon followed because local whites were furious about the Rev. Little's Garveyite crusade, which stirred up the black community. One night, a Ku Klux Klan posse descended on the Littles' home with guns and blazing torches to run them out of town. A pregnant Louise Little, who supposedly confronted the klansmen, denied the event ever occurred. Earl Little's sister Rose, who lived in Omaha at the time, likewise said the episode never took place, and accused Earl of stealing her steamer trunk and impersonating her husband to fraudulently buy clothes in his name and then skip town. Even Malcolm, who was then not yet born, gave differing accounts of that night. Whatever happened, the Littles moved to Lansing, Michigan.[18]

Soon after occupying their Lansing farmhouse, the Littles were notified that their deed contained a stipulation that the property could never be acquired by non-Caucasians. Evidently, a land development company found that the Littles were an impediment to selling adjacent lots to whites, and so convinced a judge to order their eviction "forthwith." Before the Littles vacated their home, however, an explosion ignited a raging fire that quickly consumed it. The Lansing fire department refused to help because the fire was outside the city's limits. Seemingly inexplicably, Earl Little stopped sympathetic neighbors from saving his furniture, telling them to "let it burn." Little claimed angry whites had set his home ablaze to get him to leave, but there was no need to commit arson because the eviction order was common knowledge. It was Little who was arrested for arson, once the police discovered that he had bought kerosene just hours before the fire and that Louise had lied about where the oil can was stored. The police investigation also showed that Louise had told her children not to sleep upstairs on the night of the fire. Not inconsequentially, Earl Little had bought two fire insurance policies worth $2,500, and rushed to the insurance office the morning after the fire to make a late payment. The police were convinced that Earl burned down his home either to collect on his insurance or to prevent whites from repossessing it, but such charges were impossible to prove.[19]

There was another memory that stood out for Malcolm, whose paternal uncle had been lynched. Malcolm accompanied his one-eyed father on UNIA recruiting missions in the Lansing neighborhoods, where "big shiny photographs" of Garvey were passed around:

The pictures showed that what seemed to me millions of Negroes thronged in parade behind Garvey riding in a fine car, a big black man dressed in a dazzling uniform with gold braid on it . . . wearing a thrilling hat with tall plumes. I remember hearing that he had black followers not only in the United States but all around the world, and . . . the meetings always closed with my father saying, several times, and the people chanting after him, "Up, you mighty race, you can accomplish what you will!"[20]

According to family lore, the Rev. Little's dedication to black liberation cost him his life. When Malcolm was 6-years-old, a black-robed, white supremacist group called the Black Legion allegedly crushed his father's skull and laid his body across the trolley tracks to give the appearance of an unfortunate accident. Little's life insurance company refused to pay a death benefit, claiming that he had committed suicide by throwing himself under the passing streetcar. One contemporary account suggests that Little was bludgeoned—perhaps by a car—at a remote street intersection and then transported to the streetcar tracks, where he was run over. The most careful study available supports the conclusion that Little's death was accidental, rather than a hate crime. Earl Little's left arm was crushed and his left leg nearly severed, but his head was intact. He told the police that he had tried to board a moving streetcar and missed the step, falling under the rear wheels. Little's death was ultimately ruled accidental by the state police and the coroner, but his widow steadfastly believed that whites murdered her husband, a view adopted by Malcolm and repeated in his autobiography.[21]

In the wake of Earl Little's tragic death, his family fell apart, as Louise had a nervous breakdown and was institutionalized as insane. The Little children were split up and sent to live in state institutions or with white foster families. Malcolm's sense of alienation from the larger society grew apace, especially after his dreams for a bright future were punctured. Once a promising student, Malcolm hoped to become a lawyer, but his white teacher dismissed such ambition as unrealistic for a black youngster, and suggested that he become a carpenter instead. In 1941, Malcolm left school and went to live with his older half-sister in Roxbury, Massachusetts, the black ghetto of Boston, before moving to Harlem. Nicknamed "Detroit Red" for his hair color, Malcolm worked as a shoeshine boy, soda jerk, busboy, and railroad dining car waiter, but soon gravitated to a life of crime. He turned to gambling, dope-dealing, and pimping, before being arrested and convicted of burglary. He received a seven-year prison sentence, a severe penalty, perhaps reflecting the fact that one of his accomplices was his married white girlfriend. He was not yet 21-years-old.[22]

During his first year in the Massachusetts State Prison, Malcolm continued to behave as a delinquent, baiting the guards, snorting nutmeg and other substances, and, by his own account, raging against God and the Bible to such an extent that he was called "Satan" by other inmates. But he came to respect a fellow prisoner named Bimbi, who was studious and articulate. With Bimbi's encouragement, Malcolm took correspondence classes in English and Latin, copied out an entire dictionary, and read so voraciously in his cell after lights out that he permanently impaired his vision. After transferring to another prison, Malcolm received a letter from his brother, Philbert, stating that he had discovered the "natural religion for the black man," and had joined the Nation of Islam. Philbert instructed Malcolm, "don't eat any more pork, and don't smoke any more cigarettes. I'll show you how to get out of prison." Malcolm's natural curiosity was aroused. Further letters from his siblings, three of whom were Black Muslims, and correspondence with Elijah Muhammad himself, introduced Malcolm to the Black Muslim faith. He embraced the new creed with all the enthusiasm of a convert. In addition to Black Muslim literature, he also read three classic texts—W.E.B. Du Bois' *The Souls of Black Folk*, H.G. Wells' *Outline of History*, and Will Durant's magisterial *The Story of Civilization*.[23]

Released from prison in 1952, Malcolm went directly to Detroit to meet the shy and frail Elijah Muhammad, who made him a formal member of the Nation. Malcolm took the surname "X" and advanced rapidly within the Muslim hierarchy to become assistant minister to Temple No. 1 in Detroit. He soon became the movement's most effective preacher and proselytizer. Two years later, he was given the ministry of Temple No. 7 at Lenox Avenue and 116th Street in Harlem, and quickly built a following in New York City. As a trusted minister and disciple of Elijah Muhammad, Malcolm preached orthodox Black Muslim doctrine. At a Harlem rally, he declared:

The Western World is filled with drunkenness, dope, addiction, lying, stealing, gambling, adultery, fornication, prostitution and hosts of other evils. The God of Peace and Righteousness is about to set up His Kingdom . . . here on this earth. Mr. Muhammad is trying to clean up our morals and qualify us to enter into this new Righteous Nation of God . . . stop carrying guns and knives . . . drinking whiskey, taking dope, reefers and even cigarettes. No more gambling! Elevate the black woman. . . . Your thirst for integrating makes the white man think you want only to marry his daughter. We [Muslims] who follow Mr. Muhammad don't think God ever intended for Black men to marry white women. . . . WE MUST HAVE SOME LAND OF OUR OWN . . . to become self-sustaining, economically and otherwise. How else can 20 million black people who now constitute a nation within our own right, a NATION WITHIN A NATION, expect to survive?[24]

Despite Malcolm's dedication and considerable oratical skills, the Black Muslim appeal was limited, and members had few rights. Black Muslim theology seemed bizarre even to most African Americans, while the call for racial "separation," however appealing emotionally, was vague, and to the black majority, unrealistic. Malcolm began to attract increasing attention and support from lower-class ghetto blacks, less from his exegesis of Black Muslim tenets than for his blistering condemnations of white racism and critiques of the civil rights movement's stress on nonviolence and integration. Some of his most stinging comments were reserved for Martin Luther King, Jr.'s doctrine of redemptive black suffering. Drawing an analogy with slavery, Malcolm asserted that the two classes of slaves were the "House Negro," loyal to the master, and the "Field Negro," who hated both the master and the servitude. Their modern counterparts were the "Uncle Toms"—accommodating, peaceable, and self-serving—and the "New Negro" who took pride in his color and culture, and who demanded racial separation. For Malcolm, Martin Luther King belonged firmly in the first category, an "Uncle Tom" whose "primary concern" was "preaching love the white man."[25]

When the noted psychologist Kenneth Clark asked Malcolm whether his strictures against African Americans "talking about 'love everybody' [when] they don't have any love whatsoever for their own kind" was an oblique reference to King, Malcolm replied tartly:

You don't have to criticize Reverend Martin Luther King. His actions criticize him. Any Negro who teaches other Negroes to turn the other cheek is disarming that Negro . . . of his God-given right . . . his moral right . . . his natural right . . . to defend himself. Everything in nature can defend itself . . . except the American Negro. And men like King—their job is to go among Negroes and teach Negroes "Don't fight back." He doesn't tell them, "Don't fight each other." "Don't fight the white man" is what he is saying. . . . *White* people follow King. . . . *White* people subsidize King. *White* people support King. But the masses of black people don't support King [who] is the best weapon that the white man . . . has ever gotten in this country.

Malcolm gave a similar assessment of King to Louis Lomax, a journalist: "The goal of Dr. Martin Luther King is to give Negroes a chance to sit in a segregated restaurant beside the same white man who has brutalized them for 400 years . . . to get the Negroes to forgive the people who have brutalized them for 400 years, by lulling them to sleep and making them forget what those whites have done to them, but the masses of black people today don't go for what Martin Luther King is putting down."[26]

That Malcolm was prepared to act directly against white provocation was dramatically illustrated in 1957, when he and a group of followers surrounded a Harlem police station, following the beating of a Black Muslim named Johnson Hinton by the police. Malcolm demanded the victim's release and hospitalization, and filed a $70,000 claim for damages against the New York City police department. The widely publicized action caught the attention of the media and of blacks throughout the country, and membership of the Nation increased rapidly. According to one estimate, the annual income of the Nation was $3 million in 1959; by 1961, the eight temples founded by Malcolm in the eastern states had completed payment of nearly $39,000 to the Nation's headquarters in Chicago. Malcolm's own New York Temple No. 7 contributed over $23,000.[27]

Even as Malcolm, the evangelist, built up the Nation of Islam in the North, he pursued a backdoor channel to protect its growing presence in the South. The South was a logical place for Nation expansion because black emigrationists had once been popular in Georgia, and there had been more branches of Marcus Garvey's UNIA in Louisiana and Virginia than anywhere else in the United States. At Elijah Muhammad's behest, Malcolm traveled to Atlanta on January 28, 1961, to meet with Ku Klux Klan officials, just as Garvey had once done. The entire scenario must have been deeply troubling to Malcolm, who believed that the Klan had murdered his father. According to an FBI informant, Malcolm and the klansmen agreed that racial integration was an abomination, which Malcolm blamed on a Jewish conspiracy aided by unsuspecting blacks. To undermine the drive for integration, Malcolm intimated that the Klan should murder Martin Luther King and whites who advocated race mixing. In a *quid pro quo* arrangement derisively called the "Muslim Compromise," the southern Klan promised not to attack farmers working land owned by the Nation of Islam, as long as Muslims promised not to buy farmland in "non-Negro areas." The Klan further proposed to keep the races separate by offering a 20,000-acre parcel of land in Georgia to black nationalists who would settle there. Although Malcolm dutifully informed Muhammad about the meeting, he came to regret his collusion with the Klan. As for Muhammad, he worked out some understanding of his own with George Lincoln Rockwell, the *Führer* of the American Nazi party. Such fraternization and negotiations with white supremacists by Muslim leaders could have been explosive had their followers or the public-at-large known of them.[28]

A frequent guest on television and radio programs, Malcolm X was the second most requested speaker on college campuses, the first being the 1964 Republican presidential contender, Barry Goldwater. In his numerous public addresses and in the Nation's newspaper, *Muhammad Speaks*, an increasingly confident Malcolm pointed out the major issues confronting African Americans included inadequate and expensive housing, inferior educational facilities, and political impotence. Malcolm was also increasingly uneasy with the conservatism of Elijah Muhammad, and in particular, his refusal to allow Black Muslims to participate in civil rights protests. "If I harbored any personal disappointment whatsoever," Malcolm recalled, "it was that privately I was convinced that our Nation of Islam could be an even greater force in the American black man's overall struggle if we engaged in more action. . . . I felt that, wherever black people committed themselves, in the Little Rocks and Birminghams and other places, militantly disciplined Muslims should be there—for all the world to see, and respect, and discuss. It could be heard increasingly in the Negro communities: 'Those Muslims *talk* tough, but they never *do* anything, unless somebody bothers Muslims.' "[29]

It is also clear, in retrospect, that the insularity and exclusiveness of Black Muslims, as well as their theological mysticism, no longer satisfied the intellectually mature Malcolm. The occasion of the break with the Nation was provided by John F. Kennedy's assassination in November,

1963. Disregarding Muhammad's surprising directive that Muslim representatives should express sorrow "about the death of our president,"
Malcolm blurted out that the murder was simply a matter of "chickens
coming home to roost." In his *Autobiography*, Malcolm explained what
he meant by his ill-considered and insubordinate remark: "I said that
the hate in white men had not stopped with the killing of defenseless
black people, but that hate, allowed to spread unchecked, finally had
struck down this country's Chief of State. I said it was the same thing as
had happened with Medgar Evers, with Patrice Lumumba, with Madame
Nhu's husband."[30]

When the press reported Malcolm's impolitic comments, Elijah
Muhammad censured him publicly and suspended him from the Nation
of Islam for ninety days, during which time he was forbidden to speak
as a Muslim minister. Privately, Muhammad had described Kennedy's
assassination in the same way: "That devil's death doesn't concern us; it's
time for the Christians to mourn, not the Muslims." A distraught Malcolm
suspected that his suspension was intended to curb his sizable influence
within the movement, as it also reflected the growing divergence between
his ideas and those of Minister Muhammad. Malcolm had grown
frustrated by the Nation's unwillingness to do anything other than to
denounce America's racism and by the tithing required of Black Muslims,
which allowed Muhammad's family to live extravagantly, while the
membership-at-large remained desperately poor. Moreover, Malcolm was
repulsed by his spiritual leader's serial adultery; Muhammad had fathered
thirteen children with his young secretaries, a stunning transgression
of the Nation's moral code. When Malcolm confronted his surrogate
father, Elijah Muhammad readily confessed, claiming holy exception by
pointing out that he simply followed the well-worn path of biblical
heroes. "When you read about how David took another man's wife,"
Muhammad remarked brazenly, "I'm that David. You read about Noah,
who got drunk—that's me. You read about Lot, who went and laid up
with his own daughters. I have to fulfill all of those things." With neither
side respecting or trusting the other, a break between Malcolm and
Muhammad was inevitable.[31]

Malcolm X: Muslim

In March, 1964, Malcolm resigned from the Nation of Islam, accusing
Elijah Muhammad of hypnotizing him as a "zombie" for twelve years.
Two days later, Malcolm told *Ebony* magazine that the Nation would

murder him before long: "They've got to kill me," he concluded, because "I know too much. I know where the bodies are buried, and if they press me, I'll exhume some," an apparent reference to Muhammad's embarrassing deals with the Ku Klux Klan and the American Nazi party. In the weeks before his murder, Malcolm became convinced that other groups wanted him dead, too.[32]

As he awaited his expected assassination, Malcolm announced that he would form a new religious order in New York City called the Muslim Mosque, Inc., which would adopt a black nationalist, direct-action approach to the problem of race, as well as provide a spiritual and an activist base for Muslims and non-Muslims alike. Although he publicly still endorsed Elijah Muhammad's policies of racial separatism and an ultimate return to Africa, Malcolm realized that the Nation's theology and political inactivity did not appeal to the young urban blacks. His splinter group would, therefore, "be organized in such manner to provide for the active participation of all Negroes in our political, economic, and social programs. . . . Our accent will be upon youth. . . . We are completely disenchanted with the old, adult, established politicians." Malcolm also reiterated his contention that African Americans should—and would—retaliate in self-defense when provoked: "It is criminal to teach a man not to defend himself when he is the constant victim of brutal attacks. . . . When our people are being bitten by dogs, they are within their rights to kill those dogs. We should be peaceful, law-abiding—but the time has come for the American Negro to fight back in self-defense whenever and wherever he is being unjustly and unlawfully attacked. If the government thinks I am wrong for saying this, then let the government start doing its job."[33]

From its inception, the Muslim Mosque suffered from insuperable problems. It was weak, poorly organized, and under-funded. The radical wing of the civil rights coalition—the Student Nonviolent Coordinating Committee (SNCC) and the Congress of Racial Equality (CORE)—rejected Malcolm's overtures to form a working alliance. Younger black militants initially regarded Malcolm as a lone agitator, a self-promoter, and a potential, if not actual, rival for leadership of the urban black masses. For his part, Elijah Muhammad never forgave Malcolm's apostasy, and the Nation's newspaper published weekly diatribes that compared Malcolm to such notable traitors as Judas, Brutus, and Benedict Arnold. The established black leaders, already embarrassed and angered by Malcolm's attacks, were in no mood to cooperate with him. In fact, Malcolm was now in an ambivalent position—a confirmed Black Muslim and an aspiring civil rights leader, a religious and secular black nationalist. Moreover, he was now beginning to review the plight of African Americans in a world-wide context.[34]

In 1964, Malcolm toured Middle Eastern and African nations, where he was well-received by heads of state, politicians, and students. The turning point of this tour was his pilgrimage to the Muslim holy city of Mecca, where Malcolm's exposure to the true Islamic faith broke his remaining ties with the bowdlerized version preached by Elijah Muhammad. Malcolm was particularly impressed by the fraternal relations between pilgrims of all colors and nationalities at Mecca and the interest expressed in American race relations by Arab and African leaders. He returned to the United States as a Sunni Muslim named El-Hajj Malik El-Shabazz, although he continued to be known as Malcolm X. He was convinced that if African Americans must remain in America physically, they should "return" to Africa culturally and metaphysically within the framework of pan-Africanism. This call had a special resonance with the rise of a spate of independent black nations in sub-Saharan Africa. On his return from Africa, Malcolm informed a reporter: "Every time you see another nation on the African continent become independent, you know that Marcus Garvey is alive. . . . The entire Black Nationalist philosophy here in America is fed upon the seeds that were planted by Marcus Garvey."[35]

In June, 1964, Malcolm announced the formation of the Organization of Afro-American Unity (OAAU), a secular institution that borrowed from the Organization of African Unity. The new organization declared itself "*Dedicated* to the unification of all people of African descent in this hemisphere and to the utilization of that unity to bring into being the organizational structure that will project the black people's contribution to the world." Among its objectives, the OAAU asserted the "Afro-American's right of self-defense" against all oppressors, complete independence for all black people, "a voter-registration drive to make every unregistered voter in the Afro-American community an independent voter," the "establishment of a cultural center in Harlem" to offer courses and workshops in the arts and in African-American history, and black principals for black schools. It also called for a petition to be presented to the United Nations Human Rights Commission, demanding the U.S. government be prosecuted on the grounds that the deteriorating condition of African Americans threatened world peace. As one scholar observed, the OAAU prospectus "read like a Black Power manifesto two years ahead of its time."[36]

Despite its impressive title, the OAAU was not an influential organization. It never had a thousand members, in part because the Nation of Islam intimidated those who might have been inclined to join, but also because Malcolm's message of hating whites was abandoned for the less incendiary rhetoric of hating oppressive systems. On the night before he died, Malcolm expressed hope that the OAAU would not depend on "the life of one man," but would develop effective programs which would replace his charisma as the glue holding the organization together. As a practical matter, the OAAU was more the institutional embodiment of Malcolm's changing views on the racial situation at home and abroad, rather than an activist movement in the mold of Martin Luther King's Southern Christian Leadership Conference (SCLC). OAAU rallies were public relations and educational events, during which Malcolm explained his thinking and strategies on various matters, including his opposition to the reelection of president Lyndon Johnson. He urged supporters to organize "rifle clubs" to defend the black community against white vigilantism and police brutality. Malcolm's most attractive theme for black audiences was his exposition of the history of racial discrimination in America. Like Booker T. Washington and Marcus Garvey, Malcolm alluded frequently to the debilitating effects of enslavement on the black psyche. After his break with the Nation of Islam, Malcolm did not preach the divine deliverance of African Americans from racism, but the need for blacks to deliver themselves.[37]

In a remarkable reversal of his thinking, Malcolm proffered an olive branch to liberal whites and mainline civil rights leaders who supported racial justice. He declared, "We will work with anyone, with any group, no matter what their color is, as long as they are genuinely interested in taking the type of steps necessary to bring an end to the injustices that black people in this country are afflicted by. No matter what their color is, no matter what their political, economic, or social philosophy is, as long as their aims and objectives are in the direction of destroying the vulturous system that has been sucking the blood of the black people in this country, they're all right with me." To reach out to civil rights groups, Malcolm offered vigilante assistance to Dr. King, who was then battling violent white supremacists in St. Augustine, Florida: "If the federal government will not send troops to your aid, just say the word and we will immediately dispatch some of our brothers there to organize self-defense units among our people, and the Ku Klux Klan will then receive a taste of its own medicine. The day of turning the other cheek to those brute beasts is over." No reply was forthcoming.[38]

Malcolm's attempts to "teach Negroes a new direction" on race fell on deaf ears. As to why he got nowhere in spreading his "new insights into the American black man's struggle and his problems," Malcolm had a ready target—the white press—which associated him with the racial explosions in the "long, hot summer" of 1964. He was accused of "stirring up Negroes" and "inciting violence," and he resented the charge. "It takes no one," he declared, "to stir up the sociological dynamite that stems from the unemployment, bad housing, and inferior education already in the ghettoes. This explosively criminal condition has existed for so long, it needs no fuse; it fuses itself; it spontaneously combusts from within itself." White newspapers called Malcolm " 'the angriest Negro in America,' " and he "wouldn't deny that charge":

I spoke exactly as I felt. "I *believe* in anger. The Bible says there is a *time* for anger." They called me "a teacher, a fomentor of violence." I would say point blank, "That is a lie. I'm not for wanton violence, I'm for justice. I feel that if white people were attacked by Negroes—if the forces of law prove unable, or inadequate, or reluctant to protect those whites from those Negroes—then those white people should protect and defend themselves from those Negroes, using arms if necessary. And I feel that when the law fails to protect Negroes from whites' attack, then those Negroes should use arms, if necessary, to defend themselves."

Malcolm took pains to acknowledge that he had discovered there were, after all, "sincere, well-meaning, good white people." He aimed his rhetorical firepower instead against "the white *racists*." Malcolm was convinced that "Negroes have the right to fight against these racists, by any means necessary."[39]

In his last speeches, Malcolm also made passing references to socialism. At an OAAU meeting in Harlem, he observed, "Almost every one of the countries that has gotten independence has devised some kind of socialistic system, and this is no accident. . . . You can't operate a capitalistic system unless you are vulturistic; you have to have someone's blood to suck to be a capitalist. You show me a capitalist, and I'll show you a bloodsucker." Despite such assertions, Malcolm never moved beyond a vague critique of capitalism, and never endorsed Marxism. As one confidant remarked, "He had no use for Marxism. He considered Marxism as another political ideology invented by white men for white men, to shift the seat of power from one group of white men to another group of white men. He thought it had no relevance to the black man."[40]

Essentially an inspired agitator, public moralist, and revivalist—he once called himself a "black Billy Graham"—Malcolm addressed a dispossessed and almost entirely black constituency. Unlike Martin Luther King, Jr., Malcolm never envisioned a coalition of the underprivileged across racial lines. In blunt language, he informed one interviewer that "The history of America is that working-class whites have been just as much against not only working-class Negroes, but all Negroes, period, because all Negroes are working class within the caste system. The richest Negro is treated like a working-class Negro. There never has been any good relationship between the working-class Negro and the working-class whites. . . . There can be no white/black solidarity until there's first some black solidarity. . . . I think one of the mistakes Negroes make is this worker solidarity thing. There's no such thing. It didn't even work in Russia."[41]

From his conversion to the Nation of Islam to the end of his life, Malcolm remained a black nationalist, committed to the spiritual and material elevation of African Americans through the affirmation of his own faith in the redemption of the individual. Like Booker T. Washington, Malcolm produced an authorized and inspirational account of his own life, completed shortly after his assassination on February 21, 1965, by three members of the Nation of Islam while on stage at Harlem's Audubon Ballroom. Published after his death, it became a cardinal text for the emerging Black Power movement. Malcolm's posthumous *Autobiography* presented his search for identity, as well as his claim to leadership, to an audience that had been largely indifferent or actively opposed to him during his comparatively short public career. It is possible to regard Malcolm's memoir as his greatest achievement.[42]

The Autobiography of Malcolm X

Like Booker T. Washington's *Up from Slavery*, Malcolm's *Autobiography* is a black success story, but one profoundly different in content and tone. It contains candid, if not graphic, descriptions of Malcolm's youth, his subsequent criminal activities, prison experiences, conversion to the Nation of Islam, changing relationship with Elijah Muhammad, and his discovery of "true" Islam while journeying to Mecca. In many respects, it belongs to the genre of spiritual conversion autobiography, and is, in effect, a black *Pilgrim's Progress*. Malcolm describes episodes of his life in the form of parables and then draws an appropriate moral.

In a memorable passage, Malcolm describes how, as a ghetto youth, he allowed his friend Shorty to "straighten" his hair at home, with a near-lethal mixture of lye, eggs, and other ingredients. The experience seared his scalp and his consciousness: "The congolene just felt warm when Shorty started combing it in. But then my head caught fire. I gritted my teeth and tried to pull the sides of the kitchen table together. The comb felt as if it was raking my skin off. My eyes watered, my nose was running. I couldn't stand it any longer; I bolted to the washbasin. I was cursing Shorty with every name I could think of when he got the spray going and started soap-lathering my head." When the painful operation was completed, Malcolm looked in the mirror and the sight "blotted out the hurting. . . . [O]n top of my head was this thick, smooth sheen of shiny red hair—real red—as straight as any white man's." To the intellectually-mature Malcolm, the episode was revealing and cautionary: "This was my first really big step toward self-degradation: when I endured all of that pain, literally burning my flesh to have it look like a white man's hair. I had joined the multitude of Negro men and women in America who are brainwashed into believing that the black people are 'inferior'—and white people 'superior'—that they will even violate and mutilate their God-created bodies to try to look 'pretty' by white standards."[43]

Throughout his memoir, Malcolm shrewdly adjusts his language to parallel and evoke the particular stages of his life. Recounting his career as a street-wise hustler, running narcotics, working the "numbers" racket, and procuring black prostitutes for white customers, Malcolm wrote, "Shorty would take me to groovy, frantic scenes in different chicks' and cats' pads, where with the lights and the juke down mellow, everybody blew gage and juiced back and jumped. I met chicks who were as fine as May wine, and cats who were hip to all happenings." Malcolm then adds laconically, "That paragraph is a bit deliberate of course; it's just to display a bit more of the slang that was used by everyone I respected as 'hip' in those days."[44]

As in his public speeches and addresses, so too in the *Autobiography*, Malcolm could employ parody and satire. In a devastating passage, he conveys and mocks blacks in Boston's Roxbury section who pretentiously imitated the white middle class: "I'd guess that eight out of ten of the Hill Negroes of Roxbury, despite the impressive-sounding job titles they affected, actually worked as menials and servants. 'He's in banking,' or 'He's in securities.' It sounded as though they were discussing a Rockefeller or a Mellon—and not some gray-headed, dignity-posturing bank janitor or bond-house messenger. 'I'm with an old family,' was the euphemism used to dignify the professions of white folks' cooks and maids who talked so affectedly among their own kind in Roxbury that you couldn't even understand them. I don't know how many forty- or fifty-year-old errand boys went down the Hill dressed like ambassadors in black suits and white collars, to downtown jobs 'in government,' 'in finance,' or 'in law.' It has never ceased to amaze me how so many Negroes, then and now, could stand the indignity of that kind of self-delusion."[45]

But, Malcolm was also prepared to admit that, as a teenager, he had himself slavishly conformed to sartorial trends and fashions. In a hilarious account, he recalled his purchase of a "zoot" suit: "I was measured, and the young salesman picked off a rack a suit that was just wild: sky-blue pants thirty inches in the knee and angle-narrowed down to twelve inches at the bottom, and a long coat that pinched my waist and flared out below my knees. As a gift, the salesman said, the store would give me a narrow belt with my initial 'L' on it. Then he said I ought to buy a hat, and I did—blue, with a feather in the four-inch brim. Then the store gave me another present: a long, thick, gold-plated chain that swung down lower than my coat hem." Again a moral is drawn: "I was," Malcolm recalls ironically, "sold forever on credit."[46]

Following his conversion to the Nation of Islam, Malcolm's life-story adopts a more formal, sober, and suitably dignified form. "Never in prison have I studied and absorbed so intensely as I did now under Mr. Muhammad's guidance," Malcolm wrote. "I went to bed every night ever more awed. If not Allah, who else could have put such wisdom into the little humble lamb of a man from the Georgia fourth grade and sawmills and cotton patches. The 'lamb of a man' analogy I drew for myself from the prophecy in the Book of Revelations of a symbolic lamb with a two-edged sword in its mouth. Mr. Muhammad's two-edged sword was his teachings, which cut back and forth to free the black man's mind from the white man. My adoration of Mr. Muhammad grew, in the sense of the Latin root word *adorare*."[47]

After his break with the Nation and conversion to orthodox Islam, Malcolm reflected on his slavish attachment to his longtime mentor: "I guess it would be impossible for anyone ever to realize fully how complete was my belief in Elijah Muhammad. I believed in him not only as a leader in the ordinary *human* sense, but I also believed in him as a *divine* leader. I believed he had no human weakness or faults. . . . [While in Mecca,] I realized how very dangerous it is for people to hold any human being in such esteem, especially to consider anyone some sort of a 'divinely guided' and 'protected' person."[48]

In recounting the story of his life—whether as a schoolboy, petty criminal, autodidact, Muslim minister, or putative black leader—Malcolm, like Booker T. Washington before him, presents himself as eminently successful. In a letter written at that time, Malcolm relates his receptions in Saudi Arabia with ostensible modesty and a certain disingenuousness:

Never have I been so highly honored. . . . Who would believe the blessings that have been heaped upon an *American Negro*? A few nights ago, a man who would be called in America a "white" man, a United Nations diplomat, an ambassador, a companion of kings, gave me *his* hotel suite, *his* bed. . . . His Holiness Sheikh Muhammad Harkon himself okayed my visit to Mecca . . . he told me that he prayed that I would be a successful preacher of Islam in America. A car, a driver, and a guide have been placed at my disposal. . . . Never would I have even thought of dreaming that I would ever be a recipient of such honors—honors that in America would be bestowed upon a King—not a Negro.[49]

While Malcolm embraced his new faith with enthusiasm and obvious sincerity, he also retained and displayed the self-confidence and boosterism of the American entrepreneur abroad. He realized that even religion would benefit greatly from the right kind of marketing. As he wrote in his *Autobiography*, "Behind my nods and smiles . . . I was doing some American-type thinking and reflection. I saw that Islam's conversions around the world could double and triple if the colorfulness and the true spiritualness of the Hajj pilgrimage were properly advertised and communicated to the outside world. . . . The Arabs said '*insha Allah*' ('God willing')—then they waited for converts. Even by this means, Islam was on the march, but I knew that with improved public relations the number of new converts turning to Allah could be turned to millions."[50]

As I.F. Stone, a white journalist sympathetic to Malcolm, wryly observed, El-Hajj Malik El-Shabazz "had become a Hajj but remained in some ways a Babbitt, the salesman archetype of American society. A creed was something to sell. Allah, the Merciful, needed better merchandising." In a real sense, in his *Autobiography*, Malcolm was "merchandizing" himself, attempting to reassure his readers that as a consequence of the experiences described, he was no longer a threat to society, but rather a figure of integrity and stature. He was, however, prepared to admit to Alex Haley, his transcriber, that certain incidents had been exaggerated in the telling to increase their dramatic impact. For example, as a young gang leader, concerned to establish his credentials, he had not actually played Russian roulette with a pistol, but had palmed the bullet. When Haley offered to amend the passage, Malcolm replied that it should stand since he did not want to be regarded as a bluffer.[51]

Throughout the book, Malcolm presents himself as a man constantly in motion and the process of change, who only came to rest—physically and metaphysically—in Mecca, Islam's holiest city. His sense of spiritual kinship with fellow pilgrims is conveyed in the following passage: "The Muslim world's customs no longer seemed strange to me. My hands now readily plucked up food from a common dish shared with brother Muslims; I was drinking without hesitation from the same glass as others; I was washing from the same little pitcher of water; and sleeping with eight or ten others on a mat in the open. I remember one night . . . I lay awake amid sleeping Muslim brothers and I learned that pilgrims from every land—every color, and class, and rank; high officials and the beggar alike—all snored in the same language."[52]

Malcolm's autobiography does not end with his spiritual and political illumination at Mecca, but rather in passages expressing anxiety and uncertainty. Like Martin Luther King, Malcolm was aware that he might, at any moment, be killed either by his black or white enemies. He predicted his demise with grim accuracy: "I do not expect to live long enough to read this book in its finished form," and wondered only who "would meet a fatal catastrophe first—'non-violent' Dr. King, or so-called 'violent' me." As it turned out, Malcolm was murdered three years before his great rival, both of whom were killed at age 39.[53]

Although Martin Luther King had deplored Malcolm's apparent preoccupation with violence and advocacy of racial separatism, he also deplored Malcolm's untimely death. When a young white student informed King that his grandmother thought *The Autobiography of Malcolm X* was "a marvelous book of love," King replied, "It was tragic that Malcolm was killed, he was really coming around, moving away from racism. He had such a sweet spirit. You know, right before he was killed he came down to Selma and said some pretty passionate things against me, and that surprised me because after all it was my own territory down there. But afterwards he took my wife aside, and said he thought he could help me more by attacking me than praising me. He thought it would make it easier for me in the long run." During his lifetime, Malcolm elicited less generous responses from other leaders of the civil rights coalition.[54]

Malcolm X and his black critics

As an impassioned agitator, moralist, and cynic, Malcolm X found the integrationism, gradualism, and nonviolence espoused by the established civil rights leadership in the early 1960s to be misguided and not a little ridiculous. In a "Message to the Grassroots," Malcolm informed his audience that the contemporary civil rights movement did not qualify as a social revolution. The American, French, Russian, and Chinese revolutions had been marked by violence and bloodshed and had effected radical change. With heavy irony and emphasis, he suggested, "The only kind of revolution that is nonviolent is the Negro revolution. The only revolution in which the goal is loving your enemy is the Negro revolution. It's the only revolution in which the goal is a desegregated lunch counter, a desegregated theater, a desegregated park, and a desegregated toilet; you can sit down next to white folks—on the toilet. That's no revolution."[55]

At a Harlem rally, Malcolm declared, "I don't believe we're going to overcome [by] singing. If you're going to get yourself a .45 [caliber handgun] and start singing 'We Shall Overcome,' I'm with you." Asked about his view of the activities of Martin Luther King and SCLC in Birmingham, Alabama, Malcolm replied harshly: "Martin Luther King is a chump not a champ. Any man who puts his women and children on the front lines is a chump, not a champ." Nationally recognized African-American leaders, Malcolm maintained, had betrayed their constituents. He informed a Detroit conference that the civil rights movement had reached its nadir when King had failed to desegregate Albany, Georgia. "King became bankrupt almost, as a leader," Malcolm maintained. As for other nationally-known civil rights leaders, Malcolm dismissed them as "fallen idols" who were unable "to stir up the masses," as were local activists. "Negroes of national stature . . . control you, they contain you, they have kept you on the plantation."[56]

Asked in an interview about his attitude toward "Christian-Gandhian groups," Malcolm retorted, "Christian? Gandhian? I don't go for anything that's non-violent and turn-the-other-cheekish. . . . I've never heard of a non-violent revolution or a revolution that was brought about by turning the other cheek, and so I believe that it is a crime for anyone to teach a person who is being brutalized to continue to accept the brutality without doing something to defend himself. If this is what the Christian-Gandhian philosophy teaches, then it is criminal—a criminal philosophy."[57]

Again, Malcolm's insistence on separatism and identification with Africa was at odds with the integrationism and "Americanism" of the civil rights movement. In a conversation with Robert Penn Warren, the southern literary critic, Malcolm derided the possibility that "the political and economic system of this country" could produce "freedom, justice . . . equality and human dignity for twenty-two million Afro-Americans," declaring, "I believe that a psychological, cultural, and philosophical migration back to Africa will solve our problems. Not a physical migration, but a cultural, psychological, philosophical migration back to Africa—which means restoring our common bond—will give us the spiritual strength and the incentive to strengthen our political and social and economic position right here in America. . . . And at the same time this will give incentive to many of our people to also visit and even migrate physically back to Africa, and those who stay here can help those who go back and those who go back can help those who stay here, in the same way as the Jews who go to Israel."[58]

Such statements by Malcolm, whether as a Black Muslim or independent minister, earned him the condemnation of most African-American leaders. The substance of much of their criticism echoed that of earlier black indictments of Marcus Garvey. Malcolm, it was generally conceded, had touched the sensitivities of urban blacks by exhorting them to reassert racial pride and to resist white oppression and denigration. Even Martin Luther King understood Malcolm's appeal, remarking to a friend: "I just saw Malcolm X on television. I can't deny it. When he starts talking about all that's been done to us, I get a twinge of hate, of identification with him." But King also deplored Malcolm's apparent obsession with violence, asserting that "violence is not going to solve our problem. And, in his litany of articulating the despair of the Negro without offering any positive, creative alternative, I feel that Malcolm has done himself and our people a great disservice. Fiery, demagogic oratory in the black ghettos, urging Negroes to arm themselves and prepare to engage in violence, as he has done, can reap nothing but grief."[59]

In the last months of his life, Malcolm was also seen by his African-American critics—with some justification—as confused and uncertain. Bayard Rustin, a leading civil rights strategist who organized the March on Washington, thought that Malcolm was only a marginal figure: "He has very little in the way of an organization—practically nothing. They're a few frustrated youngsters and a few confused writers . . . but even before he left here, these Sunday meetings which he was always having got smaller and smaller, because he doesn't have any real answers to the immediate problems which Negroes want an answer to." Whitney Young of the National Urban League believed that despite frequent appearances in headlines and on television, "there aren't ten Negroes who would follow Malcolm X to a separate state. The only appeal he has is to give a Negro who's been beaten down all day a chance to get a vicarious pleasure out of hearing someone cuss out the white people." James Farmer of the Congress of Racial Equality felt that "Malcolm has done nothing but verbalize—his militancy is a matter of posture, there has been no action." NAACP executive director Roy Wilkins regarded Malcolm as foolishly misguided in believing that the "the only way you could judge things was whether you did the thing that was manly, no matter if it was suicidal or not. A prosecutor like Malcolm has to be able to put himself in the shoes of people who did the best they could under the circumstances," and this, Wilkins believed, Malcolm was congenitally unprepared or unwilling to do. Only after Malcolm's death and canonization as the patron saint of Black Power by younger activists were established African-American leaders prepared to offer more favorable estimates of Malcolm X.[60]

Assessment

Throughout his public career, Malcolm X was consistently dedicated to the spiritual regeneration of African Americans. He employed the rhetoric of racial separatism to affirm the resolve of blacks to exist on their own terms within—but culturally and mentally apart from—the surrounding white society. An accomplished, polished, and artful public speaker, Malcolm portrayed and analyzed the plight of African Americans with remarkable vividness and clarity. His speeches were filled with visual images, metaphors, slogans, and allusions to black history, music, and folklore, all of which struck an immediate chord with his audiences. In the following exchange with a white writer, Malcolm responds to a question about indiscriminate reprisals against whites with a chilling parable: "If I go home . . . and my child has blood running down her leg and someone tells me a snake bit her, I'm going out and kill the snake. And when I find the snake, I'm not going to look and see if he has blood on his jaws":

Reporter: You mean you'd kill any snake you could find?

Malcolm X: I grew up in the country on a farm and . . . whenever someone said even that a snake was eating or bothering the chickens, we'd kill snakes. We never knew whether that was the snake that did it.

Reporter: To read your parable then, you would advocate non-selective reprisal? Kill any white person around.

Malcolm X: I'm not saying that. I'm just telling you about snakes.

In Malcolm's imagery, society was a jungle, infested with snakes, foxes, wolves, and vultures, yet black "leaders" themselves, were often no more than "parrots," repeating "what the [white] man says."[61]

An impressive feature of Malcolm's remarkable life was his capacity for intellectual growth. From the parochial and simplistic outlook of his Black Muslim phase, he came to embrace a more sophisticated and informed spiritual and political worldview by the time of his death. But he never abandoned his role as an evangelist for a form of black nationalism that owed much to Marcus Garvey's example. As a Black Muslim minister, Malcolm energized and greatly increased the membership of what had been a relatively obscure and largely elderly sect. By 1963, he had become increasingly impatient with the political disengagement forced on the Nation of Islam by Elijah Muhammad. Simultaneously, he pointed out the weaknesses in the objectives and achievements of a civil rights coalition that, after some successes in the South, had come to regard racial integration as a panacea. As an independent minister, Malcolm voiced the feelings of a younger black generation either hostile or indifferent to Martin Luther King's philosophy of nonviolence and the power of redemptive suffering. And, before King's own move to the left, Malcolm highlighted the socio-economic condition and needs of African Americans, and the failure of the civil rights movement to effect meaningful change in the lives of ghetto inhabitants. Malcolm espoused and personified black leadership from the grassroots of local organizations, free from the domination of the middle classes.[62]

Bayard Rustin conceded that Malcolm had brought a kind of psychic satisfaction and compensation to the dispossessed: "King had to be measured by his victories. But what King did, what the NAACP did, what Roy Wilkins did, all that was for the benefit of the Southern Negro. There were no obtainable, immediate results for the Northern ghettoized black, whose housing is getting worse; who is unable to find work; whose schools are deteriorating. . . . He . . . must find victory somewhere, and he finds victory within. He needed Malcolm, who brought him an internal victory, precisely because the external victory is beyond his reach. What can bring satisfaction is the feeling that he is black, he is a man, he is internally free. King had to win victories in the real world. Malcolm's were the kind you can create yourself."[63]

Sociologist C. Eric Lincoln expressed a similar view of Malcolm's appeal and achievement: "He was always challenging the white man, always debunking the white man. I don't think he was ever under any illusion that a powerless black minority could mount a physical challenge to a powerful white majority and survive. But they could mount a psycho-logical challenge, and if they were persistent, they might at least produce some erosion in the attitudes and the strategies by which the white man has always protected himself and his interests. His challenge was to prove that you are as great as you say you are . . . as moral as you say you are . . . as kind as you say you are . . . as loving as you say you are . . . as altruistic as you say you are . . . as *superior* as you say you are."[64]

Like Marcus Garvey, Malcolm X has been claimed as a revolutionary and a reactionary, a black nationalist and a black racist, a prophet and a demagogue. Like Garvey also, Malcolm had many more followers than those who belonged to the organization he last headed—the Organization of Afro-American Unity. Where Garvey spoke to the despairing mood of the 1920s, Malcolm spoke to the hopelessness of the enduring black ghettos of the 1960s, which he sought to transform into centers of black consciousness, enterprise, and spiritual liberation.

Two estimates of Malcolm, both delivered after his assassination, illustrate his essentially psychological appeal. Asked why he eulogized Malcolm X, Ossie Davis, the celebrated African-American actor, director, and playwright, replied, "We used to think that protocol and common sense required that Negroes stand back and let the white man speak up for us, defend us, and lead us from behind the scenes in our fight. This was the essence of Negro politics. But Malcolm said to hell with that! Get up off your knees and fight your own battles. . . . That's the way to make the white man respect you. Malcolm . . . was refreshing excitement. . . . He could make you angry as hell, but he could also make you proud. It was impossible to remain defensive and apologetic about being a Negro in his presence. . . . I never doubted that Malcolm X, even when he was wrong, was always the rarest thing in the world among us Negroes: a true man." Novelist James Baldwin observed that Malcolm had never been a "racist": "His intelligence was more complex than that. . . . What made him unfamiliar and dangerous was not his hatred for white people but his love for blacks, his apprehension of the horror of the black condition,and the reasons for it, and his determination so to work on their hearts and minds that they would be enabled to see their condition and change it for themselves."[65]

Although Martin Luther King rejected Malcolm's racial separatism and advocacy of retaliatory violence, King's widow believed that Malcolm and King occupied some common ground. Coretta Scott King wrote that Martin "shared with Malcolm the fierce desire that the black American reclaim his racial pride, his joy in himself and his race—in a physical, a cultural, and a spiritual rebirth. He shared with the nationalists the sure knowledge that 'black is beautiful' and that, in so many respects, the quality of the black people's scale of values was far superior to that of the white culture which attempted to enslave us. . . . Martin too believed that white Christianity had failed to act in accordance with its teachings. Martin also believed in nonviolent Black Power. He believed that we must have our share of the economy, of education, of jobs, of free choice."[66]

In the wake of the murders of Malcolm X and Martin Luther King, the urban riots of the 1960s, and the fragmentation of the civil rights coalition on the rocks of Black Power and the polarization caused by the Vietnam war, American society was in profound turmoil. Legislation designed to improve the citizenship status of blacks—notably, the Civil Rights Act of 1964 and the Voting Rights Act of 1965—served to heighten black expectations. Yet in 1966, the unemployment rate for blacks was twice the national average, with 40 percent of black families earning less than $3,000 a year. Ten years after the U.S. Supreme Court's historic decision on school desegregation, the U.S. commissioner of education could report that the majority of American children still attended racially segregated schools. Most disturbingly, perhaps, the nation's black ghettos, despite Martin's and Malcolm's efforts, remained as appalling reminders of the persistence, if not the intensification, of white racism impervious to the appeals of either integrationists or black nationalists.[67]

The disillusioned mood of urban blacks was most frighteningly revealed in the wave of "civil disorders" that engulfed the nation's major cities in the 1960s. Harlem and Rochester, New York (1964); Los Angeles, California (1965); Newark, New Jersey; Detroit, Michigan; and Cleveland, Ohio (1967–1968), all suffered major racial disturbances which resulted in over 200 deaths, mostly of African Americans, with at least 10,000 injured and 60,000 arrested, and the widespread destruction of property. Opinion polls indicated that while most African Americans agreed that rioters and looters were guilty of criminal acts, many of them also regarded rioting as a justifiable form of political protest against police brutality, unremitting white racism, and dreadful conditions within the black ghettos. As president Lyndon Johnson's National Advisory Commission on Civil Disorders reported, "What white Americans have never fully understood—but what the Negro can never forget—is that white society is deeply implicated in the ghetto. White institutions created it. . . . Our nation is moving toward two societies, one black, one white— separate and unequal."[68]

PLATE 1 *Booker T. Washington*
Source: Courtesy of Library of Congress, Harris & Ewing Collection

PLATE 2 *W.E.B. Du Bois*

Source: Courtesy of Library of Congress, photo by Cornelius M. Battey, 1918

PLATE 3 *Marcus Garvey*

Source: © Underwood & Underwood/Corbis

PLATE 4 *Martin Luther King, Jr.*
Source: © Everett Collection Inc/Alamy

PLATE 5 *Malcolm X*
Source: © Bettman/CORBIS

PLATE 6 *Mary McLeod Bethune*

Source: © CORBIS

PLATE 7 *Jesse Jackson*
Source: © Michael Brennan/CORBIS

PLATE 8 *Barack Obama*
Source: © Alliance Images/Alamy

References

1 George Breitman, ed., *Malcolm X Speaks: Speeches and Statements* (1965), p. 12.

2 James H. Cone, *Martin & Malcolm & America: A Dream or a Nightmare* (1991), p. 39.

3 C. Eric Lincoln, "The Meaning of Malcolm X," in John Henrik Clarke, ed., *Malcolm X: The Man and His Times* (1969), p. 10.

4 Harvard Sitkoff, *A New Deal for Blacks: The Emergence of Civil Rights as a National Issue, the Depression Decade* (2008); Gunnar Myrdal, *An American Dilemma: The Negro Problem and American Democracy* (1944).

5 David Levering Lewis, *W.E.B. Du Bois: The Fight for Equality and the American Century* (2000), pp. 335–347.

6 William Z. Foster, et al., *The Communist Position on the Negro Question* (1947); Mark Solomon, *The Cry Was Unity: Communists and Afro-Americans, 1917–1936* (1998), pp. 95–310.

7 Joseph E. Holloway and Herbert H. Booker, II, *Noble Drew Ali and the Moorish Science Temple Movement* (2007).

8 Jill Watts, *God, Harlem U.S.A.: The Father Divine Story* (1992); Robert Weisbrot, *Father Divine and the Struggle for Racial Equality* (1983); Kenneth E. Burnham, *God Comes to America: Father Divine and the Peace Mission Movement* (1979); E.U. Essien-Udom, *Black Nationalism: America: A Search for Identity in America* (1995), p. 45.

9 Reginald Kearney, *African American Views of the Japanese: Solidarity or Sedition?* (1998); Michael W. Fitzgerald, " 'We Have Found a Moses': Theodore Bilbo, Black Nationalism, and the Greater Liberia Bill of 1939," *Journal of Southern History* 63 (May, 1997): 293–320; "Races: Mr. Bilbo's Afflatus," *Time* 33 (8 May 1939): 14–15.

10 Karl Evanzz, *The Messenger: The Rise and Fall of Elijah Muhammad* (2001), pp. 62–67, 398.

11 Ibid., pp. 72–84, 96, 402–405; Claude Andrew Clegg III, *An Original Man: The Life and Times of Elijah Muhammad* (1998), pp. 34, 41–73.

12 Evanzz, *The Messenger*, pp. 114–115, 408, 416–417; Clegg, *An Original Man*, pp. 33–34.

13 C. Eric Lincoln, *The Black Muslims in America* (1994), p. 69; Clegg, *An Original Man*, pp. 77–87; Elijah Muhammad, *Message to the Blackman in America* (1965), p. 183.

14 Clegg, *An Original Man*, pp. 88–105.

15 Elijah Muhammad, "The Muslim Program," in John H. Bracey, et al., *Black Nationalism in America* (1970), pp. 404–407.

16 Clegg, *An Original Man*, pp. 109–115.

17 Bruce Perry, *Malcolm: The Life of a Man Who Changed Black America* (1991), p. 4.

18 Perry, *Malcolm*, pp. 3–4; Manning Marable, *Malcolm X: A Life of Reinvention* (2011), pp. 16, 20–23.

19 Perry, *Malcolm*, pp. 9–11; Marable, pp. 25–26.

20 Malcolm X, *The Autobiography of Malcolm X, as told to Alex Haley* (1965), p. 7.

21 Ibid., pp. 11–14; Marable, pp. 30–32.

22 Peter Goldman, *The Death and Life of Malcolm X* (1974), p. 75.

23 Malcolm X, *Autobiography*, pp. 154–178.

24 Bracey, et al., *Black Nationalism in America*, pp. 410–420.

25 Peter Goldman, *The Death and Life of Malcolm X* (1974), p. 75.

26 Kenneth B. Clark, *The Negro Protest: James Baldwin, Malcolm X, Martin Luther King Talk with Kenneth B. Clark* (1963), pp. 26–27; Louis E. Lomax, *When the World is Given: A Report on Elijah Muhammad and the Black Muslim World* (1964), p. 174.

27 Perry, *Malcolm*, pp. 164–165.

28 Clegg, *An Original Man*, pp. 152–157, 165–166; Perry, *Malcolm*, p. 358; Evanzz, *The Messenger*, pp. 226–227.

29 Malcolm X, *Autobiography*, pp. 294–298.

30 Ibid., p. 307; Evanzz, pp. 270–273.

31 Goldman, *Life and Death of Malcolm X*, p. 120; Malcolm X, *Autobiography*, pp. 300–312; Perry, *Malcolm*, pp. 230–232, 239–244; Evanzz, *The Messenger*, pp. 256–282.

32 Allan Morrison, "Who Killed Malcolm X?," *Ebony* 20 (October, 1965): 135–136, 138–140, 142.

33 Gordon Parks, "I Was a Zombie Then—Like All Muslims, I was Hypnotized," *Life* 58 (5 March 1965): 28–30; George Breitman, ed., *Malcolm X Speaks: Selected Speeches and Statements* (1965), pp. 18–22.

34 Perry, *Malcolm*, pp. 251–252; Breitman, ed., *Malcolm X Speaks*, pp. 18–22.

35 Malcolm X, *Autobiography*, pp. 325–370; Robert G. Weisbord, *Ebony Kinship: Africa, Africans, and the Afro-American* (1973), p. 82.

36 Malcolm X, "Statement of the Basic Aims and Objectives of the Organization of Afro-American Unity," in Bracey, et al., *Black Nationalism in America*, pp. 421–427; Goldman, *The Death and Life of Malcolm X*, p. 190; George Breitman, *The Last Year of Malcolm X: The Evolution of a Revolutionary* (1967), pp. 70–81.

37 William W. Sales, *From Civil Rights to Black Liberation: Malcolm X and the Organization of Afro-American Unity* (1994), pp. 99–161.

38 Breitman, *The Last Year of Malcolm X* (1967), p. 46; Taylor Branch, *Pillar of Fire: America in the King Years, 1963–65* (1998), p. 381.

39 Malcolm X, *Autobiography*, pp. 373–374.

40 Thomas L. Blair, *Retreat to the Ghetto: The End of a Dream?* (1977), p. 46; Goldman, *The Death and Life of Malcolm X*, p. 234.

41 Breitman, *The Last Year of Malcolm X*, p. 46.

42 Peniel Joseph, *The Black Power Movement: Rethinking the Civil Rights-Black Power Era* (2006), p. 46.

43 Malcolm X, *Autobiography*, pp. 54–58.

44 Ibid., p. 59.

45 Ibid., p. 43.

46 Ibid., p. 54.

47 Ibid., pp. 215–216.

48 Ibid., pp. 372–373.

49 Ibid., p. 348.

50 Ibid., p. 351.

51 I.F. Stone, *In a Time of Torment: 1961–1967* (1967), p. 117.

52 Malcolm X, *Autobiography*, p. 350.

53 Ibid., pp. 385, 389.

54 David Halberstam, "When 'Civil Rights' and 'Peace' Join Forces," in C. Eric Lincoln, ed., *Martin Luther King, Jr.: A Profile* (1972), pp. 66–67.

55 Breitman, ed., *Malcolm X Speaks*, p. 9.

56 Lomax, *When the World is Given*, p. 74; Archie Epps, ed., *The Speeches of Malcolm X at Harvard* (1969), p. 70.

57 George Breitman, ed., *By Any Means Necessary: Speeches, Interviews, and a Letter by Malcolm X* (1970), pp. 8–9.

58 Robert Penn Warren, *Who Speaks for the Negro?* (1965), p. 259.

59 Stephen B. Oates, *Let the Trumpet Sound: The Life of Martin Luther King, Jr.* (1982), p. 253.

60 Warren, *Who Speaks for the Negro?*, pp. 161, 197, 244; Goldman, *The Death and Life of Malcolm X*, p. 385.

61 Warren, *Who Speaks for the Negro?*, p. 261; Epps, *The Speeches of Malcolm X at Harvard*, p. 49.

62 Perry, *Malcolm*, pp. 206–212.

63 Peter Goldman, "*Malcolm X: Witness for the Prosecution*," in John Hope Franklin and August Meier, eds., *Black Leaders of the Twentieth Century*, p. 311.

64 Ibid., p. 312.

65 Ossie Davis, "Why I Eulogized Malcolm X," in John Henrik Clarke, ed., *Malcolm X: The Man and His Times* (1969), pp. 128–131; James Baldwin, *No Name in the Street* (1972), pp. 66–67.

66 Coretta Scott King, *My Life with Martin Luther King, Jr.* (1970), pp. 256–257.

67 Bruce J. Dierenfield, *The Civil Rights Movement* (2008), pp. 127–135.

68 *Report of the National Advisory Commission on Civil Disorders* (1968), p. 1.

CHAPTER SEVEN

African-American Women: Heroines and Trailblazers

I had reasoned dis out in my mind; there was one of two things I had a right to, liberty or death; if I could not have one, I would have de oder, for no man should take me alive.[1]

[Harriet Tubman]

Not until the Negro rises in his might and takes a hand in resenting such cold-blooded murders, if he has to burn up whole towns, will a halt be called in wholesale lynching.[2]

[Ida B. Wells-Barnett]

When I liberate myself, I liberate others. If you don't speak out, ain't nobody going to speak out for you.[3]

[Fannie Lou Hamer]

I think education is power. I think that being able to communicate with people is power. One of my main goals on the planet is to encourage people to empower themselves.[4]

[Oprah Winfrey]

Perspectives: African-American women as leaders

An oft-repeated observation is that the constraints operating against African-American men operated twice over for black women, who endured the double burdens of race and gender. For generations of slavery and segregation, black women bore the brunt of a white, male-dominated society dedicated to profit and prejudice, one that demeaned and exploited them at the most basic level. Not even their bodies, husbands, or babies were their own. As novelist Toni Morrison put it, "she had nothing to fall back on; not maleness, not whiteness, not ladyhood, not anything. And out of the profound desolation of her reality she may well have invented herself." Despite their bondage, black women somehow drew upon a deep reservoir of inner strength steeped in religion to overcome the degradation imposed upon them, thereby sustaining a vital sense of community and showing the way to a better life as circumstances changed. An admiring W.E.B. Du Bois wrote, "I most sincerely doubt if any other race of women could have brought its fineness up through so devilish a fire." Displaying incredible fortitude, black women eventually took their rightful place in American society, transformed that society, and rose to become pillars and pace-setters in that society.[5]

In the slave period, African women in America faced innumerable, sometimes insuperable, obstacles. Ripped away from their native lands and cultures, African women were forced to adapt to a new society that devalued them except as farmhands, house servants, nursemaids, and child-bearers. Enslaved women were experts at household tasks, and coped with a range of fieldwork under a blazing sun, disease-ridden swamps, lashings with cat-o-nine whips, damp shacks, and a fat-laden diet, all of which ensured a life of misery, if not despair. Because enslaved Africans were chattel, they were bought, sold, traded, bequeathed, or moved as the owner wished. Black women in slavery were not allowed to marry legally and sometimes witnessed their children being sold "down river" to the Deep South. White planters offered incentives, such as a new dress, a larger food ration, or a promotion to housework, if enslaved women bore, say, a sixth child—valued at several hundred dollars—for his growing "livestock." Because enslaved women had no control over their bodies, they could be made to endure forcible sexual intercourse, bear children, or nurse the children of others. The rape of black women by white men was commonplace in the slave South, which accounted for most of the racial "mixing" that whites condemned so vociferously.[6]

It was during slavery that the well-worn stereotype of Mammy arose, demeaning black women as morbidly obese, dark-skinned, preternaturally happy and loyal domestics who emasculated their husbands and neglected their own family to serve whites. As a result of these stereotypes, black women were viewed by whites as incompetent workers or mothers, or else immoral. The truth is that black women struggled against and ultimately survived a brutally exploitive, repressive system to carve out lives that protected their independence and their families as best as circumstances allowed. African-American women possessed intelligence, integrity, and imagination; were industrious and self-reliant; and were important carriers of black culture. Against all odds, they created flexible, extended kinship groups and became a powerful, but often unacknowledged, force in American society.[7]

Enslaved women resisted their captivity through individual and corporate actions. Small, often hidden, forms of resistance to the slave system on plantations included theft, foot-dragging, food poisoning, running away, and feigning illness. In these ways, women could claim a measure of control over their lives. To deny their masters another enslaved baby, black women used camphor and cotton roots as contraceptives or abortifacients. In rarer circumstances, women reportedly suffocated their newborn babies, rather than consign them to a lifetime of backbreaking fieldwork and numbing abuse.[8]

To release their millions of sisters and brothers in captivity, free black women in the North played major roles in the abolitionist movement of the early 19th century, a time when traditional gender expectations circumscribed their actions. Influenced by David Walker and William Lloyd Garrison, Maria Stewart defied societal conventions in delivering the first public lectures before racially mixed audiences, calling for emancipation, economic independence, and education for African Americans. She chastised black men for lacking "ambition and requisite courage" to revolt against slavery, a provocative charge that likely forced her early retirement from public life. Like many of her abolitionist peers, Mary Ann Shadd Cary grew up in an antislavery household, with her father selling subscriptions to Garrison's the *Liberator*. Her abolitionist fervor was distinguished by its call for a free black exodus to Canada, which she trumpeted in her own newspaper, the *Provincial Freeman*, making her the first black woman editor. Sarah Parker Remond grew up in a Salem, Massachusetts, household that hosted leading abolitionists, including Garrison and Wendell Phillips, as well as freedom-seeking slaves, and her brother was the first black lecturer for the American Anti-Slavery Society. Remond herself became a physician and, like her brother, lectured widely for the American Anti-Slavery Society, raising money from places as far away as Great Britain. The treatment that women abolitionists received spurred some of them to embrace feminism alongside abolitionism. Foremost among these was Sojourner Truth, a former slave to a Dutch family in New York, who is remembered particularly for her stirring speech, "Ain't I a Woman."[9]

American slavery ended formally in 1865 with the Union's victory over the Confederacy and the ratification of the 13th Amendment. But white assumptions of black inferiority persisted long afterwards, maiming the personalities and limiting the life options of black women and men. These racist assumptions were institutionalized through the enactment of comprehensive segregation ordinances. As a result, African Americans focused mainly on physical and emotional survival. The mercantile and industrial economy of the late 19th and early 20th centuries shut out black women, as they could not be clerks, cashiers, telephone operators, or steel workers. Black women therefore worked as domestic servants to white families or served the black community as teachers, nurses, and so on. There were efforts to mobilize black women in the club movement, as well as in black churches and the National Association of Colored Women (NACW), which spearheaded care for the infirm, orphans, and children of working mothers. In addition, women helped form the National Association for the Advancement of Colored People (NAACP) and led many of the local chapters in fighting laws and customs that inhibited black life. To help southern black migrants adjust to the wholly different rhythms of northern urban life, black women also worked in settlement houses and for the National Urban League (NUL).[10]

This wide-ranging set of organizational experiences well prepared African-American women for civil rights activism. Before the epic Civil Rights Act of 1964, black women greatly outnumbered men in civil rights groups. Black men risked losing their jobs and perhaps their lives, if they were connected to the campaign for civil rights, but black women had a long history of involvement in service and religious groups, as well as schools, that gave them organizational skills and community contacts. Because black women were more likely to be teachers, they also appreciated the importance of quality education. To attack Jim Crow practices, women registered to vote, offered themselves as plaintiffs, formulated legal arguments, raised money, lobbied politicians, distributed leaflets, joined marches, and crossed the color line in schools and restaurants. As the civil rights movement gained ground in the 1960s, black women became national figures in the political arena. The first black women in Congress were Shirley Chisholm of New York, whose West Indian father idolized Marcus Garvey, and Barbara Jordan of Texas; Carol Moseley Braun of Illinois broke the color/gender barrier in the U.S. Senate.[11]

Leaving aside these pioneering politicians, the core of this chapter focuses on the lives of six African-American women who demonstrated exceptional, if not formidable, leadership in different times, fields, and methods—abolitionist Harriet Tubman, anti-lynching reformer Ida B. Wells, educator Mary McLeod Bethune, civil rights activist Fannie Lou Hamer, diplomat Condoleezza Rice, and entertainer Oprah Winfrey. All of them came from the South, five from the Deep South. All of them were or are religious, with Christianity serving as their bedrock faith. Four of them received a college education of varying lengths. Four of them married and raised children. All but Rice have been consciously race leaders. Their stories, like so many other African-American women, have been ones of persistence and progress.

Harriet Tubman

A former slave, Harriet Tubman gained international acclaim for her remarkable exploits as an Underground Railroad operator, abolitionist, Civil War spy and nurse, suffragist, and humanitarian. For dedicating her long life to helping others, particularly in freeing scores of African Americans from enslavement, Tubman earned the nickname "Moses"—a reference to the Old Testament prophet who led enslaved Hebrews out of Egypt to freedom—and a place among America's most famous historical figures. Abolitionist Frederick Douglass wrote to her, "Excepting John Brown—of sacred memory—I know of no one who has willingly encountered more perils and hardships to serve our enslaved people than you have."[12]

Originally named Araminta, or "Minty," Harriet Greene was born into the misery of slavery in the early 1820s on a plantation on Maryland's Eastern Shore. Her parents, who had descended from the Asante people in West Africa, watched as several of their eleven children were sold to planters in the Deep South. Finally, Harriet's mother threatened to wield an axe to split open the head of any slaver who tried to sell her youngest son. As a 5-year-old, Harriet was rented to cruel and negligent neighbors who whipped her repeatedly, leaving welts and permanent scars on her back. To survive, Harriet stole a lump of sugar, and then hid in a neighbor's pig sty for five days, fighting with animals for scraps of food. When she was assigned to check muskrat traps in marshes with waist-deep, ice-cold water, she soon became too sick to work, suffering from exposure and malnutrition. Eventually, Harriet was assigned to field work, driving oxen, plowing, and hauling logs. Though farming was harsher than nursing, she preferred it, because it allowed her to escape constant beatings. When she had free time, her father took her into the woods to hunt, fish, and trap animals, valuable survival skills in later years.[13]

One day, an irate overseer threw a stone or iron weight at a runaway slave, only to have it strike 13-year-old Harriet in the forehead. She was left bleeding and unconscious, but was ordered to return to the fields without medical care two days later. The traumatic brain injury caused Harriet to have disabling seizures, pounding headaches, powerful dreams, and sleeping spells. As a devout Christian, the now-disfigured Harriet ascribed her visions to premonitions from God.[14]

In 1844, Harriet married John Tubman, a free man, but she still had to work for her master. About this time, Harriet's father was freed, and Harriet learned that her mother should have been freed as well, which embittered Harriet about the injustice of slavery. When Harriet told her husband she wanted to be free, he advised her to accept the status quo, noting that he would face death for helping a slave—including his wife—to escape captivity. Harriet was undeterred. When Harriet became ill, her owner, Ed Brodess, tried to sell her. Harriet prayed for divine intervention to change Brodess's mind, but he still brought prospective buyers to look her over. A desperate Harriet changed her prayer: "Oh, Lord, if you ain't never going to change that man's heart, kill him, Lord, and take him out of the way." A week later, Brodess died as Harriet petitioned, but his widow moved ahead with plans to sell Harriet just the same. To prevent this sale, Harriet escaped with two of her brothers in 1849, but they felt the risk was too great and returned to the plantation. In the end, only Harriet left slavery—alone and on foot—in the middle of the night, and traveled ninety miles to free land in Pennsylvania by following the North Star. At one safe haven, Harriet was told to sweep the yard to look as if she worked for the family. That night, Harriet was hidden in a cart with a burlap sack over her, and silently taken to the next friendly house. Upon reaching free soil, a relieved Harriet remarked, "I looked at my hands to see if I was the same person now I was free. There was such a glory over everything . . . and I felt like I was in heaven."[15]

Realizing how alone she was, Harriet vowed to help her family and friends gain their freedom as well. She went to Philadelphia to earn a living as a maid, and saved money to finance rescue trips for others. She also became involved in Philadelphia's large abolitionist community, which included organizers of the Underground Railroad, a clandestine network of houses, tunnels, and roads by which enslaved people escaped bondage in the South on their way to freedom in the North and southern Ontario. Working with Quakers and Methodists, Harriet Tubman made hazardous trips to the South by differing routes once or twice a year to assist slaves interested in escaping bondage. Dressed in various disguises—

once as an apparently mentally-impaired homeless man—she would either dictate messages to nearby slaves or sing out in her strong voice to make it known that she was nearby. Her signature song was, "Dark and thorny is the pathway where the pilgrim makes his ways/But beyond this vale of sorrow lie the fields of endless days." Tubman called for freedom seekers to depart on a Saturday evening, because travel on the Sabbath usually meant the risk of immediate detection was lessened or, if their absence was detected, a day's delay in organizing a posse or publicizing a reward. Armed with a sedative to silence crying babies and carrying a loaded gun, the gnome-like Tubman warned her escapees that she would shoot any of them who would surrender or return to slavery. "Keep going. A dead nigger tell no tales. Either you go on or die." A slave who gave up and returned to slavery could identify the trip organizers, the means by which messages were passed along, and the paths used for escaping.[16]

Her careful planning, ingenuity, and stamina allowed her to boast of her record. "In all my years as a railroad conductor, I never ran my train off the track and I never lost a passenger." The dangers were great indeed, for Congress had passed the Fugitive Slave Act of 1850, making it illegal to help freedom-seeking African slaves. Indeed, Tubman herself risked being returned to slavery, and twice she spotted her former owners, forcing her to improvise. On a return trip, she went to her husband's cabin to convince him to flee with her, but he had remarried and would not leave. She rescued her sister and nieces in 1850, one brother in 1851, three other brothers in 1854, and her parents in 1857, who settled on the outskirts of Auburn, New York, on land purchased from U.S. senator William Seward. As her fame spread, furious slaveholders offered large sums for her capture, but she was never betrayed. Word of her courage and success led prominent northerners, including suffragist Susan B. Anthony, educator Horace Mann, Transcendentalist lecturer Ralph Waldo Emerson, and writer Bronson Alcott to contribute to her escape fund.[17]

In 1858, Tubman helped John Brown prepare for his raid on Harpers Ferry, Virginia, the home of a federal arsenal. Brown claimed divine inspiration to make a surprise attack on the arsenal and distribute the weapons to nearby slaves to touch off a nationwide slave rebellion. A new state for freed African Americans would follow. Tubman, whom Brown called "General," raised money in Canada and recruited soldiers, but did not participate in the raid. Why she did not is uncertain, with hypotheses ranging from illness to recruiting more escaped slaves in Canada, to rescuing more family members in Maryland, to doubts about the plan's viability. Brown's sons and supporters were shot that day, and Brown was later hung for treason. Tubman mourned the deaths of her friends, and said that Brown had "done more in dying, than 100 men would in living."[18]

During the Civil War, Tubman contributed to the Union army in a variety of ways. She was a cook, laundress, nurse, scout, and spy behind Confederate lines. After the war erupted, she went to the South to assist "contrabands"—escaped slaves who were protected by the Union army. In 1862, she moved to Beaufort, South Carolina, which was occupied by the Union army, and helped hundreds of Sea Islander slaves make the transition from bondage to freedom. She also organized a cadre of black male spies and gathered information herself, identifying potential targets for the army, such as cotton stores and ammunition storage areas. The next year, she became the first American woman to command an armed military raid, when she guided a battalion of South Carolina blacks up the Combahee river, routing Confederate outposts; destroying stockpiles of cotton, feed, and weapons; and liberating 700 slaves, most of whom joined the Union army. Throughout the war, she provided desperately needed nursing care to black soldiers and hundreds of newly liberated slaves who crowded into Union camps suffering from dysentery and smallpox. Tubman spent her first paycheck to construct a laundry where freed black women could be paid for cleaning military uniforms. When the military shortchanged Tubman financially, she supported herself and her work by selling baked goods and root beer.[19]

After the war, Tubman continued her lifelong commitment of assisting others. She helped destitute children, raised money for schools to educate freedpeople, and transformed her New York residence into the Home for Aged and Indigent Colored People. She believed that her nonstop humanitarian efforts were God's lifelong directive to her: "Now do you suppose he wanted me to do this just for a day, or a week? No! The Lord who told me to take care of my people meant me to do it just so long as I live, and so I do what he told me to do." In 1869, two years after her first husband died, Tubman married Nelson Davis, a Union veteran half her age who had boarded at her home. Tubman apparently never had any children of her own, but did raise an adopted daughter with Davis.[20]

In the 1890s, Tubman embraced another cause—women's suffrage—which she believed vital to preserving the freedom of African Americans. When a white woman once asked Tubman whether she believed women should have the vote, Tubman replied, "I suffered enough to believe it." In this cause, Tubman worked with Susan B. Anthony, Emily Howland, and Elizabeth Cady Stanton, and toured the country speaking about her experiences as "Moses" and the sacrifices of other women as demonstrating the equality of the sexes. When the 15th Amendment to the U.S. Constitution was ratified, Tubman was unimpressed because it granted suffrage for black men but not women. Seeking an avenue for black women to show their own brand of leadership, Tubman co-founded and was the keynote speaker at the first annual convention of the National Association of Colored Women, which opposed lynching and Jim Crow laws, and supported women's suffrage, expanded education, and improved care for children and the elderly. Before she spoke, Tubman was introduced as the "Black Joan of Arc."[21]

Denied a military pension, Tubman struggled financially for the rest of her life. At one point, she fell prey to con artists who promised her gold hidden in the Civil War South for a discount price. She was lured into the woods, knocked out with chloroform, and robbed. Desperate to recover financially, she worked with a writer to publish two autobiographical accounts—*Scenes in the Life of Harriet Tubman* (1869) and *Harriet, The Moses of Her People* (1886). She also relied on a meager widow's pension, a Civil War nurse's pension, and a monthly $25 contribution from the NACW. Having survived brain surgery without anesthesia, Tubman died of pneumonia in 1913, probably in her early nineties, and was buried with a full military funeral. The next year, the city of Auburn closed down as a memorial tribute to Tubman, and Booker T. Washington delivered an address as her monument was dedicated: "It is most fitting and proper from every point of view that the name of Harriet Tubman should be perpetuated by means of this tablet so that her memory and deeds can live in the minds and hearts of the present generation, and can be held up as an object lesson for all time to the generations that follow."[22]

Ida B. Wells

One of the greatest of all African-American women leaders, Ida B. Wells came of age in the post-Reconstruction South, when Jim Crow was being institutionalized and racial violence was at its zenith. An influential journalist, outspoken lecturer, and social activist, she co-founded the NAACP and was a fearless and powerful voice against the barbarism of lynching; racial discrimination, especially in housing and public accommodations; and disfranchisement of women and black men. Her uncompromising message and aggressive style stood in stark contrast to the dominant black leader of the time—Booker T. Washington.[23]

A native of Holly Springs, Mississippi, Ida B. Wells was born into slavery during the Civil War to religiously devout parents who instilled in her an intense race consciousness. Her father, a carpenter, was his master's son; her mother, the daughter of an Indian man, was a cook. Both kept working for their master after they were freed. Ida's father was known as a "race man" because of his interest in politics and was named a trustee of Shaw University (now Rust College), a freedpeople's school that emphasized industrial education. Ida later enrolled at Shaw, but found its domestic science curriculum quite limiting, because she had already read Shakespeare, Dickens, and other classic works of literature. While there, she absorbed the school's missionary spirit, which reinforced the religious training she had received from her family. Eventually, Ida was expelled for confronting the school's white president, whom she accused of paying too much attention to a light-skinned African-American woman student.[24]

In 1878, a deadly yellow fever epidemic swept through Mississippi, killing Ida's parents and her infant brother. To prevent her surviving younger siblings from being assigned to different households, 16-year-old Ida supported them by becoming a teacher and taking in washing. Two years later, after her brothers were placed as apprentices, Ida took her two younger sisters to live with a relative in Memphis, Tennessee, a "hick town" on the bluff of the Mississippi river. One of its leading citizens had been Nathan Bedford Forrest, a Confederate cavalry general who had made a fortune trading slaves before serving as grand wizard of the Ku Klux Klan. With few choices available to black women, Ida obtained a teaching position, though she never liked the demanding profession. In the summers, she attended classes at Fisk University.[25]

Young Ida B. Wells soon became a civil rights crusader of the first rank. In 1883, she purchased a first-class ticket on the Chesapeake, Ohio & Southwestern Railroad for a commuter trip to her elementary teaching job north of Memphis. The conductor ordered Wells to move from the "ladies' car" to the smoky, second-class car, but she refused to relinquish her seat. When the conductor grabbed her by the arm, she resisted with all her might and bit his hand. It took three white men to forcibly remove the 5-foot Wells, who disembarked from the train at the next stop. In a remarkable stroke, she sued the railroad for failing to provide the first-class accommodations that she had paid for. She was the second African American, after Sojourner Truth, to file such a suit. Months later, the city newspaper reported that Wells—"a darky damsel"—won a judgment of $500. The victory proved short-lived, because the Tennessee Supreme Court ruled that the railroad had complied with the statute requiring "like accommodations" for African Americans. Ida was crushed: "I felt so disappointed because I had hoped [for] such great things from my suit for my people generally. I [had] firmly believed all along that the law was on our side and would, when we appealed to it, give us justice. I feel shorn of that belief and utterly discouraged, and just now, if it were possible, I would gather my race in my arms and fly away with them."[26]

Awakened by this incident, Wells used her pen to expose other areas of racial injustice. As a reporter, editor, and partner of the *Memphis Free Speech and Headlight*, a militant newspaper owned by a black Baptist minister, she found a vehicle to voice her strongly held opinions and ideas. She railed against the South's sharp escalation of racial violence and the acquiescence of blacks to Jim Crow. She created a stir when she defended African Americans in Georgetown, Kentucky, who had avenged the lynching of a black man by setting fire to the town. She also criticized the Memphis school system that employed her as a teacher. In a series of articles, she singled out a white school board member, who, she alleged, was having an affair with a black woman. Her outspokenness led to her dismissal as a teacher and to a full-time career in journalism as a tool in the crusade for black civil rights. Dubbed the "Princess of the Press," Wells claimed the writer's identity of "Exiled," portraying herself as an outcast or fugitive from the United States.[27]

In 1892, an ugly incident occurred that changed her life. Three black businessmen—Thomas Moss, Calvin McDowell, and William Stewart—established the People's Grocery Store in a black section of Memphis that dared to compete with a white-owned store across the street. White thugs attacked the black grocery store, which led to an indictment against the black businessmen for maintaining a nuisance. White deputy sheriffs dressed in civilian attire converged on the People's store after dark, prompting a group of blacks to fire on whites whom they believed to be vandals. Several deputies were wounded, leading to the arrest of a hundred black men, including the new grocery store owners. A black militia called the Tennessee Rifles stood guard over the jail, but a judge disarmed them, opening the way for a white posse to break open the black grocers' cell, abduct them, and barbarously shoot them, as punishment for allegedly raping white women.[28]

One of the black grocers was the father of Wells' goddaughter, and Ida knew him and his partners to be upstanding citizens. Wells channeled her anger into a series of inflammatory articles that denounced the lynchings and dismissed "the old thread-bare lie that Negro men rape white women." The real reason for the lynchings, Wells declared, was economic success. She suggested that African Americans flee Memphis for the newly opened Oklahoma territory, which she had visited. She wrote, "There is . . . only one thing left that we can do, save our money and leave a town which will neither protect our lives and property, nor give us a fair trial in the courts, but take us out and murder us in cold blood when accused by a white person." Heeding Wells' call, thousands of blacks headed for Oklahoma. For those who remained behind, she called for a black boycott of white-owned businesses and the segregated public transportation system that had humiliated her. By summer's end, the streetcar line was nearly bankrupt. To protect herself from angry white men, she bought a pistol and insisted that blacks must be ready to defend themselves by violent means.[29]

For the rest of her life, Wells denounced lynching as state-sponsored terrorism which allowed whites to kill African Americans with impunity. For her, social, political, and economic justice were not simply civil rights; rather, they were intrinsic to the basic tenets of Christian ideals, righteousness, and self identity. The denial of black civil rights, the lynching of black men, and the rape of black women, Wells believed, were immoral acts that contradicted her notions of civilized behavior and Christian values. In scathing articles, Wells not only excoriated the white perception that lascivious black men were everywhere raping virtuous white women, she intimated that white women might freely consent to a sexual relationship with black men. The white community was incensed, and before long, a mob broke into her newspaper office to destroy her presses. Civic leaders warned Wells that if she returned to Memphis, she would be hanged in front of the courthouse. Forced from her home, she migrated from the South, along with thousands of other African Americans. Seeking employment and refuge, she joined the staff of T. Thomas Fortune's *New York Age* as a "journalist in exile." Fortune soon recognized that if Wells were a man, she would be a force in politics, for "she has plenty of nerve, and is sharp as a steel trap." Undeterred by death threats, Wells spread her anti-lynching crusade beyond the confines of the black press to whites in the Northeast and in Britain in the early 1890s. Wells thus brought the plight of African Americans to an international audience. After all, she needed to convince the white majority that the evil of lynching was widespread and that white pressure could end it.[30]

Upon returning from Britain, Wells moved to Chicago, Illinois, where she remained for the rest of her life. There, she worked with Frederick Barnett, a black lawyer and founding editor of the *Chicago Conservator*, the city's first black newspaper. Despite long ambivalence about marriage, Wells married Barnett, a widower with two children, and bore him four more. Refusing to relinquish her identity, she hyphenated her last name, shared ownership of the *Conservator*, and combined child-rearing with public activism. When the Barnetts moved to a predominantly white neighborhood and were threatened by white toughs, Ida emerged from her house and told them she had a gun and was ready to use it to defend her family.[31]

In the early 1890s, Ida B. Wells-Barnett wrote invaluable accounts of lynching episodes, which occurred during the greatest such period in American history. Her first book was *Southern Horrors: Lynch Law in All Its Phases*, and the second was *A Red Record: Tabulated Statistics and Alleged Causes of Lynchings in the United States, 1892–1893–1894*, which graphically described the hanging, burning, and mutilation of blacks, often in front of smiling whites who watched the savagery in their Sunday-best clothes. With many white northerners unaware or dismissive of the extent and causation of lynching, Wells-Barnett compiled damning fact after fact to reveal that barbarism. A key finding was that black-on-white rape or the allegation of such rape comprised a small fraction of the reasons given by mobs for killing black men. Given the frequency of lynching, Wells-Barnett advised that "a Winchester rifle should have a place of honor in every Black home, and it should be used for that protection that the law refused to give." She believed that whites would never respect black lives until blacks themselves adopted a radically different mindset toward racial violence. "The more the Afro-American yields and cringes and begs," she declared, "the more he has to do so, the more he is insulted, outraged and lynched."[32]

After the publication of these books, Wells-Barnett worked within organizations and politics to advance the standing of African Americans. She established her local and national identity as a clubwoman with the creation of the Ida B. Wells Club—the nation's first black women's civic club—which set up a kindergarten for Chicago's black community. In 1896, Wells-Barnett helped form the National Association of Colored Women, which adopted the motto, "Lifting as We Climb," to demonstrate to "an ignorant and suspicious world that our aims and interests are identical with those of all good aspiring women." The organization's ambitious and forward-thinking agenda focused on job training, wage equity, child care, kindergartens, vocational schools, summer camps, and retirement homes. In addition, the NACW opposed segregated transportation systems and was a strong supporter of the anti-lynching movement. In subsequent years, the NACW endorsed women's suffrage and underwrote a national scholarship fund for college-bound African-American women.[33]

From 1898 to 1902, Wells-Barnett served as secretary of the Afro-American Council, the first national civil rights organization to discuss racial matters and to denounce lynching and Jim Crow. The brainchild of publisher T. Thomas Fortune, the council held its first meeting in

Rochester, New York, after the dedication of a statue commemorating the late abolitionist Frederick Douglass. The council's distinguished list of members included Booker T. Washington; his nemesis, Boston publisher William Monroe Trotter; activist and orator Mary Church Terrell; and professor W.E.B. Du Bois, among many others. It was one of the first organizations to treat men and women equally and provided a seat for women from every state in the Union. This premier organization of African Americans demanded that president William McKinley take action in the case of a black postmaster lynched in South Carolina. After a few years, the Afro-American Council collapsed in the wake of infighting and insufficient funds.[34]

Still, Wells-Barnett continued to make her mark. In 1900, she worked with Jane Addams in successfully blocking the establishment of segregated schools in Chicago. In 1909, along with Mary Church Terrell, Wells-Barnett called for a national conference on African Americans after three days of shocking racial violence in Springfield, Illinois. She became a founding member of the resulting NAACP and was placed on its executive committee. She called for the NAACP to have its own publication to express its views, which led to the establishment of the *Crisis*, ably edited by W.E.B. Du Bois for many years. Wells-Barnett later broke with the association because of its predominantly white board and its timidity in confronting racial issues. A firm believer in agitation, Wells-Barnett blamed whites for racial oppression, opposed Booker T. Washington's doctrines of compromise and accommodation, and allied herself with more radical black leaders, especially Du Bois. By the end of her career, the anti-lynching campaign, once a mainstay of female reform, had transferred to the domain of the male-dominated NAACP, an organization dedicated to professionalization and local and state control.[35]

During president Woodrow Wilson's administration, Wells-Barnett continued her activism. She joined a delegation that urged Wilson to end discrimination in assigning government jobs, but Wilson had instituted such segregation in the first place. Wells-Barnett was elected as chair of the Chicago Equal Rights League, and organized legal aid for victims of the Chicago race riots after World War I. Wells-Barnett strongly supported the efficacy of voting, and urged black men to exercise their right to vote. To secure woman suffrage, she founded the Alpha Suffrage Club of Chicago in 1913, which voted for Oscar DePriest, a "conscientious race man," as the city's first black alderman, and later as the first black U.S. congressman of the 20th century. In working for woman suffrage, Wells-Barnett planned to march in a Washington parade, only to be assigned to the rear.

Defiantly, she declared, "I shall not march at all unless I can march under the Illinois banner." She then stepped from the crowd of spectators and took her place in the Illinois state contingent. When African Americans in Chicago were denied access to existing social services, including those provided by the Young Men's and Women's Christian Associations, Wells-Barnett founded the Negro Fellowship League and a settlement house to assist southern black migrants in search of jobs and temporary shelter. As part of her work with troubled young people, Wells-Barnett served as a probation officer in a legal experiment that sought to avoid incarcerating them. As Wells-Barnett continuously searched for organizational vehicles to help African Americans, she praised Marcus Garvey's Universal Negro Improvement Association for restoring black racial pride, which led the U.S. Secret Service to brand her as a dangerous radical.[36]

In the last decade of her life, Ida B. Wells-Barnett was in poor health and was unable to exercise her leadership in a formal way. In 1924, she lost an election as president of the NACW to Mary McLeod Bethune. She later lost an election to become a representative to the Illinois state senate. By then, the uncompromising Wells-Barnett was marginalized, isolated, and sometimes maligned. Possessed of a powerful temper and characterized as a perennial outsider, she constantly wrestled with institutional barriers, male hegemony, and racism before her death from kidney failure in March, 1931. She was largely unappreciated and forgotten when she died. Decades later, when her autobiography, *Crusade for Justice* (1970), appeared, Wells-Barnett put her uncompromising attitude in a nutshell: "I felt that one had better die fighting against injustice than die like a dog or a rat in a trap."[37]

Mary McLeod Bethune

One of America's foremost black educators, Mary McLeod Bethune wore many hats in her extraordinary public career—teacher, administrator, civil rights leader, presidential adviser, government official, and humanitarian. A powerful orator of the early 20th century, she created or held leadership positions in a black college, several black women's organizations, the NAACP and the National Urban League (NUL), and the federal government. Called "the First Lady of the Struggle," Bethune was unflinching in her advocacy of a better life for African Americans through education and economic and political empowerment. She was arguably the most influential black woman in American history, comparable in stature to Frederick Douglass, W.E.B. Du Bois, and Martin Luther King, Jr.[38]

Mary McLeod Bethune was born to freed slaves in 1875 on a farm near Mayesville, South Carolina, the fifteenth of seventeen children and the first to be freeborn. Once terrorized by witnessing the lynching of a black man, Mary spent her youth picking cotton and attending a Presbyterian mission school for blacks that was five miles from her home. A star pupil, Mary received a scholarship to attend a seminary and boarding school in North Carolina that emphasized religious and industrial education, including household chores, and prepared many of its students to teach other African Americans. Mary's mother instilled in her the confidence that with an education she could succeed and that God did not discriminate among peoples. Mary became a true believer, convinced that education was the key to black advancement. Like Booker T. Washington, Bethune personified the American notion of self-help and pulling oneself up by her bootstraps.[39]

Bethune subsequently enrolled as the only black student at evangelist Dwight Moody's Institute for Home and Foreign Missions in Chicago, Illinois. She planned on becoming a missionary to Africa, but no church was willing to sponsor her because of her race. It was the greatest disappointment in her life. She returned to the South to teach black students— one of the few professional avenues available to educated black women. She recognized that "Africans in America needed Christ and school just as much as Negroes in Africa. . . . My life work lay not in Africa but in my own country." Bethune taught at several Presbyterian schools in Georgia and South Carolina, which she saw as the principal means of racial uplift. In 1898, she married Albertus Bethune, a dry goods clerk, with whom she had a son the following year. The marriage did not change Mary Bethune's priorities, because she saw no need to compromise her race work. Indeed, Bethune only intensified her mission after motherhood. Albertus wanted a traditional relationship—meaning, the husband in charge—and he soon abandoned Mary to live with his sister. This sour experience may have convinced Mary Bethune that marriage and family were secondary considerations to race advancement.[40]

After moving to Florida, Bethune observed that railroad workers and live-in maids who traveled with their wealthy employers needed a boarding school for their families. In 1904, she established the Daytona Educational and Industrial Institute for Negro Girls at a time when education for African Americans was frowned upon. The school was designed to recreate her seminary experience by educating young black women to be pious keepers of the home. Opening her school with "five little girls, a dollar and a half, and faith in God," Bethune made do with dry goods boxes for benches, charred splinters of burned logs for pens, and elderberry juice for ink. The school operated out of the head-heart-hand tradition popularized by Tuskegee educator Booker T. Washington, which in Bethune's case involved academic study, Bible study, and vocational training, especially food production and household chores at the school. Bethune expected students would raise sugar cane and other crops to put on the school's table and add money to its coffers. Eventually, the school expanded to include a nursing school and a hospital because her students were barred from the local whites-only hospital. Most of Bethune's graduates earned their livings as maids, cooks, seamstresses, and teachers.[41]

Financial support remained crucial to the school's success. As a black woman, Bethune had to work harder than black men, such as Booker T. Washington, to get financial support, even though she had the same vision and determination. Describing her most important job as "to be a good beggar," Bethune raised money by holding chicken dinners and marching her students into hotels to sing spirituals in front of tourists, and then making eloquent pleas for donations. White industrialists with summer homes in the area, including James Gamble of Procter and Gamble Company, provided financial assistance to the school, beginning Bethune's long association with prominent whites. She also made numerous trips to the North, where she met wealthy whites and spoke at churches and clubs. Booker Washington heard of Bethune's school and made several visits to Florida to see it for himself. Despite all her efforts, the Daytona Institute was always strapped for funds.[42]

Bethune made several crucial decisions to ensure her school's growth. In the 1920s, she affiliated the school with the Methodist Episcopal Church and merged it with the Cookman Institute for black men in Jacksonville, Florida, to become coeducational Bethune-Cookman College, the only historically black institution founded by a black woman. Its motto was "Enter to Learn/Depart to Serve." Increasingly, the school offered post-secondary courses, especially teacher training. As its enrollment increased, Bethune-Cookman won full accreditation as a junior college, and then as a four-year college in 1941. As the only woman of her generation to create and sustain an institution for disadvantaged youth and transform it into a college, president Bethune was awarded the NAACP's coveted Spingarn Medal.[43]

To elevate black women, Mary McLeod Bethune became a pillar in the women's club movement, which was devoted to charitable and civic work. She hosted state and regional conclaves, secured considerable resources for nonprofit organizations, and served as president of state, regional, and national federations, beginning with Florida's Association of Colored Women. During World War I, she organized food drives for American troops, bought Liberty bonds to finance the war, and donated money to American Red Cross chapters. At the same time, she pressured the Red Cross to desegregate, and was active in anti-lynching campaigns. After the 19th Amendment to the U.S. Constitution was ratified to give suffrage to women, she set an example by bringing her school's entire faculty and staff to register to vote, despite intimidation by the Ku Klux Klan. Among other objectives, Bethune rallied black women to demand adequate health and education facilities for children. She also worked closely with white women and the regional Commission on Interracial Cooperation. One of the more pressing issues of the day was to provide a rehabilitation facility for delinquent black girls, and Bethune created one when the state did not.[44]

In 1924, Bethune was elected president of the National Association of Colored Women, the highest position that an African-American woman could then achieve. She defeated Ida Wells-Barnett because the members thought Wells-Barnett was too confrontational. The NACW was the premier secular organization for black women, and it was the first all-black group to operate in the nation's capital. During her term, Bethune was far from passive or conformist, expecting the NACW to act as a voice for black women the world over. She called on members to think of the national organization before their state affiliations. Bethune also pushed for black women to participate in public affairs, bought a home in Washington, D.C., to serve as the NACW's national headquarters, paid an executive secretary to run the organization, and affiliated with predominantly white voluntary associations, including the National Council of Women (NCW), General Federation of Women's Clubs, National Council of Jewish Women, and National Council of Catholic Women. Bethune demanded that all NCW events be desegregated. When that policy was violated, a furious Bethune and other NACW members walked out. Bethune also raised scholarship funds so that young black women could help to emancipate the masses by teaching.[45]

When the NACW persisted in operating as a largely state and local organization unable to unite behind national issues, the 60-year-old Bethune poured her energies into the presidency of the new National Council of Negro Women (NCNW), which would become the largest organization of and for African-American women. Founded in 1935, the NCNW presented a unified and authoritative voice of a half million black women to the federal government to secure a fairer slice of the social welfare pie and to condemn lynching, job discrimination, disfranchisement in

the United States, and colonialism in Africa. Borrowing an idea from
W.E.B. Du Bois, Bethune succeeded in placing black women leaders
in the Children's Bureau, Council of National Defense, Farm Security
Administration, U.S. Housing Authority, Office of Civilian Defense, and
National Youth Administration. When black women were excluded from
the War Department, Bethune protested the slight: "We cannot accept any
excuse that the exclusion of Negro representation was an oversight. . . .
We are incensed!" The War Department bowed to Bethune's demand
and accepted the NCNW as a member of its women's advisory council
for government programs.[46]

During the Great Depression, Bethune became the point person for
African Americans in Franklin D. Roosevelt's (FDR) administration—the
first black person to be a presidential adviser. Roosevelt appointed her as
director for Negro affairs of the National Youth Administration (NYA),
the most influential position a black woman had ever held in the federal
government. At one point, Bethune spoke fervently to Roosevelt about
the need for presidential action: "We have been taking the crumbs for
a long time. We have been eating the feet and head of the chicken long
enough. The time has come when we want some white meat." Among
her accomplishments, she spent large sums to help black students and
secured jobs for African Americans, particularly as assistants to state
NYA directors. She also supported equal pay for NYA employees and
sought to ensure that blacks participated in NYA programs in proportion
to the general population. To recruit a cohort of thirty competent black
staffers, Bethune established an informal Federal Council on Negro
Affairs—the "Black Cabinet"—which advised FDR to strengthen black
support of the New Deal, decrease racial discrimination, and increase
the number of government jobs for African Americans, not to mention
black voters for Roosevelt's Democratic party. When the president was
preoccupied or uninterested in Bethune's racial requests, she went straight
to her dear friend Eleanor Roosevelt.[47]

With only one African American in Congress, Bethune held the unofficial
title of "race leader at large," serving in a leadership role of the NCNW,
the NAACP, the Urban League, and the Association for the Study of
Negro Life and History, as well as being president of her college. She
also served on the boards of Planned Parenthood and the Girl Scouts,
and was a member of the League of Women Voters. She operated with
consummate political skills, using her charismatic personality, superb
speaking ability, and keen insight into racial relations to advance her
views. Her activities in the short term helped to win for African Americans

specific exceptions to unfavorable governmental practices; in the long term, they helped to place civil rights on the national agenda. Bethune conceded that the doors of opportunity were not yet open wide enough, but she told African Americans that a new day had dawned and that the New Deal deserved their continuing support, despite its imperfect record on civil rights.[48]

World War II presented another opportunity for African Americans to make racial progress, and Bethune was a central player in this effort. She remarked, "If we accept and acquiesce in the face of discrimination, we accept the responsibility ourselves and allow those responsible to salve their conscience by believing they have our acceptance and concurrence. We should, therefore, protest openly everything . . . that smacks of slander." She joined with A. Philip Randolph in the March on Washington Movement in 1941, which successfully pressured FDR to sign Executive Order 8802, directing U.S. war industries to hire a million African Americans during the duration of the conflict. She played a key role in establishing the Fair Employment Practice Committee, a temporary, federal watchdog agency designed to reduce, if not eliminate, job discrimination during wartime; it served as a template for the permanent Equal Employment Opportunity Commission created under president Lyndon Johnson. In addition, Bethune found a way to give black pilots training and pressured the secretary of war to commission black women as officers of the Women's Army Auxiliary Corps (WAAC).[49]

After World War II, Bethune attended the San Francisco Conference, which led to the organization of the United Nations and the writing of the United Nations Charter. At first, the U.S. State Department refused to make the NCNW part of the U.S. delegation, which had no black groups. Bethune persisted, and she was the only black woman with official status at this pivotal meeting. Along with W.E.B. Du Bois, Bethune represented African-American concerns in the coalition of world leaders, which included people of color from Europe, Africa, and the Caribbean. Bethune regarded the United Nations' work as of the highest priority because through it, "the Negro" became "integrated into the structure of peace and freedom of all people, everywhere." After the conference, Bethune concluded, "We still have a long way to go," but the NCNW did work closely with the UN's Commission on the Status of Women.[50]

After World War II ended, Bethune took charge with her customary zeal, working to improve conditions for African Americans in the boom period. Under her leadership the NCNW addressed the problems of unemployment, low wages for laborers, inadequate housing and health care for the poor, rising prices for consumer goods, the poll tax on voting, and social security coverage that excluded domestics and farmers. Bethune pointed out that the United States could not defeat communism or avoid the charge of hypocrisy in the Cold War era unless it lived up to its ideals of justice for all by ending racial segregation and discrimination. America could not, she maintained, "find and bring to down-trodden nations the Holy Grail of peace and international accord while our hands are soiled with the lyncher's rope and the bull whip." She acknowledged that blacks had "made some well defined gains in many areas" but were "still, to a large extent, a subject people—men and women with little more than colonial status in a democracy." She called on African Americans to change this deplorable state of affairs with the ballot.[51]

At age 80, Mary McLeod Bethune died of a heart attack in her home in 1955, the same year that Rosa Parks touched off the Montgomery bus boycott. Bethune had become the nation's preeminent symbol of black dignity and achievement. Her last will and testament included the following passage: "I leave you love. I leave you hope. I leave you the challenge of developing confidence in one another. I leave you a thirst for education. I leave you a respect for the use of power. I leave you faith. I leave you racial dignity. I leave you a desire to live harmoniously with your fellow men. I leave you, finally, a responsibility to our young people." The media acknowledged the passing of this educator, women's leader, and civil servant extraordinaire. *Time* noted, "nothing on earth could stop Mary Bethune." The nondenominational *Christian Century* asserted that "the story of her life should be taught every school child for generations to come." The *Washington Post* affirmed, "So great were her dynamism and force that it was almost impossible to resist her. . . . Not only her own people but all America has been enriched and ennobled by her courageous, ebullient spirit." Commenting on Bethune's improbable rise to influence, the *Daytona Beach Evening News* editorialized: "To some she seemed unreal, something that could not be. . . . What right had she to greatness? . . . The lesson of Mrs. Bethune's life is that genius knows no racial barriers."[52]

Fannie Lou Hamer

Fannie Lou Hamer became the female face of the civil rights movement of the 1960s, and helped change America's perspective on democracy. In one sense, she was typical of the grassroots movement—the foot soldiers—who mobilized in southern communities to destroy racism. Her desperately poor native state of Mississippi had a black population of 40 percent, but only 6.7 percent of the voters were black, and in some counties with a large black majority, none of the voters was black. After three tries, Hamer succeeded in registering to vote, but paid a terribly steep price for doing so. A short, stout figure with a strong bearing and a thunderous voice, Hamer was an unforgettable and inspirational figure, with a penchant for lapsing into song as she led others to register. Her signature line was, "I'm sick and tired of being sick and tired," which encapsulated her hard-scrabble life and her burning desire for a better one.[53]

Born in 1917, Fannie Lou Townsend was the granddaughter of a slave and the youngest of twenty children born to a homemaker and a Baptist minister who was also a bootlegger. Fannie Lou contracted polio as an infant, leaving her with a permanent limp. The next year, her parents moved to Sunflower County in the Mississippi delta, where they worked as sharecroppers, dependent on whites for nearly everything, including their land, ramshackle housing, and supplies. Fannie Lou's parents scraped up enough money to buy a cow and several mules, but a malicious white neighbor poisoned their animals with insecticide to prevent the Townsends from succeeding. As a result, Fannie Lou grew up hungry in a tar paper shack that lacked electricity, plumbing, or hot water; she slept on a cotton sack filled with straw; and she wore shoes made of pieces of cloth wrapped around her feet. Observing the relative ease of white life, Fannie Lou concluded that "to make it you had to be white." Her mother responded sharply: "I don't ever want to hear you say that again, honey. Don't you say that, because you're black! You respect yourself as a little child, a little black child. And as you grow older, respect yourself as a black woman. Then one day, other people will respect you." Such respect would be long in coming. One day, the plantation owner offered 6-year-old Fannie Lou a can of sardines, a box of Crackerjacks, and a gingerbread cookie if she would pick 30 pounds of cotton in a week. Fannie Lou gladly took the bribe and settled into the world of field work. By age 12, Fannie Lou could pick as much as her parents—200–300 pounds of cotton a day—so she dropped out of school to help full-time.[54]

In 1942, Fannie Lou married a tractor driver named Perry "Pap" Hamer, who lived on the same plantation outside of Ruleville, Mississippi. Fannie Lou Hamer spent the next 18 years chopping cotton and serving as the plantation's timekeeper and bookkeeper. To survive, Pap Hamer made and sold liquor in a small juke joint. After Fannie Lou suffered at least one miscarriage, the couple adopted two neighborhood girls whose parents were unable to care for them. One of their girls died of chronic malnutrition and internal bleeding. Hamer's hope of bearing children herself ended when she was sterilized without her knowledge or consent. She had been diagnosed with a small cyst in her stomach, and so checked into a hospital to have it removed. But the operating physician took the liberty of performing a complete hysterectomy, even though there was no medical indication that this procedure was necessary. This "Mississippi appendectomy" was a common phenomenon in the rural South, as white doctors decided, with state government encouragement, that many poor black women were unfit to reproduce.[55]

In August, 1962, Fannie Lou Hamer, then 45-years-old, was stunned to hear from civil rights activists that black people had a constitutional right to vote, if they were registered. She had always understood that politics was "white folks' business." Hamer volunteered to register, thinking, "The only thing they could do to me was to kill me, and it seemed like they'd been trying to do that a little bit at a time ever since I could remember." When she went to the county clerk's office, she was given the usual runaround, and she failed the literacy test that required black applicants to read, copy, and interpret part of the state constitution to the satisfaction of a white clerk. After she left, the clerk telephoned her landowner, who gave Hamer a choice—either stop attempting to register to vote or be fired from her job and be evicted from her home. Hamer replied, "I didn't try to register for you. I tried to register for myself." In that one instance of defiance, her life was forever changed. The house she sought refuge in was riddled with bullets, but Hamer realized that when "they kicked me off the plantation, they set me free."[56]

After Hamer registered on her third try, she joined the Student Nonviolent Coordinating Committee (SNCC) as a field secretary-at-large and received $10 a week to help other African Americans register to vote. Risking death while singing a favorite song, "This Little Light of Mine," she went into their homes, fields, and churches to explain the importance of voting and the process of voter registration. In June, 1963, Hamer led a group of African Americans to an out-of-state literacy workshop. On the way home, the bus stopped in Winona, Mississippi, so the passengers could eat. State troopers attacked them with billy clubs and arrested them for disorderly conduct. At the county jail, they were cursed at, shoved, and kicked. Hamer heard the screams of her friends, and then it was her turn. Her tormentors told her, "You, bitch, you, we gon' make you wish you was dead." Two large black prisoners were ordered to beat her with a blackjack until she was left battered and bleeding, suffering permanent damage to her kidneys and left eye. Hamer overheard white policemen talk about ditching their bodies in a nearby river. On learning of Hamer's arrest, Martin Luther King, Jr. called the Southern Christian Leadership Conference (SCLC) headquarters in Birmingham, Alabama, to drive to Mississippi to post bond. Once freed, Hamer, by now only half conscious, was brought to a doctor, who stitched and bandaged her wounds.[57]

Fannie Lou Hamer's close encounter with death strengthened her resolve to tear down the racist system in Mississippi. Utterly fearless, Hamer would exercise her own brand of leadership until she died fifteen years later. Through song and plainly-spoken words, she urged her neighbors to educate themselves, register to vote, join the civil rights movement, and work collectively, both economically and politically, to change their lives. Hamer believed that all black women, regardless of class, were obliged to support justice: "Whether you have a Ph.D., D.D., or no D, we're in this bag together. And whether you're from Morehouse [College] or Nohouse, we're still in this bag together." Hamer became convinced that real change required political leverage, principally by electing black people in areas with a black majority. Because most African Americans were not allowed to vote and could not belong to the Democratic party or run for office, wealthy plantation owners—such as U.S. senators John Stennis and James O. Eastland (who came from Hamer's Sunflower County)—won reelection to Congress repeatedly. Their seniority allowed them to chair important committees, giving them inordinate power over the nation's political affairs. Hamer and others had concluded that the only way to oppose the segregated Mississippi political machine was to establish a racially integrated state Democratic party, which they did in April, 1964, with the Mississippi Freedom Democratic Party (MFDP).[58]

In the summer of 1964, SNCC activists organized a new kind of voter registration drive. The drive was the brainchild of Bob Moses, who directed the Council of Federated Organizations (COFO), a coalition of civil rights groups. The key idea was to recruit hundreds of northerners—mainly whites—who could bring a greater visibility to the campaign for black voting and Freedom Schools where children would receive tutoring in the fundamentals of education. At orientation, Hamer candidly warned volunteers about the grave dangers they faced and urged the fearful to leave before putting their lives on the line. In June, the first contingent of volunteers arrived in Meridian, Mississippi, and one of them—Andrew Goodman of New York was murdered that first day of summer, along with fellow activists Michael Schwerner, another New Yorker, and James Chaney, a local black plasterer.[59]

During what came to be known as Freedom Summer, civil rights volunteers blanketed the state of Mississippi, and signed up 80,000 unregistered black "voters" who were denied the ballot by local officials. Precinct and county primaries were held, and delegates to a state convention were elected. At the MFDP state convention, sixty-four blacks and four whites were chosen as delegates to the upcoming Democratic National Convention in Atlantic City, New Jersey. Aaron Henry, a black pharmacist, was elected chair and Hamer, vice-chair of the MFDP. The MFDP's stated goal was to challenge the seating of the regular party's all-white Mississippi delegation and to be seated in its place as the state's rightful delegation. This scenario infuriated president Lyndon Johnson, whose greatest concern was to beat the Republican candidate, U.S. senator Barry Goldwater of Arizona, in the general election. Johnson worried that he would lose white southern political support if MFDP members were seated. He well remembered how president Harry Truman had barely won reelection in 1948 after southern Democrats had backed diehard segregationist Strom Thurmond of South Carolina. Having played an instrumental part in the passage of the monumental Civil Rights Act of 1964, Johnson could not comprehend why black southerners were not satisfied, and he ordered the Federal Bureau of Investigation (FBI) to keep tabs on Freedom Democrats. While the new law outlawed racial discrimination in public places, it did not secure black voting rights, which Hamer and many others felt was at the heart of the civil rights struggle.[60]

On August 22nd, the Democratic party's credentials committee met before a national television audience to hear MFDP's request to be seated. Many civil rights leaders testified, including Martin Luther King, but it was Hamer's tearful testimony that riveted the nation. She described the hard life of Mississippi blacks and the way they were locked out of the political process. She explained that in her own county, 80 percent of the 8,000 white residents of voting age were registered, while only 1.1 percent of the 13,000 black residents of voting age were registered. She told of her beating in the Winona jail. She challenged the committee to do the right thing, saying, "If the Freedom Democratic Party is not seated now, I question America. Is this America, the land of the free and the home of the brave, where we have to sleep with our telephones off the hook because our lives be threatened daily, because we want to live as decent human beings—in America?" It was one of the most moving and important speeches of the civil rights era. But president Johnson denounced that "illiterate woman," and ordered an impromptu press conference to pull television cameras off of Hamer.[61]

Johnson pressured his expected vice-presidential running-mate, U.S. senator Hubert Humphrey of Minnesota, a well-known liberal on race, to quiet the reformers. In a Faustian bargain, Humphrey compromised his principles and orchestrated a proposal that denied the MFDP's petition to supplant the lily-white Mississippi delegation. The credentials committee would select two "Freedom Democrats"—Aaron Henry, president of Mississippi's NAACP, and Ed King, the white chaplain of the all-black Tougaloo College—to sit in the convention as delegates-at-large with no voting rights. The electrifying Hamer was blackballed for stirring up trouble. In addition, it was determined that at future conventions, no delegations would be allowed from states that discriminated against black voters. Even so, the MFDP found the offer of two token seats insulting. At a face-to-face meeting, Hamer scolded Humphrey for his all-consuming ambition: "Well, Mr. Humphrey, do you mean to tell me that your position is more important to you than four hundred thousand black people's lives? . . . I'm going to pray to Jesus for you." Humphrey started crying, as did Hamer. Martin Luther King, along with Roy Wilkins of the NAACP, James Farmer of Congress of Racial Equality (CORE), and Bayard Rustin, favored accepting the proposal, believing that African Americans could not afford to alienate the Democratic party which had just pushed through the sweeping Civil Rights Act. The president had control of the convention, and he forced the proposal through. SNCC, angered by the treatment of the MFDP, drew increasingly away from the "conservatism" of King and SCLC.[62]

After her appearance at the Democratic Convention, Hamer worked on a multitude of issues, including educational opportunity, an end to hunger, and low-cost housing, which amounted to community building. Hamer obtained a Head Start school, raised funds for a low-income housing project, started a low-income daycare center, and brought a garment factory to town to create jobs. As day laborers replaced sharecroppers, Hamer organized the Mississippi Freedom Labor Union and a 680-acre Freedom Farm Corporation, a nonprofit cooperative that helped hundreds of needy families raise food and livestock. She had concluded that government programs, while well intentioned, only kept poor people dependent on them. In addition to these initiatives, Hamer was a founder of the National Welfare Rights Organization and the National Women's Political Council. Like Martin Luther King, Hamer connected the Vietnam war and continuing poverty in America. "We want," she said, "to end the wrongs such as fighting a war in Vietnam and pouring billions over there, while people in . . . Mississippi and Harlem and Detroit are starving to death." In running for Congress as a regular Mississippi Democrat in 1965, she cast her first official vote, for herself, in a losing campaign that included death threats; she later lost a race for the Mississippi state senate. She also served as the plaintiff in a lawsuit that resulted in the overturning of election results in two Mississippi counties because African Americans had been denied the vote. In 1968, Hamer was part of the Mississippi state delegation that headed triumphantly to the Democratic party's national convention, which gave her a standing ovation.[63]

Before Fannie Lou Hamer died of cancer in 1977 at age 59, an interviewer asked her if she had faith that the system would "ever work properly." Hamer replied, "We have to make it work. Ain't nothing going to be handed to you on a silver platter, nothing. That's not just black people, that's people in general—[the] masses. See, I'm with the masses. . . . You've got to fight. Every step of the way, you've got to fight." At her funeral, Hamer was recognized as a truly great leader of her time, one who "shook the foundations of this nation," according to Andrew Young, one of Martin Luther King's closest aides. "None of us would be here now, if she hadn't been there then. She was a great woman who refused to be turned around and she helped turn the nation around."[64]

Condoleezza Rice

Rising from her youth in the segregated South, Condoleezza Rice became a Stanford University professor and top American foreign policymaker, the second woman and second African American to serve as national security adviser, and the first black woman and second African American to serve as secretary of state, both under president George W. Bush. As Bush's trusted confidante, she became one of the prominent faces of the United States around the world and one of its most influential women, especially after the radical Islamic attacks of September 11, 2001, on American soil. Rice played a crucial part in shaping the most aggressive U.S. foreign policy in modern history, with wars launched against Afghanistan and Iraq during her time in office. Because of Rice's steely demeanor, forceful posture on world problems, and her penchant for dressing fashionably, she earned the nickname of "Warrior Princess." By overcoming the obstacles of race and gender in the age of segregation, Rice's rise to power in diplomatic circles was in some sense almost as remarkable as Barack Obama's odyssey to the White House.[65]

Born soon after the *Brown* school desegregation decision of 1954, Condoleezza ("Condi") Rice was the only child of John Wesley Rice,

Jr., a college-educated high school gym teacher and football coach in Birmingham, Alabama, and a Presbyterian minister on Sundays at the small church founded by his father. When he went to register to vote, local Democrats administered a "civics test" that required black applicants to guess the number of beans in a large jar on the registrar's desk. Rice was insulted and joined the Republican party. Her mother, Angelena, was a music and science teacher and church organist who loved opera, and so named Condoleezza after an Italian musical term, *con dolcezza*, which means to play "with sweetness." One of Angelena Rice's students was baseball Hall-of-Famer Willie Mays, and another was Richard Arrington, Jr., Birmingham's first black mayor.[66]

Condoleezza grew up in Titusville, Alabama, a middle-class neighborhood of black educators, physicians, and government workers, many of whom worked in Birmingham, the city that Martin Luther King, Jr. called "by far the worst big city in race relations in the United States." As a child, Condoleezza could not use dressing rooms in department stores; was barred from going to the circus, amusement parks, and the city's swimming pools; and was intentionally served bad food at restaurants. During this time, the Birmingham Ku Klux Klan unleashed a violent reign of terror that included arson, bombings, and burning crosses in order to frighten, if not kill, African Americans. A prime target was the Rev. Fred Shuttlesworth, the fearless minister of Bethel Baptist Church and a founder of the SCLC, whose home and church were bombed while he slept. A bomb also destroyed the home of civil rights attorney Arthur Shores, soon after he won the right of black children to attend Birmingham's public schools.[67]

Despite Birmingham's deep-seated racism, Condoleezza remembered, "My parents had me absolutely convinced that . . . you may not be able to have a hamburger at Woolworth's but you can be President of the United States." To insulate their daughter from that hate-filled world, the fiercely protective Rices had Condoleezza use their bathroom at home, rather than accept the indignity of Jim Crow arrangements. Because the Rices owned an automobile, Condoleezza never had to ride in the back of a segregated bus. In the bootstrap tradition of Booker T. Washington, the watchwords in the Rice household were self-reliance and self-improvement. The Rices advised their daughter that she would have to know white culture better than whites did and be "twice as good" as whites in order to overcome racism built into American society. A quick study, Condoleezza soon mastered their Steinway grand piano, figure skating, and French, and also took years of lessons in ballet, deportment, and the violin. Her father, the football coach, taught Condoleezza strategy and tactics, which led her to love football and adopt football thinking when viewing global politics. In school, Condoleezza earned excellent grades from the outset, skipping the first and seventh grades.[68]

In 1963, Martin Luther King, Jr. organized demonstrations in Birmingham against racism, and some of the demonstrators were John Rice's young students, who were subjected to angry police dogs and powerful fire-hoses. Rice sometimes brought his daughter to watch the protests unfold, but he had no intention of allowing his daughter to join King's risky children's crusade. Years later, Condoleezza asked her father why he had not marched with King. The elder Rice replied, "If somebody strikes me, I'm going to fight back, and then I would have ended up dead, and you would have been left without a father." According to Fred Shuttlesworth, Rice was afraid his small church would be destroyed and could not be rebuilt. After a federal court ordered Birmingham's schools to desegregate, the Klan murdered four girls attending the Sixteenth Street Baptist Church on a Sunday morning. Condoleezza felt the shudder of the bomb blast as she sat in her father's church pew two miles away; she had been a playmate of one of the girls who died. To forestall more violence, her father joined an armed patrol at night. Many Birmingham blacks blamed King for the bombings, but King would have none of it. "What murdered these four girls?" he asked rhetorically. "The apathy and the complacency of many Negroes who will sit down on their stools and do nothing and not engage in creative protest to get rid of this evil."[69]

Condoleezza's father made a series of career changes that left Birmingham's racism behind, thereby opening doors to his daughter. When Condoleezza was a teenager, he became an assistant dean of admissions at the University of Denver in Colorado, a far more racially tolerant community than Birmingham. Dean Rice increased scholarship funds for minority students, initiated an exchange program with historically black colleges, advocated recruitment of black faculty, and organized a seminar series "to bring the real story of the American Negro to the Denver community." One of the speakers was civil rights legend Fannie Lou Hamer. It was in this environment of heightened racial consciousness that Condoleezza attended an integrated Catholic school. Condoleezza was always a classic overachiever, but her school's guidance counselor offered the stunning assessment that she was not college material. Rice's parents assured their daughter that the assessment, which was based on her first standardized test, was wrong and urged her to persevere. She entered the University of Denver at the age of 15—the same age that

Martin Luther King started at Morehouse College. At one point, a professor expounded on physicist William Shockley's theory that African Americans were devolving, provoking Condoleezza to stand up and cry out, "I'm the one who speaks French. I'm the one who plays Beethoven. I'm better at your culture than you are. This can be taught!"[70]

At first intent upon becoming a concert pianist, Condoleezza switched majors after being inspired by the professor she called her "intellectual father"—political scientist Josef Korbel, a Czech refugee and a Soviet specialist who taught a class on international politics. His daughter, Madeleine Albright, became U.S. secretary of state under president Bill Clinton. About her change in career plans, Condoleezza quipped, "Instead of studying Russian composers, I decided to study Russian generals." Put another way, she became a student—and ultimately, a practitioner—of power. Condoleezza graduated from the University of Denver with Phi Beta Kappa honors and then earned a master's degree at the University of Notre Dame. At a time when the United States and the Soviet Union signed the Anti-Ballistic Treaty and the Strategic Arms Limitation Talks (SALT) I, followed by the Soviet invasion of Afghanistan, Rice returned to Denver to complete a doctoral degree in international studies. Her dissertation investigated the relationship between the Czechoslovak Communist party and its army.[71]

Even before finishing graduate school, Rice received a fellowship from Stanford University to study at its Center for International Security and Arms Control. She was the first woman to receive this fellowship. Fluent in French and Russian, with an expertise in the Soviet Union, she made a highly favorable impression, and was offered an assistant professorship of political science at Stanford. She filled her lectures on war with football references, and became a popular, award-winning instructor. She also published her dissertation and another book entitled, *The Gorbachev Era*, an account of the leadership of Mikhail Gorbachev, the Soviet Union's reformist head of state. Such accomplishments helped Rice obtain fellowships from the Hoover Institution from Stanford, the Ford Foundation, and the Council on Foreign Relations. Aside from playing her piano, Rice was a workaholic. She was engaged once to a professional football player, but she never married and has no children.[72]

Rice benefited from connections she made with white Republican administration officials, including former secretary of state George Schultz and general Brent Scowcroft, who had been national security adviser. Scowcroft was so impressed with Rice's understanding of Soviet ideology and her insights on nuclear planning that when he became national security adviser again, this time under president George H.W. Bush, he appointed Rice to the National Security Council as its Soviet expert. Along with secretary of state James Baker, Rice studied the dramatic events of the late 1980s, including the end of the Cold War, the dissolution of the Eastern Bloc's Warsaw Pact, and the collapse of the Soviet Union. Rice helped Bush prepare for his summit meetings with Gorbachev, where the topics of conversation included arms control, expansion of trade, and the transition of Eastern European nations away from totalitarianism. Bush proudly introduced Rice to Gorbachev, "This is Condoleezza Rice. She tells me everything I know about the Soviet Union."[73]

To preserve her job at Stanford, Rice resigned from the National Security Council in 1991, and soon became Stanford's youngest, first female, and first non-white provost—the administrator who oversees the school's budget and academic programs—a post she held for six years. In appointing her, Stanford's president later acknowledged Rice's "exceptional talents," but added it "would be disingenuous for me to say that the fact that she was a woman, the fact that she was black, and the fact that she was young weren't in my mind." Her responsibilities included eliminating a large budget deficit and defending the institution from accusations of misusing government grant money intended for military research. There was some faculty dissension about Rice's governing style. "I told people," she explained, "I don't do committees." In addition, she drew protests when she stopped applying affirmative action to tenure decisions and unsuccessfully sought to consolidate the university's ethnic community centers. She did succeed in turning the school's record deficit into a record surplus. "That was the toughest job I ever had," Rice told an interviewer. Her demanding duties did not prevent her from remaining in the public eye, publishing scholarly works and editorials for *Time* and major newspapers.[74]

When Texas governor George W. Bush, the former president's son, ran for president himself, Rice tutored him on foreign affairs. At the Republican national convention which picked Bush as its nominee in 2000, Rice delivered a speech laying out her conviction that "America's armed forces are not a global police force. They are not the world's 911," a reference to the nation's emergency telephone number. The indefatigable Rice became Bush's trusted national security adviser, and worked 15-hour days gathering relevant information for the president. In her conception of the office, she "rarely" told the president her private opinions.[75]

On September 11, 2001, a shadowy Islamic fundamentalist group known as al-Qaeda (Arabic for "the foundation") orchestrated the deadliest attack on American soil by hijacking commercial airliners and flying them into New York City's World Trade Center towers and the Pentagon, America's military nerve center near Washington, D.C. At first, Rice and other officials retreated into an underground bunker, where she handled the crisis with her trademark calm, telephoning world leaders that the U.S. government was still functional. Responding to the 9/11 attacks, Rice supported sending American troops to Afghanistan—the apparent retreat for al-Qaeda mastermind Osama bin Laden—as well as to Iraq, then ruled by the despotic hand of Saddam Hussein, who was believed by the Bush administration to have weapons of mass destruction powerful enough to reach the United States. In an unprecedented move, Congress asked Rice to explain why the administration was caught unprepared for a disaster of this magnitude.[76]

America's invasion of Iraq was initially successful, taking U.S. troops just a hundred hours in March, 2003, to liberate the capital of Baghdad from Hussein's iron grip. As it turned out, the defeat of Hussein was relatively easy, compared to the instability, chaos, and deadly bombings by al-Qaeda that followed. These serious postwar problems in no way dissuaded Rice from justifying the American invasion of Iraq: "There are those who say, 'Well, if you didn't go into Iraq, there wouldn't be terrorists there.' They weren't some place drinking tea and playing Scrabble. These are hardened jihadists who will fight us some place. And if they want to fight us in Iraq, where we are 140,000 strong, better there than in New York City again." After the invasion disproved claims that Hussein had nuclear weapons—the pretext for war—critics called Rice's claims a "hoax," a "deception," and a "demagogic scare tactic."[77]

Rice was not seriously tarnished by such criticisms, and became U.S. secretary of state after general Colin Powell resigned the office in 2004. In this position, Rice followed a pragmatic policy of "transformational diplomacy," which had several components. One component dealt with American diplomats. She relocated them to the places where they were needed most, including China, India, Brazil, Egypt, Nigeria, Indonesia, South Africa, and Lebanon. She also required them to serve in hardship posts in Afghanistan, Angola, Iraq, and the Sudan; to gain expertise in at least two regions; and to become fluent in two foreign languages, such as Arabic, Chinese, and Urdu. For Rice, certain seemingly intractable problems, such as terrorism, drug trafficking, and diseases, necessitated regional solutions. Rice also believed that the U.S. and its allies should build and sustain stable, democratic nations the world over, especially in the Middle East. In addition, Rice called for the United States to work individually with nations to improve their infrastructure in order to reduce their dependence on U.S. foreign aid. The net effect of transformational diplomacy, Rice asserted, would be to "maintain security, fight poverty, and make democratic reforms" in the targeted countries and improve their legal, economic, health care, and education systems. Similarly, Rice identified certain countries, such as Belarus, Burma, Cuba, Iran, North Korea, and Zimbabwe, as "outposts of tyranny" that threatened world peace and human rights, and insisted that the United States should foster freedom in these countries. As she initiated diplomatic efforts around the world on behalf of the Bush administration, she continued the style of diplomacy defined by Henry Kissinger and James Baker, two Republican secretaries of state.[78]

Critics faulted Rice for a lack of a coherent foreign policy vision and an inability to prevent a complete breakdown in relations between the U.S. State Department and secretary Donald Rumsfeld's U.S. Defense Department. Some white men questioned the competency of Rice, the first black woman to direct U.S. foreign policy. Relying on her considerable intelligence and ability, Rice reminded her critics of powerful world leaders who were women: "Haven't they heard of [former English prime minister] Margaret Thatcher, [former Indian prime minister] Indira Gandhi, or Cleopatra [the Queen of Egypt] for that matter?" At the same time, Rice was never identified with so-called "black issues," which led some African Americans to view her with suspicion. *Washington Post* columnist Eugene Robinson asked, "How did [Rice] come to a worldview so radically different from that of most black Americans". *Black Commentator* thought Rice suffered from "profound personal disorientation," and was "a black woman who doesn't know how to talk to black people." Rice defended herself from such criticisms, remarking, "Why would I worry about something like that? . . . The fact of the matter is I've been black all my life. Nobody needs to tell me how to be black." Several other prominent African Americans, including former politicians Mike Espy, Andrew Young, and Kweisi Mfume, along with journalist Clarence Page and Dorothy Height of the National Council of Negro Women, defended Rice and her worthiness to work on an international stage.[79]

After her government service concluded with the end of the second Bush administration, Rice returned to Stanford University as a professor and senior fellow at the Hoover Institution. *Newsweek* writer Evan Thomas offered this assessment of Rice's life and career: "At an early age, she drove right through the boundaries of race and chased excellence and accomplishment all the way to the northwest corner office of the West

Wing." During her tenure as secretary of state, *Forbes* ranked Condoleezza Rice as the most powerful woman in the world.[80]

Oprah Winfrey

Talk-show host, actor, and producer, Oprah Winfrey rose from a troubled inner-city background to become the most famous and richest African-American woman in history. As the "queen of the talk shows," her influence on American popular culture has been pervasive, stemming from her uncanny style of hosting her Emmy Award-winning television program and her extraordinary generosity for humanitarian causes. Her message of love, redemption, and forgiveness possesses a universal appeal, and she believes it will change the world, one person at a time.[81]

In 1954, Oprah Winfrey—her name was to be "Orpah," after a biblical character—was born in Kosciusko, Mississippi, to Vernita Lee, an unmarried teenager, and, reportedly, a farmer who had fought in World War II. Oprah's mother soon looked for work in the North, leaving Oprah to live with her grandmother, Hattie Mae Lee. Watching her grandmother cleaning, doing yard work, and washing clothes in a pot of boiling water convinced Oprah that her life "won't be like this; it will better." Grandmother Lee taught Oprah to read at an early age, and she recited long poems and Bible verses in her Baptist church, where she was dubbed "preacher" and "little Jesus." When she was 6-years-old, Oprah went to live with her mother, who was working as a maid and living on welfare in Milwaukee, Wisconsin. While her mother worked, young Oprah was allegedly raped repeatedly by a cousin and an uncle. This continuing emotional trauma and lack of a stable family life made Oprah increasingly uncontrollable, and she stole money, destroyed property, used drugs, and traded sexual favors for money. At age 14, Oprah was pregnant, but the premature baby boy died soon after birth.[82]

Even as her life spiraled out of control, Oprah retained hope. Seeking refuge, she went to live in Nashville, Tennessee, with Vernon Winfrey, a barber whom she believed to be her biological father. Strict but encouraging, Winfrey imposed a curfew and required her to read a book a week and then write a report on it. Oprah flourished in this structured environment, becoming a popular honors student. After she placed second in the nation in dramatic interpretation, a local radio station hired her to read newscasts during her senior year of high school. Winfrey received a full scholarship to study speech and the performing arts at Tennessee State University, a historically black school. In her first year at college, the 17-year-old

Oprah won the Miss Black Tennessee beauty pageant. She later dropped out of college to pursue a broadcasting career, this time as a television reporter and news anchor.[83]

After a false start in Baltimore, Maryland, Winfrey's career flourished when she moved to Chicago, Illinois, in 1984 to host *AM Chicago*, a faltering half-hour, early morning talk show. She changed the show's subject matter from lightweight fare to topical and controversial issues. It quickly surpassed the long-running *Phil Donahue Show* to become the city's top-ranked talk show. A year later, it was expanded to an hour and renamed the *Oprah Winfrey Show*. Oprah improvised on her show, removing cue cards and scripts and empathizing with her emotional guests, sometimes by holding their hand, sometimes by revealing a trauma from her life. The values that Oprah consistently emphasized were ones that black women had long relied upon over the course of centuries of oppression, namely, community, family, religious convictions, and education. The more intimate, confessional-style show was broadcast nationally, and became one of the most successful and highest-ranked television programs in history, with a weekly viewership of 20 million Americans and additional millions in a hundred countries worldwide. The *Oprah Winfrey Show* was especially popular among white women, Democrats, political moderates, Baby Boomers, Generation Xers, and Americans in the South and along the East coast.[84]

Winfrey's show earned three daytime Emmy Awards in its first year—Outstanding Host, Outstanding Talk/Service Program, and Outstanding Direction—the first of many such awards. *Time* wrote, "Few people would have bet on Oprah Winfrey's swift rise to host of the most popular talk show on TV. In a field dominated by white males, she is a black female of ample bulk. . . . What she lacks in journalistic toughness, she makes up for in plainspoken curiosity, robust humor and above all empathy. Guests with sad stories to tell are apt to rouse a tear in Oprah's eye. . . . They, in turn, often find themselves revealing things they would not imagine telling anyone, much less a national TV audience. It is the talk show as a group therapy session." The *Wall Street Journal* coined the term "Oprahfication," meaning public confession as a form of therapy. TV columnist Howard Rosenberg described Oprah Winfrey as "a roundhouse, a full course meal, big, brassy, loud, aggressive, hyper, laughable, lovable, soulful, tender, low-down, earthy and hungry."[85]

In its early years, the *Oprah Winfrey Show* imitated the model of other daytime talk shows, which featured sensational stories and controversial, if not outrageous, guests to attract viewers. But since the 1990s, with popular tabloid talk shows such as *Jerry Springer* and *Jenny Jones* appealing to base instincts with programs on pornography, prostitutes, and psychopaths, Oprah reinvented her show, focusing on self-help, healthy living, and spirituality, drawing an even larger audience. She hosted shows about heart disease in women, homeopathy, the paranormal phenomenon, New Age religion, gift-giving, and home decoration. Winfrey also addressed formerly taboo subjects, including rape, incest, drug abuse, and crime. With a half-brother who died of AIDS, she was particularly interested in problems faced by gays and lesbians. On one program, Winfrey had members of the audience stand up one after another, giving their names and announcing their sexual orientation. When the subject of gay marriage arose, a woman in Oprah's audience complained that gays constantly flaunted their sex lives and that she was tired of it. Winfrey had an immediate rejoinder: "You know what I'm tired of? Heterosexual males raping and sodomizing young girls. That's what I'm tired of." The audience erupted into a screaming, standing ovation.[86]

Although Winfrey was criticized for promoting a kind of societal narcissism and controversial self-help fads, many viewers identified with Winfrey's ongoing battles to overcome adversity. One theme was her weight, which fluctuated widely, and she often brought her chef and personal trainer on the program to discuss better health. This was no small matter in a society where thin body types are the ideal. Winfrey confessed that overeating helped her deal with the pain of a long string of abusive relationships. At one point, Winfrey went on a 400-calories a day liquid diet and lost 67 pounds. A triumphant Winfrey paraded around her television studio in tight-fitting blue jeans, pulling a little red wagon with the amount of beef fat she had lost. Within a year, Winfrey gained all her weight back. She nevertheless posed for an entertainment magazine as a sexy, sequin-clad millionaire; in reality, her head was superimposed over Swedish-American actor Ann-Margret's colorized body.[87]

Despite her record of yo-yo dieting, Oprah's lifetime theme of personal transformation made her a pop psychologist for America's masses. She was dubbed America's "moral monitor," "today's Billy Graham," the "high priestess" of the New Age movement, and "a really hip and materialistic Mother Teresa." At the same time, she did not repudiate the Christianity in which she was raised: "As I study the New Age movement, it all seems to say exactly what the Bible has said for years, but many of us were brought up with a restricted, limited understanding of what the Bible said." A few nuggets of her wisdom follow:

"I believe you're here to live your life with passion. Otherwise, you're just traveling through the world blindly—and there's no point to that."

"Don't complain about what you don't have. Use what you've got. To do less than your best is a sin. Every single one of us has the power for greatness, because greatness is determined by service—to yourself and to others."

"I am a woman in progress. I'm just trying like everyone else. I try to take every conflict, every experience, and learn from it. All I know is that I can't be anybody else. And it's taken me a long time to realize that."

"I always feel if you do right, right will follow."[88]

Winfrey became so popular that top entertainers, politicians, and authors coveted invitations to appear on her program. Winfrey often managed to get these prominent guests to talk about issues that affected them directly, such as cancer, charity work, or substance abuse. Her prime-time interview with reclusive pop singer Michael Jackson drew 100 million viewers, the fourth most watched program in television history. As the years rolled along, some of her regular guests, including "Dr. Phil" McGraw, a psychologist, Dr. Mehmet Oz, a cardiologist, and Rachael Ray, a celebrity chef, went on to host enormously successful television shows of their own.[89]

Winfrey's dominance of the daytime talk-show field did not satisfy her acting and producing itch, especially for classic African-American literature. For her poignant portrayal of Sofia, the distraught housewife, in film director Steven Spielberg's adaptation of Alice Walker's novel, *The Color Purple*, Winfrey received Oscar and Golden Globe nominations. Winfrey received positive reviews for her performance in *Native Son*, a movie version of Richard Wright's classic novel. She also produced and starred in the feature film *Beloved*, an adaptation of the book written by Nobel prize-winning novelist Toni Morrison; a film adaptation of Zora Neale Hurston's novel, *Their Eyes Were Watching God*; and a successful Broadway musical version of *The Color Purple*. In addition to her film and theater roles, Winfrey produced and appeared in several dramatic television productions, including *The Women of Brewster Place*, *There Are No Children Here*, and *Before Women Had Wings*.[90]

Oprah Winfrey's influence on American society and culture was significant and measurable. When she hosted a program about mad cow disease, a horrified Winfrey suddenly exclaimed to her nationwide audience that she would never eat another hamburger. Beef sales plummeted, and the Texas cattle industry sued Winfrey for damages, only to lose in court.

A relieved Winfrey greeted her adoring fans outside the courthouse to say, "Free speech not only rules, it rocks!" In 1996, she launched the wildly influential "Oprah's Book Club." She endorsed the works of authors she admired, a majority of whom were women, including Toni Morrison and Oprah's longtime friend, Maya Angelou. When Winfrey endorsed books by largely unknown authors, their books reached the top of the bestseller lists overnight, sometimes selling a million more copies. She became the most powerful book marketer in the United States, a role usually held by white men. Winfrey received an honorary National Book Award for her influential contribution to reading, and the National Book Foundation gave her a gold medal for the same reason. Her book club later shifted gears, endorsing classic works, such as Alan Paton's *Cry, The Beloved Country*.[91]

Winfrey's business and personal interests have been wide ranging, and almost every endeavor has been successful. Haunted by memories of abuse, Oprah Winfrey championed children's rights and animal rights. In 1994, president Bill Clinton signed a bill into law that Winfrey had proposed, creating a nationwide database of convicted child abusers. To help track down accused child molesters, she initiated "Oprah's Child Predator Watch List." Apart from being a successful talk-show host, a producer, and an actor, Winfrey co-founded "Oxygen Media" in 1998, a cable channel and interactive network for "independent minded, high-achieving women." Two years later, Winfrey and the Hearst Corporation published *O, The Oprah Magazine*, the most successful start-up in the history of the industry. *O* carried Winfrey's trademark message of hope and empowerment for "women for the 21st century," as her magazine's mission statement put it. Both Oxygen Media and *O* are aimed at "busy" women between 18 and 49 years old, the most desirable demographic from a business perspective. Indeed, *O* subscribers tend to be professional women who do not have time to watch Oprah's television show. In a shrewd move, Winfrey established Oprah.com, an interactive website, which offered a cross-purpose platform linking her talk show, magazine, and book club.[92]

Oprah Winfrey managed her career superbly, and she became the highest-paid performer on television. At its height, the *Oprah Winfrey Show* made $150 million a year, and as owner and producer of that show, Winfrey paid herself $100 million. In 2003, *Forbes* disclosed that Winfrey was the first African-American woman to become a billionaire and, later, the richest self-made woman of any color. Much of Winfrey's wealth came from her company, Harpo ("Oprah" spelled backwards)

Productions, Inc., which produced the *Oprah Winfrey Show*, making Winfrey one of three women in the history of television and film—along with Mary Pickford and Lucille Ball—to own their own production studios. Ownership of the syndication rights made Winfrey even wealthier. Winfrey explained her success by referring to heroic black women who preceded her: "I am where I am today because of the bridges that I crossed. Sojourner Truth was a bridge. Harriet Tubman was a bridge. Ida B. Wells was a bridge. Madame C.J. Walker was a bridge. Fannie Lou Hamer was a bridge."[93]

Oprah Winfrey's extraordinary wealth allowed her to live luxuriously, with a 42-acre ocean-front estate in California and homes in Hawaii and the Caribbean island of Antigua, but she has also been an exceedingly generous philanthropist, donating more than a tithe of her annual income to charity. She contributed millions of dollars toward education at her alma mater, Morehouse College, and the United Negro College Fund, as well as the Oprah Winfrey Scholars Program for African Women at New York University's Robert F. Wagner Graduate School of Public Service. Her Angel Network of 150,000 contributors donated $80 million for charitable programs in thirty countries, such as building dozens of new schools and rebuilding homes after Hurricane Katrina devastated the Gulf coast. She spent $40 million of her own money to build the Oprah Winfrey Leadership Academy for Girls near Johannesburg, South Africa, and $5 million more for a state-of-the-art Boys & Girls Club building in her hometown in Mississippi. Winfrey also presented a $100,000 "Use Your Life Award' to people who used their lives to benefit the lives of others. *BusinessWeek* identified her the greatest black philanthropist in American history, with $300 million in gifts. The National Academy of Television Arts and Sciences named Winfrey as its first recipient of the Bob Hope Humanitarian Award.[94]

Winfrey used her considerable clout to endorse Barack Obama for the presidency. It was her first foray into politics. She hosted a fundraiser for Obama and appeared with him at campaign events. She told one large crowd, "Dr. [Martin Luther] King dreamed the dream. But we don't have to just dream the dream any more. We get to vote that dream into reality by supporting a man who knows not just who we are, but who we can be." According to Gallup polls, Winfrey's endorsement made some whites uneasy, if not angry, with this apparent racial bonding with the sole black candidate, and her favorable ratings slipped from 74 to 66 percent, and her unfavorability ratings increased by 50 percent. One analysis estimated that Winfrey delivered a million votes to Obama as he defeated Hillary

Clinton in a close race for the Democratic party's nomination. On election night, a tearful Winfrey remarked, "My job was to make people, or allow people, to be introduced to Obama who might not have been at the time. I wanted him elected, and I think I did that."[95]

Winfrey inspired people worldwide with her example of overcoming great odds to achieve great success financially, spiritually, and socially. Her rise was not unlike Booker T. Washington's example of rising from slavery to become the most popular and influential African American of his day. Winfrey has been honored with superlatives and showered with awards, including more than forty Emmys for best daytime television show. The National Academy of Television Arts and Sciences finally retired the Emmy for Winfrey, recognizing her one more time with an award for lifetime achievement: "For her profound influence over the way people the world over read, eat, exercise, and think about themselves and the world around them, Oprah Winfrey has been called 'the most powerful woman in the world.' " *Time* named her one of the "100 Most Influential People of the 20th Century," and *New York Times* columnist Maureen Dowd concurred with this assessment: "[Oprah] is the top alpha female in this country. She has more credibility than the president. Other successful women, such as Hillary Clinton and [home decorator] Martha Stewart, had to be publicly slapped down before they could move forward. Even Condi [Rice, the secretary of state] has had to play the protégé with Bush. None of this happened to Oprah—she is a straight ahead success story." *Vanity Fair* wrote, "Oprah Winfrey arguably has more influence on the culture than any university president, politician, or religious leader, except perhaps the Pope."[96]

After her television program appeared 5,000 times over a quarter century, Winfrey announced a career change. In 2011, she undertook a $200 million broadcasting venture with the Discovery Health Channel, which was renamed the Oprah Winfrey Network (OWN). Her ambitious goal, she declared, was a 24/7 network with mostly original programming that would "inspire and entertain people around issues of money, weight, health, relationships, spirit, helping people to raise their children and give back, teaching people to be all that they can be in the world."[97]

Assessment

For much of African-American history, women remained largely in the background, as males assumed leadership roles. The black church has almost always been headed by men, but women have filled the pews and collection plates, sat on committees, and organized events. The reform organizations, such as the NAACP, CORE, and SCLC, as well as black nationalist groups, such as the Nation of Islam and the Black Panthers, were invariably headed by men, but the foot soldiers who did the difficult work of motivating local people to get involved in the struggle were women more often than not. Women created the possibility for change by holding their families together in often dire circumstances and providing financial support for activists. The tactics that black women used to build and strengthen their communities included raising families and filling a variety of roles, including teaching, organizing, protesting, fund-raising, government service, and media appearances. After the Civil War, black women established their own organizations to add weight to their hopes for a better life, including the NACW and the NCNW. The issues remained remarkably similar over the generations, as women fought against dehumanization and racial violence and for education, the franchise, equal employment opportunity, and an end to Jim Crow in public life.

Some black women leaders, such as Harriet Tubman, Ida B. Wells, and Fannie Lou Hamer, showed raw courage in risking their lives for freedom, while Oprah Winfrey and other current leaders have reaped the benefits of the freedom their forebears won. All of the women profiled in this chapter were shrewd, skillful speakers, who sought to change the world as they found it. Most of them were indefatigable activists in the drive to upend the unjust, oppressive, and racist system into which they had been born. In many ways, black women leaders, like their black male counterparts, depended on white support, such as that offered by abolitionist Thomas Garrett, New York governor William Seward, settlement house activist Jane Addams, businessman James Proctor, First Lady Eleanor Roosevelt, and presidents Franklin D. Roosevelt and George W. Bush. In the final analysis, however, these women transcended the restrictive sphere that limited African Americans and succeeded because of their own vision, intelligence, and drive. They refused to accept either a subordinate or peripheral position for themselves or for African-American women as a whole. Fannie Lou Hamer once addressed the role and responsibility of black women "to support whatever is right, and to bring in justice where we've had so much injustice."[98]

References

1 Sarah Bradford, *Harriet, The Moses of Her People* (1886), p. 29.

2 James West Davidson, *"They Say": Ida B. Wells and the Reconstruction of Race* (2008), p. 122.

3   Elsia Kelly, *The Melting Pot* (2008), p. 72.

4   Brian Lanker, *I Dream a World: Portraits of Black Women Who Changed America* (1999), p. 66.

5   Paula J. Giddings, *When and Where I Enter: The Impact of Black Women on Race and Sex in America* (1984), p. 33; Dawn Keetley and John Pettegrew, eds., *Public Women, Public Words: A Documentary History of American Feminism*, vol. 3 (2002), p. 74.

6   Deborah Gray White, *Ar'n't I a Woman? Female Slaves in the Plantation South* (1999); Jacqueline Jones, *Labor of Love, Labor of Sorrow: Black Women, Work, and the Family from Slavery to the Present* (1986).

7   Jeanne Noble, *Beautiful, Also, Are the Souls of My Black Sisters: A History of the Black Woman* (1978), pp. 77–88.

8   Giddings, *When and Where I Enter*, pp. 39–46; Liese M. Perrin, "Resisting Reproduction: Reconsidering Slave Contraception in the Old South," *Journal of American Studies* 35 (2001): 255–274.

9   Shirley J. Yee, *Black Women Abolitionists: A Study in Activism, 1828–1860* (1992); Marilyn Richardson, ed., *Maria W. Stewart: America's First Black Woman Political Writer, Essays and Speeches* (1987); Jane Rhodes, *Mary Ann Shadd Cary: The Black Press and Protest in the Nineteenth Century* (1998); Nell Irvin Painter, *Sojourner Truth: A Life, A Symbol* (1996), pp. 112–120.

10   Giddings, *When and Where I Enter*, pp. 89–117, 135.

11   Ibid., pp. 261–297; Shirley Chisholm, *Unbought and Unbossed* (1970); Mary Beth Rogers, *Barbara Jordan: American Hero* (2000).

12   Bradford, *Harriet*, pp. 134–135.

13   Kate Clifford Larson, *Bound for the Promised Land: Harriet Tubman, Portrait of an American Hero* (2004), pp. 8–10, 15–41.

14   Sarah Bradford, *Scenes in the Life of Harriet Tubman* (1869), pp. 14–15.

15   Ibid., p. 19.

16   Jean Humez, *Harriet Tubman: The Life and the Life Stories* (2003), pp. 19–22; David S. Reynolds, *Waking Giant: America in the Age of Jackson* (2008), p. 183; Darlene Clark Hine and Kathleen Thompson, *A Shining Thread of Hope: The History of Black Women in America* (1998), pp. 89, 115–117; Noble, *Beautiful, Also, Are the Souls of My Black Sisters*, p. 45.

17   Catherine Clinton, *Harriet Tubman: The Road to Freedom* (2004), p. 192.

18   Larson, *Bound for the Promised Land*, pp. 158–159, 161–166, 174, 177; Clinton, *Harriet Tubman*, pp. 126–128, 132, 134–135; Jean Humez, *Harriet Tubman*, p. 39.

19 Clinton, *Harriet Tubman*, pp. 147–149, 156–157, 164–166, 186–187,
    193–195; Larson, *Bound for the Promised Land*, pp. 195, 204, 209–216,
    225–226, 276–279.

20 Humez, *Harriet Tubman*, p. 260; Clinton, *Harriet Tubman*, p. 198; Larson,
    Bound for the Promised Land, p. 260.

21 Clinton, *Harriet Tubman*, pp. 191–192; Larson, *Bound for the Promised
    Land*, pp. 273, 275, 287; Beverly Lowry, *Harriet Tubman: Imagining a Life*
    (2007), p. 372.

22 Larson, *Bound for the Promised Land*, pp. 255–259, 264–265, 282; Clinton,
    Harriet Tubman, pp. 196, 201, 215–216.

23 Henry Louis Gates, Jr. and Cornel West, eds., *The African-American
    Century: How Black Americans Have Shaped Our Country* (2000),
    pp. 35–38.

24 Ida B. Wells-Barnett, *Crusade for Justice: The Autobiography of Ida B.
    Wells*, ed. Alfreda M. Duster, (1970), pp. 7–14; Linda O. McMurry, *To
    Keep the Waters Troubled: The Life of Ida B. Wells* (2000), pp. 3–14; Paula
    J. Giddings, *Ida: A Sword Among Lions: Ida B. Wells and the Campaign
    Against Lynching* (2009), pp. 30–31.

25 McMurry, *To Keep the Waters Troubled*, pp. 14–23.

26 Ibid., pp. 24–31; Mia Bay, *To Tell the Truth Freely: The Life of Ida B. Wells*
    (2007), p. 55.

27 Wells-Barnett, *Crusade for Justice*, pp. 35–66 *passim*.

28 Ibid., pp. 47–52.

29 Ibid., p. 63; Bay, *To Tell the Truth Freely*, p. 89.

30 Wells-Barnett, *Crusade for Justice*, pp. 61–63, 85–102, 107–113.

31 Ibid., pp. 239–243, 247, 249.

32 Ida B. Wells, *Southern Horrors: Lynch Law in All Its Phases* (1892); Ida B.
    Wells, *A Red Record: Tabulated Statistics and Alleged Causes of Lynchings
    in the United States, 1892–1893–1894* (1895).

33 McMurry, *To Keep the Waters Troubled*, pp. 248–252, 267–268; Patricia
    A. Schechter, *Ida B. Wells-Barnett & American Reform, 1880–1930* (2001),
    pp. 179, 181; Philip S. Foner and Robert James Branham, eds., *Lift Every
    Voice: African-American Oratory, 1787–1900* (1998), p. 799; Giddings,
    When and Where I Enter, pp. 410–432.

34 Wells-Barnett, *Crusade for Justice*, pp. 242–245, 256–268, 328–329.

35 Ibid., pp. 322–328, 342, 392–394, 401.

36 McMurry, *To Keep the Waters Troubled*, pp. 293–303; Schechter, *Ida B.
    Wells-Barnett & American Reform*, pp. 4–5, 155–156, 161–162, 170–171,
    186–199, 202–213, 221, 304–305.

37 Bay, *To Tell the Truth Freely*, pp. 9, 314–328.

38 Gates and West, eds., *The African-American Century*, pp. 42–45.

39 Rackham Holt, *Mary McLeod Bethune: A Biography* (1964), pp. 1–32.

40 Amy Alexander, *Fifty Black Women Who Changed America* (1999), p. 46;
Joyce A. Hanson, *Mary McLeod Bethune & Black Women's Political
Activism* (1999), pp. 51–53.

41 Hanson, *Mary McLeod Bethune*, pp. 56–65.

42 Ibid., pp. 65–74.

43 Ibid., 83–90; "Mrs. Bethune: Spingarn Medalist," *Crisis* 42 (July, 1935):
202, 212.

44 Hanson, *Mary McLeod Bethune*, pp. 78–79, 91–99.

45 Ibid., pp. 99–101, 104–113, 116.

46 Ibid., pp. 165–166; Tracey A. Fitzgerald, *The National Council of Negro
Women and the Feminist Movement, 1935–1975* (1985), pp. 1–25; Bettye
Collier-Thomas, *N.C.N.W., 1935–1980* (1981), pp. 1–7, 27–28; Paula J.
Giddings, *When and Where I Enter*, p. 229; Dorothy Height, *Open Wide
the Gates: A Memoir* (2003), pp. 82–87, 93–94; Hine and Thompson,
A Shining Thread of Hope, pp. 250–252.

47 Hanson, *Mary McLeod Bethune*, pp. 120–163; Joyce B. Ross, "Mary
Bethune and the National Youth Administration: A Case Study of Power
Relationships in the Black Cabinet of Franklin D. Roosevelt," *Journal of
Negro History* 60 (1975): 1–28; Nancy J. Weiss, *Farewell to the Party of
Lincoln: Black Politics in the Age of FDR* (1983), pp. 136–156.

48 Kwame Anthony Appiah and Henry Louis Gates, Jr., *Africana: Civil Rights,
An A-to-Z Reference of the Movement that Changed America* (2004), p. 70;
Hanson, *Mary McLeod Bethune*, pp. 4, 179.

49 Audrey Thomas McCluskey and Elaine M. Smith, *Mary McLeod
Bethune: Building a Better World, Essays and Selected Documents*,
(1999), p. 26.

50 Hanson, *Mary McLeod Bethune*, pp. 192–193.

51 Ibid., p. 193.

52 Polly Welts Kaufman, *National Parks and the Woman's Voice: A History*
(2006), p. 227; Elaine Smith, "Introduction," *Mary McLeod Bethune Papers:
The Bethune Cookman College Collection, 1922–1955*. Black Studies
Research Sources microfilm project (1995).

53 Gates and West, eds., *The African-American Century*, pp. 249–251;
Jerry DeMuth, " 'Tired of Being Sick and Tired,' " *The Nation* 198
(1 June 1964): 549.

54 Kay Mills, *This Little Light of Mine: The Life of Fannie Lou Hamer* (1993), pp. 3–13; Rosetta E. Ross, *Witnessing & Testifying: Black Women, Religion, and Civil Rights* (2003), pp. 90–97.

55 Ross, *Witnessing & Testifying*, pp. 97–98; Chana Kai Lee, *For Freedom's Sake: The Life of Fannie Lou Hamer* (1999), pp. 18–22; Joyce A. Ladner, "Fannie Lou Hamer: In Memoriam," *Black Enterprise* 7 (May, 1977): 56.

56 Mills, *This Little Light of Mine*, p. 119; Lee, *For Freedom's Sake*, pp. 23–34.

57 Lee, *For Freedom's Sake*, pp. 45–60.

58 Ibid., pp. 61–68; Manning Marable and Leith Mullings, eds., *Let Nobody Turn Us Around: Voices of Resistance, Reform, and Renewal, An African American Anthology* (2009), p. 398.

59 Eric R. Burner, *And Gently He Shall Lead Them: Robert Parris Moses and Civil Rights in Mississippi* (1994), pp. 133–160; Bruce Watson, *Freedom Summer: The Savage Season that Made Mississippi Burn and Made America a Democracy* (2010), pp. 63–64, 77–104.

60 Burner, *And Gently He Shall Lead Them*, pp. 160–168; Lee, *For Freedom's Sake*, pp. 85–87.

61 Lee, *For Freedom's Sake*, pp. 87–90.

62 Ibid., pp. 90–100; Timothy Thurber, *The Politics of Equality: Hubert H. Humphrey and the African American Freedom Struggle* (1999), p. 155.

63 Lee, *For Freedom's Sake*, pp. 103–162; Neil A. Hamilton, *American Social Leaders & Activists* (2002), p. 182.

64 Interview of Fannie Lou Hamer, Civil Rights Documentation Project, University of Southern Mississippi, 14 April 1972; Ladner, "Fannie Lou Hamer: In Memoriam."

65 Elisabeth Bumiller, *Condoleezza Rice: An American Life, A Biography* (2007), pp. xxi–xxii.

66 Bumiller, *Condoleezza Rice*, pp. 3–10; Antonia Felix, *Condi: The Condoleezza Rice Story* (2002), p. 7; Condoleezza Rice, *Extraordinary, Ordinary People: A Memoir of Family* (2010), pp. 20–29.

67 Laura Flanders, *Bushwomen: Tales of a Cynical Species* (2004), pp. 31–32; Taylor Branch, *Parting the Waters: America in the King Years, 1954–63* (1988), p. 684; Bumiller, pp. 11–13; Rice, *Extraordinary, Ordinary People*, pp. 83–87.

68 Bumiller, *Condoleezza Rice*, pp. 13–18, 23–25; Felix, *Condi*, p. 36.

69 Bumiller, *Condoleezza Rice*, pp. 26–35; Rice, *Extraordinary, Ordinary People*, pp. 88–100.

70 Flanders, *Bushwomen*, pp. 37–38; Marcus Mabry, *Twice as Good: Condoleezza Rice and Her Path to Power* (2007), pp. 93–94.

71 Bumiller, *Condoleezza Rice*, pp. 47–78.

72 Ibid., pp. 79–93.

73 Felix, *Condi*, p. 7.

74 Leslie Montgomery, *The Faith of Condoleezza Rice* (2007), p. 143.

75 Mabry, *Twice as Good*, pp. 150–157, 169–177.

76 Bumiller, *Condoleezza Rice*, pp. 131–172.

77 Ibid., pp. 199–229.

78 Maria Pinto Carland and Candace Faber, eds., *Careers in International Affairs*, 8th ed., (2008), p. 107. For on-site reporting of Rice's work as secretary of state, see Glenn Kessler, *The Confidante: Condoleezza Rice and the Creation of the Bush Legacy* (2007).

79 "Expert on Soviets Named to National Security Council," *Jet* 76 (17 April 1989): 25.

80 Evan Thomas, "Their Faith and Fears," *Newsweek* 140 (11 September 2002): 36.

81 Gates and West, eds., *The African-American Century*, pp. 379–382.

82 Kitty Kelley, *Oprah: A Biography* (2010), pp. 18–40; Helen S. Garson, *Oprah Winfrey: A Biography* (2004), pp. 7–29.

83 Kelley, *Oprah*, pp. 41–74; Garson, *Oprah Winfrey*, pp. 29–32.

84 Bernard M. Timberg, *Television Talk: A History of the TV Talk Show* (2002), pp. 136–138; Janice Peck, *The Age of Oprah: Cultural Icon for the Neoliberal Era* (2008), p. v.

85 Garson, *Oprah Winfrey*, p. 35; Timberg, *Television Talk*, p. 327.

86 Peck, *The Age of Oprah*, pp. 1–8; Joshua Gamson, *Freaks Talk Back: Tabloid Talk Shows and Sexual Nonconformity* (1999), pp. 55–56, 111, 114, 116, 202.

87 Jeffrey Louis Decker, *Made in America: Self-Styled Success from Horatio Alger to Oprah Winfrey* (1997), pp. 117–119.

88 Ann Oldenburg, "The Divine Miss Winfrey?: Many See Oprah as Spiritual Leader; Others Don't Believe," *USA Today* (11 May 2006), p. D1; Marcia Z. Nelson, *The Gospel According to Oprah* (2005); Maria McGrath, "Spiritual Talk: The Oprah Winfrey Show and the Popularization of the New Age," in Jennifer Harris and Elwood Watson, eds., *The Oprah Phenomenon* (2007), pp. 125–145; Janet Lowe, *Oprah Winfrey Speaks: Insights from the World's Most Influential Voice* (2001), pp. 124, 134, 167.

89 Peck, *The Age of Oprah*, p. 206.

90 Kitty Kelley, *Oprah: A Biography* (2010), pp. 124–125, 166, 188, 210–211, 220–224, 324–325, 353, 355; Helen S. Garson, *Oprah Winfrey: A Biography* (2004), pp. 8, 19, 89.

91 Cecilia Konchar Farr, *Reading Oprah: How Oprah's Book Club Changed the Way America Reads* (2005); Malin Pereira, "Oprah's Book Club and the American Dream," in Harris and Watson, eds., *The Oprah Phenomenon*, pp. 191–205.

92 Peck, *The Age of Oprah*, pp. 103, 189, 202–203.

93 Kelley, *Oprah*, pp. 213–220; Melanie L. Campbell, " 'Whispering Out Loud' Series Marks Bridge to Change, Champions Concerns of Women," *Washington Afro* (11 March 2009), http://ncbcp.org/news/in_the_news/whispering_out_loud_melanie/, (3 December 2010); Alexander, *Fifty Black Women Who Changed America*, p. 283.

94 Oprah's Angel Network, http://oprahsangelnetwork.org/ 2010 (24 November 2010); Nelson, *The Gospel According to Oprah*, p. xii.

95 Kelley, *Oprah*, pp. 430–440; Audie Cornish, "Oprah and Obama Tour Early-Voting States," National Public Radio, 10 December 2007, http://www.npr.org/templates/story/story.php?storyId=17067193 (3 December 2010); Peck, *The Age of Oprah*, pp. 223–224; Trystan T. Cotten, "Irony and Contradiction in Harpo's Production of Their Eyes Were Watching God," in Trystan T. Cotten and Kimberly Springer, eds., *Stories of Oprah: The Oprahfication of American Culture* (2010), p. 176.

96 "Oprah Winfrey's Official Biography: Honorary Achievements," 10 September 2010, http://www.oprah.com/pressroom/Oprah-Winfreys-Official-Biography/10; Susie Mackenzie, "Woman of Mass Derision," *Guardian* (11 March 2006), p. 28.

97 David Lieberman, "Oprah Gets Her Own Cable Network, Launching in '09," *USA Today* (15 January 2008), http://www.usatoday.com/money/media/2008-01-15-oprah-cable-channel_N.htm.

98 Jacquelyn Grant, "Fannie Lou Hamer," in Jesse Carney Smith, ed., *Notable Black American Women* (1992), p. 443.

CHAPTER EIGHT

Jesse Jackson: The Rainbow Man

I've always developed a tension—a tension in my own mind about the place I'm assigned to and the place I deserve to be. That's why I resist the press calling me a black leader.... I'm a moral leader who just happens to be black.[1]

[Jesse Jackson]

We can move from the slave ship to the championship! From the guttermost to the uppermost! From the outhouse to the courthouse! From the state house to the White House![2]

[Jesse Jackson]

Jackson's rise to prominence...was fueled by a number of factors; central among them were his impressive knack for self-promotion and the dispirited and uncertain conditions prevailing within the Afro-American population.[3]

[Adolph L. Reed, Jr.]

Perspectives: From Black Power to political power, 1960s

By the mid-1960s, the black protest movement had achieved its most notable victories. The Civil Rights Act of 1964 and the Voting Rights Act of 1965 abolished the formal practices of segregation and eliminated literacy and other tests that had been used to prevent African Americans from registering as qualified voters. Yet there were divisions within the civil rights coalition. The older, established organizations and their leaders resented the publicity given to younger elements, such as the Congress of Racial Equality (CORE) and the Student Nonviolent Coordinating Committee (SNCC), and there were tensions and jealousies between the leaders themselves. Roy Wilkins of the National Association for the Advancement of Colored People (NAACP), for example, resented Martin Luther King, Jr.'s preeminence as the primary symbol and spokesperson of the civil rights struggle. At one point, U.S. attorney general Robert Kennedy reminded president John F. Kennedy that the administration should keep in mind that "Roy Wilkins hates Martin Luther King."[4]

Nor were younger activists satisfied with the state of the civil rights movement. SNCC field secretaries believed that King's style of leadership discouraged grassroots organization, and they rejected integration as the proper goal of militant black protest, preferring instead to create autonomous political and economic institutions. As SNCC evolved, it disavowed nonviolence and spurned alliances with white liberals. CORE likewise excluded whites from its membership; it also sanctioned the use of violence in self-defense, called for economic boycotts, and urged all-black businesses and financial institutions to be based within the ghettos. In general, black radicals rejected the assumptions of integration, criticized the civil rights movement as a subterfuge for the maintenance of white supremacy, and stressed the virtues of black lifestyles and black consciousness.[5]

At the end of the black ideological spectrum, the Nation of Islam continued to denigrate Malcolm X as an apostate. In an editorial published years after Malcolm's assassination, the Nation's newspaper, *Muhammad Speaks* warned that:

Some people want to build a backward nation by goading unstable youths to violence. . . . Such people are attempting to use Malcolm to mislead his sincere admirers. His good qualities—the long hard study put in under the guidance of Mr. Muhammad—are ignored. . . . [W]hat youths are really being told is that by being a degenerate, hustler, and quick-to-kill, they are being "revolutionary" like the "real Malcolm," the pre-Muslim Malcolm. Other young blacks are being told that Malcolm discovered some great, abstract . . . "humanistic" "Truth" in the last eleven months of his life. This nameless, mythical abstraction they would have impressionable Blacks substitute for a program of real social progress . . . for dignity bestowed on hard work . . . which are consistently advanced by Messenger Muhammad year in year out.

The Nation expressed concern over the growing cult of Malcolm X's
disciples. In many respects, Malcolm was the inspiration for a revitalized
nationalism that began as a slogan and gradually acquired a supporting
rationale—the ideology of Black Power.[6]

Black Power: "Old Wine in New Bottles"?

During James Meredith's "March Against Fear" in the summer of 1966,
SNCC's Stokely Carmichael whipped up a crowd of African Americans
in Greenwood, Mississippi: "The only way we gonna stop them white
men from whuppin" us is to take over. . . . We been saying 'freedom' for
six years and we ain't got nothing. What we gonna start saying now," he
shouted, "is Black Power! We . . . want . . . Black . . . Power!" In mesmeriz-
ing fashion, Carmichael and crowd went back and forth shouting ever
louder their insistence on "Black Power." Precisely what that insurgent
slogan meant was unclear. Julius Lester, a former SNCC field secretary,
offered a simplistic interpretation of the concept in his half-humorous,
but sharply bitter, account—*Look Out, Whitey! Black Power's Gon' Get
Your Mama!* Black Power, Lester explained, meant that "Black People
would control their own lives, destinies, and communities." He ridiculed
the 1963 March on Washington as "a great inspiration to those who think
that something is being accomplished by having black bodies next to
white ones." "The March," he declared, "was nothing but a giant therapy
session that allowed Dr. King to orate about his dreams of a nigger eating
at the same table with some Georgia cracker, while most black folks just
dreamed about eating."[7]

As a black nationalist ideology, Black Power acquired a variety of
connotations. It was most obviously a reaction against persistent white
racism and paternalism, which viewed integration as either "tokenism"
or "assimilationism." Stokely Carmichael and Charles Hamilton, in their
elucidation of Black Power, asserted, "The goal of black people must not
be to assimilate into middle-class America, for that class, as a whole,
is without a viable conscience as regards humanity." They rejected the
notion of an equal working partnership with whites in the black protest
movement, and dismissed the efforts of "many young, middle-class, white
Americans, [who] like some sort of Pepsi-Cola generation, have wanted
to 'come alive' through the black community and black groups." Black
Power also represented a disillusionment with the limited legislative
achievements of the civil rights coalition—a recognition that its apparent
victories had not discernibly changed the lives of most African Americans.

Black Power reasserted racial pride and rejected white standards of physical and cosmetic beauty, as was evident in the slogan "Black is Beautiful" and the vogue of "natural" African-American hairstyles or wigs adopted by entertainers, such as James Brown and Nina Simone. In music, the sound of black jazz grew harsher, as the work of Miles Davis, Sonny Rollins, and John Coltrane revealed. There was also a renewed interest in the African heritage of African Americans, together with demands on college campuses for black studies programs, black instructors, and separate facilities for black students. In politics, Black Power was synonymous with independent black action, either through the creation of a black political party or control of the political machinery within the ghettos. Economically, Black Power called for the creation of self-sufficient black business enterprises through the encouragement of African-American entrepreneurs and the formation of black cooperatives. In the area of education, Black Power theoreticians demanded local control of public schools in predominantly African-American neighborhoods.[8]

Essentially, Black Power stressed self-help, racial unity, and voluntary segregation. Owing a great deal to Malcolm X's black nationalist sentiments, Black Power, as president Lyndon Johnson's Commission on Civil Disorders concluded, was in some respects also "Old Wine in New Bottles": "Black Power advocates feel that they are the most militant group in the Negro protest movement. Yet they have retreated from a direct confrontation with American society on the issue of integration and, by preaching separatism, unconsciously function as an accommodation to white racism. Much of their economic program, as well as their interest in Negro history, self-help, racial solidarity and separation, is reminiscent of Booker T. Washington. The rhetoric is different, but the programs are remarkably similar."[9]

From its inception, Black Power was never a coherent ideology. It failed to formulate demands that were supported by a majority of its proponents. It also contained disturbing elements of anti-Semitism, which many American commentators chose to ignore. Moreover, as historian Manning Marable observed, Black Power was quickly appropriated by conservative interests, black and white. When Clairol corporation co-sponsored a Black Power conference in June, 1968, its white president endorsed the concept as meaning black "ownership of apartments, ownership of homes, ownership of businesses, as well as equitable treatment for all people." That same year, Republican presidential candidate Richard Nixon defined Black Power as another form of "free enterprise": "What most of the militants are asking for is not separation, but to be included in—not as supplicants, but as owners, as entrepreneurs—to have a share of the wealth and a piece of the action. . . . [The federal government's] central target of the new approach ought to be . . . oriented toward more black ownership, for from this can flow the rest—black pride, black jobs, black opportunity and yes, Black Power—in the best, the constructive sense of that often misapplied term." In these formulations, Black Power had been transmuted into black capitalism. Historian Theodore Draper suggested plausibly that "both the strengths and weaknesses of the Black Power slogan may be traced to its ambiguity. . . . It sprang from a nationalist urge without getting into any of the nationalist dilemmas. It avoided trouble by the simple expedient of leaving undefined what kind of 'power' it had in mind. Black capitalists, as well as black separatist revolutionaries, could adopt it for very different purposes."[10]

The Black Panther party, which Huey Newton and Bobby Seale founded in Oakland, California, in 1966, was an extreme example of Black Power in action. Its original "Ten Point Program" set forth the following demands:

1 We want freedom. We want power to determine the destiny of our black community.

2 We want full employment for our people.

3 We want an end to robbery by the white man of our black community.

4 We want decent homes, for shelter of human beings.

5 We want education of our people that exposes the true nature of this decadent American society. We want education that teaches us our true history and our role in the present day society.

6 We want all black men to be exempt from military service.

7 We want an immediate end to *police brutality* and *murder* of black people.

8 We want freedom for all black men held in federal, state, county, and city prisons and jails.

9 We want all black people when brought to a trial to be tried in court by a jury of their peer group of people from their black communities, as defined by the Constitution of the United States.

10 We want land, bread, housing, education, clothing, justice and peace.[11]

With its armed patrols, black berets, and menacing Black Panther emblem, the new party spread rapidly across the country, and appeared to threaten law and order. In fact, the Panthers were initially reformist rather than revolutionary. Early on, they initiated a free breakfast program for African-American children, and offered medical advice to ghetto residents. But by the end of the decade, the Panthers had become a revolutionary Marxist-Leninist party, advocating the overthrow of capitalist America. As a consequence of police and FBI infiltration and harassment in the early 1970s, the party's leaders were dead, imprisoned, or, as in the case of Eldridge Cleaver, the Panthers' minister of information, in exile abroad.[12]

The Nation of Islam also underwent significant changes in the 1970s. After Elijah Muhammad's death in 1975, his son, Warith Deen Muhammad, assumed leadership of the sect, and sharply modified or, according to some, "Malcolmized," its tenets. Successively named the World Community of Islam in the West, the American Muslim Mission, and the American Society of Muslims, the revamped group embraced the orthodox teachings of Sunni Islam, repudiated the deification of W. Fard Muhammad, disbanded the paramilitary Fruit of Islam, abolished the Nation's dress code, and promoted the establishment of a collectivist capitalism. Warith Muhammad stunned the faithful by denying that his father Elijah had ever been a prophet, much less the "Messenger of Allah." Whites were invited to join the movement which had earlier castigated them as "devils." The notion of a "homeland" for African Americans was considerably played down in favor of a more conventional form of pan-Islamism. In recognition of this ideological shift, Warith Muhammad received a large sum from the United Arab Emirates to build a mosque and a school. He also obtained a contract to package food and supplies for the U.S. army, a public show of support from the government. Not all black Muslims accepted these innovations. In 1978, Minister Louis Farrakhan announced his intention to return the Nation to the precepts and practices of Elijah Muhammad, hastening the fragmentation and decline of the black nationalist sect.[13]

A year before his assassination, Malcolm X remarked that the legal victories achieved by the civil rights movement in the 1960s made African Americans more politically conscious and assertive. During the 1970s and 1980s, many blacks appeared to believe that voting and political power were the most effective means to realize further racial advancement. Accordingly, the strategies employed by African-American leaders turned increasingly away from demonstrations, confrontations, and boycotts towards greater use of the ballot gained by the Voting Rights Act. In

1966, there were six black members in Congress and 97 African Americans serving in state legislatures; by 1979, African Americans held 4,607 elected offices—two-thirds of which were in the South—and there were 191 black mayors and 313 state legislators. The Democratic party responded to this upsurge in political activity by significantly increasing the number of black delegates to the party's 1972 National Convention, where black U.S. congresswoman Shirley Chisholm campaigned unsuccessfully for the Democratic presidential nomination. In the 1976 presidential election, over 90 percent of black voters supported the Democratic nominee, Jimmy Carter of Georgia. As president, Carter appointed African Americans to high office, most notably, Andrew Young, as U.S. ambassador to the United Nations, Patricia Harris as secretary of Housing and Urban Development, and John Reinhardt to the International Communications Agency. Willie Brown, the African-American speaker of the California state legislature, observed that "black leadership" had become more diffuse: "Now the politicians who are black are providing one aspect of black leadership, the religious community another, and the professional organizations another. This adds up to even greater institutional change than could ever have been brought about by a Martin Luther King rally or a Roy Wilkins boycott."[14]

Black political power did not translate into significant socioeconomic change for many African Americans. African Americans had gained "power" in large urban centers precisely when their migration to metropolitan areas prompted an exodus of affluent whites to the suburbs and the sunbelt, making inner cities politically less significant. One study found that in 23 out of 26 cities with black mayors, 16 ranked in the top third of all American cities based on their rates of poverty. Despite the growth of the black middle class, black unemployment rates were at least double those of whites, life expectancy for African Americans was shorter than that for whites, black infant mortality rates were greater, and 70 percent of poor black families were headed by women. According to John Hope Franklin, the dean of African-American historians, "so many black families . . . were unemployed and on welfare that it was quite likely that the nation would spawn an entire generation of blacks who had simply never worked to support themselves."[15]

Carter was followed into the presidency by former California governor Ronald Reagan, a conservative Republican who had little sympathy for minority groups or civil rights. In its first six months in office, the Reagan administration filed only five lawsuits relating to racial discrimination, as compared to twenty-four suits under Nixon and seventeen under Carter at that same point in their tenures. Reagan insisted that enforcement of civil rights should be left to the individual states, and he curtailed laws against housing discrimination and reduced the numbers of those eligible for social welfare programs, such as unemployment compensation, Medicaid, food stamps, and Aid to Families with Dependent Children. Only after intense pressure from the Congressional Black Caucus and civil rights sympathizers, did Reagan agree to sign the bill which commemorated Martin Luther King's birthday (January 15th) as a national holiday. At a White House ceremony in 1983, Reagan declared in the presence of the King family that "traces of bigotry still mar America. So each year on Martin Luther King day, let us not only recall Dr. King, but rededicate ourselves to the commandments he believed in and sought to live every day." Even if Reagan was unconvincing in endorsing King's precepts and practices, an aspiring African-American leader had already laid claims to being his true successor.[16]

Jesse Jackson: From A&T to Rainbow/PUSH

Jesse Louis Jackson was born in Greenville, South Carolina, in 1941, to Helen Burns, a 16-year-old high school student whose singing talent had brought college scholarship offers, and Noah Robinson, a married, former professional boxer in his thirties, who lived next door with his three stepchildren. Jackson bluntly explained what happened: "My father wanted a man-child of his own. His wife would not give him any children. So he went next door." Helen's doctor urged her to have an abortion, but she decided against it after speaking to her minister. Jackson's ancestry, which includes Africans, Cherokees, and an Irish plantation owner, gave him acorn-brown skin with some freckles on his face. He was, as one biographer put it, "a kind of walking Rainbow Coalition." Though well-to-do, Jackson's biological father was not involved in Jesse's upbringing, leading neighbors and classmates to taunt him with chants of derision: "There goes Noah's bastard" and "Jesse ain't got no daddy, you ain't nothing but a nobody."[17]

These boyhood taunts and his primitive living conditions greatly influenced Jackson's life and explain his affinity for the downtrodden: "That's why I have always been able to identify with those the rest of society labels as bastards, as outcasts and moral refuse. I know people saying you're nothing and nobody and can never be anything. I understand when you have no real last name. I understand." Jesse's mother, a beautician, eventually married a shoeshine attendant named Charles Jackson, who was not at all theatrical. When Helen and Charles had a child of their own, Jesse was forced to live with his grandmother in a shack around the corner until he was a teenager. When Noah Robinson moved into a better house, Jesse wandered over to look at it for long periods, even peeking in the windows, searching for his almost mythic father. Finally, Jesse's mother interceded and convinced her husband to adopt her 13-year-old son.[18]

According to one biographer, "Every teacher Jesse came into contact with took note of his insecurities, masked by a stoic sense of superiority. They never perceived him as brilliant, but rather each saw him as a charmer, a spirited, fierce competitor with an almost uncanny drive to prove himself by always winning, always being number one in everything." With the encouragement of his extended family, Jackson developed an extraordinary drive to overcome his circumstances and insecurities. In high school, Jackson was elected as president of his class, the honor society, and the student council, served as a state officer of Future Teachers of America, graduated tenth in his class, and lettered in football, basketball, and baseball.[19]

One of the circumstances with which the young Jackson had to cope was the Jim Crow system. He described his youth in South Carolina as one of "Humiliation":

Humiliation: go to the back of the bus even though you pay the same fare.

Humiliation: no public parks or libraries you can use even though you pay taxes.

Humiliation: upstairs in movies. Back doors in hotels and cafes. . . .

Humiliation: all white police with no police warrants who were so absolute in their power until they were called "the law."

Humiliation: a dual school system. Black teachers and white teachers working the same hours, only the Black teachers taught more students and taught double shifts and received less pay. . . . We used books exactly three years after white students used them. We used desks exactly four years after whites used them. There were no Black school board members. . . . We were rewarded for docility and punished for expressing manhood. Men were called boys. Women called girls. We called white children "Master" and "Missy."[20]

In 1959, Jackson rejected a professional baseball contract in order to attend the University of Illinois on an athletic scholarship. By this point, Jackson had seen enough of the segregated South and was eager to escape to the "Promised Land of the North." Jackson lasted a year at Illinois, upset about being passed over as starting quarterback on the football team, demoted from a public speaking competition, excluded from social events, and, for the first time in his life, called a "nigger." The common ingredient in these developments, Jackson maintained, was racism, although the football team did start another black quarterback that year. He was also on academic probation, perhaps a byproduct of the escalating tensions around him and the resulting isolation and alienation he felt. Leaving these problems behind, Jackson transferred to the all-black North Carolina Agricultural and Technical (A&T) State University, where he became involved in the Greensboro student sit-in movement directed against segregated lunch counters, libraries, and other public places. A. Knighton Stanley, a young black minister serving the A&T campus, recognized that the flashy Jackson—a football star who was also the student body president—would be a valuable addition to the protests. Stanley later recalled, "We needed Jesse as a football player the girls loved. . . . We woke him up one day and told him to protest with us and he has been protesting ever since." Recruited to act as a marshal for downtown marches, Jackson soon became identified as a sit-in leader. On one occasion, he led hundreds of demonstrators to city hall and declared that local blacks would "take over" Greensboro. When Jackson was arrested and put in jail, leaflets were printed with the headline, "Your great leader has been arrested."[21]

After graduating with a sociology degree, Jackson attended theological seminary, but soon dropped out to immerse himself in the civil rights movement. In 1965, Jackson joined Martin Luther King's campaign in Selma, Alabama, and, the following year, he worked in the Chicago Freedom Movement, which pressed for open housing and school integration in Illinois' largest city. Chicago turned out to be far different than Selma, because Chicago mayor Richard Daley, Sr., expressed sympathy with racial justice, all the while maintaining the racial status quo. In addition, many black Chicagoans were uninterested in racial change or had been bought off by the Daley machine, which liberally doled out patronage. In other ways, Chicago and Selma were alike, especially in the raw racism expressed toward and violence perpetrated upon civil rights demonstrators. King and Jackson were nearly stoned to death by white ethnics who waved Nazi flags, screamed "you monkeys" and "White Power," and threatened Catholic nuns and priests who demanded social justice. Afterward, King told the press that in all his marches in the South, "I have never seen so much hatred and hostility on the faces of so many people . . . as I've seen here today." The most apt comparison to the ill-starred Chicago campaign, King thought, was Hitler's Germany.[22]

Despite his reservations, King appointed Jackson to head Operation Breadbasket in Chicago, an organization affiliated with the Southern Christian Leadership Conference (SCLC) and dedicated to improving economic conditions in black communities. Jackson recruited black ministers and entrepreneurs to the cause, and pressured local businesses to hire African Americans and purchase goods and services from black contractors. Businesses that did not cooperate were subjected to black boycotts, called "selective buying," an idea pioneered by T.R.M. Howard, a wealthy surgeon and entrepreneur originally from Mississippi. Jackson urged blacks to buy products from black-owned businesses that appeared on store shelves. "You will show your blackness," he declared, "by buying Grove Fresh orange juice. Say it loud. I'm black and I'm proud and I buy Grove Fresh orange juice." Within a year, Jackson had helped to obtain 2,200 jobs for African Americans in white-owned firms and was named national director of the organization. Knowing poverty first-hand, Jackson was unusually devoted to the campaign to ensure jobs and food for destitute African Americans.[23]

Because of his rapid ascent within SCLC, the charismatic Jackson was regarded by many of his colleagues as an upstart and a self-promoter. Martin Luther King shared some of these reservations about Jackson, and questioned Jackson's failure to appreciate the need for a wholesale restructuring of the American economy. Andrew Young remembered that King, despite being impressed by Jackson's performance with Operation Breadbasket, was "quite rough on Jesse because [King] said that . . . Breadbasket would not solve the problem . . . that jobs would finally have to be provided by the public sector rather than the private sector, and that Breadbasket was essentially a private sector program." On another occasion, King remarked in exasperation: "Jesse Jackson's so independent, I either want him in SCLC or out. . . . [H]e's a part of SCLC or he's not a part of SCLC." William Rutherford, a black Chicago businessman and SCLC member, believed that King's displeasure with Jackson was more than a disagreement over ideology: "He didn't trust Jesse, he didn't even like Jesse. . . . If you ask me if there was any suspicion about Jesse's motives and even devotion to the movement, I would say categorically yes, there was—considerable." Another SCLC executive remembered that King used to say, "Jesse, you have no love."[24]

When Martin Luther King was assassinated at the Lorraine Motel in Memphis, Tennessee, in April, 1968, Jackson aroused bitterness—even disbelief—within SCLC by appearing on national television the next morning, intimating that he had cradled the dying leader in his arms, heard his last words, and had his shirt stained by King's blood. Thus did Jackson boldly lay claim to the crucified King's mantle of civil rights leadership. In fact, Jackson had been talking to musicians in the parking lot below the motel balcony at the moment King was shot, not by his side. Even so, with Jackson's charisma, stirring oratory, quick wit, and uncompromising stands for racial justice, the media anointed him as King's *de facto* successor. Two months later, Jackson suddenly filled out his resume by being ordained into the ministry, even though he never completed his formal seminary training. The question of who would officially succeed the slain King as head of SCLC consumed the organization for years, but in the end the grandstanding Jackson was passed over. Ultimately, however, Jackson accomplished what King could not—firmly establish SCLC in the North.[25]

At the time of his murder, King had devised an audacious tactical gambit—a Poor People's Campaign—to demand that the federal government divert money from the Vietnam war to feed the hungry and abolish poverty. In his speeches, he called for economic justice, by which he meant the redistribution of wealth, a guaranteed annual income for all Americans, government ownership of basic industries, and affirmative action for minorities seeking employment. Although King thought he might well be murdered for these ideas, he continued to promote them. King's alarmed advisers thought he had become irrational. Black ministers criticized his plans, and an angry president Lyndon Johnson and SCLC— King's own organization—repudiated him over his stance on Vietnam. A depressed King guzzled more whiskey than ever and could be heard banging hotel walls, shouting, "I don't want to do this anymore! I want to go back to my little church!" By now, King understood that his brand of leadership had become increasingly irrelevant to a fractured and stymied movement.[26]

As King feared, he was soon murdered. His longtime lieutenant and SCLC vice-president, Ralph David Abernathy, took over the Poor People's Campaign, remarking, "We are not going to let the white man put us down any more." The centerpiece of this bold initiative to broaden the civil rights movement was to be a "Resurrection City" in Washington, D.C., that would create a model community of the disadvantaged of all races. This multiracial army of protesters would launch a series of sit-ins and demonstrations in the nation's jittery capital, which looked like a war zone from the riots following King's murder. In May and June of 1968, the tent and plywood shantytown along the Washington Mall attracted thousands of idealistic African Americans, along with some Latinos and Indians, as well as some whites. The operation was soon plagued by infighting, disorganization, and heavy rains that left the site awash in a sea of mud. Violent gangs from Chicago, Memphis, and Milwaukee, Wisconsin, descended on the Mall, and quickly found the trouble they were looking for. Beatings and robberies were commonplace. Expecting an apocalyptic outcome, the FBI and U.S. army infiltrated the encampment and kept federal agencies closely informed. News of the murder of U.S. senator Robert Kennedy, a presidential candidate with a liberal record on race and class, in Los Angeles, California, on June 5th, dispirited the protesters further. Not even Bayard Rustin and Stanley Levison could help the ill-starred campaign. After six weeks of chaos, the National Park Service razed the encampment and billed SCLC $71,000 for the damage caused to the Mall. The omnipresent Jesse Jackson was the manager of Resurrection City, but the media charged Abernathy with ineptitude for this fiasco. In truth, the white liberal consensus on race had fractured as soon as the civil rights movement put economic considerations on the reform agenda—before Resurrection City had even been erected.[27]

Despite the fiasco of Resurrection City, the self-aggrandizing Jackson continued to enjoy the media spotlight. He aroused considerable jealousy among the civil rights leadership when he appeared on the cover of *Time* in an issue devoted to "Black America 1970." Characterized as "one leader among many," Jackson was, nevertheless, given an extensive profile:

Tall and sensuously attractive, Jackson is the kind of leader who suggests both a dignity of bearing in his brooding dedication to his cause and a sense of brotherly warmth in his casual Levi's, boots and open sports shirts. He possesses what he himself matter-of-factly accepts as charisma, and he inspires devotion among a wide range of followers. . . . At 28, he effectively bridges the widening gulf between the young activists and the old-style moralistic preachers. His strength is his use of evangelistic fervor to achieve pragmatic ends. . . . Jackson expounds his opinions forcefully in public. He does not arouse a crowd as readily as King did, but he employs cadence, sweeping hand gestures, a penetrating gaze and abrupt changes in volume to command attention. He deliberately mangles grammar and throws in mild profanity to develop rapport with audiences. He is hopelessly addicted to preacherly metaphors. . . . He has a host of adoring admirers as well as caustic critics. But he is still too young to assume a black leadership role on a national scale.[28]

Within SCLC itself, there was opposition to Ralph Abernathy's assumption of leadership, particularly from Jackson. Matters came to a head in 1971 when Jackson organized an entrepreneurial and entertainment fund-raising extravaganza called "Black Expo," ostensibly under the aegis of SCLC. Abernathy discovered that Jackson had committed financial "irregularities" in operating the exposition, and suspended him from SCLC. Abernathy remarked, "I have considered the liberation of the black and the poor people much more important than dissipating energies and resources seeking to deal with . . . Reverend Jackson. . . . We have been bogged down with matters of getting America to feed its hungry, house its poor, and redirect its national priorities. This has had to take precedence over everything else." In the wake of his suspension, Jackson abruptly resigned altogether from SCLC.[29]

In the decade following his purging from SCLC, Jackson engaged in a carefully planned campaign of self-advertisement. He addressed hundreds of civic and professional groups, appeared on television talk shows, addressed labor union rallies, campaigned for liberal political candidates, and became a syndicated columnist. Jackson also founded Operation PUSH (People United to Save Humanity—later changed to People United to *Serve* Humanity) with its headquarters in Chicago. The organization pursued black self-help in several ways, including operating youth programs for reading and job placement, and facilitating agreements for affirmative action with corporations that did considerable business in black communities. As the head of PUSH, Jackson threatened boycotts of major companies, including Coca-Cola, Heublein, Burger King, and Ford Motor, that did not offer sufficient opportunities for African Americans. He even threatened to compare their largely white corporate cultures to apartheid in South Africa. When actor Bill Cosby, a popular pitchman for Coke, sided with Jackson, Coca-Cola capitulated. So did General Foods, Kentucky Fried Chicken, Miller Brewing, Nike, and 7-Eleven convenience stores. These companies hired more black managers, granted more franchises and dealerships to African Americans, deposited more money in black banks, allocated more money to black insurance companies, hired more black law firms, took out more advertisements in black newspapers, bought more supplies from black medical companies, and signed more contracts with black construction firms to renovate their plants. Jackson's escalating demands led Coca-Cola and Budweiser to try to placate him by awarding distributorships to his half-brother and two sons, leading critics to accuse him of being more of an opportunist than a leader.[30]

With distinct echoes of Booker T. Washington's ideas concerning the promotion of black capitalism, Jackson remarked: "When we organized Operation PUSH, our stated objective was to help effect and direct a transformation of the Human Rights Movement from emphasis on Civil Rights to one on Civil Economics." While PUSH was a non-profit corporation, it was not tax exempt, allowing it to be actively involved in political matters. PUSH grew rapidly to consist of seventy chapters with over 80,000 members. PUSH allowed Jackson, as he put it, to be a "father to a community."[31]

To fuel the momentum for change, Jackson held weekly PUSH rallies on Saturday mornings to avoid competing with other ministers for Sunday worship services. Despite travelling 200,000 miles a year, the self-described "Country Preacher" always returned to Chicago to orchestrate three-hour productions that had the flavor of old-fashioned tent revivals. A 100-voice choir led the audience in singing traditional hymns that were given new rhythms and syncopation. The lights brightened and dimmed as people shouted, danced, swayed, and clapped to the music. Large pictures of Jesse Jackson and Martin Luther King were placed behind the podium to reinforce Jackson's claim that he was King's heir. The star of the production, of course, was the muscular 6-foot 2-inch, 220-pound Jackson, who wore a dashiki, bell-bottom trousers or jeans, a turtleneck, and a gold-plated medallion commemorating King. Jackson's soaring oratory was delivered in the chants and cadences of the black church, and the aroused listeners, which included a nationwide radio audience, worshipped the preacher. The highlight of the service came when Jackson led the audience in the following chant:

> I am—Somebody!
> I may be poor, but I am—Somebody!
> I may be on welfare, but I am—Somebody!
> I may be uneducated, but I am—Somebody!
> I may be in jail, but I am—Somebody!
> I am—Somebody![32]

Jackson followed PUSH with a school ministry called PUSH for Excellence (PUSH-Excel), a campaign begun in 1975 to promote parent-teacher cooperation and to address drugs, teenage pregnancy, and truancy among black youngsters. He called on students to sign pledges to study at least two hours a night, on parents to shut off television and radio during study time, and on teachers to distribute their phone numbers to parents. An impassioned orator, Jackson delivered his message of personal responsibility to male students far and wide: "You are not a man because you can make a baby. They can make babies through artificial insemination. Imbeciles can make babies. Fools can make babies. You're a man only if you can raise a baby, protect a baby, and provide for a baby." When black teenagers told Jackson that he didn't understand their lives, Jackson retorted, "I *do* understand. I was born to a teenage mother, who was born to a teenage mother. How do I understand? I never slept under the same roof with my natural father one night in my life. I *understand*."[33]

Jackson's rousing oratory to schoolchildren combined elements of uplift and militancy, and attracted a large following. "What does it matter," Jackson exhorted his young listeners, "if the doors of opportunity are now wide open if you still too uneducated to find your way through that door? If you too high or too drunk to stagger through it?"

Just 'cause you were born in the slum doesn't mean the slum was born in you, you can rise above it. . . . To those who say you can only play ball and can't think, say, 'Bring 'em on!' Let the challenges come. You can rise up to where God made and meant you to be. Up to you now! Education and success are not going to kidnap you, you got to get them for yourselves. Up to you now! Want you to repeat after me: My mind is a pearl . . . I can learn anything . . . in the whole world! . . . Nobody will save us . . . for us . . . but us!

This Calvinist refrain of discipline, hard work, and morality sounded distinctly like Booker T. Washington nearly a century earlier. Critics noted that electrifying speeches did not produce higher test scores, but truancy, fighting, and vandalism in predominantly black schools declined somewhat, and more black students enrolled in advanced academic courses. More than once, Jackson angrily defended himself from the charge that he had no "follow-through": "I play the role of a catalyst. If I bring inspiration and direction, it is the job of the people who work there to develop the actual programs. We're trying to change *attitudes*." More succinctly, Jackson explained, "I'm a tree-shaker, not a jelly-maker."[34]

By the end of the 1970s, Jesse Jackson was America's most well-known African-American leader, having appeared on television shows and in newspapers and magazines, especially *Jet*, almost weekly. His services, rallies, and media appearances were carefully staged. "I'm a preacher," Jackson said, "but primarily I'm an organizer and a programer. In a sense the civil rights movement is a drama, but you have to keep setting the stage and creating scenes that people can act their way out of if they are to make maximum progress." For his hyperactive moral leadership, Jackson was sometimes referred to as the "Black Jesus," the "Black Messiah," and the "Black Moses," as many in the black community looked to anoint its latest leader.[35]

Inevitably, Jackson's higher profile and successful campaign to pressure major corporations to invest in the black community drew criticism and government scrutiny. Project PUSH-Excel, which was designed to motivate black students, was initially successful in gaining donations from private foundations, the federal government, and even the Arab League. But it soon encountered criticism for its failure to file acceptable financial reports, as required by state and federal laws. The Reagan administration, responding to Jackson's attacks on its policies on Central America and South Africa, launched an investigation of Operation PUSH's finances, and claimed that PUSH had "misused" over $1.7 million in government contracts.[36]

Economic clout was one thing, political power another. On the 20th anniversary of the March on Washington, Jackson reminded African Americans of their unrealized potential at the ballot box, pointing to the outcome of the 1980 presidential election: "Reagan won Alabama by 17,500 votes, but there were 272,000 unregistered blacks. He won Arkansas by 5,000 votes, with 85,000 unregistered blacks. He won Kentucky by 17,800 votes, with 62,000 unregistered blacks. . . . So the numbers show that Reagan won through a perverse coalition of the rich and the unregistered." Jackson insisted that the upcoming election would be "a new day" because "hands that picked cotton in 1884 will pick the president in 1984." He repeated the same message across the country, and it became clear that Jackson himself would be a contender for the Democratic party's presidential nomination, even though he had never held elective office. Jackson demonstrated his political savvy and clout by organizing a large voter-registration drive which delivered votes for Harold Jackson, the first African American to win election as mayor of Chicago. Despite the criticisms of some black leaders, including Benjamin Hooks of the NAACP, John Jacob of the Urban League, and Coretta Scott King, that a black candidacy would split the Democratic vote and produce a white backlash at the polls, Jackson shrugged and remarked that "some leaders have a very static view of the possible political options." He thought that all black political candidates would benefit from a Jackson presidential bid.[37]

Presidential contender

Eliciting and responding to his audiences' shouts of "Run, Jesse, Run," the flamboyant Jackson campaigned for the 1984 Democratic nomination. His was the second nationwide campaign by an African American for the presidency, the first being congresswoman Shirley Chisholm of New York in 1972. Jackson's appeal rested largely on his platform of social programs, voting rights, and affirmative action for those neglected by Reaganomics, including the poor, the disabled, African Americans, Native Americans, women, and immigrants. One of Jackson's major goals was to increase voter registration among these disadvantaged groups, which he, like Robert Kennedy before him, hoped would invigorate the Democratic party. Initially, the strategy appeared to work. In the New York state primary election, Jackson won 34 percent of the Puerto Rican vote, and was the only candidate for the Democratic nomination to address the National Congress of American Indians. One Native American journalist wrote that Jackson was "a national minority leader who has captured the imagination of people of color, other than blacks." Among white voters, Jackson earned the support of left-wing activists, liberals, blue-collar workers, and the unemployed. African Americans also responded to Jackson's campaign, which, according to one estimate, was endorsed by more than 90 percent of all black clergy within weeks of his announced candidacy. Although Jackson's appeal to minority groups was considerable, many moderate African-American leaders, including mayors Tom Bradley of Los Angeles, California, and Andrew Young of Atlanta, Georgia, did not support him. They were convinced that Jackson's candidacy would divide the Democratic party and thereby benefit the Republicans in the national election.[38]

In the area of foreign policy, Jackson called for a reduction of the American and Soviet armory, the removal of cruise missiles from Europe, normalized diplomatic relations with Cuba, and an end to United States intervention in Central America. In a daring move, Jackson went to Syria to ask president Hafez al-Assad for the release of Lt. Robert Goodman, a young African-American navigator who was taken prisoner when his reconnaissance plane had been shot down on a bombing run over Lebanon. After meeting with Jackson, Assad released Goodman to Jackson's custody, and the two men were given heroes' welcomes by president Reagan at the White House. This dramatic episode boosted Jackson's popularity as an American patriot and momentarily improved his chances as a presidential aspirant. Months later, Jackson negotiated the release of twenty-two Americans in Fidel Castro's Cuba, but by now critics were accusing Jackson of interfering in the conduct of U.S. foreign policy.[39]

Jackson's disturbing anti-Semitism also aroused heavy criticism. In an off-the-record remark to a reporter, Jackson referred to Jews as "Hymies" and New York City as "Hymietown." The public's reaction was instantaneous and explosive, prompting a Jackson staffer to remark that "it was like somebody dropped an atomic bomb right in the middle of our campaign." When Jackson finally admitted saying these words, he insisted that no slur was intended. But the derogatory remark, together with his refusal to reject the support of Black Muslim Minister Louis Farrakhan who had called Judaism "a gutter religion," offended many American Jews and white liberals, who were already disturbed by the connection between PUSH and Arab groups. Nor had Jews forgotten Jackson's 1979 visit to the Middle East, when he characterized Israeli prime minister Menachem Begin as a "terrorist" and met with Yasser Arafat, head of the Palestine Liberation Organization, which had orchestrated persistent violent attacks against Israel. Adding fuel to the fire, Jackson remarked to the editor of *Israel Today* that "it's about time American Jews stopped putting Americans on a guilt trip about the Holocaust."[40]

By the time of the Democratic National Convention in San Francisco in July, 1984, Jackson had garnered 3.2 million primary votes, or 18.2 percent of the total, winning five primaries and caucuses. Jackson was far more than the "fringe" candidate that pundits had predicted. Although his competitive showing was unprecedented for an African-American candidate, he lost handily to former vice-president Walter Mondale, a lackluster campaigner who had the backing of the party machinery. Jackson graciously endorsed the nominee and gave a rousing speech to answer his critics: "If in my low moments, in word, deed, or attitude, through some error of temper, taste, or tone, I have caused anyone discomfort, created pain, or revived someone's fears, that was not my truest self. . . . I am not a perfect servant. I am a public servant doing my best against the odds. As I develop and serve, be patient. God is not finished with me yet." If Jackson was auditioning for the vice-presidential slot, Mondale had other ideas, and balanced his ticket by gender, not race. Mondale selected Geraldine Ferraro, a white U.S. representative from New York as the woman to run for that office on a major party label. Jackson supported the ill-fated Democratic ticket, which went down to a crushing defeat with the re-election of the popular Ronald Reagan. But Jackson's candidacy undoubtedly contributed to a large black voter turnout that fall. An estimated 3 million African Americans voted in the Democratic primaries, and over 10 million—89 percent of whom supported Mondale—participated in the November elections.[41]

Four years later, Jackson again sought the Democratic party nomination for president. This time, the media and pundits immediately wrote him off as unelectable. Jackson's 1988 campaign was better organized and better financed than his previous effort, and he distinguished himself as the most "radical" of all candidates. His long list of proposed domestic reforms included jobs for all Americans, reversing the Reagan tax cuts for the rich, creating a single-payer system of universal health care, ratifying the Equal Rights Amendment for women, targeting bankers who allegedly funded the drug epidemic, giving reparations to descendants of enslaved African Americans, resurrecting New Deal programs to support family farms, and providing free community college education to all. Jackson also took liberal positions in foreign affairs, including designating the white-supremacist South Africa as a rogue state, creating statehood for the Palestinians, and instituting an immediate nuclear freeze and initiating disarmament talks with the Soviet Union. Except for the call to adopt sanctions against South Africa for its apartheid policy, none of these positions was adopted by the Democratic party platform committee.[42]

Despite impressive performances in the presidential primaries doubling his 1984 results, the charismatic Jackson again lacked the support of party leaders. Massachusetts governor Michael Dukakis, another lackluster white candidate, won the Democratic nomination, and, in a move that stunned Jackson, used geography, not race, to balance the party ticket. Dukakis correctly assumed that most African Americans would continue to vote for the Democrats, regardless of whom he selected as his running-mate. This calculation resulted in the selection of U.S. senator Lloyd Bentsen from Texas—a state that was a rich prize in the Electoral College—as the Democrats' vice-presidential nominee, rather than Jackson. The Dukakis ticket lost the November election in a landslide to Republican George H.W. Bush, Reagan's vice-president, who played the race card against the Democrats. Bush ran advertisements reminding white voters that Dukakis had allowed first-degree murderers in Massachusetts to participate in a weekend furlough program, from which a black man serving a life sentence without parole escaped and brutally raped a white woman.[43]

Once again, Jackson proved to be a divisive figure in presidential politics, because of his focus on the dispossessed. To his admirers, Jackson demonstrated his ability to appeal to a "Rainbow Coalition" of the

American electorate—he gained three times as many white votes in the 1988 primaries than he had in 1984—and was the Democrats' most progressive figure. To his detractors, Jackson projected confusing and contradictory images: a self-declared successor of Martin Luther King, Jr and a political opportunist, a color-blind populist and a confirmed anti-Semite, a preacher and a demagogue, an idealist and a "hustler," a champion of the poor and an ardent black capitalist. At the same time, Jackson energized the black electorate for all political races, and had shown that many white voters would support a black candidate for national office. In this last respect, Jesse Jackson paved the way for the nation's first African-American president twenty years later.[44]

To many, Jackson was now the unofficial president of Black America. His legacy as a "black leader"—a characterization which he rejected—was comparable to that of Booker T. Washington, Marcus Garvey, and Malcolm X. As conservative critic Garry Wills observed, Jackson was the only nationally active and visible black leader in the Age of Reagan, the one an entire generation of blacks grew accustomed to. Many of the objections often made about Jackson—"symbolic leadership, lack of electoral validation, concern for larger issues than black welfare, moral appeals to a broad spectrum of clashing interests—marked King's life and work." So too were claims that Jackson encouraged a cult of personality. And, Wills might have added, these and similar charges were also made against Booker T. Washington, W.E.B. Du Bois, Marcus Garvey, and Malcolm X. Certainly the highly-charged responses which Jackson consistently evoked from his audiences—black and white—brings to mind sociologist John Dollard's observation, made in 1937, that "No more exhilarating form of leadership of human beings exists than that possible between the Negro preacher and his congregation."[45]

As a two-time loser in the presidential sweepstakes, Jackson watched his window of political opportunity effectively closed. Despite this new reality, Jackson maintained a high profile on the national and international stage. He directed Operation PUSH and, in 1986, founded the National Rainbow Coalition, a nonprofit advocacy group of the poor and powerless. Jackson explained the group's rationale: "Our flag is red, white and blue, but our nation is a rainbow—red, yellow, brown, black and white—and we're all precious in God's sight." He traveled widely, putting a spotlight on international problems and undertaking private diplomacy in hostage situations. He spoke out against apartheid in South Africa, urged statehood for the Palestinians, and helped broker the release of American soldiers and civilians from Syria, Iraq, Bosnia, and Sierra Leone.

He also interceded with Muammar Gaddafi over Libya's conviction of foreign medical workers on the absurd charge of infecting Libyan children with HIV. Jackson later received a presidential appointment as a special envoy to Africa to promote human rights and democracy. While some pundits and government officials frowned on his diplomatic missions as meddlesome and self-serving, Jackson also won praise for his successes.[46]

After the 1988 election, Jackson moved his home from Chicago to Washington, D.C. When Washington mayor Marion Barry was forced out of office by a cocaine drug scandal, many observers thought Jackson would replace him, but Jackson declined to run. He did accept a new unpaid, nonvoting position as statehood senator—popularly called "shadow senator"—to lobby Congress for statehood for the District of Columbia, which had a large African-American majority. For black residents of the nation's capital, statehood would finally empower them to make political decisions as first-class citizens in American democracy. *Washington Post* editor Ben Bradlee was perplexed as to why Jackson would agree to the post: "This is a dogshit position he's got here. A nonpaying job to get statehood for the District, which is a lost cause. Why does he want to do that?" Desperate to keep his presidential hopes alive, Jackson nonetheless served as statehood senator for Washington during much of the 1990s, but the question of statehood was never considered seriously. Jackson's presidential prospects evaporated altogether when fellow Democrat Bill Clinton captured the presidency in 1992 and promoted more centrist policies on race.[47]

After his stint as Washington's shadow senator ended, Jackson turned his attention to the nation's financial capital. He recognized that minorities needed to attract the attention of New York City's Wall Street to effect real economic change. He had to find a way to force America's leading corporations to provide more business and employment for minorities. Jackson's approach to injustice had always been to organize protests to shame or intimidate unresponsive organizations and businesses, but an incident involving racist comments by Texaco employees opened his mind to another option. Jackson contacted New York State comptroller H. Carl McCall to join him in picketing Texaco. McCall, an African American responsible for the state's huge investments, responded, "Jesse, when you own a million shares you don't have to picket." Black investors, Jackson now understood, could quietly wield far more power than noisy protesters. So, Jackson founded the Wall Street Project in 1997, telling African Americans that "We empower politically with our vote. Now we must empower economically with our dollar." Economic empowerment required purchasing company stock to gain access to board meetings where company policy was made. In making this transition, Jackson announced, "we have gone from sharecroppers to shareholders. We say to corporate America: We don't want to be just consumers and workers, but investors and partners."[48]

At the same time, Jackson faced serious personal problems. In 2001, the 60-year-old minister, a married father of five, admitted to an affair with Karin Stanford, the director of the Washington PUSH offices, who bore him a daughter named Ashley. According to Stanford, the affair lasted four years, and she was pregnant with Jackson's child at the time Jackson was U.S. president Clinton's "spiritual adviser" during the Monica Lewinsky sex scandal that ended in Clinton's impeachment. Jackson thus continued the family tradition of an older married man fathering an illegitimate child. The Rainbow/PUSH Coalition had paid Stanford to keep quiet, but word leaked to the press anyway. Jackson finally admitted paternity and personally paid child support.[49]

Although rumors linking Jackson with a "galaxy" of women had been around for decades, charges of hypocrisy in the Stanford affair flew fast and furious, as many newspapers saw an opportunity for an editorial roasting. The press had protected Martin Luther King from public disgrace over his infidelities, as it had president Kennedy, mainly because of different journalistic standards a generation earlier, King's apparent indispensable leadership of the movement, and King's focus on chastising a racist society, not licentious black teenagers. The *Chicago Sun-Times* wrote: "Jackson has held others to the highest and most stringent standards, delivering his judgments often in harsh and very memorable phrases. . . . Now it is obvious Jackson has not lived up to the high standards he insisted upon for others." Pulitzer prize-winning columnist Clarence Page, an African American, wrote, "First to evaporate is Jackson's credibility as a moral icon and role model for young people." Harlem resident Maxine Jones also chastised Jackson: "He sits up there talking about wearing a condom and abstinence and he's doing worse than the teenagers. I'm so disappointed." But by this time, many Americans, including many African Americans, had long-since stopped listening to his message of race-based politics.[50]

Jackson found a more receptive audience abroad, traveling to speaking engagements in Britain, Venezuela, and West Africa. When the 2004 presidential campaign opened, Jackson surprised observers by declining to support either black candidate—the Rev. Al Sharpton or former U.S. senator Carol Moseley Braun of Illinois. As Jackson became increasingly irrelevant, a new and very different African-American leader was about to be crowned, and his name was Barack Obama.[51]

Assessment

Critics have charged Jesse Jackson with being little more than a cheerleader of causes, and to be sure, he has often been a whirlwind force on many different issues. His economic boycotts were criticized by some businesspeople as extortion and by some reformers as half-hearted. Political scientist Adolph Reed, Jr. observed that Jackson's prime motive was to help himself: "This is the long-term pattern of Jackson's politics. He has always sought to operate and be recognized as a political insider, as a leader without portfolio or without accountability to any constituency that he claims to represent." As for PUSH, Reed charged that that organization was "a simple extension of his will, and he has sought to ensure that the Rainbow Coalition would be the same kind of rubber stamp, a letterhead and front for his mercurial ambition."[52]

For all his critics—and they have been legion—Jesse Jackson has been a powerful African-American leader, one of the most significant in American history. His burning drive to succeed has made him a tireless worker, fiercely committed to his many causes. He was much more than his oratory, however. Whereas Booker T. Washington expected black southerners to earn their way to a better place in society, Jackson called for the federal government to recognize the humanity of African Americans. Whereas Marcus Garvey promoted a new black identity, Jackson crafted a rainbow coalition of the powerless. Like Harlem preacher Adam Clayton Powell, Jr., in the 1930s, Jackson not only called for affirmative action hiring, he pressured some of America's leading corporations to sign contracts to hire and promote African Americans and to deal more fairly in their business practices. Though hardly the first African-American leader to do so— certainly his mentor, Martin Luther King, at the end of his life comes to mind—Jackson identified economic inequality as the fundamental cause of discrimination. In so doing, he redefined the nature of the civil rights struggle. More than any other African-American leader, Jackson succeeded in having minorities hired and promoted in the workplace and in having corporate America realize that good business meant investing in black neighborhoods.

Since Martin Luther King's death, no one else on the national stage can remotely equal Jesse Jackson's record of helping African Americans to register to vote, get a job or a promotion or a business franchise, and secure major funding from major corporations for black businesses. In this regard, Jackson followed in King's footsteps, but he went well beyond it. Writing in *Essence*, Jackson observed, "People who are victimized may not be responsible for being down, but they must be responsible for getting up. Slave masters don't retire; people who are enslaved change their minds and choose to join the abolitionist struggle. . . . Change has always been led by those whose spirits were bigger than their circumstances. . . . I do have hope. We have seen significant victories during the last 25 years." What distinguishes Jackson from many other leaders—white or black—is that he has been a man of action, while others talk of action. In a 1996 speech to the Democratic National Convention, Jackson summarized his philosophy: "If you go along and get along, you're a coward. Only by principled engagement can you be a force for change and hope." For all his insecurities, egotism, and ambition, Jackson has been deeply committed to this truth.[53]

References

1　Marshall Frady, *Jesse: The Life and Pilgrimage of Jesse Jackson* (1996), p. 449.

2　Walter Isaacson, "Seeking Votes and Clout," *Time* 122 (22 August 1983): 20.

3　Adolph L. Reed, Jr., *The Jesse Jackson Phenomenon: The Crisis of Purpose in Afro-American Politics* (1986), p. 106.

4　Adam Fairclough, *Better Day Coming: Blacks and Equality, 1890–2000* (2001), pp. 236, 282, 292–293, 310–315.

5　Charles W. Eagles, ed., *The Civil Rights Movement in America* (1986), p. 62; August Meier and Elliott Rudwick, *CORE: A Study in the Civil Rights Movement, 1942–1968* (1973), pp. 379–393.

6　C. Eric Lincoln, *The Black Muslims in America* (1973), p. 212.

7　Milton Viorst, *Fire in the Streets: America in the 1960s* (1979), p. 374; Julius Lester, *Look Out, Whitey! Black Power's Gon' Get Your Mama!* (1968), pp. 100, 104.

8　Stokely Carmichael and Charles V. Hamilton, *Black Power: The Politics of Liberation in America* (1967), pp. 54, 95.

9　*Report of the National Advisory Commission on Civil Disorders* (1968), p. 235.

10　Manning Marable, *Race, Reform, and Rebellion: The Second Reconstruction in Black America, 1945–1982* (1984), pp. 108–109; Theodore Draper, *The Rediscovery of Black Nationalism* (1970), p. 125.

11 John H. Bracey, et al., *Black Nationalism in America* (1970), pp. 531–532.

12 Peniel E. Joseph, *Waiting 'Til the Midnight Hour: A Narrative History of Black Power in America* (2006); Jeffrey O. G. Ogbar, *Black Power: Radical Politics and African American Identity* (2004).

13 Clifton E. Marsh, *The Lost-Found Nation of Islam* (2000), pp. 67–128.

14 John Hope Franklin and Alfred A. Moss, Jr., *From Slavery to Freedom: A History of African Americans* (2000), pp. 557, 559–560; Kenneth M. Pierce, et al., "Goodbye to the Old Guard," *Time* 118 (21 September 1981): 20–21.

15 Franklin and Moss, *From Slavery to Freedom*, p. 561.

16 Ibid., pp. 564–569.

17 Barbara A. Reynolds, *Jesse Jackson: America's David* (1985), pp. 17–31; Frady, *Jesse*, pp. 82–87.

18 Frady, *Jesse*, pp. 86–89, 94–96; Reynolds, *Jesse Jackson*, pp. 22–24.

19 Reynolds, *Jesse Jackson*, pp. 32–36.

20 Manning Marable, *Black American Politics: From the Washington Marches to Jesse Jackson* (1985), p. 258; Karin L. Stanford, *Beyond the Boundaries: Reverend Jesse Jackson in Foreign Affairs* (1997), p. 42.

21 William H. Chafe, *Civilities and Civil Rights: Greensboro, North Carolina and the Black Struggle for Freedom* (1980), pp. 125, 142–143.

22 Reynolds, *Jesse Jackson*, pp. 45–80; Marshall Frady, *Martin Luther King, Jr.* (2002), p. 176.

23 Reynolds, *Jesse Jackson*, pp. 105–153.

24 Adam Fairclough, *To Redeem the Soul of America: The Southern Christian Leadership Conference and Martin Luther King, Jr.* (1987), pp. 353–354; David J. Garrow, *Bearing the Cross: Martin Luther King, Jr., and the Southern Christian Leadership Conference* (1986), pp. 585–586.

25 Reynolds, *Jesse Jackson*, pp. 313–314.

26 Taylor Branch, *At Canaan's Edge: America in the King Years, 1965–1968* (2006), p. 641.

27 Gerald McKnight, *The Last Crusade: Martin Luther King, Jr., the FBI, and the Poor People's Campaign* (1998), pp. 107–139; Ralph David Abernathy, *And the Walls Came Tumbling Down: An Autobiography* (1991), pp. 494–539.

28 "Jesse Jackson: One Leader among Many," *Time* 95 (6 April 1970): 11–16, 21–24, 27.

29 Abernathy, *And the Walls Came Tumbling Down*, pp. 409–410.

30 Reynolds, *Jesse Jackson*, pp. 312–356; Juan Williams, *Enough: The Phony Leaders, Dead-End Movements, and Culture of Failure that are Undermining Black America—and What We Can Do About It* (2006), p. 51; Ken Timmerman, *Shakedown: Exposing the Real Jesse Jackson* (2002).

31 Marable, *Black American Politics*, p. 262, Jesse Jackson, *Straight from the Heart*, eds. Roger D. Hatch and Frank E. Watkins (1987), pp. xi–xiii.

32 Roger Bruns, *Jesse Jackson: A Biography* (2005), p. 65.

33 Ernest R. House, *Jesse Jackson & the Politics of Charisma: The Rise and Fall of the PUSH/Excel Program* (1988), pp. 21–113; Eddie Stone, *Jesse Jackson: A Biography* (1988), p. 137; Frady, *Jesse*, p. 76.

34 Frady, *Jesse*, pp. 290–296.

35 Reynolds, *Jesse Jackson*, pp. 9–11, 13; Frady, *Jesse*, p. 135; House, *Jesse Jackson & the Politics of Charisma*, pp. 15–16.

36 House, *Jesse Jackson & the Politics of Charisma*, pp. 92, 110, 169; Frady, *Jesse*, pp. 325–326.

37 Joanne Ball, "Jesse Jackson's PUSH for Power," *Black Enterprise* 14 (November, 1983): 44–46, 48, 50; "Seeking Votes and Clout," *Time* 122 (22 August 1983): 20–24, 26.

38 Marable, *Black American Politics*, pp. 275–276.

39 Michael Preston, "The 1984 Presidential Primary Campaign: Who Voted for Jesse Jackson and Why," in Lucius J. Barker and Ronald W. Walters, eds., *Jesse Jackson's 1984 Presidential Campaign: Challenge and Change in American Politics* (1989), pp. 129–146; Frady, *Jesse*, pp. 334–341, 354–355.

40 Rick Atkinson, "Peace with American Jews Eludes Jackson," *Washington Post* (13 February 1984), pp. A1, A4; Frady, *Jesse*, pp. 343–349.

41 Jackson, *Straight From the Heart*, pp. 4–5; Jesse Jackson's 1984 Democratic National Convention Address, http://www.americanrhetoric.com/speeches/jessejackson1984dnc.htm; Michael Preston, "The 1984 Presidential Campaign: Who Voted for Jesse Jackson and Why," in Lucius J. Barker and Ronald W. Walters, eds., *Jesse Jackson's 1984 Presidential Campaign: Challenge and Change in American Politics* (1989), pp. 129–146.

42 Allen D. Hertzke, *Echoes of Discontent: Jesse Jackson, Pat Robertson, and the Resurgence of Populism* (1993), pp. 59–80; Frady, *Jesse*, pp. 378–401.

43 Hertzke, *Echoes of Discontent*, p. 177; Frady, *Jesse*, pp. 402–417; Steve Takesian, *Willie Horton: True Crime and Its Influence on a Presidential Election* (2002).

44 Sheila D. Collins, *From Melting Pot to Rainbow Coalition* (1986).

45 Garry Wills, *Under God: Religion and American Politics* (1990),
   pp. 235–244; John Dollard, *Caste and Class in a Southern Town* (1937),
   p. 242.

46 Sheila D. Collins, *The Rainbow Challenge: The Jackson Campaign and the
   Future of U.S. Politics* (1986), pp. 302–332; Stanford, *Beyond The
   Boundaries* (1997).

47 Frady, *Jesse*, pp. 471–483; Robin Toner, "Jackson to Run for Lobby Post in
   Washington," *New York Times* (6 July 1990), p. A9.

48 Eric L. Smith, "The Wall Street Project: What Does It Mean for You?"
   Black Enterprise 29 (October, 1998): 111–112, 114, 116.

49 Pam Belluck, "Rainbow Coalition Paid $35,000 to Woman in Jackson
   Affair," *New York Times* (20 January 2001), p. 9.

50 Frady, *Jesse*, pp. 326–330; William K. Piotrowski, "Hide, Jesse, Hide,"
   Religion in the News 4 (Spring, 2001): 18–30.

51 Stephen J. Wayne, *The Quest for the 2004 Nomination and Beyond* (2004).

52 Adolph Reed, "Jesse's Snake Oil," *Progressive* 59 (April, 1995): 18–20.

53 Jesse Jackson, "Renewing Our Minds," *Essence* 26 (May, 1995): 76; Jesse
   Jackson, "We Must Seek a New Moral Center," *Vital Speeches* 62
   (15 September 1996): 717.

CHAPTER NINE

Barack Obama: America's First Black President

Change will not come if we wait for some other person or some other time. We are the ones we've been waiting for. We are the change that we seek.[1]

[Barack Obama]

The secret of Mr. Obama is that he isn't really very good at politics, and he isn't good at politics because he doesn't really get people. . . . He was good at summoning hope, but he's not good at directing it and turning it into something concrete that answers a broad public desire. . . . He is not a devil, an alien, a socialist. He is a loser. And this is America, where nobody loves a loser.[2]

[Peggy Noonan]

Perspectives: The newest African-American leaders

Jesse Jackson's political star began falling after his second consecutive unsuccessful run for the presidency in 1988, and for a generation, no African-American leader of truly national stature emerged. There were pretenders to the proverbial leadership throne, including Minister Louis Farrakhan of the Nation of Islam and the Rev. Al Sharpton, but they lacked widespread appeal, chiefly because their polarizing messages were circumscribed by race.

The son of Caribbean parents, Louis Farrakhan had succeeded Malcolm X as the Nation of Islam's spokesman, but Farrakhan soon became mired in a succession fight to lead the organization. In an attempt to strengthen his hand, Farrakhan condemned a favorite target—the Jews—which exposed his anti-Semitism and made him a pariah in mainstream American society. Some commentators referred to Farrakhan as a "Black Hitler." Farrakhan was also dogged by persistent rumors that he, not J. Edgar Hoover's Federal Bureau of Investigation, was responsible for Malcolm X's murder, either to protect Elijah Muhammad and the Nation or to advance his own standing within it. Malcolm had once been Farrakhan's mentor and Farrakhan the godfather of Malcolm's children, but two months before Malcolm's murder in 1965, Farrakhan called Malcolm a traitor for criticizing Minister Muhammad. "The die is set, and Malcolm shall not escape," Farrakhan wrote in the Nation's newspaper. "Such a man is worthy of death." Malcolm had no doubt that the Nation was gunning for him, especially after the Nation ordered him evicted from his home and firebombed it when he refused to leave. Within days, three known Nation enforcers killed Malcolm in a hail of gunfire during a speech. Decades later, matters came to a head when Malcolm's widow, Betty Shabazz, publicly accused Farrakhan of killing her husband, and Malcolm's daughter Qubilah was charged with plotting to avenge her father's life by hiring a hit-man to kill Farrakhan. Qubilah avoided jail by accepting court-ordered psychological counseling and drug treatment.[3]

Insisting he "truly loved" Malcolm, Farrakhan attempted to recover lost ground by offering an indirect acknowledgement that his earlier comments might have made him "complicit" in the murder. In a further effort to make amends, Farrakhan organized a Million Man March in October, 1995, to portray black men in a positive light and to unite the African-American community in the face of serious continuing socioeconomic problems, including a staggering poverty rate of 40 percent. Although cynics dismissed Farrakhan's proposed rally as a mere public relations ploy, the turnout apparently dwarfed Martin Luther King's march on Washington, though it likely fell well short of the announced goal. The attendees at Farrakhan's march heard an impressive roster of speakers, including civil rights icon Rosa Parks, Jesse Jackson, National Association for the Advancement of Colored People (NAACP) leader Ben Chavis, Martin Luther King, III, and Betty Shabazz. After the march, Farrakhan remained a figure on the national stage, refraining from public rants and refashioning his deracialized message of redemption to encompass all of humankind. Still, he in no way approached the stature or influence of

Malcolm X or indeed any other major African-American figure discussed in this book, from Booker T. Washington to Barack Obama.[4]

Meanwhile, Al Sharpton, a Pentecostalist-turned-Baptist minister, positioned himself to become the new dominant voice of African Americans. For him, race is the "American Dilemma," and is at the heart of the nation's political, social, and economic problems, especially in New York, which he viewed as America's most racist city. Inspired by Adam Clayton Powell, Jr., a popular minister and U.S. congressman from Harlem, Sharpton joined the Southern Christian Leadership Conference and participated in many demonstrations for civil rights, particularly against the A&P grocery store chain, which stood accused of discriminatory hiring and business practices. As a teenager, Sharpton was appointed youth director of New York City's Operation Breadbasket, a national organization led by Jesse Jackson and dedicated to improving the economic condition of black communities across America. Like Jackson, Sharpton gravitated to the limelight, working with boxing promoter Don King and pop singer Michael Jackson, speaking in colorful language, and appearing, seemingly, everywhere, always available for questions from any television reporter. Sharpton once explained his penchant for the limelight by observing that "a preacher is part religious leader, social leader, social worker, and entertainer." Because Sharpton addressed many problems simultaneously, he found it difficult to be ideologically consistent, calling simultaneously for revolution, liberal reform, and a Booker T. Washington-brand of black capitalism. He invited all people to work together for change and still embraced black leaders who insisted on excluding whites.[5]

Steeped in the traditions of civil rights and black power, Sharpton responded with alacrity to any racial incident, including the New York City subway shootings of several young black panhandlers by Bernard Goetz. Sharpton rose to national prominence in December, 1986, when he led a sizable march that protested the severe beating (and one death) of several black men after they ate in a pizzeria in the upscale, virtually all-white Howard Beach neighborhood of Queens, New York. Sharpton's most memorable case involved the alleged rape of 15-year-old Tawana Brawley in a small town north of New York City. Brawley claimed that a gang of young white men, including a police officer, had raped her in the woods, scrawled racial epithets on her body, rubbed feces in her hair, and left her in a garbage bag. When a grand jury determined that Brawley had fabricated the entire scenario—perhaps to avoid another beating from her stepfather—many whites concluded that Sharpton followed racial trouble like a shark follows blood in the water. Sharpton unapologetically pointed out that he was defending black womanhood, which had long endured sexual abuse at the hands of white men. In yet another episode, Sharpton organized a series of rallies to protest the killing of a young black man in the Bensonhurst neighborhood of Brooklyn, New York, only to be pelted with watermelons and racial epithets, and stabbed in the chest with a knife.[6]

Among African Americans, Sharpton received a mixed reception, with poorer blacks applauding his uncompromising defense of the race and professional blacks chagrined by his race-baiting, boorishness, and all-consuming greed. Some black scholars, such as Harvard sociologist Orlando Patterson, accused Sharpton of being a "racial arsonist" who poisoned race relations with his polarizing invective. Shelby Steele, a fellow of Stanford University's public-policy think-tank called the Hoover Institution, dismissed Sharpton as a street hustler whose moral authority comes from "simply being black." Sharpton had been, after all, indicted for tax evasion, grand larceny, misappropriation of funds, and falsifying business records. While Sharpton never apologized for the Brawley fiasco, he gained a measure of respectability by choosing his causes more carefully, improving his physical appearance, and speaking in more measured tones, even if the message itself remained provocative. In 1991, Sharpton formed the Harlem-based National Action Network to address leading issues of the day, including chronic unemployment, racial profiling, police brutality, and AIDS awareness, and it attracted 200,000 members in forty-two cities. Harvard law professor Charles Ogletree described the new Sharpton as "a conduit between the disadvantaged and powerful leaders, and he has access to both the streets and the suites, to make sure that the people who are voiceless, faceless, and powerless finally have some say." Sharpton parlayed his activist experience, his high media visibility, and growing organizational membership into a run for the presidency in 2004, but his campaign for the Democratic party's nomination never caught fire. He withdrew in favor of U.S. senator John Kerry of Massachusetts, the eventual nominee.[7]

For a time, it appeared that four-star army general Colin Powell, the son of Jamaican immigrants, might fill the bill as race leader. Public opinion polls reported that he was widely admired among nearly all groups and classes in American society and was a prohibitive favorite to become the first African-American president. Certainly, he had substantial credentials. He had served with distinction in two tours of duty in Vietnam, the start of a highly-decorated, thirty-five year career in the U.S. army.

Upon his return from southeast Asia, Powell moved up the military chain of command with lightning speed. Under president Ronald Reagan, Powell broke the color barrier as national security adviser and chairman of the Joint Chiefs of Staff. Powell preferred to rely on diplomacy rather than military force, leading to his nickname, the "Reluctant Warrior." But when Reagan's successor, George H.W. Bush, called for Operation Desert Storm to liberate Kuwait from Iraqi domination, Powell organized a massive military machine in 1991 that defeated the overmatched Iraqi army in a hundred hours. The use of overwhelming force was dubbed the "Powell Doctrine." Because Powell was America's premier soldier-statesman, both political parties recruited him as a presidential candidate, but he declined to run, insisting that he lacked an all-consuming passion to campaign for the position.[8]

Under president George W. Bush, the elder Bush's son, Powell became the first African-American secretary of state, and he was called on to lead the nation's response to al-Qaeda's deadly attack of September 11, 2001, on the World Trade Center towers in New York City and the Pentagon, which houses the U.S. Defense Department in northern Virginia. It was his assignment to persuade the United Nations and world opinion generally that Iraq was connected to the terrorists. As a "good soldier," Powell had to provide evidence that Iraqi dictator Saddam Hussein had weapons of mass destruction, which would justify an American-led invasion to topple Hussein's regime. In a display of candor seldom seen in American public life, Powell described the UN speech as a painful "blot" on his record, because evidence subsequently showed that Iraq had no nuclear capability. Despite justifying the invasion of a country that had not directly attacked the United States, Powell still occupied the position of respected elder statesman whose independence of thought seemed to elevate him above race, party, or self-interest.[9]

Dreams from My Father

In 2004, a charismatic, yet enigmatic, new figure took the national stage—Barack Hussein Obama II, a Democratic state senator from Illinois. In some ways, Obama's life story was quintessentially American and parallels Booker T. Washington's biography, but it was unique in other respects. Barack ("blessed by God" in Arabic) was born in 1961 to a Luo tribesman with the same name from the British colony of Kenya, then in the throes of becoming an independent nation, and an idealistic white woman named Stanley Ann Dunham, a Kansas native of Irish descent who ended up in the new, multi-ethnic state of Hawaii. As an only child, Stanley Ann received a masculine first name because her father—a furniture salesman named Stanley—had wanted a son. Dunham met her brilliant and bombastic husband in a Russian language class when they were students at the University of Hawaii. The 24-year-old pipe-smoking Obama was the university's first African student, and his natty appearance, booming baritone voice, and provocative dancing were unforgettable. No one knew that the flirtatious Obama was married to an African woman named Kezia who had borne him two children, an inconvenient truth he kept largely hidden as he married thrice more.[10]

When Barack Obama and an unsuspecting Ann Dunham eloped, as her parents had done a generation earlier, she was 18-years-old and pregnant, which led her to leave school to raise their infant son, Barack junior. At the time, an interracial marriage would have been illegal in much of the American mainland. The hasty marriage—which under American law, though not Luo custom, made Obama a bigamist—deeply angered both families. Dunham's mother thought Obama was "straaaaaange" and was frightened that her daughter might be beheaded if she moved to Kenya during the Mau Mau rebellion; Obama's father did not want his black African bloodline "sullied by a white woman". The marriage was doomed from the start, and Obama and Dunham separated almost immediately. Obama, a Phi Beta Kappa graduate but a deadbeat dad, soon departed Hawaii to earn a doctorate in economics at Harvard University, part of his grandiose plan to "reshape the destiny of Africa." Obama passed his doctoral qualifying examinations to continue his studies, but his "playboy ways" and white fears of miscegenation finally cost him the opportunity to complete his dream degree. In a double whammy, Harvard's International Office cut off Obama's financial aid and the federal government's Immigration and Naturalization Service quickly deported this "very slippery character" from the United States. Demoralized, Obama returned to Kenya, where he worked as a government economist and married and divorced another American woman.[11]

Ann Dunham subsequently married Lolo Soetoro, a geology student from Indonesia. Soetoro, followed by his new wife and stepson, returned to Indonesia when the government called home all of its citizens studying abroad. It was in Jakarta that young Barack played in rice paddies; rode water buffalo; ate dog, snake, and roasted grasshopper; and had a backyard menagerie that included a cockatoo, an ape, and crocodiles. He also witnessed dire poverty first hand, which left a powerful imprint on him. In far-off Indonesia, where fatalism was a necessary strategy for survival, Dunham became, her son later wrote, "a lonely witness for secular humanism, a soldier for New Deal, Peace Corps, position-paper liberalism." Dunham was determined to make her "black" son into somebody. Before going to work as a secretary, she awoke Barack at 4:00 a.m. each weekday to give him three hours of English lessons. Nor did she neglect his African-American heritage, surrounding Barack with books on the heroes of the civil rights movement and recordings of the speeches of Martin Luther King and the soul music of Mahalia Jackson. To his mother, Obama remembered, "every black man was Thurgood Marshall or Sidney Poitier; every black woman Fannie Lou Hamer or Lena Horne." "To be black," Barack learned as he searched for his racial identity, "was to be the beneficiary of a great inheritance, a special destiny, glorious burdens that only we were strong enough to bear."[12]

Dunham's second marriage collapsed when Soetoro, who worked for an American petroleum company, spent his time drinking whiskey and playing golf and tennis with his company pals. As Soetoro upset Dunham by embracing Western ways, Dunham upset her husband by refusing to attend business dinners and was indifferent about her appearance, immersing herself instead in Javanese culture. Despite the birth of a daughter, the Soetoros barely spoke to each other but remained in a loveless marriage for years before divorcing. Dunham concluded that 10-year-old Barack was better off in Hawaii, and shipped him there to live with his maternal grandparents and to have access to modern medicine, while she remained in Indonesia to complete her field work for a doctorate in cultural anthropology. During this period of family turmoil, grandmother Madelyn, a World War II factory worker who became the first female vice-president of the Bank of Hawaii, instilled in Barack her Midwestern values of prudence, hard work, and pragmatism.[13]

From a continent away, Barack's father wrote to him occasionally, but saw him in person only once more before he died. The elder Obama was a distant and intimidating figure, whose professional life was stunted by Kenyan politics mired in cronyism and corruption and whose personal life dissolved in whiskey, philandering, and wife-beating. Frustrated and embittered, he died after crashing his car into a eucalyptus tree while driving drunk. Later, the younger Barack visited his relatives in Kenya and saw first-hand how difficult their lives were: "I was probably lucky not to have been living in his house as I was growing up. I do think that part of my life has been a deliberate attempt to not repeat mistakes of my father," whom, in any case, he hardly knew. "Every man," Obama continued, "is trying to live up to his father's expectations or make up for his mistakes.

In my case, both things might be true." It was his mother, not his father, who gave Barack his mind, temperament, empathy, and audacity before she died in 1995 of ovarian cancer at age 52.[14]

To continue his education, Barack won a scholarship to the Punahou School, Hawaii's top college preparatory academy, which was founded in Honolulu in 1841 for the children of Christian missionaries. There, Barack was one of three blacks in a student body of 1,200. He endured racial taunts as he grew up, but racial prejudice in the diverse state of Hawaii was mild compared to that on the mainland. As a youngster, Barack—then called "Barry"—played basketball with a passion, experimented with drugs, and learned how to be "black" thousands of miles away from the centers of African-American culture. As Obama reflected on it, his use of alcohol, marijuana, and cocaine helped him "push questions of who I was out of my mind."[15]

Obama's quest to define himself remained a preoccupation. He listened to musical recordings of Marvin Gaye and Stevie Wonder, watched *Soul Train* and comedian Richard Pryor on television, and read celebrated African-American writers, including poet Langston Hughes, essayists W.E.B. Du Bois and James Baldwin, and novelists Richard Wright and Ralph Ellison. In studying the panoply of black leaders, Obama was most fascinated by Malcolm X. In his memoir, Obama wrote that Du Bois, Hughes, and Baldwin finally gave up their fight for racial justice and withdrew from the mainstream of American life, "all of them exhausted, bitter men, the devil at their heels." "Only Malcolm X's autobiography," Obama concluded, "seemed to offer something different. His repeated acts of self-creation spoke to me; the blunt poetry of his words, his unadorned insistence on respect, promised a new and uncompromising order, martial in its discipline, forged through sheer force of will." Obama concluded that "all the other stuff" that was part of Malcolm's fiery rhetoric, "the talk of blue-eyed devils and apocalypse, was incidental to that program." Such searching reflected Obama's deep desire to find out who he was.[16]

As a teenager, Obama confessed to a "troubled heart," one that reflected "the mixed blood, the divided soul, the ghostly image of the tragic mulatto trapped between two worlds." NAACP co-founder W.E.B. Du Bois had spoken of the "two-ness" that every African American felt a century ago, but he meant a division between being American and black; Obama was divided by his own biracial heritage, with a black father and white mother. "Where did I belong?" Obama kept wondering. "If I had come to understand myself as a black American, and was understood as such, that understanding remained unanchored to place. What I needed was a community . . . that cut deeper than the common despair that black friends and I shared when reading the latest crime statistics or the high fives that I might exchange on a basketball court." When Obama shared his reading with some African-American friends, one told him curtly, "I don't need no books to tell me how to be black." Henceforth, Obama kept private his quest for finding himself. He became adept at slipping back and forth between his black and white worlds, "understanding that each possessed its own language and customs and structures of meaning, convinced that with a bit of translation on my part the two worlds would eventually cohere."[17]

The search for selfhood continued for Obama as he pursued higher education on the mainland. At Occidental College in California, Obama wanted "to avoid being mistaken for a sellout," so he associated with "politically active black students, the foreign students . . . the Marxist professors and structural feminists and punk-rock performance poets," and stayed up late into the night in his dormitory discussing "neocolonialism, Frantz Fanon, Eurocentrism, and patriarchy." He admits he was "alienated." After two years, he transferred across country to Columbia University, a prestigious institution located next to Harlem's poor black neighborhoods in New York City. There, Obama undertook "a lot of spiritual exploration" to reconcile his rational side with his yearning for transcendence. He attended the famed Abyssianian Baptist Church once led by Adam Clayton Powell, Jr., but otherwise "withdrew from the world in a fairly deliberate way." Adopting a monkish lifestyle, he fasted, went for days without speaking to another person, and read books by Augustine, the 4th-century North African bishop whose writings helped build the Christian Church; Friedrich Nietzsche, the 19th-century German philosopher who espoused existentialism; and Graham Greene, the Roman Catholic Englishman whose novels discuss pain and ambivalence. He also immersed himself in books about Martin Luther King and the civil rights movement. At Columbia, Obama majored in political science and listened to activists Jesse Jackson and Stokely Carmichael (Kwame Ture) offering their solutions to the racial dilemma, but he found their remarks unhelpful or irrelevant.[18]

After his father died, Obama became driven to make his "mark" on society. "I wanted," he recalled, "to devote myself to something larger than making money or having a good time." Obama had spent his youth searching for his identity and his place in the world, and he concluded that his place was in the public arena. At first, Obama stayed in New York to work for a consumer advocacy group established by Ralph Nader.

Determined to help poor African Americans and inspired by the election of Harold Washington—Chicago's first black mayor—Obama accepted a position as a Saul Alinsky-type community organizer in the impoverished South Side of Chicago. This assignment helped him fill the hole left by his father's absence, chastened him about the dead ends he might have taken as a young black man, and allowed him to contribute to the legacy of the civil rights movement he admired. "It was a promise of redemption," Obama admitted. Obama was too late to be a black Moses like Harriet Tubman, Marcus Garvey, or Martin Luther King, Jr., but he could be a Joshua—Moses' successor—and help the poor. Despite his inexperience, Obama achieved modest successes while directing the Developing Communities Project, which was run by Roman Catholic priests. A talented motivator, Obama expanded the staff and budget, established a tenants' rights group, organized voter registration drives, and implemented programs for job-training, college preparatory tutoring, and drug treatment; but the South Side remained a deeply troubled neighborhood. The assignment tested Obama's mettle, and he learned quickly that idealism was no substitute for street-smart politics.[19]

After three years of organizing, Obama entered Harvard University law school in 1988 "to find out more about power. How do powerful people think? What kind of networks do they have? How do they connect to each other?" Underlying these questions was Obama's conviction that government, not community activism alone, could solve urban ills. Several years older than most of his classmates, Obama moved swiftly to make an impact at Harvard, the same school his absent father and W.E.B. Du Bois had attended. The younger Obama wrote articles for the *Harvard Civil Rights-Civil Liberties Law Review*, was active in the anti-apartheid movement on campus, served on the board of directors of the Black Law Students Association, and became the first African-American president of the *Harvard Law Review*, in part because of his ability to navigate between liberals and conservatives.[20]

A high-powered law career was within his grasp, but he spurned a U.S. Supreme Court clerkship, opting instead to return to Chicago. There, Obama met and married a well-connected, Harvard-educated lawyer named Michelle Robinson, with whom he had two daughters. In quick order, he received a publication advance for a book on race, tentatively titled "Journeys in Black and White"; was hired by the University of Chicago to teach in its law school; and joined a law firm specializing in civil rights litigation and neighborhood economic development. At the same time, Obama directed Illinois Project Vote, which dispatched hundreds of volunteers to enroll 150,000 low-income African Americans, resulting in black registrants outnumbering whites in Chicago for the first time. Intended to combat the Reagan administration's rollback of social programs, Project Vote helped elect Carol Moseley Braun to the U.S. Senate—the first black woman—and put Illinois in the Democratic column for Bill Clinton, the first time the Democrats had carried the state in a presidential race in three decades. Power brokers in Chicago began to think that Obama just might be the first black president.[21]

Increasingly, the ever-restless Obama realized that practicing and teaching law did not affect people's lives as powerfully as enacting legislation did. Seeing an opportunity to help the dispossessed, Obama sought political office from Chicago's South Side. Playing hard-ball politics to deny the incumbent a spot on the ballot, he was elected to three terms in the Illinois state senate, where he demonstrated an inclination for avoiding histrionics and controversy—thus the nickname "No-drama Obama"—and a willingness to study the issues and to work across the political aisle. His early political career was devoted to reforming laws relating to ethics, health care, welfare, and the death penalty; increasing tax credits for low-income workers and subsidies for childcare; ending predatory lending practices to forestall home mortgage closures; and monitoring police interrogations of suspects.[22]

As he ascended the political ladder, the 33-year-old Obama finished his book on race, which had evolved into an autobiography, *Dreams from My Father: A Story of Race and Inheritance*, a poignant coming-of-age account of alienation and rebellion that was published in 1995. The publisher had expected that the manuscript would appeal to "multicultural" readers, but Obama's personal story proved to have universal appeal. One reviewer described Obama's book as perhaps "the best-written memoir ever produced by an American politician," and Obama even received a Grammy Award for the audio book edition. Critics analyzed the book more deeply and found that Obama's memoir romanticized his life story. Journalist David Remnick described Obama's autobiography as "a mixture of verifiable fact, recollection, recreation, invention and artful shaping." Each section, for example, ends with Obama in tears—dreaming of his father, discovering his spiritual roots inside a church sanctuary, and visiting his father's grave in Kenya. Although this moving account about racial identity focuses on his father and his African past, the younger Obama knew him more as a myth than a man.[23]

In 2000, Obama set his sights on Congress, but lost to the popular four-term incumbent, Bobby Rush—a one-time Black Panther—in what remains the only election Obama ever lost. It was a strategically foolish move on the 38-year-old Obama's part because he was still learning how to be a candidate in a party primary contest where challengers seldom win. The upstart Obama was stiff on the stump, pedantic, even arrogant, in reminding voters of his sacrifices as a community organizer, when he could have been a high-priced corporate attorney. Rush mocked Obama as inauthentic, meaning he was insufficiently black. Obama, said Rush, had attended an Ivy League school and "became an educated fool" who imagined he was an expert on civil rights. Another primary opponent accused Obama of being a "white man in black face." Word on the street was that Obama was a carpetbagger "sent by the white man . . . to break up and rape the black community," not unlike Clarence Thomas, the African-American judge who became a dyed-in-the-wool conservative on the U.S. Supreme Court. Rush had the support of most black leaders, including Jesse Jackson, who sensed that Obama might become a political rival to his son, Jesse Jackson, Jr., and so Rush won in a landslide. "Completely mortified and humiliated" at losing, Obama attributed his political thrashing to several circumstances, including the fatal shooting of Rush's oldest son in front of their South Side home by drug dealers, which created enormous sympathy among voters with just a month remaining before election day; the press's pillory of Obama when he missed a key legislative vote on gun-control in order to extend a Hawaiian vacation; and president Clinton's endorsement of Rush.[24]

Even as his congressional campaign imploded, Obama made one thing clear to his disheartened staffers: he was addicted to politics and would continue seeking a prominent elective office. A Chicago reporter recognized Obama's soaring ambition and warned that Obama's winning smile masked another side of him: "What the public has yet to see clearly is his hidden side: his imperious, mercurial, self-righteous and sometimes prickly nature, each quality exacerbated by the enormous career pressures he has inflicted upon himself. . . . He is an extraordinarily ambitious, competitive man with . . . a career reach that seems to have no bounds. He is, in fact, a man of raw ambition so powerful that even he is still coming to terms with its full force."[25]

Black man headed to the White House

In 2004, Barack Obama attracted national attention for the re-release of his autobiography, which became a run-away best-seller, and for delivering the keynote address at the Democratic party's national convention. The speech was a plum assignment, because Obama was then only a state senator running for the U.S. Senate. On the appointed day, Obama walked around Boston, Massachusetts, the convention city, with a successful black businessman who marveled at the growing crowd accompanying them: "This is incredible. You're like a rock star." Obama replied to his friend, "You think it's bad today, wait until tomorrow." When asked what he meant, Obama replied, "My speech is pretty good." To a reporter, Obama was nonchalant about the entourage gathering around him: "I'm LeBron [James], baby," referring to a talented professional basketball player. "I can play on this level. I got some game." As predicted, Obama stole the show, speaking movingly of his maternal grandfather's service in general George Patton's Third Army and the benefits that same grandfather later received from the GI Bill and the Federal Housing Authority. Obama also spoke about changing the federal government's social and economic priorities, and questioned the conduct of the Iraq war, which, he reminded voters, he had opposed.[26]

Calling for a new day in politics, Obama implored Americans to find unity in diversity:

There's not a liberal America and a conservative America; there's the United States of America. There's not a black America and white America and Latino America and Asian America; there's the United States of America. The pundits . . . like to slice and dice our country into red states and blue States: red states for Republicans, blue States for Democrats. But I've got news for them, too. We worship an awesome God in the blue states, and we don't like federal agents poking around our libraries in the red states. We coach little league in the blue states and, yes, we've got some gay friends in the red states. There are patriots who opposed the war in Iraq, and there are patriots who supported the war in Iraq. We are one people, all of us pledging allegiance to the stars and stripes, all of us defending the United States of America. In the end, that's what this election is about. Do we participate in a politics of cynicism, or do we participate in a politics of hope?

Obama then laid out his vision of a new kind of politics that would appeal to Americans of every background and color:

I'm talking about something more substantial. It's the hope of slaves sitting around a fire singing freedom songs; the hope of immigrants setting out for distant shores; the hope of a young naval lieutenant bravely patrolling the Mekong Delta; the hope of a millworker's son who dares to defy the odds; the hope of a skinny kid with a funny name who believes that America has a place for him, too. Hope in the face of difficulty, hope in the face of uncertainty, the audacity of hope: In the end, that is God's greatest gift to us, the bedrock of this nation, a belief in things not seen, a belief that there are better days ahead.

The hall erupted in applause, and the public mobbed Obama wherever he went. Pundits spoke of an "Obama phenomenon" and dubbed him as the Democratic party's rising star, a Democratic Colin Powell who offered a refreshing mix of races and cultures, as well as liberal ideas with traditional values. Ethel Kennedy, Robert Kennedy's widow, told Obama, "The torch is being passed to you," and a chill shot up Obama's spine.[27]

That fall, Obama won his race for a U.S. Senate seat by trouncing the last-minute Republican candidate in what was the largest margin of victory for statewide office in Illinois history. Obama was the fifth African American, and the third popularly elected, to serve in the Senate. On Capitol Hill, Obama voted "liberal" 90 percent of the time, but his legislative record was unimpressive, evidently because he concluded that he could get little done as a member of the party out of power. He introduced two initiatives that bore his name, one to track federal spending and the other to use international cooperation to reduce conventional weapons. He also supported measures to criminalize deceptive practices in federal elections, divest state pension funds from Iran's oil industry, reduce the risk of international terrorism, and provide job protection for family members caring for soldiers afflicted with injuries from combat. Obama established a reputation for high intelligence, but not a keen interest in the political process, and most of his legislation remained mired in committee. In this regard, Obama followed in the steps of another junior senator in his forties—John F. Kennedy—who tired of political wrangling in the "world's greatest deliberative body," and ran for president instead.[28]

Just two years into his first term in the Senate, Obama plunged into the 2008 race for the U.S. presidency. It was an audacious decision on his part, given his short political resume by presidential standards. As a result, he would run on his ability to inspire voters with his optimistic rhetoric. His campaign slogan was "Change We Can Believe In," which resonated well with many Americans. Obama's presidential ambition was also audacious because several African Americans had already made a symbolic race for the ultimate prize in American politics and lost. In recent decades, a partial list of black presidential aspirants included journalist George Edwin Taylor, 1904; trade unionist Clifton DeBerry, 1964; comedian

Dick Gregory, communist activist Charlene Mitchell, and Black Panther party leader Eldridge Cleaver, 1968; U.S. congresswoman Shirley Chisholm of New York, 1972; Margaret Wright, a socialist and World War II shipyard worker, 1976; Jesse Jackson, twice in the 1980s; developmental psychologist Lenora Fulani, 1988; former diplomat Alan Keyes, 1996 and 2000; and Al Sharpton and Carol Moseley Braun, 2004. Martin Luther King, Jr. had been asked to run for president on a third-party ticket in 1968, but he declined because he would undoubtedly lose, damaging his influence and legacy. Unlike Jesse Jackson's bids, Obama would not organize his presidential campaign around a black base and a rainbow coalition of liberal ethnics, gays, and union members, espousing instead a center-left political philosophy.[29]

To lay out his policy positions on a host of issues, Obama wrote a second best-selling book, a manifesto called, *The Audacity of Hope: Thoughts on Reclaiming the American Dream*. Challenging readers to shelve their biases as they read his book, Obama went on record as opposing the Iraq war and supporting a plan for universal health care, a woman's right to choose an abortion, a revamped educational system with merit pay and more teacher accountability, and higher fuel-efficiency standards in automobiles. He conceded that racial discrimination was a fact of life in corporations, unions, and government offices, but maintained that African Americans, especially the black poor, must take collective and individual responsibility for their welfare. In any event, Obama wrote, "white guilt has largely exhausted itself in America." One of Obama's most revealing passages is one he learned from his mother: "I reject a politics that is based solely on racial identity, gender identity, sexual orientation, or victimhood generally." A reviewer wrote that *The Audacity of Hope* does not contain "boldly innovative policy prescriptions that will lead the Democrats out of their wilderness," but it does show Obama's potential to "construct a new politics that is progressive but grounded in civic traditions that speak to a wider range of Americans."[30]

Throughout the presidential primary campaign, Obama proposed a reform agenda that liberal Democrats had championed since Franklin D. Roosevelt's New Deal during the Great Depression, namely, an enlarged social safety net. Several Democratic candidates were more experienced in that cycle, including John Edwards, the former U.S. senator from North Carolina who ran for vice-president in 2004. Edwards, a trial lawyer by trade, made a populist appeal, but his candidacy never gained widespread support, and finally imploded when he confessed to adultery, while his wife was battling incurable cancer. Obama's most formidable opponent was Hillary Rodham Clinton, the junior U.S. senator from New York and heir to the Clinton political dynasty. Hillary Clinton held a Yale law degree, actively supported children's issues, and spearheaded her husband's unsuccessful bid to secure health care reform. She appealed especially to women and, as a reliable liberal, to the Democratic party's old guard. On the hustings, Clinton presided over an undisciplined campaign effort, but nevertheless did well in party primaries, where turnout depended on party machinery and union organization. Much of the press hailed Clinton's party nomination as "inevitable," but the Democratic nominating process then included numerous party caucuses that selected delegates to the convention. Obama shrewdly mastered the complicated and labor-intensive caucus mechanism in what would become one of the most formidable political operations in American history.[31]

As an inspirational figure and experienced community organizer, with an increasingly large following among young people and intellectuals, Obama repeatedly bested Hillary Clinton in the caucuses. "Are you FIRED UP? Are you READY TO GO?" he asked his adoring crowds. "FIRED UP! READY TO GO!" the crowd responded. As the likely voters streamed out of the rally, Obama exhorted them, "Let's go change the world." In the eyes of some older supporters, Obama was a black Jack Kennedy, sporting the same youthfulness, obvious intelligence, and popular appeal. Perhaps a closer comparison was Bobby Kennedy, whose charisma, ambition, and mixture of idealism and bare-knuckle politics also described Obama. Obama tapped his popular appeal by raising record amounts of campaign cash, especially by insistent appeals made on computer internet sites. Obama was so successful raising donations for his Hopefund that he became the first major-party presidential candidate to reject public financing in the general election since the system was created in 1976. Even after declining to accept public money, he outspent all of his competitors combined.[32]

To capture the Democratic party's nomination, Obama endured withering criticism of his background and his political philosophy, as some white opponents went into overdrive to discredit his candidacy. At their most base level, these attacks centered on the claim that Obama was disloyal, because, it was alleged, he was a foreigner and a Muslim who consorted with terrorists. Activists in the crackpot Birther Movement posed the canard that Obama was constitutionally precluded from being president because they claimed that he had been born in Indonesia or, perhaps, Kenya. Fake hospital certificates appeared, purporting to "prove" Obama's foreign birth. Some right-wingers associated Obama with Muslim terrorist cells in the Middle East. His last name, "Obama," sounded like "Osama," as in Osama bin Laden, the Saudi Arabian mastermind of the terrorist attack on New York City's World Trade Center. Cartoons appeared of Obama's face morphed into bin Laden's. Obama's middle name "Hussein" reminded critics of another Muslim—Saddam Hussein—the late tyrant of Iraq, whom the United States had defeated in a brief war during George W. Bush's presidency. Rumors spread that Obama was a secret Muslim. None of these allegations was true.[33]

Still others criticized Barack Obama's patriotism, noting that he had never served in the military, had voted against the "war on terror" in Iraq, and had refused, for a time, to wear an American flag pin in his lapel. Some detractors pointed to his work as a community organizer in Chicago to suggest that he was somehow subversive. Moreover, conservatives painted Obama as a radical with a bevy of radical friends and mentors. Two of these associates stood out. Barack Obama knew William Ayers, a onetime leader of the Weather Underground, an anti-Vietnam war group which used bombs against government buildings to stop what was then America's longest war. One of these bombs killed three people. Some quibblers claimed that Ayers had ghostwritten Obama's memoir, *Dreams from My Father*. There is no doubt that Obama had known Ayers, but major news publications concluded that Obama had no ongoing relationship with him. Unlike the autobiographies of Booker T. Washington and Malcolm X, no evidence has been produced to prove that anyone other than Obama wrote his memoir.[34]

As incendiary as the alleged Ayers association was, Obama was tarnished just as much, if not more, by his longtime membership in the Rev. Jeremiah Wright's Trinity United Church of Christ. Wright, a Vietnam veteran, delivered jeremiads against racial injustice and trumpeted a motto of "unashamedly black and unapologetically Christian." He blended scriptural references, Afrocentrism, and a call for social justice to build a 6,000-member congregation. Obama had come to Wright's megachurch in a circuitous manner. Obama's mother was raised in the liberal Unitarian Society by "non-practicing Methodists and Baptists," as Obama put it, and she was turned off by organized religion. At the same time, Obama described his mother as "in many ways the most spiritually awakened person that I have ever known." His father, Barack, Sr., was "raised a Muslim" but was a "confirmed atheist" by the time his parents met. Obama's Indonesian stepfather viewed religion as "not particularly useful." Obama came to religion through his work as a community organizer, when he saw "the power of the African-American religious tradition to spur social change." Seeing religion in this new light and continuing to define his own sense of blackness, Obama was baptized at Trinity Church. Rev. Wright later officiated at Obama's wedding and baptized his daughters. It was one of Wright's sermons that gave Obama the title of his book on campaign issues—*The Audacity of Hope*.[35]

Rev. Wright never shied from controversy. His church gave a "greatness" award to the Nation of Islam's Louis Farrakhan, an anti-Semitic demagogue. At one worship service, Wright was videotaped in an anti-American outburst: "God damn America—that's in the Bible—for killing innocent people. God damn America, for treating our citizens as less than human. God damn America, as long as she tries to act like she is God, and she is supreme. The United States government has failed the vast majority of her citizens of African descent." That explosive recording, which expounded on Martin Luther King's denunciations of American genocide and imperialism, was replayed endlessly on radio and television airwaves and made available on computer websites. Critics who listened to Wright's diatribe against the United States concluded that Obama was mentored by a minister consumed, not with a love of God, but with racial bitterness and national self-hatred.[36]

To prevent these damaging charges from sinking his campaign, Obama acted quickly. His responses showed that he was a calculating politician prepared to take decisive action to save his reputation. Obama released a copy of his birth certificate, which proved to all but the Birther Movement that he was born in Kapi'olani Hospital in Honolulu, Hawaii, and moved to Indonesia as a boy. With regard to Ayers, Obama dismissed the claim that he was close to the former Weatherman, who had long since become a valued member of the community as a professor at the University of Illinois at Chicago. Obama condemned Ayers' past and insisted that he had known Ayers only casually, serving on community boards with him.[37]

It was harder to dismiss the Wright connection because of the damning videotape, photographs of a smiling Obama standing next to Wright, and Obama's twenty-year membership in Wright's church. When the imbroglio would not subside, Obama gave a remarkably candid speech on race entitled, "A More Perfect Union," which condemned Wright's comments but placed them in historical context. Wright's racially-charged sermons, Obama said, were relics of an earlier era when progress for African Americans was all but impossible. Obama compared Wright to "an old uncle" who could not be disowned, in the same way that he could not disown the black community or his white grandmother—"a woman who helped raise me, a woman who sacrificed again and again for me, a woman who loves me as much as she loves anything in this world, but a woman who once confessed her fear of black men who passed her by on the street, and who on more than one occasion has uttered racial or ethnic stereotypes that made me cringe. These people are a part of me. And they are a part of America, this country that I love." Conservatives thought the speech was a "brilliant fraud," while liberals deemed it the finest address since Martin Luther King's "I Have a Dream" masterpiece. The controversy had begun to fade when Wright angrily defended himself in public and obliquely attacked Obama. Finally, Obama could take no more, and repudiated his longtime pastor as he resigned from Trinity Church. Obama's speech changed the conversation in the campaign and stopped the bloodletting touched off by the Wright tape.[38]

Some of Obama's critics were powerful because they controlled influential media outlets. Bill Kristol, a top official in the Reagan and Bush I administrations, published the *Weekly Standard*, a magazine that attracted some of the brighter and abler conservative journalists. Far less restrained were conservative broadcasters on daily radio and television programs. Rush Limbaugh, a college dropout and former disc jockey with a penchant for histrionics, had the largest listening audience of all radio talk shows, and was tabbed by former president Ronald Reagan as "the Number One voice for conservatism in our Country." In one memorable insult and fabrication, Limbaugh labeled Obama as a "Halfrican American" of Arab descent who was intent on providing blacks with reparations for slavery and subverting capitalism in favor of socialism. Limbaugh imitators, including Bill O'Reilly, Jr., Sean Hannity, and Glenn Beck, filled the airwaves on the Fox cable television channel. At one point, Beck described Obama as a man who has "a deep-seated hatred for white people or the white culture." These often demagogic talk-show hosts reinforced right-wing fears of a radical takeover of America. The steady drumbeat of questioning Obama's loyalty bore fruit during the campaign, with demented people shouting, "kill him," "terrorist," "communist," "traitor," "socialist," and "off with his head."[39]

As criticism against him mounted, Obama's patience grew thin, especially with the working class. At a private California fundraiser, he explained why lower-class whites in the industrial Northeast—not a few of whom had been unemployed for years—opposed his candidacy: "It's not surprising, then, they get bitter, they cling to guns or religion or antipathy to people who aren't like them or anti-immigrant sentiment or anti-trade sentiment as a way to explain their frustrations." This simplistic analysis about class differences weakened his claim that he was the best candidate to unify the country. Hillary Clinton, who was raised in a church-going family in the Midwest, described Obama's remarks as "elitist," "out of touch," and "demeaning," adding that they were "not reflective of the values and beliefs of Americans." She added, "People don't need a president who looks down on them. They need a president who stands up for them." Accused of arrogance and condescension, Obama tried to quell the furor by conceding that his remarks were ill-advised, noting that what really made Americans angry was a government that ignored its people.[40]

Other critics wondered about Obama's experience and toughness to become the leader of the Free World. In the Democratic primary, Hillary Clinton ran television commercials on this theme, repeatedly asking Americans whom they would prefer to answer an emergency alarm in the dead of night. But Obama had more experience than Abraham Lincoln did when the Great Emancipator became president, and Obama had several times shown his ability to play a sharp-elbowed game of politics when it suited his purpose. His hard inner core and unyielding ambition belied his good luck, smiling countenance, and soft-spokenness. "This campaign cannot be about me," Obama told a cheering crowd in Chicago. "I am an imperfect vessel for your hopes and dreams." In point of fact, Obama's campaign was almost entirely about him and the compelling idea of transformation that he embodied.[41]

Obama transcended criticisms and innuendoes to wage an often-inspiring campaign marked by soaring rhetoric that inspired a generation of young people. "Change you can believe in," Obama chanted repeatedly, and many people welcomed the mantra. He promised to end the war in Iraq, increase energy independence, and provide universal health care, all without raising taxes for 95 percent of working families. Obama defended himself, especially for voting against the Iraq war: "I don't oppose all wars. What I am opposed to is a dumb war. What I am opposed to is a rash war." Obama's liberal agenda made him the darling of the Hollywood set, and he received the blessing of television's favorite afternoon host, Oprah Winfrey, a billionaire African-American media mogul who lived in Chicago and who was therefore endorsing her own U.S. senator. In front of 18,000 fans in Des Moines, Iowa, the Queen of Daytime TV delivered this proclamation: "There are those who say it's not his time, that he should wait his turn. I'm sick of politics as usual. We need Barack Obama."[42]

Unsurprisingly, race was one of the issues in the presidential campaign, although Obama, as a living metaphor for an increasingly diverse America, tried mightily to become a post-racial candidate. Simple voting math demonstrated that a black presidential candidate had to attract a sizable percentage of white voters to win office. In some ways, race became a secondary issue because African Americans were more accepted in the larger society than ever before. A majority of African Americans had reached the middle class for the first time, and they had been integrated into American society by civil rights laws and affirmative action programs. Obama benefited from a long line of high-achieving black students in largely white suburban schools, black news anchors on television, and thousands of black officials elected before him, not to mention an enriched school curriculum that included black history and literature, such as *Narrative of the Life of Frederick Douglass, an American Slave.* Obama represented the assimilated black who was not an exotic figure, but a known and unthreatening quantity.[43]

Obama reassured many whites by his complete assimilation into American society. He was, as U.S. Senate majority leader Harry Reid, a fellow Democrat, indelicately put it, "light-skinned," which was significant because, traditionally, the darker one's skin color in America, the more suspicion it aroused among whites. Obama had received the best education that America had to offer and, Reid continued, had no trace of a "Negro dialect unless he wanted to have one." Obama could, and did, speak in a different way to different audiences. U.S. Senator Joe Biden of Delaware described Obama as "the first mainstream African American who is articulate and bright and clean and a nice-looking guy . . . that's a storybook." In addition, Obama never became angry, at least in public, and he seldom spoke about racial issues. The campaign kept what it termed "radioactive" blacks, such as Jesse Jackson and Al Sharpton, off of platforms with Obama.[44]

On the surface, it appeared that Obama allowed white America to disregard race. In truth, this was not a color-blind election, for many white Americans voted for Obama precisely because he was black—a safe black. Black conservative writer Shelby Steele viewed Obama as quite different from racial "hucksters" such as Jackson and Sharpton, who periodically stirred the racial pot to maintain their visibility and maintain a steady flow of donations. Obama, in this understanding, professed to condemn racial divisiveness, while adroitly using it to his advantage. He offered a great bargain to whites who felt guilty about the legacy of racism and discrimination that stained American civilization. Obama subtly told whites that if they voted for him, they would be forever cleansed of the damning charge of racism. It was a perverse way of being born again, Steele suggested.[45]

Within the black community, Obama attracted little support at first. The reasons were obvious. Obama's campaign included many white staffers, notably his campaign manager, media strategist, communications director, and finance chair. Moreover, Obama was the son of a white mother, had graduated from an Ivy League school, and spoke little of racial matters. He did not embrace the standard list of civil rights demands, such as protecting affirmative action, ending capital punishment, and enacting laws punishing "hate crimes." Further, Obama highlighted the racial diversity of his extended family, which included a white grandmother, six half-siblings from Kenya, and a half-sister from Indonesia. His mother had ancestors who were Native Americans, as well as distant relatives of Jefferson Davis, president of the Confederacy during America's civil war. "When we get together for Christmas or Thanksgiving," Obama said, "it's like a little mini-United Nations. I've got relatives who look like [black comedian] Bernie Mac, and I've got relatives who look like [former British prime minister] Margaret Thatcher." Puzzled by questions as to whether he was "black enough," Obama told a convention of the National Association of Black Journalists that "we should ask ourselves why that is. It is not because of my physical appearance presumably. It's not because of my track record." Obama lamented the continuing reality that "we're still locked in this notion that if you appeal to white folks then there must be something wrong." Obama thought his lighter skin color and his record on racial positions should be irrelevant to African Americans. Even so, sociologist Michael Eric Dyson speculated that the key to Obama's election chances depended on figuring out "how to wink at black America while speaking to white America."[46]

Many African Americans initially preferred Hillary Clinton, who had long supported issues important to the black community. At the outset, Clinton backers included members of the Congressional Black Caucus, such as Charles Rangel and John Lewis, the lion of the civil rights movement whose blood had often been spilled in that crusade. But once Obama captured the overwhelmingly white Iowa caucuses and then the South Carolina primary, the first primary where African Americans comprised a sizable percentage of the electorate, black support nationwide swung to Obama's side. Lewis explained to the Clintons that he loved them, but he, unlike Rangel, would now support Obama. "I realized that I was on the wrong side of history," Lewis concluded. Suddenly "black enough," Obama was added to the pantheon of the civil rights generation by hip-hop rapper Jay-Z: "Rosa sat so Martin could walk; Martin walked so Obama could run; Obama is running so our children can fly." Attracted to Obama's approach of campaigning as an American "who just happens to be black," general Colin Powell defected from the Republican ranks and backed the Democratic candidate. The upshot of blacks voting for Obama and white women voting for Clinton was that the Democratic primary increasingly became one of identity politics. As the long primary season came to a conclusion, Obama earned a narrow victory. A disappointed Clinton then endorsed Obama's candidacy for president.[47]

Jesse Jackson had declared his support for Obama early on, but made snide comments about him as the campaign proceeded. A racially-charged episode in Jena, Louisiana, gave Jackson a golden opportunity to criticize Obama. In 2006, a black student crossed a perceived racial boundary when he sat under a schoolyard tree that sheltered white students. The following day, white students hung nooses from the tree's limbs, an apparent threat designed to keep blacks away. In the weeks that followed, the school was burned down and fights broke out at a nearby private dance party and gas station. As racial trouble continued, six African-American teenagers were charged with attempted murder in the beating of a white classmate who suffered concussion and multiple bruises, thus exposing one of the most sensitive fault lines in American politics. If convicted, the accused could have been sentenced to a hundred years in jail, whereas white students who got in trouble at the same time were simply suspended from school or not charged with waving guns against black youngsters. To show their solidarity with the Jena Six, Jackson, Al Sharpton, and 20,000 supporters from the Rainbow/PUSH Coalition, National Action Network, and the New Black Panther party went to Louisiana in September, 2007, to participate in a mass march. Hoping to avoid the trap of being a black-only candidate, Obama denounced this "travesty of justice" in a speech, but he kept his distance from the protest march. Jackson dismissed Obama's remarks as weak, and accused the candidate of "acting like he's white," a devastating charge in the black community. "If I were a candidate," Jackson insisted, "I'd be all over Jena. Jena is a defining moment, just like Selma [Alabama] was a defining moment" in the 1960s.[48]

Jackson, once the most popular black man in America, had many reasons not to like Barack Obama, including Obama's greater political popularity and his hectoring of black men, which, Jackson believed, was made cynically to attract white voters. One journalist recalled Obama's bottom-line approach to campaigning for white votes—"I gotta do what I gotta do"—and concluded that "Obama did not, and could not, represent the prophetic tradition: he was not Frederick Douglass or Bishop

[Henry McNeal] Turner or Malcolm. . . . He was a pragmatist, a politician." Jackson was angered by an Obama speech which accurately pointed out that most black children live in single-parent households, where they are five times more likely than whites to be poor and commit crime, nine times more likely to drop out of schools, and twenty times more likely to end up in prison. Too many black men, Obama noted, have "abandoned their responsibilities, acting like boys instead of men. And the foundations of our families are weaker because of it."[49]

Jackson himself had long harped on this sad reality, but he nonetheless muttered to a black panelist on a television program, "See, Barack been talking down to black people" about absent fathers. "I want to cut his nuts [testicles] out," said a furious Jackson, as he made a slicing gesture with his hand. Obama, whose biological father had deserted him, knew whereof he spoke, but perhaps his reproach of "irresponsible" black males hit too close to home, for Jackson himself had fathered a child who did not live with him. All the more embarrassing for Jackson, his son, Jesse Jackson, Jr., was a national co-chair of Obama's campaign. The younger son affirmed his love for his father, but rebuked him at the same time. The chastened elder Jackson apologized for his "crude," "hurtful," and "wrong" remarks, which recalled the castration often associated with lynching, and declared his "wide, deep and unequivocal" support for Obama's candidacy. In a second apology, Jackson declared that Obama "represents the redemption of our country." Obama shrugged off the offensive remark, accepted Jackson's apology, and reiterated his campaign's support for "jobs, justice, and opportunity for all."[50]

For all of Jackson's sniping, there were obvious similarities between him and Barack Obama. Both had grown up in broken homes, both had graduated from college, both had been community organizers in Chicago, both were inspiring speakers who addressed internal problems in the black community, and both had lost political campaigns. But the differences seemed even more profound. Obama, the intellectual, was born to a white American mother and black father from Kenya a generation after Jackson, the crusader, was born to two African Americans. When Obama's mother remarried, Barack spent critical years growing up in Indonesia and then Hawaii in the 1960s and 1970s, so his experience with racial discrimination and hatred was less intense than Jackson's. Jackson graduated from a black college in North Carolina that found itself in the middle of the civil rights revolution, whereas Obama graduated from the nation's finest institutions of higher learning, both of which were inter-racial, a generation after the major civil rights legislation was enacted. Barack Obama's educational opportunity and political career were possible because of the civil rights campaign headed by Martin Luther King and Jesse Jackson, among many others.

In the general election for the presidency in the fall of 2008, Obama squared off against veteran Republican U.S. senator John McCain of Arizona, a longtime prisoner of the North Vietnamese during America's prolonged, failed war in southeast Asia. McCain had gained a maverick reputation in politics, showing an occasional willingness to go against his party. McCain chided Obama for his inexperience, but selected a complete unknown for his own vice-presidential nominee—Alaska governor Sarah Palin, a self-described "hockey mom" who enjoyed hunting wild animals. McCain's selection attracted initial approval from some women, but it also undercut the Republican claim that political experience was essential to national office. Palin's political experience was limited to a stint as mayor of a small town and then a year as governor. Although Palin possessed an astounding ignorance of political and foreign policy issues, she appealed to rock-ribbed Republicans who never warmed to McCain. To compensate for his own brief career on the national stage, Obama selected U.S. senator Joe Biden of Delaware, a veteran Washington insider, as his running-mate.[51]

On November 4, 2008, Barack Obama defeated John McCain with 52.9 percent of the popular vote, a plurality of 8 million votes, which translated into a two-to-one margin in the Electoral College. Obama was the first Democrat from outside the South to win the presidency since John F. Kennedy, and Obama received the highest percentage of the popular vote of any Democratic presidential candidate since Lyndon Johnson in 1964. Obama won a majority of the votes cast by white women and Latinos, and a supermajority among Jews and the young. He received a staggering 96 percent of the African-American vote. The results made him the first African American to win the presidency in 220 years of American political history, a goal that had twice eluded Jesse Jackson. Twelve presidents before him had held African slaves, including eight while in office. In his victory speech to hundreds of thousands of joyous supporters in Chicago's Grant Park, Obama triumphantly proclaimed, "Change has come to America." A television camera captured a tender moment when it spotted an unaware Jackson in the throng, crying tears of joy. McCain, the vanquished Republican, gave a gracious concession speech that put the election into historical perspective: "A century ago, President Theodore Roosevelt's invitation to Booker T. Washington to visit—to dine at the White House—was taken as an outrage in many quarters. America today is a world away from the cruel and prideful bigotry of that time. There is no better evidence of this than the election of an African American to the presidency of the United States."[52]

Barack Obama became America's 44th president for several reasons. First, many Americans were tired of, if not embarrassed by, the presidency of George W. Bush, which had benefited early on from the anger—and patriotism—that arose in the wake of the September 11th attacks by al-Qaeda on the World Trade Center and the Pentagon. Subsequently, the Bush administration had been criticized for entering into a prolonged war in Iraq and triggering a sinking economy whose effects rippled across the globe. Second, the long-standing American practice of switching ruling parties reasserted itself. The Republicans had won the presidency seven times out of ten elections since 1968, and only Bill Clinton had won two terms as a Democrat since Franklin D. Roosevelt in the 1940s. A desire for change, if not reform, had settled upon the American electorate. Third, Obama inspired a new generation of Americans to get involved in politics to remake the political climate and institute fundamental change. At the heart of his resonant message were calls to stimulate the economy, end the Iraq war quickly, increase energy independence, and at long last provide universal health care for American citizens, a staple of Democratic rhetoric from Harry Truman to Bill Clinton. Beyond his message, Obama inspired Americans with his youth and obvious energy, an Ivy League education, and a persuasive oratorical style that was compared to Martin Luther King. Finally, Obama represented the safe African-American, one who could be trusted to handle complicated issues, because he himself was indisputably intelligent and because he did not dwell on race. He was just "black enough" and just "white enough" to pass America's racial test. In short, Obama offered himself as a transformational figure who would bring real change to American lives.[53]

The election of an African American to the presidency was one that Booker T. Washington and Martin Luther King had predicted; but many other African Americans believed that day would never come. John Lewis told a black church that only a "crazy" person would have thought a black person would have been elected in his lifetime. Recalling the vicious police attack in Alabama that badly injured him at Edmund Pettus Bridge in 1965, Lewis remarked that "Barack Obama is what comes at the end of that bridge in Selma." Although too young to have participated in the civil rights movement himself, Obama represented the prize for which Lewis and other civil rights workers had waited for their entire lives. As journalist David Remnick put it, "Obama was not a patriarch and not a prophet but the prophesied." Obama's supporters hoped that he would be a bridge between the races, between the political parties, and between African Americans who were scarred by life under Jim Crow and a new generation that reveled in a multicultural America. Lewis felt certain that the masses watching Obama inaugurated on the Washington Mall would be joined by the "saints and angels," including Harriet Tubman and Sojourner Truth; Nat Turner, Frederick Douglass, and John Brown; and W.E.B. Du Bois and Marcus Garvey. Following the swearing-in ceremony, Lewis approached the new president for his signature on a commemorative photograph. The first black president wrote, "Because of you, John. Barack Obama."[54]

Obama's presidency

Assuming office in the midst of the worst financial collapse since the Great Depression and two intractable wars a half-world away, the 47-year-old Obama expressed admiration for Franklin D. Roosevelt (FDR) and Ronald Reagan for their abilities to achieve change on a grand scale from the White House. Obama soon issued executive orders to bar the Central Intelligence Agency from operating secret prisons and torturing terrorist suspects, and to reverse a Bush-era policy that sharply limited federal funding of embryonic stem cell research. Obama also relaxed the statute of limitations for equal pay lawsuits and authorized health insurance for 4 million children. When vacancies on the U.S. Supreme Court arose, Obama nominated, and the U.S. Senate confirmed, two women—U.S. Circuit Court judge Sonia Sotomayor as the first Latina justice and U.S. solicitor general and former Harvard law dean Elena Kagan. Obama also signed legislation to expand the criteria of federal hate-crime law to include crimes motivated by a victim's actual or perceived gender, sexual orientation, or disability.[55]

At the beginning of his presidency, Barack Obama showed himself to be unsentimental, unflappable, pragmatic, and dogged in his pursuit of a changed America. As one historian phrased it, "In 'Alice in Wonderland' terms, he's the Cheshire Cat, the magical creature who saves the day just as the guillotine is about to drop." Obama adopted a style of governing that was reminiscent of FDR, who took advantage of the dire circumstances of the Great Depression to advance a reform agenda that was breath-taking in the context of American politics. Roosevelt moved the United States far down the path of government responsibility for a host of economic matters, including social welfare and business regulation.

Similarly, Obama used the circumstance of a relentless economic slide to pursue sweeping reform that, critics argued, went well beyond the demands of the moment. The administration's first legislative package appropriated $787 billion to staunch the bleeding of the American economy, though the government spent nowhere near that amount. The American Recovery and Reinvestment Act was a landmark measure that provided the largest tax cuts for the middle class since the Reagan administration, the largest infrastructure expenditure since Eisenhower's Interstate Highway Act, the most far-reaching education bill since Lyndon Johnson, the largest scientific and medical research investment in decades, and the biggest clean energy bill ever. It saved jobs, particularly in the automotive industry, but did little to restore or create jobs in a double-digit unemployment economy or to aid distressed homeowners.[56]

Following his plan to implement the change he promised, Obama ignored the advice of his aides and simultaneously tackled other monumental problems of his time. He banked his presidency on a $1 trillion bill to provide universal health care for the 45 million Americans who could not afford it. In part, his motivation was personal, for he claimed that his mother had died of cancer awaiting medical payment from her insurance company. The stakes in this battle for the Obama presidency were enormous, and the opposition was formidable. Universal health care opponents included physicians, hospitals, and powerful insurance and pharmaceutical companies. Despite compromising on several key points, a bruised and battered Obama prevailed in a drawn-out epic battle, signing the Affordable Care Act, which fulfilled the Democratic party's long promise to deliver this part of the social safety net. To address the "Great Recession," Obama signed bills to regulate Wall Street and to buy billions of dollars in sour mortgage securities that clogged the nation's credit system. The administration hoped that once banks were rid of these "toxic assets," they would stimulate the economy by resuming loans to consumers for cars, to students for education, and to entrepreneurs for business improvements.[57]

Obama might have accomplished even more in his first two years in office, but he sometimes preferred to keep a low profile or to deliver well-crafted speeches, rather than digging into the political fray. At times, he was too interested in being liked and too ready to do what was popular than to live up to the bracing rhetoric of his inaugural address. The health care bill, for example, insured millions of impoverished Americans, but it fell short of its original intent of insuring all Americans or containing costs by offering a government health care option to compete with large insurance companies. This missed opportunity has many explanations, not the least of which is that Obama turned the assignment over to a group of bungling congressional Democrats and largely ignored fuming Republicans, who saw this fight as a splendid opportunity to cripple the young president. The Republicans insisted—falsely—that "ObamaCare" would require government "death panels" which would ultimately decide who would live or die. Voters were also spooked by the enormous cost of the health-care scheme, especially at a time when the nation's deficit was doubling to $14 trillion.[58]

Preoccupied by a slumping economy and congressional infighting over health care, Obama was caught flat-footed by a major oil spill in the Gulf of Mexico. In April, 2010, a drilling rig owned by the British Petroleum (BP) Company exploded, dumping millions of barrels of crude oil into the Gulf's waters. The Obama administration initially assigned financial responsibility for the disaster to BP, but did not cap the well itself. Meanwhile, millions of barrels of crude oil gushed out day after day, infecting the food chain, layering wetlands and vast areas of the ocean floor with tar deposits, and damaging local businesses, especially the shrimp, fishing, and tourism industries. The United States declined international offers to help collect the oil, and BP was cautious in placing a cap on the gusher. It became the worst oil spill in American history, and critics charged the Obama administration with acting indecisively as environmental and economic problems mounted. The man-made calamity resulted in a public outcry for safer offshore drilling regulations, but oil lobbyists worked hand-in-glove with Congress to block the robust overhaul of industry safeguards that Obama promised.[59]

One issue that Obama did not tackle from the Oval Office was race. Although Obama created the White House Office of Urban Affairs, he largely avoided the subject of race altogether because he regarded himself as president of all Americans, rather than the first urban president who should, accordingly, tend to urban problems. Sociologist Michael Eric Dyson observed candidly, "This president runs from race like a black man runs from a cop." This neglect mattered a great deal to a fractured black community which was hard hit by the AIDS epidemic and, as Jesse Jackson pointed out, was first in high school dropouts, first in infant mortality, and first in homicides. Some majority-black American cities had become human cesspools, where social pathologies, such as drug use and gang warfare, remained the norm. In Detroit, for example, the murder rate was among the nation's highest, twice that of Chicago's and six times that of New York City's. With an official unemployment rate of 24 percent, compared to a rate of 6.7 percent a decade earlier, Detroit struggled to pay its municipal employees and keep its parks open. Middle-class neighborhoods hired private security patrols because police assistance was questionable at best. Detroit's schools collapsed, with 44 percent of Michigan adults unable to read or compute at even an elementary level to fill high-tech jobs. Obama told a black audience that he wanted to create "an economy that lifts up all Americans," but it remained a truism in American life that African Americans and Latinos suffer the most.[60]

Just a half year into his presidency, Obama was, to the surprise of nearly everyone, named the Nobel peace prize laureate for 2009. Norwegian prime minister Jens Stoltenberg insisted that Obama deserved the prize for providing leadership on key issues facing the world, such as disarmament, nuclear nonproliferation, and global warming. Many observers saw the award as a sharp rebuke of the bellicose George W. Bush. Obama had "no doubt" that others were more deserving of the award, but he nonetheless accepted it with "great humility." In his Nobel speech, which diverged dramatically from Martin Luther King, Jr.'s address, Obama spoke of the limits of nonviolence and defended warlike means to achieve peaceful ends. He could hardly do otherwise as he presided over two wars simultaneously. "I believe," Obama intoned, "the United States of America must remain a standard bearer in the conduct of war. That is what makes us different from those whom we fight. That is a source of our strength. That is why I prohibited torture. That is why I ordered the prison at Guantanamo Bay closed. And that is why I have reaffirmed America's commitment to abide by the Geneva Conventions. We lose ourselves when we compromise the very ideals that we fight to defend." To achieve real and lasting peace, Obama asserted that nations must provide economic security and opportunity for their peoples. Protesters outside the awards venue questioned whether Obama was worthy of the Nobel prize, with one sign reading, "Obama: You won it. Now earn it!"[61]

Obama had, in fact, sought change in the international arena, starting with a goodwill tour of the world. According to *Time*'s White House correspondent Michael Scherer, Obama's vision was "a hodgepodge of classic realpolitik, diplomatic determination, community-organizer idealism and charismatic leadership. He presented what he hopes will become a new public identity for the U.S.: less global leader than global facilitator, less savior than responsible partner." Under the guiding hand of secretary of state Hillary Clinton, Obama restored diplomacy as vital to American foreign policy and generally pursued the war on terrorism in a judicious, restrained manner that relied on global intelligence-gathering, assassinations, and limited interventions in other countries. Some successes occurred, including an agreement with Russia to reduce long-range nuclear weapons, several popular revolts in the Arab world that overthrew longtime dictatorships, and the deaths of leading terrorists. But the world remained a troublesome place, in large measure because the United States lost considerable leverage from its weakened economic position and from the rise of other powerful nations, and because it had to resort to nation-building in unstable areas before diplomacy could begin to produce results. Meanwhile, Israel refused to freeze its settlements on the West Bank; China ignored calls for human rights; the climate-change summit in Denmark produced little of consequence; the Russians remained largely uninterested in refashioning relations with the United States; and North Korea and Iran edged ever closer to nuclear weaponry—if they did not have them already—with its likely destabilizing effects in their respective regions.[62]

Obama had never put on a military uniform, but he intended to follow the constitutional prerogative that the president is the commander-in-chief. After the most intensive White House national security meetings since Kennedy's Cuban Missile Crisis in 1962, Obama increased American troops in Afghanistan to fight Muslim terrorists, including al-Qaeda and the Taliban. As the internal deliberations dragged on, many observers charged the president with dithering on a war which he said was crucial to American security. Such indecisiveness, the argument went, demonstrated that Obama remained a small-time community organizer with no inclination to be a decisive leader in the mold of Harry Truman. This time, the critics underestimated Obama. When general Stanley McChrystal—a counterinsurgency expert—publicly questioned Obama's leadership in the decade-long $500 billion war in Afghanistan, Obama reprimanded the general before relieving him of his command. It was the tensest situation between a military officer and the civilian commander-in-chief since Truman fired an insubordinate 5-star general named Douglas MacArthur.[63]

Obama compiled a mixed record in his first two years as president. He secured landmark legislation in stimulating the economy, health care, and banking regulation, though these measures were heavily compromised as they moved through Congress. The automotive industry stabilized with massive government help, and General Motors began repaying its loans to the federal treasury. But the Obama administration was unable to lower the national unemployment rate to 9 percent. Rhetoric aside, there was no grand public works program in the tradition of FDR to provide desperately needed jobs. Nor did the administration make good on the Justice Department's Operation Broken Trust, a much-ballyhooed campaign to hold criminally liable the greedy and irresponsible financial sector that gamed the nation's economy to near devastation. The sagging economy, the laggard response to the BP oil spill, the populist anger over illegal immigration from Mexico, and the prolonged war in Afghanistan harmed Obama, who saw his public approval numbers sink below 50 percent by the mid-term elections. He lost support from every demographic category, including African Americans, whose support of Democratic presidents since Franklin D. Roosevelt had always been strong, if not decisive.[64]

It seemed unlikely that political realities would allow Obama to accomplish much more. Following a longtime pattern, the midterm congressional elections swept into power the opposition party, which typically produces gridlock. The Republicans gained a majority in the U.S. House of Representatives, due in part to an insurgent Tea Party movement that demanded a smaller, more fiscally responsible, federal government. Senate Minority leader Mitch McConnell of Kentucky told the *National Journal* that "the single most important thing we want to do is for President Obama to be a one-term president," and that intention virtually ensured a legislative logjam. Among the planks of the Obama agenda destined for the political scrapheap were tax increases for stimulating the economy, ever-increasing budget deficits, and the overhaul of the nation's environmental policy—dubbed "cap and trade"—for limiting carbon emissions from industrial production. With the economy still burdened by an overhang of consumer debt, a stagnant housing market, and the after-effects of the financial crisis that began on Wall Street, Obama would be hard pressed to preserve the legislative gains he already made, including universal health care coverage, parts of which some judges already ruled unconstitutional.[65]

Obama admitted that he had been given a "shellacking" in the midterm elections, but his political obituary was premature. In the lame-duck session between that election and the inauguration of the new, more conservative Congress, Obama demonstrated remarkable political skills. To continue middle-class tax cuts and government assistance to the long-term unemployed, Obama reluctantly accepted the Bush tax cuts for Americans who earned at least $250,000 annually. To appease his liberal base and to expand the notion of equality still one more step, Obama threw his weight behind the successful repeal of the Clinton administration's controversial "Don't Ask, Don't Tell" policy which forced gay and lesbian members of the armed forces to conceal their sexual orientation. In the realm of foreign affairs, Obama pressed for U.S. Senate approval of the latest START arms treaty with Russia, which reduced the number of strategic nuclear missile launchers by half and the number of deployed strategic nuclear warheads by 30 percent over the previous agreement. The START treaty had the endorsement of every living Republican secretary of state, secretary of defense, and national security adviser, and the Senate dutifully concurred, despite the vocal opposition of its Republican leaders. Obama's lame-duck record was a *tour de force*, unmatched in decades. Observers marveled at this turn of events, predicting it would give Obama a new lease on his presidency in the run-up to the 2012 election.[66]

After the lame-duck session ended, however, a beleaguered Obama struggled to revive the stagnant economy and to secure national debt relief. Obama warned repeatedly of economic catastrophe unless Congress raised the debt ceiling to stratospheric levels and raised additional tax revenues, primarily by taxing the wealthy—a favorite liberal target. Sensing a wounded president, congressional Republicans drew a line in the sand, vowing not a penny in new taxes from anyone and demanding trillions of dollars in federal government spending cuts. Both sides dug in their heels, until president Obama capitulated. He signed a debt deal in which Republicans took him to the cleaners, and the national debt was downgraded for the first time in American history. Noting high unemployment and home foreclosure rates among African Americans, a furious Black Congressional Caucus described the deal as "a sugar-coated satan sandwich" that would abandon communities that were already struggling. Cornel West, a political philosopher at Princeton University and an adviser to Obama's first presidential campaign, saw the deal as just another example of how "Brother Obama" was a "black mascot of Wall Street oligarchs and a black puppet of corporate plutocrats."[67]

Pundits scratched their hands as to why Obama surrendered to obdurate Republicans on such a vital matter a year from his reelection. Their suggestions ranged from Obama's need to attract independent voters in the coming election, to Obama's core political ideology (which was arguably not liberal, but moderate), to Obama's temperament as incapable of being confrontational. Another explanation for Obama's timid leadership was that the president's governing philosophy called for rule by consensus in an age of extreme political polarization. Put another way, Obama subscribed to the by-now quaint belief advanced by the Founding Fathers that leaders must work together through reasoned debate for the common good. In 2008, Obama had promised to be a transformational president, meaning that he would transform governance by working across the political aisle in Congress. Recall his famous speech to the 2004 Democratic national convention, in which he said "there's not a liberal America and a conservative America, there's the United States of America."[68]

As the economy remained stuck in neutral and the stock market fluctuated wildly, Obama appeared unable to address this fundamental problem, putting his reelection in doubt. Public opinion polls showed that the American people believed their country was adrift as political wrangling brought government action to a standstill. Some liberals and leftists felt betrayed by a president who made a practice of conceding unilaterally to Republicans who controlled only one house of Congress, and whispers could be heard that Obama was "Bush III." Obama championed health care reform, but abandoned single-payer insurance and abortion coverage. He accepted the scientific consensus over global warming, promising a strict limit on industrial emissions into the ozone layer, but canceled plans for enforcement, in violation of the Clean Air Act. He called for phased troop withdrawal from Afghanistan—by then the longest war in American history—but put more troops on the ground than when he took office. He denounced the Bush tax cuts for the wealthy, but then extended them. He vowed to close the detention camp for terrorist suspects at the Guantanamo Bay naval base, but it continued to operate. He once insisted that war could not be waged without congressional approval, but then joined the North Atlantic Treaty Organization in bombing dictator Muammar Gaddafi's strongholds in Libya. Obama declared that Medicare and Social Security were untouchable entitlement programs for the middle class, but then agreed that they could be modified—meaning cut—as financial considerations warranted. Adopting the Republican mindset of slashing government programs, Obama urged a cut in domestic spending to "the lowest level it's been since Dwight Eisenhower was president" in the 1950s.[69]

When Barack Obama first campaigned for the presidency, he had promised "hope" for real change in Washington politics, but increasingly the public perception of him was one of ineptitude, that he was incapable of effective governance, especially of revitalizing an anemic economy. He was, it appeared after all, fundamentally indecisive, timid, and unresponsive, a mere shadow of FDR, Lyndon Johnson, and Ronald Reagan, and less than 40 percent of Americans approved of Obama's leadership. Not even the sensational commando raid that assassinated al-Qaeda leader Osama bin Laden in Pakistan, the Hellfire missile that killed American jihadist Anwar al-Awlaki in Yemen, or the defeat and subsequent death of Libya's Gaddafi persuaded most Americans that Obama was a strong leader. In the middle of his presidency, Obama told a television interviewer that he would "rather be a really good one-term president than a mediocre two-term president," but by most lights, his performance was not "really good," raising real questions about his reelection. Since 1888, only one Democrat—the bright but ineffectual Jimmy Carter—had lost a second term as president. The question for the 2012 presidential campaign was whether Obama—the man who promised so much change—would be the next.[70]

Assessment

According to a recent intellectual biography, Barack Obama was the most "penetrating political thinker elected to the presidency" in a century. In his first two years as president, Obama had compiled a significant legislative record. For journalist Jonathan Alter, who was allowed access to White House staff and their meetings, Obama's first-year accomplishments were comparable to other path-breaking Democratic presidents—Franklin D. Roosevelt and Lyndon Johnson. Obama's domestic record in that first year, Alter concluded, made him "a figure of history far beyond the color of his skin." In Obama's second year, Reagan aide Dinesh D'Souza compared Obama to the cerebral, but complex, Richard Nixon, and thought that Obama stood "astride American politics like a colossus." But Obama's momentum soon stalled along with the continuing weak economy.[71]

The sharp fall in Obama's political standing—"the Great Disappointment," as some liberal commentators put it—can be traced to several factors. Thanks to unfunded wars, tax cuts for the rich, supply-side deficits, and regulatory permissiveness that spawned the housing and banking crises, the administration of George W. Bush left the economy in shambles. It was Obama's misfortune and duty to begin straightening it out. As Obama did so, however, congressional Republicans sabotaged much of the president's reform agenda, and relabeled every Bush-era failing as Obama's fault. In addition, the American people had impossible expectations of Obama. He promised "change," and the public believed that he meant wholesale and immediate change. American politics is never that simple, especially when Congress balks.[72]

Obama himself shares in the blame for his political predicament. Pulitzer prize-winning journalist Ron Suskind studied the Obama administration's response to the Wall Street debacle, and described Obama as an earnest man unprepared for power—a "brilliant amateur" who presided over a sometimes dysfunctional administration. Obama admitted that he could be remote and detached from the American people, preventing them from understanding and liking him, despite his legislative achievements. He suffered, he confessed, from "the disease" of being a policy wonk who was "very comfortable with a technocratic approach to government." As was his practice, Obama articulated principles or framed debates, but on economic issues passively allowed subordinates with oversized egos and a record of failure to handle the hard details of policy implementation. Moreover, Obama lacked certain leadership skills required by the difficult times he inherited. He failed, for example, to understand that governing in modern America is a perpetual campaign with the president as campaigner-in-chief. Columbia University historian Alan Brinkley put it this way:

Obama shares many of the qualities of our greatest modern presidents but seems to lack many others. He shares Woodrow Wilson's scholarly temperament but does not project Wilson's shining idealism. He shares Franklin Roosevelt's ability to create soaring oratory, but not his joyous (and devious) love of politics. He shares Lyndon Johnson's ambition, but not often his powers of heavy-handed persuasion. And he shares some of John Kennedy's cool, pragmatic temperament, but not (publicly at least) his wit and his sense of humor. Unfortunately, although the traits he does reveal are admirable, it is the ones he is missing that our politics demand.[73]

For conservatives, as Shelby Steele argued, Obama was a fervent practitioner of "post-'60s liberalism," whose fall from grace can be attributed to his "inexperience, ideological wrong-headedness, and an oddly undefined character." As president, Obama increased the size and scope of government, pursued income redistribution, and made Wall Street into an economic scapegoat, all part of his undeclared goal to "overcome, or at least subdue, American capitalism itself." More than simple inexperience, if not outright incompetence, Steele charged Obama with warring against American values. In this understanding, Obama believed that America's exceptional position in the world stemmed, not from its unparalleled virtues, but from "a bargain with the devil" that depended on "an indulgence in militarism, racism, sexism, corporate greed, and environmental disregard." Such thinking, Steele maintained, gravely harmed United States and contributed significantly to Obama's unpopularity, because Americans would never accept a liberal prescription for mediocrity to fulfill a perverse definition of "fairness."[74]

Partisans on the left and right of the American political spectrum complained aplenty about Obama, but he did stabilize the economy, end the torture of enemies, institute education and health care reform, and gradually disengage the United States from the war in Iraq. By extending a verbal olive branch to the Muslim world, Obama sought to remove clouds of hatred and fear through which so much of the world saw the United States during George W. Bush's presidency. This fact alone may have prompted the Nobel committee to make Obama the third African American and third sitting president to receive its peace prize. Moreover, Obama refused to concede to populist pressures within his party for more government regulations, punitive taxation, and a general protective tariff that would strangle the economy and harm entrepreneurs and workers. But with the euphoria of the 2008 election long since past, Obama's reelection seems tied to the fate of the economy, which stubbornly resisted recovery, despite prodigious—conservatives thought profligate—spending by the federal government.

"I don't quit," Obama told the nation in his second State of the Union address in January, 2010. His easy smile and easy gait belied an ambitious and determined leader who beat considerable odds to guide much of his early legislative agenda through congressional landmines to passage. No task consumed more of Obama's energy and political capital than greatly expanding health care for Americans. When victory was assured on Capitol Hill, Obama greeted thrilled White House staffers with hugs, and told them, "After nearly a hundred years of talk and frustration, we proved we are still a people capable of doing big things. . . . This is what change looks like." Whatever its merits and deficiencies, the health care bill only intensified liberal and conservative criticism of Obama, and much more of it was to come, to the president's displeasure. He told an old friend, "Who would really want this job for more than one term." Upon momentary reflection, he added, "but I have to run [for reelection] now; otherwise it'll mean letting [a Republican] step in and get credit for all the good stuff that happens after we've been through all this crap."[75]

References

1 Alan Kennedy-Shaffer, *The Obama Revolution* (2009), front cover.

2 Peggy Noonan, "They've Lost That Lovin' Feeling," *Wall Street Journal* (30 July 2011), http://online.wsj.com/article/SB10001424053111904800304576474620336602248.html.

3 Florence Hamlish Levinsohn, *Looking for Farrakhan* (1997), pp. 75,
   130–139, 193; Arthur J. Magida, *Prophet of Rage: A Life of Louis Farrakhan
   and His Nation* (1996), pp. 88–92; Karl Evanzz, *The Messenger: The Rise
   and Fall of Elijah Muhammad* (1999), p. 269.

4 Michael H. Cottman, *Million Man March* (1995); Haki R. Madhubuti
   and Maulana Karenga, eds., *Million Man March/Day of Absence: A
   Commemorative Anthology* (1996); Jeremiah A. Wright, Jr. and Colleen
   Birchett, *When Black Men Stand Up for God: Reflections on the Million
   Man March* (1997); Clarence Taylor, *Black Religious Intellectuals: The Fight
   for Equality from Jim Crow to the 21st Century* (2002), pp. 160–180.

5 Taylor, *Black Religious Intellectuals*, p. 141; Jo Renee Formicola, "The
   Reverend Al Sharpton: Pentecostal for Racial Justice," in Jo Renee Formicola
   and Hubert Morken, eds., *Religious Leaders and Faith-Based Politics: Ten
   Profiles* (2001), pp. 53–69.

6 Taylor, *Black Religious Intellectuals*, p. 126; Formicola, "The Reverend Al
   Sharpton," pp. 58–60; Jim Yardley, "After a Decade, Brawley Reappears
   and Repeats Charges," *New York Times* (3 December 1997), pp. B1, B6; Al
   Sharpton and Anthony Walton, *Go and Tell Pharaoh: The Autobiography of
   the Reverend Al Sharpton* (1996), pp. 47–48, 55–58, 121–142; Al Sharpton,
   Al on America (2002), pp. 229–239.

7 Taylor, *Black Religious Intellectuals*, p. 120; Juan Williams, *Enough: The
   Phony Leaders, Dead-End Movements, and Culture of Failure that are
   Undermining Black America—and What We Can Do About It* (2006),
   pp. 51–55. In *A Bound Man: Why We Are Excited About Obama and
   Why He Can't Win* (2008), pp. 78–79, Shelby Steele labels Al Sharpton
   "a self-appointed arbiter of the racist stigma. . . . Like a modern-day
   potentate, he can ruin or redeem a white man in one quick trip to the
   microphones. And though he has himself committed many of the sins
   that so outrage him in whites, he pays no price and loses no power when
   his hypocrisy is pointed out."

8 Colin Powell, with Joseph E. Persico, *My American Journey* (1995),
   pp. 255–542; Karen DeYoung, *Soldier: The Life of Colin Powell* (2006),
   pp. 35–208.

9 DeYoung, *Soldier*, pp. 296–520; "Colin Powell on Iraq, Race,
   and Hurricane Relief," *ABC 20/20* (8 September 2005),
   http://abcnews.go.com/2020/Politics/story?id=1105979&page=1.

10 Barack Obama, *Dreams from My Father: A Story of Race and Inheritance*
   (1995), pp. 9–10; David Mendell, *Obama: From Promise to Power* (2007),
   pp. 25–31; Janny Scott, *A Singular Woman: The Untold Story of Barack
   Obama's Mother* (2011), pp. 59–60, 80–93; Peter Firstbrook, *The Obamas:
   The Untold Story of an African Family* (2011), pp. 205–216; Sally Jacobs,

The Other Barack: The Bold and Reckless Life of President Obama's Father (2011), pp. 99–119.

11 Jacobs, *The Other Barack*, pp. 119–131, 154–161, 171–177, 192, 226–231.

12 Obama, *Dreams from My Father*, pp. 28–52.

13 Mendell, *Obama: From Promise to Power*, pp. 32–35; Scott, *A Singular Woman*, pp. 120–135.

14 Obama, *Dreams from My Father*, pp. 5, 63, 216; Mendell, *Obama*, pp. 38–40.

15 Obama, *Dreams from My Father*, p. 93; Mendell, *Obama*, pp. 35–38, 40–44.

16 Obama, *Dreams from My Father*, p. 86; Gretchen Reynolds, "Vote of Confidence," *Chicago Magazine* 42 (January, 1993): 53–54.

17 Obama, *Dreams from My Father*, pp. xv, 82, 87, 115.

18 Obama, *Dreams from My Father*, pp. 100–101, 139–140; Lisa Miller and Richard Wolffe, "Finding His Faith," *Newsweek* 152 (21 July 2008): 26–32.

19 Todd Purdum, "Raising Obama," *Vanity Fair* 50 (March, 2008): 314–325; "Transcript: Illinois Senate Candidate Barack Obama," *Washington Post* (27 July 2004), http://www.washingtonpost.com/wp-dyn/articles/A19751-2004Jul27.html; Byron York, "What Did Obama Do as a Community Organizer," *National Review Online* (8 September 2008), http://www.nationalreview.com/articles/225564/what-did-obama-do-community-organizer/byron-york?page=1.

20 Mendell, *Obama*, pp. 83–92.

21 David Remnick, *The Bridge: The Life and Rise of Barack Obama* (2010), pp. 219–227.

22 Remnick, *The Bridge*, pp. 276–293, 295–306, 338, 350–351; Mendell, *Obama*, pp. 121–128.

23 Remnick, *The Bridge*, pp. 219–255; Daren Briscoe, et al., "How He Did It," *Newsweek* 152 (5 November 2008): 38–49.

24 Remnick, *The Bridge*, pp. 313–333; Mendell, *Obama*, pp. 128–139.

25 Remnick, *The Bridge*, p. 333; Mendell, *Obama*, p. 7.

26 Evan Thomas, *"A Long Time Coming": The Inspiring, Combative 2008 Campaign and the Historic Election of Barack Obama* (2009), p. 6; John Heilemann and Mark Halperin, *Game Change: Obama and the Clintons, McCain and Palin, and the Race of a Lifetime* (2010), p. 26.

27 Briscoe, et al., "How He Did It," pp. 38–49; Mendell, *Obama*, pp. 1–3, 272–285.

28 Dan Balz and Haynes Johnson, *The Battle for America 2008: The Story of an Extraordinary Election* (2009), p. 25.

29 Brian Friel, Richard E. Cohen, and Kirk Victor, "Obama: Most Liberal Senator in 2007," *National Journal* (31 January 2008), http://nj.nationaljournal.com/voteratings/; Balz and Johnson, *The Battle for America 2008*, pp. 25–34; David J. Garrow, *Bearing the Cross: Martin Luther King, Jr., and the Southern Christian Leadership Conference* (1986), pp. 557–559. For an indispensable survey of African Americans who have ever run for the presidency, see Bruce Glasrud and Cary Wintz, eds, *African Americans and the Presidency: The Road to the White House* (2010).

30 Barack Obama, *The Audacity of Hope: Thoughts on Reclaiming the American Dream* (2006), pp. 16, 293; Michael Tomasky, "The Phenomenon," *New York Review of Books* 53 (30 November 2006): 14–18.

31 Remnick, *The Bridge*, pp. 492–495, 505–516; Heilemann and Halperin, *Game Change*, pp. 45–53, 61, 84, 98, 119, 126–144, 147–149, 153–156, 166–170, 183–185, 239–240, 256–258.

32 Robin Abcarian, "She Put Words in His Mouth: Edith Childs' Rallying Cry Has Become an Obama Signature," *Los Angeles Times* (13 December 2007), p. A16; Heilemann and Halperin, *Game Change*, pp. 327–328.

33 Remnick, *The Bridge*, pp. 502, 543; Heilemann and Halperin, *Game Change*, pp. 416, 421; Balz and Johnson, *The Battle for America 2008*, pp. 289–292, 363; Jonathan Alter, *The Promise: President Obama: Year One* (2010), pp. 20, 111–112, 130, 264.

34 Heilemann and Halperin, *Game Change*, pp. 85, 90–91, 238–242, 333, 408; Remnick, *The Bridge*, pp. 253–255.

35 Remnick, *The Bridge*, p. 157; Obama, *The Audacity of Hope*, pp. 242, 245–246; Adia Harvey Wingfield and Joe R. Feagin, *Yes We Can? White Racial Framing and the 2008 Presidential Campaign* (2010), pp. 121–126.

36 Clarence E. Walker and Gregory D. Smithers, *The Preacher and the Politician: Jeremiah Wright, Barack Obama, and Race in America* (2009), pp. 13–14, 24–51; Wingfield and Feagin, *Yes We Can?*, pp. 126–129.

37 Remnick, *The Bridge*, pp. 55, 253–254, 279–281, 545–548.

38 Walker and Smithers, *The Preacher and the Politician*, pp. 93–94, 105–119; Wingfield and Feagin, *Yes We Can?*, pp. 133–143, 145–147.

39 Remnick, *The Bridge*, pp. 254–255, 391, 525, 543–544, 578; James Bowman, "Rush: The Leader of The Opposition," *National Review* 38 (6 September 1993), http://www.nationalreview.com/articles/207702/rush-leader-opposition/james-bowman; Kelefa Sanneh, "Beyond the Pale: Is White the New Black," *New Yorker* 86 (12 April 2010), http://www.newyorker.com/arts/critics/books/2010/04/12/100412crbo_books_sanneh.

40 "Obama Concedes Remarks on 'Bitter' Working Class Voters Ill Chosen," *Chicago Sun-Times* (12 April 2008), http://www.suntimes.com/news/politics/obama/891816,obamaremarks041208.article.

41 Maureen Dowd, "The 46-Year-Old Virgin," *New York Times* (5 September 2007), p. 27; Thomas, *"A Long Time Coming,"* p. 204.

42 Remnick, *The Bridge*, pp. 346–347, Heilemann and Halperin, *Game Change*, pp. 85–89, 159.

43 Heilemann and Halperin, *Game Change*, p. 332; Balz and Johnson, *The Battle for America 2008*, p. 175.

44 Heilemann and Halperin, *Game Change*, pp. 36, 336; Remnick, *The Bridge*, p. 477.

45 Shelby Steele, "Obama's Post-Racial Promise," *Los Angeles Times* (5 November 2008), http://www.latimes.com/news/opinion/opinionla/la-oe-steele5-2008nov05,0,6049031.story.

46 Sylvester Monroe, "Obama, Clinton Headline NABJ Convention in Las Vegas," *Jet* 112 (27 August 2007): 8; Gwen Ifill, *The Break-through: Politics and Race in the Age of Obama* (2009), pp. 51–69.

47 Remnick, *The Bridge*, pp. 13–15, 507; Dan Martin, "Jay-Z: Obama's Running So We All Can Fly," *Guardian* (5 November 2008), <http://www.guardian.co.uk/music/2008/nov/05/jayz-falloutboy>; Heilemann and Halperin, *Game Change*, pp. 421–422.

48 Gabriel J. Chin, "The Jena Six and the History of Racially Compromised Justice in Louisiana," *Harvard Civil Rights-Civil Liberties Law Review* 44 (2009): 361–391; Remnick, *The Bridge*, pp. 491–492.

49 Remnick, *The Bridge*, p. 535; Barack Obama, "Obama's Father's Day Remarks," *New York Times* (15 June 2008), http://www.nytimes.com/2008/06/15/us/politics/15text-obama.html?pagewanted=print.

50 Remnick, *The Bridge*, p. 534; "Black Power Struggle: 'I Want to Cut His Nuts Out,'" *Independent* (11 July 2008), http://www.independent.co.uk/news/world/americas/black-power-struggle-i-want-to-cut-his-nuts-out-865071.html.

51 Balz and Johnson, *The Battle for America 2008*, pp. 235–246, 314–315, 325–344.

52 Ibid., pp. 371–373; Remnick, *The Bridge*, p. 560; Glasrud and Wintz, *African Americans and the Presidency*, p. 114.

53 Daren Briscoe, et al., "How He Did It," *Newsweek* 152 (5 November 2008): 38–49.

54 David Remnick, "The Joshua Generation: Race and the Campaign of Barack Obama," *New Yorker* 84 (17 November 2008): 68–83; David Remnick, "The President's Hero," *New Yorker* 84 (2 February 2009): 21–23.

55 Alter, *The Promise*, pp. xiv, 77, 328–330, 425, 428; George Packer, "Obama's Lost Year," *New Yorker* 86 (15 March 2010): 41–51; Carl Hulse, "Senate Confirms Kagan in Partisan Vote," *New York Times* (6 August 2010), p. A1.

56 Douglas Brinkley, "'The Bridge: The Life and Rise of Barack Obama' by David Remnick," *Los Angeles Times* (28 March 2010), p. E1; Alter, *The Promise*, pp. 81–94, 125–132.

57 Alter, *The Promise*, pp. 192, 201–202, 244–270, 268, 395–421.

58 Ibid., pp. 431–434.

59 Loren Steffy, *Drowning in Oil: BP & the Reckless Pursuit of Profit* (2010); Stephen Power and Tennille Tracy, "Spill Panel Finds U.S. Was Slow to React," *Wall Street Journal* (7 October 2010), http://online.wsj.com/article/SB10001424052748703735804575536042567062622.html.

60 Dinesh D'Souza, *The Roots of Obama's Rage* (2010), p. 7; Steven Gray, "Letter from Detroit: Where's the Urban President," *Time* (4 August 2010), http://www.time.com/time/nation/article/0,8599,2008623-2,00.html.

61 Alter, *The Promise*, pp. 225–227, 357–358; Jeff Zeleny, "Obama Arrives in Oslo for Nobel Ceremony," *New York Times* (10 December 2009), http://thecaucus.blogs.nytimes.com/2009/12/10/obama-arrives-in-oslo-for-nobel-ceremony/.

62 Michael Scherer, "The Five Pillars of Obama's Foreign Policy," *Washington Post* (13 July 2009), http://www.time.com/time/nation/article/0,8599,1910057,00.html; Thomas Friedman, "Barack Kissinger Obama," *New York Times*, (25 October 2011), http://www.nytimes.com/2011/10/26/opinion/barack-kissinger-obama.html.

63 Bob Woodward, *Obama's Wars* (2010); Michael Hastings, "The Runaway General: The Rolling Stone Profile of Stanley McChrystal that Changed History," *Rolling Stone* (22 June 2010), http://www.rollingstone.com/politics/news/the-runaway-general-20100622?page=6.

64 Peter Baker, "Education of a President," *New York Times* (12 October 2010), http://www.nytimes.com/2010/10/17/magazine/17obama-t.html?_r=1&pagewanted=2; Evan Thomas, "God of All Things," *Newsweek* (22 November 2010), cover story; Hendrik Hertzberg, "Electoral Dissonance," *New Yorker* (15 November 2010), http://www.newyorker.com/talk/comment/2010/11/15/101115taco_talk_hertzberg.

65 Mike Dorning, "GOP Shuts Obama's Window for Sweeping Change," *Bloomberg Businessweek* (3 November 2010), http://www.businessweek.com/bwdaily/dnflash/content/nov2010/db2010113_679513.htm; Alter, *The Promise*, pp. 129–130, 409.

66 Perry Bacon, Jr., "A Lame-Duck Session with Unexpected Victories," *Washington Post* (22 December 2010), http://www.washingtonpost.com/wp-dyn/content/article/2010/12/22/AR2010122203663.html; Lisa Lerer and Laura Litvan, "No Congress since '60s Makes as Much Law as 111th Affecting Most Americans," *Bloomberg* (22 December 2010), http://www.bloomberg.com/news/2010-12-22/no-congress-since-1960s-makes-most-laws-for-americans-as-111th.html.

67 Allison Samuels, "The Black War over Obama," *Newsweek* 158 (22 & 29 August 2011): 14–15; Michael Eric Dyson, "In the Name of King," *Time* (25 August 2011), http://www.time.com/time/nation/article/0,8599,2090428,00.html.

68 William Broyles, "Oval Office Appeaser," *Newsweek* 158 (14 August 2011): 4.

69 Dick Polman, "Is Obama in Trouble?," *Buffalo News* (16 August 2011), pp. G1–G2; Alan Brinkley, "The Philosopher President," *Democracy: A Journal of Ideas* (Winter, 2011), http://www.democracyjournal.org/19/6791.php?page=2; "Obama pulls back proposed smog standards in victory for business," *Washington Post* (4 September 2011), http://www.washingtonpost.com/national/health-science/obama-pulls-back-proposed-smog-standards-in-victory-for-business/2011/09/02/gIQAisTiwJ_story_1.html.

70 Nicholas Schmidle, "Getting Bin Laden," *New Yorker* (8 August 2011), http://www.newyorker.com/reporting/2011/08/08/110808fa_fact_schmidle?printable=true; Mark Mazzetti, Eric Schmitt, and Robert Worth, "Two-Year Manhunt Led to Killing of Awlaki in Yemen," *New York Times* (30 September 2011), http://www.nytimes.com/2011/10/01/world/middleeast/anwar-al-awlaki-is-killed-in-yemen.html?pagewanted=all.

71 James T. Kloppenberg, *Reading Obama: Dreams, Hope, and the American Political Tradition* (2011), inside flap; Alter, *The Promise*, p. 434; D'Souza, *The Roots of Obama's Rage*, p. 18.

72 Bill Keller, "Fill in the Blanks," *New York Times* (18 September 2011), http://www.nytimes.com/2011/09/19/opinion/filling-in-the-blanks.html?pagewanted=all.

73 Ron Suskind, *Confidence Men: Wall Street, Washington, and the Education of a President* (2011), pp. 459, 478–482; Brinkley, "The Philosopher President."

74 Shelby Steele, "Obama and the Burden of Exceptionalism," *Wall Street Journal* (1 September 2011), http://online.wsj.com/article/SB10001424053111904787404576532623176115558.html.

75 Alter, *The Promise*, pp. 425, 429–430, 434.

Conclusion

From colonial times to the present, African-American leaders have developed and utilized their distinctive personal qualities to improve or eliminate the inferior caste status of their people. Their shared concern has been to improve the condition of blacks through economic, educational, political, legal, and psychological progress. Whatever their differences on issues such as segregation and integration, accommodation or protest, alliances with or rejection of whites, most of the leaders discussed here displayed and promoted a sense of racial pride and identity with their followers; and they sought to lift up their race, by whatever means seemed to them most effective at a given time.

Lines of ideological continuity also link the leaders discussed. Booker T. Washington, the towering southern black figure of the late 19th and early 20th centuries, was a professed admirer of the vocational education plans favored by Frederick Douglass and Mary McLeod Bethune. On several occasions, W.E.B. Du Bois conceded that given the circumstances of his time and place, Washington had implemented a realistic, if incomplete, program of racial advancement. Moreover, before the publication of *The Souls of Black Folk*, Du Bois and Washington shared some basic convictions. Both endorsed the white middle-class virtues of thrift, sobriety, education, and capital accumulation, and emphasized the importance of economic advancement. Marcus Garvey acknowledged Washington as the inspiration for his own racial and economic philosophy, as he also castigated Du Bois' elitism and integrationism. Ironically, Du Bois came to agree with both Washington and Garvey on the necessity for a "black economy," and also shared Garvey's conviction that African Americans needed to acknowledge their African antecedents and culture. Martin Luther King, Jr., recognized the achievements, even as he deplored the limitations, of Washington, Du Bois, and Garvey, and displayed at least a grudging respect for his contemporary rival, Malcolm X, who, in turn, expressed admiration for Garvey's racial vision. Jesse Jackson, the young colleague of Martin Luther King, proclaimed himself the heir to King's legacy, and moved mountains to achieve corporate concessions on race. In like manner, Oprah Winfrey paid homage to Harriet Tubman and Fannie Lou Hamer. Barack Obama studied the writings of Du Bois, King, and Malcolm, but ultimately rejected a race-based appeal, believing that such appeals were passé, even counterproductive.

In assessing the contributions of African-American leaders to their respective causes, a historical perspective reveals the shifting connotations of such key concepts as "integration," "segregation," "separatism," and "civil rights." It also suggests that the adjectives "radical" and "conservative" when applied to black leaders and the policies they espoused, reflect particular conditions and "limited options." To his contemporary critics, Booker T. Washington's public deprecations of political action and support for the social separation of the races smacked of supine surrender to white supremacy. It may well have been a shrewd and calculated recognition of the fearful penalties which would have attended any displays of black militancy in the era of Jim Crow. From the end of Reconstruction to World War II, black southern leadership was forced to operate within the "separate but [un]equal" confines of a system predicated on and pledged to the maintenance of white supremacy. Whatever influence black southern leaders possessed was exercised through white intermediaries, who made limited concessions within the framework of segregation.

In the post-war period, a younger generation of southern black men and women began to demand changes which ran directly counter to prevailing customs and mores. The South's "rank order of discriminations," as sociologist Gunnar Myrdal observed, included racial intermarriage, first and foremost, and then encompassed "dancing, bathing, eating, drinking together, and social intercourse generally . . . segregations and discriminations in use of public facilities such as schools, churches and means of conveyance . . . discriminations in law courts, by the police, and by other public servants. Finally come discriminations in securing land, credit, jobs . . . public relief and other social welfare activities." From the 1950s onwards, and starting at the grassroots with local protests, black southerners challenged this traditional list of racial proscriptions. The civil rights movement, which brought into prominence Martin Luther King, also owed its dynamic to the continued efforts of thousands of activists, black and white, male and female. It also came to provide training, membership and leadership for the protest and reform movements which followed, namely, the anti-war movement, the student movement, and the campaigns for minority rights. Paradoxically, the civil rights movement, like earlier black protests, drew much of its strength from the sense of racial identity which segregation had inadvertently fostered. The National Association for the Advancement of Colored People (NAACP), which institutionalized black opposition to Booker T. Washington and the Tuskegee Machine, was at its inception a radical organization, pledged to securing both black political participation and racial integration. Given the tradition of black protest which existed in the northern states, such a response was feasible and timely. But the increasing shift of black Americans from the rural South to the industrialized urban centers of the North, also gave rise to conditions which fostered intense black separatist feelings, which, in turn, were capitalized upon by such leaders as Marcus Garvey, Elijah Muhammad, and Malcolm X.[1]

With the advent of the Nation of Islam, and the rise of the Black Power slogan in the 1960s, racial separatism was viewed as a "radical" response to appalling socio-economic conditions, and a younger generation of black "militants" rejected the integrationism of the NAACP, the Urban League, and the Southern Christian Leadership Conference as "assimilationism." Instead, they advocated a form of cultural pluralism— "a Negro nation within a nation"—without sufficient awareness of its historic antecedents and precedents. At the end of their respective careers, W.E.B. Du Bois, Martin Luther King, and Malcolm X, had moved beyond an exclusive concern with civil rights to formulate "radical" critiques of capitalist society, colonialism, and militarism. Jesse Jackson attempted to project his social democratic concept of a "Rainbow Coalition" of the disadvantaged and unrepresented into American politics. As for Barack Obama, he redefined the notion of black leader; he is a leader who is black, not a leader of blacks.

The fundamental aspiration of the African American, to which most black leaders have responded, was well expressed by W.E.B. Du Bois in *The Souls of Black Folk*:

He simply wishes to make it possible for a man to be both a Negro and an American, without being cursed and spit upon by his fellows, without having the doors of Opportunity closed roughly in his face . . . to be a co-worker in the kingdom of culture, to escape both death and isolation, to husband and use his best powers and his latent genius. . . . Merely a concrete test of the underlying principles of the great republic is the Negro Problem, and the spiritual striving of the freedmen's sons is the travail of souls whose burden is almost beyond the measure of their strength, but who bear it in the name of an historic race, in the name of this the land of their father's fathers, and in the name of human opportunity.[2]

The perpetual vexing question was precisely how to achieve this aspiration. Over the course of the century since Du Bois penned these words, black leaders have pursued many different methods—and often quarreled with each other over priorities—to win the fundamental rights that the 14th Amendment guaranteed them at birth. These methods have included industrial education, white philanthropy, emigration, publicity against racist deeds, lawsuits, legislative lobbying, black nationalism, civil rights demonstrations, voter-registration drives, militant self-defense, government welfare, and compensatory programs, such as affirmative action. The results have been mixed at best. A majority of African Americans have finally reached the middle class—compared to just 1 percent in 1940—and are the wealthiest black people in the world, but tens of millions more of them have long been confined to dead-end urban slums.[3]

In 2004, on the fiftieth anniversary of the epic *Brown* school desegregation decision, the NAACP held a gala celebration in Washington, D.C. The keynote speaker was 69-year-old comedian Bill Cosby, who had broken color barriers in television, earned a doctorate in education, and donated $30 million to historically black colleges. Unexpectedly, Cosby delivered a jeremiad to black America about the profound crisis it faced. Pointing to what he characterized as the destructive hip-hop culture, Cosby blasted "people with their hats on backwards, pants down around the crack," children with faux African names like "Shaniqua, Shaligua," "knuckleheads" whose fractured English included phrases such as "Why you ain't," and girls who start becoming "baby machines at age twelve, each with a different man." In 1964, in the midst of the civil rights revolution, 82 percent of black families had mothers and fathers living in the same household; forty years later, 69 percent of black children are born to unmarried women, an appalling statistic that owed much to well-intentioned, but still-destructive welfare programs that paid women more to have a child than to have a job. Cosby was also flummoxed that black America tolerated high school dropout rates of 50 percent, crack houses in their neighborhoods, and incarceration rates that made African Americans the proportional leader among ethnic groups. In light of all these social pathologies, Cosby wondered, "What the hell good is *Brown v. Board of Education* if nobody wants it?"[4]

In a nutshell, Cosby endorsed what Frederick Douglass, Booker T. Washington, W.E.B. Du Bois, Mary McLeod Bethune, Malcolm X, and Jesse Jackson, among others, had once argued: Americans of all colors can succeed if they shun self-defeating behavior and follow a self-help formula that includes discipline, educational achievement, and plain hard work.

Central to this formula is a stable family life and good parenting. Douglass understood that African Americans must prepare for a world of work, once editorializing that blacks must "Learn Trades or Starve," which journalist Juan Williams calls "the core message of black leadership in American history." The problem, as Cosby saw it, was that contemporary black leaders have convinced too many black people that they remain victims of a racist society and are therefore helpless to change their condition. "There are people," he declared in another speech, "that want you to remain in a hole, and they rejoice in your hopelessness because they have jobs mismanaging you." By implication, Cosby referred to the civil rights leadership of Jesse Jackson, Julian Bond, and Al Sharpton. The fate of black people, Cosby declared unequivocally, lies in the hands of black people themselves. His impolitic remarks brought instant condemnation, as Cosby stood accused of being a hypocrite, a "crotchety old uncle," and a black billionaire who betrayed the black underclass whom he seemed incapable of understanding.[5]

Using himself as a textbook example of self-help, president Barack Obama also urged black youth to act responsibly and to make education a high priority. At the same time, Obama did not endorse the call for reparations for slavery or special government programs for African Americans, though he did take steps to help the poor of all backgrounds. With Obama adopting a "rising tide lifts all boats" metaphor, it remains to be seen whether a new, post-civil rights generation of black leadership can work effectively to raise up the large remnant of a long-suffering people. The title of Martin Luther King's last book remains timely—*Where Do We Go from Here?*[6]

References

1 Gunnar Myrdal, *An American Dilemma* (1944), pp. 60–67.

2 W.E.B. Du Bois, *The Souls of Black Folk* (1903), p. 4.

3 Stephen Grant Meyer, *As Long As They Don't Move Next Door: Segregation and Racial Conflict in American Neighborhoods* (2000), p. 12; Juan Williams, *Enough: The Phony Leaders, Dead-End Movements, and Culture of Failure that are Undermining Black America—and What We Can Do About It* (2006), p. 73.

4 Williams, *Enough*, pp. 1–11, 221–227.

5 Ibid., 11–43; Michael Eric Dyson, *Is Bill Cosby Right? Or Has the Black Middle Class Lost Its Mind?* (2006).

6 Martin Luther King, Jr., *Where Do We Go from Here? Chaos or Community?* (1968).

Selected Bibliography

Introductory and general studies

Texts & Reference Works

Aptheker, Herbert, ed. *A Documentary History of the Negro People in the United States*. 4 vols. 1992.

Bennett, Lerone, Jr. *Before the Mayflower: A History of Black Americans*. 2003.

Berry, Mary F., and John Blassingame. *Long Memory: The Black Experience in America*. 1982.

Carson, Clayborne, et al. *African American Lives: The Struggle for Freedom*. 2005.

Clay, William L. *Just Permanent Interests: Black Americans in Congress: 1870–1992*. 1993.

Cruse, Harold. *The Crisis of the Negro Intellectual: From Its Origins to the Present*. 1967.

Ellison, Mary. *The Black Experience: American Blacks since 1865*. 1974.

Fairclough, Adam. *Better Day Coming: Blacks and Equality, 1890–2000*. 2001.

Finkelman, Paul, ed. *Encyclopedia of African American History, 1619–1895: From the Colonial Period to the Age of Frederick Douglass*. 2006.

Finkelman, Paul, ed. *Encyclopedia of African American History, 1896 to the Present: From the Age of Segregation to the Twenty-first Century*. 2009.

Franklin, John Hope, and Alfred A. Moss, Jr. *From Slavery to Freedom: A History of African Americans*. 2000.

Frazier, E. Franklin. *The Negro in the United States*. 1957.

Gates, Henry Louis, Jr., and Cornel West, eds. *The African-American Century: How Black Americans Have Shaped Our Country*. 2000.

Gates, Henry Louis, Jr., and Evelyn Brooks Higginbotham, eds. *African American Lives*. 2004.

Gerstle, Gary. *American Crucible: Race and Nation in the Twentieth Century*. 2001.

Grant, Joanne. *Black Protest: History, Documents, and Analysis, 1619 to the Present*. 1968.

Harding, Vincent. *There is a River: The Black Struggle for Freedom in America*. 1993.

Hine, Darline Clark, et al. *The African-American Odyssey*. 2002.

Holt, Thomas C. *Children of Fire: A History of African Americans*. 2010.

Horton, James Oliver, and Lois E. Horton. *Hard Road to Freedom: The Story of African America*. 2002.

Horton, James Oliver, and Lois E. Horton. *In Hope of Liberty: Culture, Community, and Protest among Northern Free Blacks, 1700–1860*. 1997.

Isaacs, Harold R. *The New World of Negro Americans*. 1963.

Klarman, Michael. *Unfinished Business: Racial Equality in American History*. 2007.

Klinkner, Philip, with Rogers M. Smith. *The Unsteady March: The Rise and Decline of Racial Equality in America*. 1999.

Logan, Rayford W. *The Betrayal of the Negro: From Rutherford B. Hayes to Woodrow Wilson*. 1965.

Manning, Marable, and Leith Mullings, eds., *Let Nobody Turn Us Around: Voices of Resistance, Reform, and Renewal, An African American Anthology*. 2009.

Myrdal, Gunnar. *An American Dilemma: The Negro Problem and Modern Democracy*. 1944.

Painter, Nell Irvin. *Creating Black Americans: African American History and Its Meanings, 1619 to the Present*. 2005.

Salzman, Jack, et al. *Encyclopedia of African-American Culture and History*. 2005.

Thernstrom, Stephan, and Abigail Thernstrom. *America in Black and White: One Nation, Indivisible—Race in Modern America*. 1997.

Thorpe, Earl E. *The Mind of the Negro: An Intellectual History of Afro-Americans*. 1970.

Trotter, Joe William, Jr. *The African American Experience.* 2001.

Tuck, Stephen G.N. *We Ain't What We Ought to Be: The Black Freedom Struggle from Emancipation to Obama.* 2010.

Williams, Michael W. *The African American Encyclopedia.* 1993.

Wright, Kai, ed. *The African-American Experience: Black History and Culture through Speeches, Letters, Editorials, Poems, Songs, and Stories.* 2009.

African-American leadership

Burgess, M. Elaine. *Negro Leadership in a Southern City.* 1960.

Franklin, John Hope, and August Meier, eds. *Black Leaders of the Twentieth Century.* 1982.

Gaines, Kevin. *Uplifting the Race: Black Leadership, Politics, and Culture in the Twentieth Century.* 1996.

Higham, John, ed. *Ethnic Leadership in America.* 1978.

Litwack, Leon, and August Meier, eds. *Black Leaders of the Nineteenth Century.* 1988.

Meier, August, Elliott Rudwick and Francis L. Broderick, eds. *Black Protest Thought in the Twentieth Century.* 1971.

Nelson, H. Viscount "Berky". *The Rise and Fall of Modern Black Leadership: Chronicle of a Twentieth Century Tragedy.* 2003.

Smith, Robert C. *We Have No Leaders: African Americans in the Post-Civil Rights Era.* 1996.

Thompson, Daniel C. *The Negro Leadership Class.* 1963.

Walters, Ronald W., and Robert C. Smith. *African American Leadership.* 1999.

Black protest and accommodation, 1800–1877

Enslaved & Free Blacks

Berlin, Ira. *Many Thousands Gone: The First Two Centuries of Slavery in North America.* 1998.

Berlin, Ira. *Slaves without Masters: The Free Negro in the Antebellum South.* 1974.

Blassingame, John, et al., eds. The Frederick Douglass Papers. 5 vols. 1979–1992.

Blassingame, John W. The Slave Community: Plantation Life in the Antebellum South. 1979.

Blassingame, John W., ed. Slave Testimony: Two Centuries of Letters, Speeches, Interviews, and Autobiographies. 1977.

Bontemps, Arna. Free at Last: The Life of Frederick Douglass. 1971.

Cornish, Dudley. The Sable Arm: Black Troops in the Union Army, 1861–1865. 1966.

Curry, Leonard P. The Free Black in Urban America, 1800–1850: The Shadow of the Dream. 1981.

Fields, Barbara Jeanne. Slavery and Freedom on the Middle Ground: Maryland during the Nineteenth Century. 1985.

Fox-Genovese, Elizabeth. Within the Plantation Household: Black and White Women of the Old South. 1988.

Genovese, Eugene. Roll, Jordan, Roll: The World the Slaves Made. 1974.

Horton, James Oliver. Free People of Color: Inside the African American Community. 1993.

Levine, Lawrence W. Black Culture and Black Consciousness: Afro-American Folk Thought from Slavery to Freedom. 1977.

King, Wilma. Stolen Childhood: Slave Youth in Nineteenth Century America. 1995.

Kolchin, Peter. American Slavery, 1619–1877. 1993.

Litwack, Leon F. North of Slavery: The Negro in the Free States, 1790–1860. 1961.

Raboteau, Albert J. Slave Religion: The "Invisible Institution" in the Antebellum South. 1978.

Stampp, Kenneth. The Peculiar Institution: Slavery in the Ante-Bellum South. 1956.

Stevenson, Brenda E. Life in Black and White: Family and Community in the Slave South. 1996.

Toll, Robert C. Blacking Up: The Minstrel Show in Nineteenth-Century America. 1974.

Woods, Peter H. Black Majority: Negroes in South Carolina from 1670 through the Stono Rebellion. 1974.

Slave Resistance

Aptheker, Herbert, ed. *American Negro Slave Revolts*. 1983.

Bacon, Jacqueline. *Freedom's Journal: The First African-American Newspaper*. 2007.

Bell, Howard Holman. *A Survey of the Negro Convention Movement, 1830–1861*. 1969.

Blockson, Charles L. *The Underground Railroad*. 1987.

Delany, Martin R. *The Condition, Elevation, Emigration, and Destiny of the Colored People of the United States, Politically Considered*. 1852.

Dick, Robert C. *Black Protest: Issues and Tactics*. 1974.

Douglass, Frederick. *The Life and Times of Frederick Douglass as Written by Himself*. 1892.

Douglass, Frederick. *My Bondage and My Freedom*. 1855.

Douglass, Frederick. *Narrative of the Life of Frederick Douglass, an American Slave*. 1845.

Egerton, Douglas R. *Gabriel's Rebellion: The Virginia Slave Conspiracies of 1800 & 1802*. 1993.

Egerton, Douglas R. *He Shall Go Out Free: The Lives of Denmark Vesey*. 1999.

Foner, Philip S. *Frederick Douglass: A Biography*. 1964.

Foner, Philip S., ed. *The Life and Writings of Frederick Douglass*, 4 vols. 1950–1955.

Franklin, John Hope, and Loren Schweninger. *Runaway Slaves: Rebels on the Plantation*. 2000.

Franklin, Vincent P. *Black Self-Determination; A Cultural History of the Faith of the Fathers*. 1984.

Genovese, Eugene D. *From Rebellion to Revolution: Afro-American Slave Revolts in the Making of the Modern World*. 1979.

Genovese, Eugene D. *In Red and Black: Marxian Explorations in Southern and Afro-American History*. 1971.

Greenberg, Kenneth S., ed. *Nat Turner: A Slave Rebellion in Story and Memory*. 2003.

Hinks, Peter P. *To Awaken My Afflicted Brethren: David Walker and the Problem of Antebellum Slave Resistance*. 1997.

Hoffer, Peter Charles. *The Great New York Conspiracy of 1741*. 2003.

Huggins, Nathan Irvin. *Slave and Citizen: The Life of Frederick Douglass*. 1980.

Lepore, Jill. *New York Burning: Liberty, Slavery, and Conspiracy in Eighteenth-Century Manhattan*. 2005.

Levine, Robert S. *Martin Delany, Frederick Douglass, and the Politics of Representative Identity*. 1997.

Litwack, Leon F. *Been In the Storm So Long: The Aftermath of Slavery*. 1972.

Martin, Waldo E., Jr. *The Mind of Frederick Douglass*. 1986.

Mayer, Henry. *All on Fire: William Lloyd Garrison and the Abolition of Slavery*. 2000.

McFeely, William S. *Frederick Douglass*. 1991.

Miller, Floyd J. *The Search for a Black Nationality: Black Emigration and Colonization, 1787–1863*. 1975.

Mullin, Gerald W. *Flight and Rebellion: Slave Resistance in Eighteenth-Century Virginia*. 1972.

Newman, Richard S. *Freedom's Prophet: Bishop Richard Allen, the AME Church, and the Founding Fathers*. 2008.

Oates, Stephen B. *The Fires of Jubilee: Nat Turner's Fierce Rebellion*. 1975.

Oates, Stephen B. *To Purge This Land with Blood: A Biography of John Brown*. 1984.

Ofari, Earl. *"Let Your Motto Be Resistance": The Life and Thought of Henry Highland Garnet*. 1972.

Pasternak, Martin B. *Rise Now and Fly to Arms: The Life of Henry Highland Garnet*. 1995.

Pease, Jane H., and William H. Pease. *They Who Would Be Free: Blacks' Search for Freedom, 1830–1861*. 1975.

Quarles, Benjamin. *Black Abolitionists*. 1969.

Quarles, Benjamin, *Frederick Douglass*. 1984.

Rasmussen, Daniel. *American Uprising: The Untold Story of America's Largest Revolt*. 2011.

Staudenraus, P.J. *The African Colonization Movement, 1816–1865*. 1961.

Sterling, Dorothy. *The Making of an Afro-American: Martin Robison Delany, 1812–1885.* 1971.

Stuckey, Sterling. *Slave Culture: Nationalist Theory and the Foundations of Black America.* 1978.

Ullman, Victor. *Martin R. Delany: The Beginnings of Black Nationalism.* 1971.

Booker T. Washington

Reconstruction

Foner, Eric. *Reconstruction: America's Unfinished Revolution, 1863–1877.* 1988.

Hahn, Steven. *A Nation under Our Feet: Black Political Struggles in the Rural South from Slavery to the Great Migration.* 2003.

Litwack, Leon. *Been in the Storm So Long: The Aftermath of Slavery.* 1979.

Logan, Rayford. *The Negro in American Life and Thought: The Nadir, 1877–1901.* 1954.

Rabinowitz, Howard N., ed. *Southern Black Leaders of the Reconstruction Era.* 1982.

Williamson, Joel. *The Crucible of Race: Black/White Relations in the South since Emancipation.* 1984.

Jim Crow Era

Arnesen, Eric. *Black Protest and the Great Migration: A Brief History with Documents.* 2002.

Blackmon, Douglas A. *Slavery by Another Name: The Re-Enslavement of Black People in America from the Civil War to World War II.* 2008.

Daniel, Pete. *The Shadow of Slavery: Peonage in the South, 1909–1969.* 1972.

Dray, Philip. *At the Hands of Persons Unknown: The Lynching of Black America.* 2002.

Grossman, James R. *Land of Hope: Chicago, Black Southerners, and the Great Migration.* 1991.

Lemann, Nicholas. *The Promised Land: The Great Black Migration and How It Changed America*. 1991.

McMath, Robert C. *Populism: A Social History, 1877–1898*. 1993.

McMillen, Neil R. *Dark Journey: Black Mississippians in the Age of Jim Crow*. 1989.

Meier, August. *Negro Thought in America, 1880–1915*. 1963.

Rabinowitz, Howard N. *Race Relations in the Urban South, 1865–1890*. 1978.

Woodward, C. Vann. *Origins of the New South*. 1951.

Woodward, C. Vann. *The Strange Career of Jim Crow*. 2001.

Booker T. Washington

Adams, Cyrus Field. *The National Afro-American Council, Organized 1898, A History*. 1902.

Baker, Ray Stannard. *Following the Color Line: American Negro Citizenship in the Progressive Era*. 1964.

Bieze, Michael. *Booker T. Washington and the Art of Self-Representation*. 2008.

Brundage, W. Fitzhugh, ed. *Up from Slavery by Booker T. Washington with Related Documents*. 2003.

Dalton, Kathleen. *Theodore Roosevelt: A Strenuous Life*. 2002.

De Marco, Joseph. *The Social Thought of W.E.B. Du Bois*. 1983.

Dyer, Thomas G. *Theodore Roosevelt and the Idea of Race*. 1980.

Engs, Robert Francis. *Educating the Disfranchised and Disinherited: Samuel Chapman Armstrong and Hampton Institute, 1839–1893*. 1899.

Fox, Stephen M. *The Guardian of Boston: William Monroe Trotter*. 1970.

Gaither, Gerald H. *Blacks and the Populist Revolt: Ballots and Bigotry in the New South*. 1977.

Gaston, Paul M. *The New South Creed: A Study in Southern Mythmaking*. 1970.

Harlan, Louis R. *Booker T. Washington: The Making of a Black Leader, 1865–1901*. 1972.

Harlan, Louis R. *Booker T. Washington: The Wizard of Tuskegee, 1901–1915.* 1983.

Harlan, Louis R., and Raymond Smock, eds. *The Booker T. Washington Papers.* 14 vols. 1972–1989.

Hawkins, Hugh, ed. *Booker T. Washington and His Critics.* 1974.

Jackson, David H., Jr. *Booker T. Washington and the Struggle against White Supremacy: The Southern Educational Tours, 1908–1912* (2008).

Kellogg, Charles F. *NAACP: A History of the National Association for the Advancement of Colored People.* 1967.

Mathews, Basil. *Booker T. Washington: Educator and Interracial Interpreter.* 1948.

McMurry, Linda O. *George Washington Carver: Scientist and Symbol.* 1981.

Meier, August. *Negro Thought in America, 1880–1915: Racial Ideologies in the Age of Booker T. Washington.* 1963.

Moore, Jacqueline M. *Booker T. Washington, W.E.B. Du Bois, and the Struggle for Racial Uplift.* 2003.

Morris, Edmund. *Theodore Rex.* 2001.

Moses, Wilson Jeremiah. *Creative Conflict in African American Thought: Frederick Douglass, Alexander Crummell, Booker T. Washington, W.E.B. Du Bois, and Marcus Garvey.* 2004.

Norrell, Robert J. *Reaping the Whirlwind: The Civil Rights Movement in Tuskegee.* 1985.

Norrell, Robert. *Up from History: The Life of Booker T. Washington.* 2009.

Smock, Raymond. *Booker T. Washington: Black Leadership in the Age of Jim Crow.* 2009.

Spencer, Samuel J. *Booker T. Washington and the Negro's Place in American Life.* 1955.

Thornbrough, Emma L. *T. Thomas Fortune: Militant Journalist.* 1972.

Thornbrough, Emma L., ed. *Booker T. Washington.* 1969.

Washington, Booker T. *Frederick Douglass.* 1906.

Washington, Booker T. *The Future of the American Negro.* 1899.

Washington, Booker T. *My Larger Education: Being Chapters from My Experience*. 1911.

Washington, Booker T. *Up from Slavery*. 1901.

Washington, Booker T. *Working with the Hands: Being a Sequel to "Up from Slavery" Covering the Author's Experiences in Industrial Training at Tuskegee*. 1904.

Weisberger, Bernard. *Booker T. Washington*. 1972.

West, Michael Randolph. *The Education of Booker T. Washington: American Democracy and the Idea of Race Relations*. 2006.

Wintz, Cary, ed. *African American Political Thought, 1890–1930: Washington, Du Bois, Garvey, and Randolph*. 1996.

W.E.B. Du Bois

Alridge, Derrick P. *The Educational Thought of W.E.B. Du Bois: An Intellectual History*. 2008.

Aptheker, Herbert, ed. *The Correspondence of W.E.B. Du Bois*. 1973–1978.

Aptheker, Herbert, ed. *W.E.B. Du Bois, Against Racism: Unpublished Essays, Papers, Addresses, 1887–1961*. 1985.

Arnold, Edwin T. *What Virtue There is in Fire: Cultural Memory and the Lynching of Sam Hose*. 2009.

Balaji, Murali. *Professor and the Pupil: The Politics and Friendship of W.E.B. Du Bois and Paul Robeson*. 2007.

Blum, Edward J. *W.E.B. Du Bois: American Prophet*. 2007.

Broderick, Francis L. *W.E.B. Du Bois: Negro Leader in a Time of Crisis*. 1959.

Byerman, Keith E. *Seizing the Word: History, Art, and Self in the Work of W.E.B. Du Bois*. 1994.

Clarke, John Henrik, et al., eds. *Black Titan: W.E.B. Du Bois, An Anthology*. 1970.

Crouch, Stanley, and Playthell Benjamin. *Reconsidering the Souls of Black Folk: Thoughts on the Groundbreaking Classic Work*. 2002.

DeMarco, Joseph P. *The Social Thought of W.E.B. Du Bois*. 1983.

Du Bois, Shirley Graham. *His Day Is Marching On: A Memoir of W.E.B. Du Bois.* 1971.

Du Bois, W.E.B. *The Autobiography of W.E.B. Du Bois: A Soliloquy on Viewing My Life from the Last Decade of Its First Century.* 1968.

Du Bois, W.E.B. *Black Reconstruction in America, 1860–1880.* 1935.

Du Bois, W.E.B. *Color and Democracy.* 1945.

Du Bois, W.E.B. *Darkwater: Voices From Within the Veil.* 1920.

Du Bois, W.E.B. *Dusk of Dawn: An Essay toward an Autobiography of a Race Concept.* 1940.

Du Bois, W.E.B. *The Negro.* 1915.

Du Bois, W.E.B. *The Philadelphia Negro.* 1899.

Du Bois, W.E.B. *The Souls of Black Folk.* 1903.

Du Bois, W.E.B. *The Suppression of the African Slave Trade to the United States of America, 1638–1870.* 1896.

Du Bois, W.E.B. *The World and Africa: An Inquiry into the Part Which Africa Has Played in World History.* 1946.

Esedebe, P. Olisanwuche. *Pan-Africanism: The Idea and Movement, 1776–1991.* 1994.

Foner, Philip S., ed. *W.E.B. Du Bois Speaks: Speeches and Addresses, 1890–1919.* 1970.

Fontenot, Chester J., Jr., and Mary Alice Morgan, eds. *W.E.B. Du Bois and Race: Essays Celebrating the Centennial Publication of the Souls of Black Folk.* 2002.

Gaines, Kevin K. *Uplifting the Race: Black Leadership, Politics, and Culture in the Twentieth Century.* 1996.

Geiss, Imanuel. *The Pan-African Movement: A History of Pan-Africanism in America, Europe, and Africa.* 1968.

Horne, Gerald. *Black and Red: W.E.B. Du Bois and the Afro-American Response to the Cold War, 1944–1963.* 1986.

Horne, Gerald. *W.E.B. Du Bois: A Biography.* 2009.

Hubbard, Dolan, ed. *The Souls of Black Folk: One Hundred Years Later.* 2003.

Hughes, Langston. *Fight for Freedom: The Story of the NAACP.* 1962.

Kahn, Jonathon S. *Divine Discontent: The Religious Imagination of W.E.B. Du Bois*. 2009.

Kirby, John B. *Black Americans in the Roosevelt Era*. 1980.

Langley, J. Ayodele. *Pan-Africanism and Nationalism in West Africa, 1900–1945*. 1973.

Lester, Julius. *The Seventh Son: The Thought and Writings of W.E.B. Du Bois*, 2 vols. 1971.

Lewis, David Levering. *W.E.B. Du Bois: Biography of a Race, 1868–1919*. 1993.

Lewis, David Levering. *W.E.B. Du Bois: The Fight for Equality and the American Century, 1919–1963*. 2000.

Lewis, David Levering. *W.E.B. Du Bois: A Reader*. 1995.

Logan, Rayford W., ed. *W.E.B. Du Bois: A Profile*. 1971.

Marable, Manning. *W.E.B. Du Bois: Black Radical Democrat*. 1986.

Moore, Jack B. *W.E.B. Du Bois*. 1981.

Rampersad, Arnold. *The Art and Imagination of W.E.B. Du Bois*. 1976.

Reed, Adolph L., Jr. *W.E.B. Du Bois and American Political Thought: Fabianism and the Color Line*. 1997.

Rudwick, Elliott. *W.E.B. Du Bois: Propagandist of the Negro Protest*. 1969.

Rudwick, Elliott. *W.E.B. Du Bois: A Study in Minority Group Leadership*. 1960.

Sullivan, Patricia. *Lift Every Voice: The NAACP and the Making of the Civil Rights Movement*. 2009.

Sundquist, Eric J., ed. *The Oxford W.E.B. Du Bois Reader*. 1996.

Walters, Alexander. *My Life and Work*. 1917.

Wilson, Sondra Kathryn, ed. *The Crisis Reader: Stories, Poetry, and Essays from the N.A.A.C.P.'s Crisis Magazine*. 1999.

Wintz, Cary, ed. *African American Political Thought, 1890–1930: Washington, Du Bois, Garvey, and Randolph*. 1996.

Wolters, Raymond. *Du Bois and His Rivals*. 2002.

Wolters, Raymond. *Negroes and the Great Depression: The Problem of Economic Recovery*. 1970.

Zamir, Shamoon. *W.E.B. Du Bois and American Thought, 1888–1903*. 1995.

Marcus Garvey

Anderson, Jervis. *A. Philip Randolph: A Biographical Portrait*. 1986.

Anderson, Jervis. *Harlem: The Great Black Way, 1900–1950*. 1982.

Barrett, Leonard E. *Soul-Force: African Heritage in Afro-American Religion*. 1974.

Bracey, John H., et al., eds. *Black Nationalism in America*. 1970.

Burkett, Randall K. *Garveyism as a Religious Movement: The Institutionalization of a Black Religion*. 1978.

Clarke, John Henrik, ed. *Marcus Garvey and the Vision of Africa*. 1974.

Cronon, E. David. *Black Moses: The Story of Marcus Garvey and the Universal Negro Improvement Association*. 1969.

Draper, Theodore. *The Rediscovery of Black Nationalism*. 1970.

Edwards, Adolph. *Marcus Garvey, 1887–1940*. 1972.

Essien-Udom, E.U. *Black Nationalism: A Search for an Identity in America*. 1962.

Essien-Udom, E.U., and Amy Jacques Garvey, eds. *More Philosophy and Opinions of Marcus Garvey*. 1977.

Fax, Elton C. *Garvey: The Story of a Pioneer Black Nationalist*. 1972.

Garvey, Amy Jacques. *Garvey and Garveyism*. 1963.

Garvey, Amy Jacques, ed. *Philosophy and Opinions of Marcy Garvey*. 1969.

Grant, Colin. *Negro with a Hat: The Rise and Fall of Marcus Garvey*. 2008.

Hill, Robert A., ed. *Marcus Garvey and Universal Negro Improvement Association Papers*. 10 vols. 1983–2006.

Hill, Robert A., and Barbara Blair. *Marcus Garvey: Life and Lessons*. 1987.

Huggins, Nathan I. *Harlem Renaissance*. 1971.

Johnson, James Weldon. *Black Manhattan*. 1930.

Kornweibel, Theodore, Jr. *No Crystal Stair: Black Life and the Messenger, 1917–1928*. 1975.

Lewis, David Levering. *When Harlem Was in Vogue*. 1981.

Lewis, Rupert. *Marcus Garvey: Anti-Colonial Champion*. 1988.

Lewis, Rupert, and Patrick Bryan, eds. *Garvey: His Work and Impact*. 1991.

Locke, Alain, ed. *The New Negro.* 1980.

Martin, Tony. *Race First: The Ideological and Organizational Struggles of Marcus Garvey and the Universal Negro Improvement Association.* 1976.

Martin, Tony. *Marcus Garvey, Hero—A First Biography.* 1983.

McKay, Claude. *Harlem: Negro Metropolis.* 1940.

Moses, Wilson Jeremiah. *Black Messiahs and Uncle Toms: Social and Literary Manipulations of a Religious Myth.* 1982.

Moses, Wilson Jeremiah, ed. *Classical Black Nationalism: From the American Revolution to Marcus Garvey.* 1996.

Moses, Wilson Jeremiah. *The Golden Age of Black Nationalism, 1850–1925.* 1978.

Nielson, David G. *Black Ethos: Northern Urban Negro Life and Thought, 1890–1930.* 1977.

Osofsky, Gilbert. *Harlem: The Making of a Ghetto, 1880–1930.* 1963.

Ottley, Roi. *"New World A-Coming": Inside Black America.* 1968.

Painter, Nell Irvin. *Exodusters: Black Migration to Kansas after Reconstruction.* 1976.

Pfeffer, Paula F. *A. Philip Randolph, Pioneer of the Civil Rights Movement.* 1990.

Pinkney, Alphonso. *Red, Black, and Green: Black Nationalism in the United States.* 1976.

Powell, Adam Clayton, Sr. *Against the Tide: An Autobiography.* 1938.

Redkey, Edwin S. *Black Exodus: Black Nationalist and Back-to-Africa Movements, 1890–1910.* 1969.

Stein, Judith. *The World of Marcus Garvey: Race and Class in Modern Society.* 1986.

Tolbert, Emory J. *The UNIA and Black Los Angeles: Ideology and Community in the Garvey Movement.* 1980.

Vincent, Theodore G. *Black Power and the Garvey Movement.* 1972.

Weisbord, Robert G. *Ebony Kinship: Africa, Africans, and the Afro-American.* 1973.

Wintz, Cary, ed. *African American Political Thought, 1890–1930: Washington, Du Bois, Garvey, and Randolph.* 1996.

Martin Luther King, Jr.

Great Depression

Bunche, Ralph. *The Political Status of the Negro in the Age of FDR.* 1975.

Burnham, Kenneth E. *God Comes to America: Father Divine and the Peace Mission Movement.* 1979.

Foster, William Z., et al. *The Communist Position on the Negro Question.* 1947.

Harris, Sara. *Father Divine: Holy Husband.* 1953.

Holloway, Joseph E., and Herbert H. Booker, II. *Noble Drew Ali and the Moorish Science Temple Movement.* 2007.

Hudson, Hosea, and Nell Irvin Painter. *The Narrative of Hosea Hudson: The Life and Times of a Black Radical.* 1993.

Kelley, Robin D.G. *Hammer and Hoe: Alabama Communists during the Great Depression.* 1990.

Kirby, John B. *Black Americans in the Roosevelt Era: Liberalism and Race.* 1980.

Naison, Mark. *Communists in Harlem during the Depression.* 1983.

Nolan, William. *Communism versus the Negro.* 1951.

Record, Wilson. *The Negro and the Communist Party.* 1951.

Record, Wilson. *Race Relations and Radicalism: The NAACP and the Communist Party in Conflict.* 1964.

Rosengarten, Theodore. *All God's Dangers: The Life of Nate Shaw.* 1974.

Sitkoff, Harvard. *A New Deal for Blacks: The Emergence of Civil Rights as a National Issue. The Depression Decade.* 1978.

Solomon, Mark. *The Cry Was Unity: Communists and Afro-Americans, 1917–1936.* 1998.

Sullivan, Patricia. *Days of Hope: Race and Democracy in the New Deal Era.* 1996.

Watts, Jill. *Harlem USA: The Father Divine Story.* 1995.

Weisbrot, Robert. *Father Divine and the Struggle for Racial Equality.* 1983.

Weiss, Nancy J. *Farewell to the Party of Lincoln: Black Politics in the Age of FDR.* 1983.

Wolters, Raymond. *Negroes and the Great Depression: The Problem of Economic Recovery.* 1970.

General Studies of the Civil Rights Movement

Appiah, Kwame Anthony, and Henry Louis Gates, Jr. *Africana: Civil Rights, An A-to-Z Reference of the Movement that Changed America.* 2004.

Bloom, Jack M. *Class, Race, and the Civil Rights Movement.* 1987.

Blumberg, Rhoda Lewis. *Civil Rights.* 1984.

Branch, Taylor. *At Canaan's Edge: America in the King Years, 1965–68.* 2006.

Branch, Taylor. *Parting the Waters: America in the King Years, 1954–63.* 1988.

Branch, Taylor. *Pillar of Fire: America in the King Years, 1963–65.* 1998.

Bullard, Sara. *Free at Last: A History of the Civil Rights Movement and Those Who Died in the Struggle.* 1993.

Carson, Clayborne, ed. *The Eyes on the Prize Civil Rights Reader.* 1991.

Cashman, Sean D. *African-Americans and the Quest for Civil Rights, 1900–1990.* 1991.

Chappell, David L. *Inside Agitators: White Southerners in the Civil Rights Movement.* 1994.

Chappell, David L. *A Stone of Hope: Prophetic Religion and the Death of Jim Crow.* 2004.

Cook, Robert. *Sweet Land of Liberty? The African-American Struggle for Civil Rights in the Twentieth Century.* 1998.

D'Angelo, Raymond. *The Civil Rights Movement: Readings and Interpretations.* 2001.

Davis, Jack E., ed. *The Civil Rights Movement.* 2001.

Dierenfield, Bruce J. *The Civil Rights Movement.* 2008.

Eagles, Charles W., ed. *The Civil Rights Movement in America.* 1986.

Estes, Steve. *I Am a Man!: Race, Manhood, and the Civil Rights Movement.* 2005.

Fairclough, Adam. *Better Day Coming: Blacks and Equality, 1890–2000.* 2001.

Garrow, David J., ed. *We Shall Overcome: The Civil Rights Movement in the United States in the 1950s and 1960s.* 1989.

Hall, Simon. *Peace and Freedom: The Civil Rights and Antiwar Movements in the 1960s.* 2005.

Hampton, Henry. *Voices of Freedom: An Oral History of the Civil Rights Movement from the 1950s through the 1980s.* 1991.

King, Richard. *Civil Rights and the Idea of Freedom.* 1992.

Klarman, Michael J. *From Jim Crow to Civil Rights: The Supreme Court and the Struggle for Racial Equality.* 2004.

Lawson, Steven F., and Charles Payne, eds. *Debating the Civil Rights Movement, 1945–1968.* 1988.

Lomax, Louis E. *The Negro Revolt.* 1962.

Lowery, Charles D., and John F. Marszalek, eds. *The Greenwood Encyclopedia of African American Civil Rights.* 2003.

Marable, Manning. *Race, Reform, and Rebellion: The Second Reconstruction in Black America, 1945–1982.* 1984.

Marsh, Charles. *The Beloved Community: How Faith Shapes Social Justice, from the Civil Rights Movement to Today.* 2005.

Meacham, Jon, ed. *Voices in Our Blood: America's Best on the Civil Rights Movement.* 2001.

Muse, Benjamin. *The American Negro Revolution: From Nonviolence to Black Power, 1963–1967.* 1968.

Nieman, Donald G. *Promises to Keep: African Americans and the Constitutional Order, 1776–Present.* 1991.

Norrell, Robert J. *The House I Live In: Race in the American Century.* 2005.

Ogbar, Jeffrey, O.G., ed. *Problems in American Civilization: The Civil Rights Movement.* 2003.

Ownby, Ted., ed. *The Role of Ideas in the Civil Rights South.* 2002.

Polsgrove, Carol. *Divided Minds: Intellectuals and the Civil Rights Movement.* 2001.

Raines, Howell, ed. *My Soul is Rested: Movement Days in the Deep South Remembered.* 1977.

Robinson, Armstead L., and Patricia Sullivan. *New Directions in Civil Rights Studies.* 1991.

Sitkoff, Harvard. *The Struggle for Black Equality, 1954–1999.* 1993.

Sugrue, Thomas J. *Sweet Land of Liberty: The Forgotten Struggle for Civil Rights in the North.* 2008.

Ward, Brian. *Just My Soul Responding: Rhythm and Blues, Black Consciousness, and Race Relations.* 1998.

Warren, Robert Penn. *Who Speaks for the Negro?* 1965.

Weisbrot, Robert. *Freedom Bound: A History of America's Civil Rights Movement.* 1990.

Wendt, Simon. *The Spirit and the Shotgun: Armed Resistance and the Struggle for Civil Rights.* 2007.

Williams, Juan. *Eyes on the Prize: America's Civil Rights Years, 1954–1965.* 1988.

Books by Martin Luther King, Jr.

King, Martin Luther, Jr. *Strength to Love.* 1963.

King, Martin Luther, Jr. *Stride toward Freedom: The Montgomery Story.* 1958.

King, Martin Luther, Jr. *Trumpet of Conscience.* 1968.

King, Martin Luther, Jr. *Where Do We Go From Here? Chaos or Community?* 1968.

King, Martin Luther, Jr. *Why We Can't Wait?* 1964.

Washington, James M., ed. *I Have a Dream: Writings and Speeches that Changed the World.* 1992.

Primary Sources on Martin Luther King, Jr.

Carson, Clayborne, ed. *The Autobiography of Martin Luther King, Jr.* 1998.

Carson, Clayborne, ed. *A Knock at Midnight: Inspiration from the Great Sermons of Reverend Martin Luther King, Jr.* 1998.

Carson, Clayborne, ed. *A Call to Conscience: The Landmark Speeches of Dr. Martin Luther King, Jr.* 2001.

Carson, Clayborne, ed. *The Papers of Martin Luther King, Jr.* 6 vols. 1992–.

Washington, James M., ed. *A Testament of Hope: The Essential Writings and Speeches of Martin Luther King, Jr.* 1986.

Biographies of Martin Luther King, Jr.

Baldwin, Lewis V. *There is a Balm in Gilead: The Cultural Roots of Martin Luther King, Jr.* 1991.

Bennett, Lerone, Jr. *What Manner of Man: A Biography of Martin Luther King, Jr.* 1964.

Burns, Stewart. *To the Mountaintop: Martin Luther King Jr.'s Sacred Mission to Save America, 1955–1968.* 2004.

Colaiaco, James A. *Martin Luther King Jr.: Apostle of Militant Nonviolence.* 1993.

Fairclough, Adam. *Martin Luther King, Jr.* 1990.

Frady, Marshall. *Martin Luther King, Jr.: A Life.* 2002.

Harding, Vincent. *Martin Luther King, Jr.: The Inconvenient Hero.* 1996.

Jackson, Troy. *Becoming King: Martin Luther King Jr. and the Making of a National Leader.* 2008.

Kirk, John A. *Martin Luther King, Jr.* 2005.

Lewis, David L. *King: A Critical Biography.* 1970.

Lincoln, C. Eric, ed. *Martin Luther King, Jr.: A Profile.* 1970.

Ling, Peter J. *Martin Luther King, Jr.* 2002.

Miller, William R. *Martin Luther King, Jr.* 1969.

Oates, Stephen B. *Let The Trumpet Sound: The Life of Martin Luther King, Jr.* 1982.

Reddick, Lawrence D. *Crusader without Violence: A Biography of Martin Luther King, Jr.* 1964.

Sitkoff, Harvard. *King: Pilgrimage to the Mountaintop.* 2008.

Martin Luther King, Jr.'s Views and Beliefs

Ansbro, John G. *Martin Luther King, Jr.: The Making of a Mind.* 1982.

Baker-Fletcher, Garth. *Somebodyness: Martin Luther King, Jr., and the Theory of Dignity.* 1993.

Baldwin, Lewis V. *There Is a Balm in Gilead: The Cultural Roots of Martin Luther King, Jr.* 1991.

Baldwin, Lewis V. *Toward the Beloved Community: Martin Luther King, Jr., and South Africa.* 1995.

Baldwin, Lewis V. *To Make the Wounded Whole: The Cultural Legacy of Martin Luther King, Jr.* 1992.

Clark, Kenneth B. *The Negro Protest: James Baldwin, Malcolm X, Martin Luther King Talk with Kenneth B. Clark.* 1963.

Cone, James H. *Martin & Malcolm & America: A Dream or Nightmare.* 1991.

Downing, Frederick L. *To See the Promised Land: The Faith Pilgrimage of Martin Luther King, Jr.* 1986.

Edelman, Marian Wright. *Lanterns: A Memoir of Mentors.* 1999.

Erskine, Noel L. *King among the Theologians.* 1994.

Hanigan, James P. *Martin Luther King, Jr., and the Foundations of Militant Nonviolence.* 1984.

Ivory, Luther D. *Toward a Theology of Radical Involvement: The Theological Legacy of Martin Luther King, Jr.* 1997.

Jackson, Thomas F. *From Civil Rights to Human Rights: Martin Luther King, Jr., and the Struggle for Economic Justice.* 2007.

Kapur, Sudarshan. *Raising Up a Prophet: The African-American Encounter with Gandhi.* 1992.

King, Richard. *Civil Rights and the Idea of Freedom.* 1992.

Long, Michael G. *Against Us, But for Us: Martin Luther King, Jr. and the State.* 2002.

Moses, Greg. *Revolution of Conscience: Martin Luther King, Jr., and the Philosophy of Nonviolence.* 1997.

Smith, Kenneth L., and Ira G. Zepp, Jr., *Search for the Beloved Community: The Thinking of Martin Luther King, Jr.* 1974.

Walton, Hanes, Jr. *The Political Philosophy of Martin Luther King, Jr.* 1971.

Watley, William D. *Roots of Resistance: The Nonviolent Ethic of Martin Luther King, Jr.* 1985.

Zepp, Ira G., Jr. *The Social Vision of Martin Luther King, Jr.* 1989.

Martin Luther King, Jr.'s Preaching & Rhetoric

Bass, Patrik Henry. *Like a Mighty Stream: The March on Washington, August 28, 1963.* 2002.

Calloway-Thomas, Carolyn, and John Louis Lucaites, eds. *Martin Luther King, Jr., and the Sermonic Power of Public Discourse.* 1993.

Gentile, Thomas. *March on Washington: August 28, 1963.* 1983.

Hansen, Drew. *The Dream: Martin Luther King, Jr., and the Speech That Inspired a Nation.* 2003.

Lischer, Richard. *The Preacher King: Martin Luther King, Jr., and the Word that Moved America.* 1995.

Rieder, Jonathan. *The Word of the Lord Is Upon Me: The Righteous Performance of Martin Luther King, Jr.* 2008.

Sundquist, Eric. *King's Dream: The Legacy of Martin Luther King's "I Have a Dream" Speech.* 2009.

Martin Luther King, Jr.'s Plagiarism

Dyson, Michael Eric. *I May Not Get There with You: The True Martin Luther King, Jr.* 2000.

Miller, Keith D. *Voice of Deliverance: The Language of Martin Luther King, Jr., and Its Sources.* 1992.

Pappas, Theodore. *Plagiarism and the Culture War: The Writings of Martin Luther King, Jr., and Other Prominent Americans.* 1998.

Martin Luther King, Jr.'s Assassination

Dyson, Michael Eric. *April 4, 1968: Martin Luther King, Jr.'s Death and How It Changed America.* 2008.

Frank, Gerald. *An American Death: The True Story of the Assassination of Martin Luther King, Jr., and the Greatest Manhunt in Our Time.* 1972.

Huie, William B. *He Slew the Dreamer: My Search, with James Earl Ray, for the Truth About the Murder of Martin Luther King, Jr.* 1997.

Lane, Mark, and Dick Gregory. *Murder in Memphis: The FBI and the Assassination of Martin Luther King.* 1993.

Pepper, William F. *Orders to Kill: The Truth Behind the Murder of Martin Luther King, Jr.* 1996.

Posner, Gerald. *Killing the Dream: James Earl Ray and the Assassination of Martin Luther King, Jr.* 1998.

Sides, Hampton. *Hellhound on His Trail: The Stalking of Martin Luther King, Jr. and International Hunt for His Assassin.* 2010.

Witcover, Jules. *The Year the Dream Died: Revisiting 1968 in America.* 1997.

Civil Rights Memoirs

Abernathy, Ralph D. *And the Walls Came Tumbling Down: An Autobiography.* 1989.

Ashmore, Harry S. *Civil Rights and Wrongs: A Memoir of Race and Politics, 1944–1994.* 1994.

Bates, Daisy. *The Long Shadow of Little Rock: A Memoir.* 1962.

Beals, Melba Pattillo. *Warriors Don't Cry: A Searing Memoir of the Battle to Integrate Little Rock's Central High.* 1994.

Blackwell, Unita. *Barefootin': Life Lessons from the Road to Freedom.* 2006.

Boynton, Amelia P. *Bridge across Jordan: The Story of the Civil Rights Struggle in Selma.* 1979.

Campbell, Will. *Brother to a Dragonfly.* 1977.

Carawan, Guy, and Candie Carawan, eds. *Freedom Is a Constant Struggle: Songs of the Freedom Movement with Documentary Photographs.* 1968.

Carmichael, Stokely, with Ekwueme Michael Thelwell. *Ready for Revolution: The Life and Struggles of Stokely Carmichael (Kwame Ture).* 2003.

Chestnut, J.L., and Julia Cass. *Black in Selma: The Uncommon Life of J.L. Chestnut, Jr.* 1990.

Clark, Septima. *Echo in My Soul.* 1962.

Curry, Constance, et al. *Deep in Our Hearts: Nine Women in the Freedom Movement.* 2000.

Davis, Angela. *Angela Davis: An Autobiography.* 1988.

Evers-Williams, Mylie, and Manning Marable. *The Autobiography of Medgar Evers.* 2006.

Farmer, James. *Lay Bare the Heart: An Autobiography of the Civil Rights Movement.* 1985.

Forman, James. *The Making of Black Revolutionaries: A Personal Account.* 1972.

Good, Paul. *The Trouble I've Seen: White Journalist—Black Movement.* 1975.

Graetz, Robert. *A White Preacher's Memoir: The Montgomery Bus Boycott.* 1999.

Gray, Fred D. *Bus Ride to Justice: Changing the System by the System.* 1999.

Greenberg, Jack. *Crusaders in the Court: How a Dedicated Band of Lawyers Fought for the Civil Rights Revolution.* 1994.

Henry, Aaron, with Constance Curry. *Aaron Henry: The Fire Ever Burning.* 2000.

Horton, Myles, with Judith Kohl and Herbert Kohl. *The Long Haul: An Autobiography.* 1991.

King, Christine Farris. *My Brother Martin: A Sister Remembers Growing Up with the Rev. Dr. Martin Luther King, Jr.* 1992.

King, Coretta Scott. *My Life With Martin Luther King, Jr.* 1970.

King, Dexter Scott. *Growing Up King: An Intimate Memoir.* 2003.

King, Martin Luther, Sr., with Clayton Riley, *Daddy King: An Autobiography.* 1980.

King, Mary. *Freedom Song: A Personal Story of the 1960s Civil Rights Movement.* 1987.

LaNier, Carlotta Walls. *A Mighty Long Way: My Journey to Justice at Little Rock Central High.* 2009.

Lewis, John, with Michael D'Orso. *Walking with the Wind: A Memoir of the Movement.* 1998.

May, Benjamin E. *Born to Rebel: An Autobiography*. 1987.

McKinstry, Carolyn Maull, with Denise George. *While the World Watched*. 2011.

McKissick, Floyd. *Three-Fifths of a Man*. 1969.

McWhorter, Diane. *Carry Me Home: Birmingham, Alabama—The Climactic Battle of the Civil Rights Revolution*. 2001.

Meredith, James. *Three Years in Mississippi*. 1966.

Morgan, Charles, Jr. *A Time to Speak*. 1964.

Parks, Rosa, with Jim Haskins. *Rosa Parks: My Story*. 1992.

Peck, James. *Freedom Ride*. 1962.

Powers, Georgia Davis. *I Shared the Dream: The Pride, Passion, and Politics of the First Black Woman Senator from Kentucky*. 1995.

Powledge, Fred. *Free at Last?: The Civil Rights Movement and the People Who Made It*. 1992.

Roberts, Terrence. *Lessons from Little Rock*. 2009.

Robinson, Amelia Platts Boynton. *Bridge across Jordan*. 1991.

Robinson, Jo Ann Gibson. *The Montgomery Bus Boycott and the Women Who Started It: The Memoir of Jo Ann Gibson Robinson*, ed. David Garrow. 1987.

Rowan, Carl. *Breaking Barriers: A Memoir*. 1992.

Seay, Solomon S. *I Was There by the Grace of God*. 1990.

Sellers, Cleveland. *The River of No Return: The Autobiography of a Black Militant and the Life and Death of SNCC*. 1973.

Smiley, Glenn. *Nonviolence: The Gentle Persuader*. 1991.

Walker, Wyatt Tee. *"Somebody's Calling My Name": Black Sacred Music and Social Change*. 1979.

Watters, Pat. *Down to Now: Reflections on the Southern Civil Rights Movement*. 1971.

Webb, Sheyann, and Rachel West Nelson, as told to Frank Sikora. *Selma, Lord, Selma: Girlhood Memories of the Civil Rights Days*. 1980.

White, Walter. *A Man Called White: The Autobiography of Walter White*. 1948.

Wilkins, Roger. *A Man's Life: An Autobiography*. 1982.

Wilkins, Roy, with Tom Matthews. *Standing Fast: The Autobiography of Roy Wilkins.* 1982.

Wofford, Harris. *Of Kennedys and Kings: Making Sense of the Sixties.* 1980.

Young, Andrew. *An Easy Burden: The Civil Rights Movement and the Transformation of America.* 1996.

Biographies of Other Civil Rights Figures

Anderson, Jervis. *A. Philip Randolph: A Biographical Portrait.* 1973.

Anderson, Jervis. *Bayard Rustin: Troubles I've Seen, A Biography.* 1997.

Ball, Howard. *A Defiant Life: Thurgood Marshall and the Persistence of Racism in America.* 2001.

Bass, Jack. *Unlikely Heroes: The Dramatic Story of the Judges of the Fifth Circuit Who Translated the Supreme Court's Decision into a Revolution for Equality.* 1981.

Blake, John. *Children of the Movement.* 2004.

Burner, Eric R. *And Gently Shall He Lead Them: Robert Parris Moses and Civil Rights in Mississippi.* 1994.

Clark, Septima Poinsette. *Ready from Within: Septima Clark and the Civil Rights Movement.* Ed. and with an introduction by Cynthia Stokes Brown. 1986.

Curry, Constance. *Silver Rights.* 1995.

D'Emilio, John. *Lost Prophet: The Life and Times of Bayard Rustin.* 2003.

Dennis, Michael. *Luther P. Jackson and a Life for Civil Rights.* 2004.

Dickerson, Dennis C. *Militant Mediator: Whitney M. Young.* 1998.

Duberman, Martin Bauml. *Paul Robeson: A Biography.* 1989.

Eagles, Charles W. *Outside Agitator: Jon Daniels and the Civil Rights Movement in Alabama.* 2000.

Fleming, Cynthia Griggs. *Soon We Will Not Cry: The Liberation of Ruby Doris Smith Robinson.* 1998.

Foner, Philip S., ed. *Paul Robeson Speaks: Writings, Speeches, and Interviews, 1918–1974.* 1978.

Grant, Joanne. *Ella Baker: Freedom Bound.* 1998.

Haines, Herbert H. *Black Radicals and the Civil Rights Mainstream, 1954–1970.* 1988.

Halberstam, David. *The Children.* 1998.

Hamilton, Charles V. *Adam Clayton Powell, Jr.: The Political Biography of an American Dilemma.* 2002.

Haygood, Will. *King of the Cats: The Life and Times of Adam Clayton Powell, Jr.* 1993.

Howlett, Duncan. *No Greater Love: The James Reeb Story.* 1966.

James, Rawn, Jr. *Root and Branch: Charles Hamilton Houston, Thurgood Marshall, and the Struggle to End Segregation.* 2010.

Levine, Daniel. *Bayard Rustin. Bayard Rustin and the Civil Rights Movement.* 2000.

Lewis, Andrew B. *The Shadows of Youth: The Remarkable Journey of the Civil Rights Generation.* 2009.

Long, Michael G. *Billy Graham and the Beloved Community.* 2006.

Longnecker, Stephen. *Selma's Peacemaker: Ralph Smelzer and Civil Rights Mediation.* 1987.

Manis, Andrew. *A Fire You Can't Put Out: The Civil Rights Life of Reverend Fred Shuttlesworth.* 1999.

May, Gary. *The Informant: The FBI, the Ku Klux Klan, and the Murder of Viola Liuzzo.* 2005.

Pfeffer, Paula F. *A. Philip Randolph, Pioneer of the Civil Rights Movement.* 1990.

Ransby, Barbara. *Ella Baker and the Black Freedom Movement: A Radical Democratic Vision.* 2003.

Stanton, Mary. *From Selma to Sorrow: The Life and Death of Viola Liuzzo.* 1998.

Stanton, Mary. *Journey toward Justice: Juliette Hampton Morgan and the Montgomery Bus Boycott.* 2006.

Tyson, Timothy B. *Radio Free Dixie: Robert F. Williams and the Roots of Black Power.* 1999.

Weiss, Nancy. *Whitney M. Young, Jr. and the Struggle for Civil Rights.* 1989.

Whitfield, Stephen J. *A Death in the Delta: The Story of Emmett Till.* 1988.

Williams, Juan. *Thurgood Marshall: American Revolutionary.* 2000.

The Media in the King Years

Clowse, Barbara B. *Ralph McGill: A Biography.* 1998.

Donovan, Robert J., and Ray Scherer. *Unsilent Revolution: Television News and American Public Life.* 1992.

Fisher, Paul L., and Ralph Lowenstein, eds. *Race and the News Media.* 1967.

Graham, Allison. *Framing the South: Hollywood, Television, and Race during the Civil Rights Struggle.* 2001.

Graham, Hugh Davis. *Crisis in Print: Desegregation and the Press in Tennessee.* 1967.

Lentz, Richard. *Symbols, the News Magazines, and Martin Luther King.* 1990.

Lyon, Danny. *Memories of the Southern Civil Rights Movement.* 1992.

Roberts, Gene, and Hank Klibanoff. *The Race Beat: The Press, the Civil Rights Struggle, and the Awakening of a Nation.* 2007.

Savage, Barbara Dianne. *Broadcasting Freedom: Radio, War, and the Politics of Race, 1938–1948.* 1999.

State & Local Studies

Aickin, Mary. *A Case of Black and White: Northern Volunteers and the Southern Freedom Summers, 1964–1965.* 1982.

Anderson, Alan B., and George W. Pickering, *Confronting the Color Line: The Broken Promise of the Civil Rights Movement in Chicago.* 1986.

Arsenault, Raymond. *Freedom Riders: 1961 and the Struggle for Racial Justice.* 2006.

Barnes, Catherine A. *Journey from Jim Crow: Desegregation of Southern Transit.* 1983.

Bayor, Ronald H. *Race and the Shaping of Twentieth-Century Atlanta.* 1996.

Beifuss, Joan Turner. *At the River I Stand: Memphis, the 1968 Strike, and Martin Luther King.* 1985.

Biondi, Martha. *To Stand and Fight: The Struggle for Civil Rights in Postwar New York City.* 2001.

Brown-Nagin, Tomiko. *Courage to Dissent: Atlanta and the Long History of the Civil Rights Movement.* 2011.

Burns, Stewart, ed. *Daybreak of Freedom: The Montgomery Bus Boycott.* 1997.

Button, James W. *Blacks and Social Change: Impact of the Civil Rights Movement in Southern Communities.* 1989.

Chafe, William H. *Civilities and Civil Rights: Greensboro, North Carolina, and the Black Struggle for Freedom.* 1980.

Colburn, David. *Racial Change and Community Crisis: St. Augustine, Florida, 1877–1980.* 1985.

Countryman, Matthew. *Up South: Civil Rights and Black Power in Philadelphia.* 2006.

Crosby, Emilye. *A Little Taste of Freedom: The Black Struggle in Claiborne County, Mississippi.* 2005.

Culpepper, E. Clark. *The Schoolhouse Door: Segregation's Last Stand at the University of Alabama.* 1993.

Dittmer, John. *Local People: The Struggle for Civil Rights in Mississippi.* 1994.

Dollard, John. *Caste and Class in a Southern Town.* 1937.

Eick, Gretchen Cassel. *Dissent in Wichita: The Civil Rights Movement in the Midwest, 1954–72.* 2001.

Eskew, Glen T. *But for Birmingham: The Local and National Movements in the Civil Rights Struggle.* 1997.

Fager, Charles E. *Selma 1965: The March that Changed the South.* 1974.

Fager, Charles. *Uncertain Resurrection: The Poor People's Washington Campaign.* 1969.

Fairclough, Adam. *Race and Democracy: The Civil Rights Struggle in Louisiana, 1915–1972.* 1995.

Fleming, Cynthia Griggs. *In the Shadow of Selma: The Continuing Struggle for Civil Rights in the Rural South.* 2004.

Gaillard, Frye. *Cradle of Freedom: Alabama and the Movement that Changed America*. 2004.

Garrow, David J., ed. *Birmingham, Alabama, 1956–63: The Black Struggle for Civil Rights*. 1989.

Garrow, David J., ed. *Chicago 1966: Open Housing Marches, Summit Negotiations, and Operation Breadbasket*. 1989.

Garrow, David J. *Protest at Selma: Martin Luther King, Jr., and the Voting Rights Act of 1965*. 1978.

Garrow, David J., ed. *St. Augustine, Florida, 1963–1964: Mass Protest and Racial Violence*. 1989.

Garrow, David J., ed. *The Walking City: The Montgomery Bus Boycott, 1955–1956*. 1989.

Grady-Willis, Winston A. *Challenging U.S. Apartheid: Atlanta and Black Struggles for Human Rights, 1960–1977*. 2006.

Green, Laurie B. *Battling the Plantation Mentality: Memphis and the Black Freedom Struggle*. 2007.

Greene, Christina. *Our Separate Ways: Women and the Black Freedom Movement in Durham, North Carolina*. 2005.

Holt, Len. *The Summer that Didn't End*. 1965.

Honey, Michael K. *Going Down Jericho Road: The Memphis Strike, Martin Luther King's Last Campaign*. 2007.

Jacoway, Elizabeth. *Turn Away Thy Son: Little Rock, the Crisis that Shocked the Nation*. 2007.

Kirk, John A. *Redefining the Color Line: Black Activism in Little Rock, Arkansas, 1940–1970*. 2002.

Korstad, Robert Rodgers. *Civil Rights Unionism: Tobacco Workers and the Struggle for Democracy in the Mid-Twentieth-Century South*. 2003.

Levy, Peter B. *Civil War on Race Street: The Civil Rights Movement in Cambridge, Maryland*. 2003.

Lovett, Bobby L. *The Civil Rights Movement in Tennessee: A Narrative History*. 2005.

McAdam, Doug. *Freedom Summer*. 1988.

McKnight, Gerald D. *The Last Crusade: Martin Luther King, Jr., the FBI, and the Poor People's Campaign*. 1998.

Mills, Nicolaus. *Like a Holy Crusade: Mississippi 1964—The Turning of the Civil Rights Movement in America*. 1992.

Morris, Aldon D. *The Origin of the Civil Rights Movement: Black Communities Organizing for Change*. 1984.

Noble, Phil. *Beyond the Burning Bus: The Civil Rights Revolution in a Southern Town*. 2003.

Norrell, Robert J. *Reaping the Whirlwind: The Civil Rights Movement in Tuskegee*. 1985.

O'Brien, Gail Williams. *The Color of the Law: Race, Violence, and Justice in the Post-World War II South*. 1999.

Payne, Charles. *I've Got the Light of Freedom: The Organizing Tradition and the Mississippi Freedom Struggle*. 1995.

Ralph, James J., Jr. *Northern Protest: Martin Luther King, Jr., Chicago, and the Civil Rights Movement*. 1993.

Rogers, Kim Lacy. *Righteous Lives: Narratives of the New Orleans Civil Rights Movement*. 1993.

Sikora, Frank. *Until Justice Rolls Down: The Birmingham Church Bombing Case*. 2005.

Sugarman, Tracy. *Stranger at the Gates: A Summer in Mississippi*. 1966.

Thornton, J. Mills, III. *Dividing Lines: Municipal Politics and the Struggle for Civil Rights in Montgomery, Birmingham, and Selma*. 2002.

Tuck, Stephen G.N. *Beyond Atlanta: The Struggle for Racial Equality in Georgia, 1940–1980*. 1999.

Watson, Bruce. *Freedom Summer: The Savage Season that Made Mississippi Burn and Made America a Democracy*. 2010.

Woodruff, Nan Elizabeth. *American Congo: The African American Freedom Struggle in the Delta*. 2003.

Zinn, Howard. *The Southern Mystique*. 1964.

Politics & Public Policy in the King Years

Bartley, Numan V., and Hugh D. Graham. *Southern Politics and the Second Reconstruction*. 1975.

Berman, William C. *The Politics of Civil Rights in the Truman Administration*. 1970.

Beschloss, Michael R., ed. *Reaching for Glory: Lyndon Johnson's Secret White House Tapes, 1964–1965*. 2002.

Beschloss, Michael R., ed. *Taking Charge: The Johnson White House Tapes, 1963–1964*. 1997.

Black, Earl. *Southern Governors and Civil Rights: Racial Segregation as a Campaign Issue in the Second Reconstruction*. 1976.

Brauer, Carl M. *John F. Kennedy and the Second Reconstruction*. 1977.

Broussard, Albert S. *Black San Francisco: The Struggle for Racial Equality in the West, 1900–1954*. 1993.

Burk, Robert F. *The Eisenhower Administration and Black Civil Rights*. 1984.

Button, James W. *Blacks and Social Change: Impact of the Civil Rights Movement in Southern Communities*. 1989.

Davidson, Chandler, and Bernard Grofman, eds. *Quiet Revolution in the South: The Impact of the Voting Rights Act, 1965–1990*. 1994.

Dierenfield, Bruce J. *Keeper of the Rules: Congressman Howard W. Smith of Virginia*. 1987.

Frederickson, Kari. *The Dixiecrat Revolt and the End of the Solid South, 1932–1968*. 2001.

Gardner, Michael. *Harry Truman and Civil Rights: Moral Courage and Political Risks*. 2002.

Garfinkel, Herbert. *The March on Washington Movement in the Organizational Politics for FEPC*. 1969.

Graham, Hugh D. *The Civil Rights Era: Origins and Development of National Policy, 1960–1972*. 1990.

Harvey, James C. *Black Civil Rights during the Johnson Administration*. 1973.

Harvey, James C. *Civil Rights during the Kennedy Administration*. 1971.

Karabel, Zachary. *The Last Campaign: How Harry Truman Won the 1948 Election*. 2001.

Kotz, Nick. *Judgment Days: Lyndon Baines Johnson, Martin Luther King, Jr., and the Laws that Changed America*. 2005.

Kousser, J. Morgan. *Colorblind Injustice: Minority Voting Rights and the Undoing of the Second Reconstruction*. 1999.

Lawson, Steven F. *Black Ballots: Voting Rights in the South, 1944–1969*. 1976.

Lawson, Steven F. *In Pursuit of Power: Southern Blacks and Electoral Politics, 1965–1982*. 1985.

Lawson, Steven F. *Running for Freedom: Civil Rights and Black Politics in America since 1941*. 1997.

Loevy, Robert D. *The Civil Rights Act of 1964: The Passage of a Law that Ended Racial Segregation*. 1997.

Loevy, Robert D. *To End All Segregation: The Politics of the Passage of the Civil Rights Act of 1964*. 1990.

Mann, Robert. *When Freedom Would Triumph: The Civil Rights Struggle in Congress, 1954–1968*. 2007.

Marable, Manning. *Black American Politics from the Washington Marches to Jesse Jackson*. 1985.

McAdam, Doug. *Political Process and the Development of Black Insurgency, 1930–1970*. 1982.

McCoy, Donald R., and Richard T. Ruetten. *Quest and Response: Minority Rights and the Truman Administration*. 1973.

McCullough, David. *Truman*. 1992.

Nichols, David A. *A Matter of Justice: Eisenhower and the Beginnings of the Civil Rights Revolution*. 2007.

O'Reilly, Kenneth. *Nixon's Piano: Presidents and Racial Politics from Washington to Clinton*. 1995.

Rosenberg, Jonathan, and Zachary Karabell. *Kennedy, Johnson, and the Quest for Justice: The Civil Rights Tapes*. 2003.

Schlesinger, Arthur M., Jr. *Robert Kennedy and His Times*. 1978.

Schlesinger, Arthur M., Jr. *A Thousand Days: John F. Kennedy in the White House*. 1965.

Stern, Mark. *Calculating Visions: Kennedy, Johnson, and Civil Rights*. 1992.

Thurber, Timothy. *The Politics of Equality: Hubert H. Humphrey and the African American Freedom Struggle*. 1999.

Watson, Denton. *Lion in the Lobby: Clarence Mitchell, Jr.'s Struggle for the Passage of Civil Rights Laws*. 1990.

Watters, Pat, and Reese Cleghorn. *Climbing Jacob's Ladder: The Arrival of Negroes in Southern Politics.* 1967.

Whalen, Charles W., and Barbara Whalen. *The Longest Debate: A Legislative History of the 1964 Civil Rights Act.* 1985.

Wolk, Allan. *The Presidency and Black Civil Rights: Eisenhower to Nixon.* 1971.

Civil Rights Groups & Organizations

Adams, Frank, and Myles Horton. *Unearthing Seeds of Fire: The Idea of Highlander.* 1975.

Bell, Inge Powell. *CORE and the Strategy of Nonviolence.* 1968.

Carson, Clayborne. *In Struggle: SNCC and the Black Awakening of the 1960's.* 1981.

Fairclough, Adam. *To Redeem the Soul of America: The Southern Christian Leadership Conference and Martin Luther King, Jr.* 1987.

Findlay, James F. *Church People in the Struggle: The National Council of Churches and the Black Freedom Movement, 1950–1970.* 1993.

Garrow, David J. *Bearing the Cross: Martin Luther King, Jr., and the Southern Christian Leadership Conference.* 1986.

Glen, John M. *Highlander: No Ordinary School.* 1996.

Greenberg, Cheryl, ed. *A Circle of Trust: Remembering SNCC.* 1998.

Hill, Lance. *The Deacons for Defense: Armed Resistance and the Civil Rights Movement.* 2004.

Hogan, Wesley. *Many Minds, One Heart: SNCC's Dream for a New America.* 2007.

Hughes, Langston. *Fight For Freedom: The Story of the NAACP.* 1962.

Jacoway, Elizabeth, and David Colburn, eds. *Southern Businessmen and Desegregation.* 1982.

Kellogg, Charles F. *NAACP: A History of the National Association for the Advancement of Colored People.* 1967.

Klarman, Michael J. *From Jim Crow to Civil Rights: The Supreme Court and the Struggle for Racial Equality.* 2004.

Kluger, Richard. *Simple Justice: The History of Brown v. Board of Education and Black America's Struggle for Equality.* 1975.

Kreuger, Thomas A. *And Promises to Keep: The Southern Conference for Human Welfare, 1938–1948*. 1967.

Meier, August, and Elliot Rudwick. *CORE: A Study in the Civil Rights Movement*. 1973.

Newman, Mark. *Getting Right with God: Southern Baptists and Desegregation, 1945–1995*. 2001.

Patterson, James T. *Brown v. Board of Education: A Civil Rights Milestone and Its Troubled Legacy*. 2001.

Salmond, John A. *Southern Struggles: The Southern Labor Movement and the Civil Rights Struggle*. 2004.

Skocpol, Theda, et al. *What a Mighty Power We Can Be: African American Fraternal Groups and the Struggle for Racial Equality*. 2006.

Sutherland, Elizabeth, ed. *Letters from Mississippi*. 1965.

Tushnet, Mark V. *The NAACP's Legal Strategy Against Segregated Education, 1925–1950*. 1987.

Vose, Clement E. *Caucasians Only: The Supreme Court, the NAACP, and the Restrictive Covenant Cases*. 1959.

Weiss, Nancy J. *The National Urban League: 1910–1940*. 1974.

Zangrando, Robert L. *The NAACP's Crusade Against Lynching, 1909–1950*. 1980.

Zinn, Howard. *SNCC: The New Abolitionists*. 1965.

Cold War and Civil Rights

Anderson, Carol. *Eyes Off the Prize: The United Nations and the African American Struggle for Human Rights, 1944–1955*. 2003.

Borstelmann, Thomas. *The Cold War and the Color Line: American Race Relations in the Global Arena*. 2001.

Dudziak, Mary. *Cold War, Civil Rights: Race and Image of American Democracy*. 2000.

Layton, Azza Salama. *International Politics and the Civil Rights Policies in the United States, 1941–1960*. 2000.

Von Eschen, Penny M. *Race against Empire: Black Americans and Anticolonialism, 1937–1957*. 1997.

Opposition to the Civil Rights Movement

Bartley, Numan V. *The Rise of Massive Resistance: Race and Politics in the South during the 1950s.* 1969.

Bass, Jonathan S. *Blessed Are the Peacemakers: Martin Luther King, Jr., Eight White Religious Leaders, and the "Letter from Birmingham City Jail."* 2001.

Belknap, Michal R. *Federal Law and Southern Order: Racial Violence and Constitutional Conflict in the Post-Brown South.* 1987.

Blackstock, Nelson. *COINTELPRO: The FBI's Secret War on Political Freedom.* 1975.

Carter, Dan T. *The Politics of Rage: George C. Wallace, the Origins of the New Conservatism, and the Transformation of American Politics.* 2000.

Chalmers, David. *Backfire: How the Ku Klux Klan Helped the Civil Rights Movement.* 2003.

Chalmers, David. *Hooded Americanism: The History of the Ku Klux Klan.* 1987.

Cohodas, Nadine. *Strom Thurmond and the Politics of Southern Change.* 1993.

Dickerson, James. *Dixie's Dirty Secret: The True Story of How the Government, the Media, and the Mob Conspired to Combat Integration and the Vietnam Antiwar Movement.* 1998.

Frady, Marshall. *Wallace.* 1968.

Friedly, Michael, and David Gallen. *Martin Luther King, Jr.: The FBI File.* 1993.

Garrow, David J. *The FBI and Martin Luther King, Jr.: From "Solo" to Memphis.* 1981.

Lewis, George. *Massive Resistance: The White Response to the Civil Rights Movement.* 2006.

McMillen, Neil R. *The Citizens' Council: Organized Resistance to the Second Reconstruction, 1954–1964.* 1971.

Nelson, Jack. *Terror in the Night: The Klan's Campaign against the Jews.* 1993.

Newton, Michael. *The Ku Klux Klan in Mississippi: A History.* 2010.

Nunnelley, William. *Bull Connor*. 1991.

O'Brien. Gail Williams. *The Color of the Law: Race, Violence, and Justice in the Post-World War II South*. 1999.

O'Reilly, Kenneth. *"Racial Matters": The FBI's Secret File on Black America, 1960–1972*. 1989.

Theoharis, Athan. *Spying on Americans: Political Surveillance from Hoover to the Huston Plan*. 1978.

Wade, Wyn Craig. *The Fiery Cross: The Ku Klux Klan in America*. 1987.

Webb, Clive, ed. *Massive Resistance: Southern Opposition to the Second Reconstruction*. 2005.

Webb, Clive. *Rabble Rousers: The American Far Right in the Civil Rights Era*. 2010.

Woods, Jeff. *Black Struggle, Red Struggle: Segregation and Anti-Communism in the South, 1948–1968*. 2004.

Black Power

Brown, H. Rap. *Die Nigger Die!* 1969.

Bush, Rod. *We Are Not What We Seem: Black Nationalism and Class Struggle in the American Century*. 1999.

Carmichael, Stokely, and Charles V. Hamilton, *Black Power: The Politics of Liberation in America*. 1967.

Fanon, Frantz. *The Wretched of the Earth*. 1968.

Joseph, Peniel. *Waiting 'Til the Midnight Hour: A Narrative History of Black Power in America*. 2007.

Lester, Julius. *Look Out, Whitey! Black Power's Gon' Get Your Mama!* 1968.

Ogbar, Jeffrey O.G. *Black Power: Radical Politics and African American Identity*. 2004.

Pearson, Hugh. *The Shadow of the Panther: Huey Newton and the Price of Black Power in America*. 1994.

Van Deburg, William L., ed. *Modern Black Nationalism: From Marcus Garvey to Louis Farrakhan*. 1996.

Van Deburg, William L. *New Day in Babylon: The Black Power Movement and American Culture, 1965–1975.* 1992.

Williams, Robert F. *Negroes with Guns.* 1962.

Urban Riots

Bloom, Jack M. *Class, Race, and the Civil Rights Movement.* 1987.

Conot, Robert E. *Rivers of Blood, Years of Darkness: The Unforgettable Classic Account of the Watts Riot.* 1967.

Feagin, Joe R., and Harlan Hahn. *Ghetto Revolts: The Politics of Violence in American Cities.* 1973.

Fine, Sidney. *Violence in the Model City: The Cavanaugh Administration, Race Relations and the Detroit Riot of 1967.* 1989.

Fogelson, Robert M. *Violence as Protest: A Study of Riots and Ghettoes.* 1971.

Franklin, Raymond S. *Shadows of Race and Class.* 1991.

Hayden, Tom. *Rebellion in Newark: Official Violence and the Ghetto Response.* 1967.

Horne, Gerald. *Fire This Time: The Watts Uprising and the Meaning of the 1960s.* 1995.

Kerner Commission. *Report of the National Advisory Commission on Civil Disorders.* 1968.

Viorst, Milton. *Fire in the Streets: America in the 1960s.* 1979.

White Backlash

Appleborne, Peter. *Dixie Rising: How the South Is Shaping American Values, Politics, and Culture.* 1996.

Brennan, Mary C. *Turning Right in the Sixties: The Conservative Capture of the GOP.* 1995.

Carter, Dan T. *From George Wallace to Newt Gingrich: Race in the Conservative Counterrevolution, 1963–1994.* 1996.

Durr, Kenneth D. *Behind the Backlash: White Working-Class Politics in Baltimore, 1940–1980.* 2003.

Edsall, Thomas Byrne, with Mary D. Edsall. *Chain Reaction: The Impact of Race, Rights, and Taxes on American Politics.* 1991.

Feldman, Glenn. *Before Brown: Civil Rights and White Backlash in the Modern South.* 2004.

Formisano, Ronald. *Boston against Busing: Race, Class, and Ethnicity in the 1960s and 1970s.* 1991.

Hardisty, Jean. *Mobilizing Resentment: Conservative Resurgence from the John Birch Society to the Promise Keepers.* 1999.

Kruse, Kevin. *White Flight: America and the Making of Modern Conservatism.* 2005.

Lassiter, Matthew. *The Silent Majority: Suburban Politics in the Sunbelt South.* 2005.

Lukas, J. Anthony. *Common Ground: A Turbulent Decade in the Lives of Three Boston Families.* 1985.

Wicker, Tom. *Tragic Failure: Racial Integration in America.* 1996.

Malcolm X

Ali, Drew N. *The Holy Koran of the Moorish Holy Temple of Science.* 1914.

Barboza, Steven. *American Jihad: Islam after Malcolm X.* 1993.

Blair, Thomas L. *Retreat to the Ghetto: The End of a Dream?* 1977.

Bracey, John H., et al., eds. *Black Nationalism in America.* 1970.

Breitman, George. *The Last Year of Malcolm X: The Evolution of a Revolutionary.* 1967.

Breitman, George, et al., *The Assassination of Malcolm X.* 1968.

Breitman, George. *Malcolm X: By Any Means Necessary.* 1970.

Breitman, George, ed. *By Any Means Necessary: Speeches, Interviews, and a Letter By Malcolm X.* 1970.

Breitman, George, ed. *Malcolm X Speaks: Selected Speeches and Statements.* 1990.

Carmichael, Stokely, and Charles V. Hamilton. *Black Power: The Politics of Liberation in America.* 1969.

Carson, Clayborne. *Malcolm X: The FBI File.* 1991.

Clarke, John Henrik, ed., *Malcolm X: The Man and His Times.* 1969.

Clegg, Claude A. III. *An Original Man: The Life and Times of Elijah Muhammad.* 1997.

Collins, Rodnell, P., with A. Peter Bailey. *Seventh Child: A Family Memoir of Malcolm X*. 1998.

Cone, James H. *Malcolm and Martin and America: A Dream or a Nightmare*. 1991.

DeCaro, Louis A., Jr. *On the Side of My People: A Religious Life of Malcolm X*. 1996.

Draper, Theodore. *The Rediscovery of Black Nationalism*. 1970.

Dyson, Michael Eric. *Making Malcolm: The Myth & Meaning of Malcolm X*. 1995.

Epps, Archie, ed. *The Speeches of Malcolm X at Harvard*. 1969.

Essien-Udom, E.U. *Black Nationalism: A Search for Identity in America*. 1962.

Essien-Udom, E.U. *Black Nationalism: The Rise of the Black Muslims in the USA*. 1966.

Evanzz, Karl. *The Judas Factor: The Plot to Kill Malcolm X*. 1992.

Evanzz, Karl. *The Messenger: The Rise and Fall of Elijah Muhammad*. 1999.

Friedly, Michael. *Malcolm X: The Assassination*. 1992.

Gallen, David, ed. *Malcolm X: As They Knew Him*. 1992.

Goldman, Peter. *The Death and Life of Malcolm X*. 1974.

Joseph, Peniel E. *Waiting 'Til the Midnight Hour: A Narrative History of Black Power in America*. 1986.

Lee, Martha F. *The Nation of Islam: An American Millenarian Movement*. 1988.

Lester, Julius. *Look Out Whitey! Black Power's Gon' Get Your Mama!* 1968.

Lincoln, C. Eric *The Black Muslims in America*. 1973.

Lomax, Louis E. *When the Word is Given: A Report on Elijah Muhammad and the Black Muslim World*. 1964.

Malcolm X. *The Autobiography of Malcolm X, as told to Alex Haley*. 1965.

Marable, Manning. *Malcolm X: A Life of Reinvention*. 2011.

Marsh, Clifton E. *From Black Muslims to Muslims: The Transition from Separatism to Islam, 1930–1980*. 1984.

Marsh, Clifton E. *The Lost-Found Nation of Islam in America*. 1996.

Muhammad, Elijah. *Message to the Blackman in America*. 1965.

Muhammad, Elijah. *The Supreme Wisdom: Solution to the So-Called Negro's Problem*. 1957.

Perry, Bruce. *Malcolm X: The Last Speeches*. 1989.

Perry, Bruce. *Malcolm: The Life of a Man Who Changed Black America*. 1991.

Pinkney, Alphonso. *Red, Black, and Green: Black Nationalism in the United States*. 1978.

Rashad, Adib. *The History of Islam and Black Nationalism in the Americas*. 1976.

Sales, William M., Jr. *From Civil Rights to Black Liberation: Malcolm X and the Organization of Afro-American Unity*. 1994.

Stone, I.F. *In a Time of Torment, 1961–1967*. 1967.

Strickland, William. *Malcolm X: Make It Plain*. 1994.

Wolfenstein, Eugene Victor. *The Victims of Democracy: Malcolm X and the Black Revolution*. 1981.

Wood, Joe. *Malcolm X: In Our Image*. 1992.

Black women leaders

General Studies

Alexander, Amy. *Fifty Black Women Who Changed America*. 1999.

Felder, Deborah G. *The 100 Most Influential Women of All Time: A Ranking of Past and Present*. 2001.

Giddings, Paula J. *When and Where I Enter: The Impact of Black Women in Race and Sex in America*. 1996.

Hine, Darlene Clark, ed. *Black Women in American History: From Colonial Times through the Present*. 4 vols. 1990.

Hine, Darlene Clark. *A Shining Thread of Hope: The History of Black Women in America*. 1998.

Hine, Darlene Clark, ed. *Black Women in America*. 2005.

Jones, Jacqueline. *Labor of Love, Labor of Sorrow: Black Women, Work, and the Family from Slavery to the Present*. 1986.

Lerner, Gerda, ed. *Black Women in White America: A Documentary History*. 1992.

Loewenberg, Bert James, and Ruth Bogin, eds. *Black Women in Nineteenth-Century American Life*. 1976.

Lyman, Darryl. *Great African-American Women*. 1999.

Noble, Jeanne. *Beautiful, Also, Are the Souls of My Black Sisters: A History of the Black Woman in America*. 1978.

Salem, Dorothy C. *African American Women: A Biographical Dictionary*. 1993.

Smith, Jessie Carney. *Black Heroes*. 2001.

Smith, Jessie Carney, ed. *Notable Black American Women*. 3 vols. 1992–2003.

Sterling, Dorothy. *We Are Your Sisters: Black Women in the Nineteenth Century*. 1984.

Tate, Gayle T. *Unknown Tongues: Black Women's Political Activism in the Antebellum Era, 1830–1860*. 2003.

White, Deborah Gray. *Too Heavy a Load: Black Women in Defense of Themselves, 1894–1994*. 1999.

Harriet Tubman

Blockson, Charles L. *The Underground Railroad: First Person Narratives of Escapes to Freedom in the North*. 1987.

Bordewich, Fergus. *Bound for Canaan: The Epic Story of the Underground Railroad, America's First Civil Rights Movement*. 2006.

Bradford, Sarah Hopkins. *Harriet, the Moses of Her People*. 1886.

Bradford, Sarah Hopkins. *Scenes in the Life of Harriet Tubman*. 1869.

Clinton, Catherine. *Divided Houses: Gender and the Civil War*. 1992.

Clinton, Catherine. *Harriet Tubman: The Road to Freedom*. 2004.

Conrad, Earl. *Harriet Tubman*. 1943.

Frost, Karolyn Smardz. *I've Got a Home in Glory Land: A Lost Tale of the Underground Railroad*. 2007.

Humez, Jean. *Harriet Tubman: The Life and Life Stories*. 2003.

Larson, Kate Clifford. *Bound for the Promised Land: Harriet Tubman, Portrait of an American Hero.* 2004.

Lowry, Beverly. *Harriet Tubman: Imagining a Life.* 2007.

Petry, Ann. *Harriet Tubman: Conductor of the Underground Railroad.* 1955.

Still, William. *Still's Underground Rail Road Records, Revised Edition, With a Life of the Author. Narrating the Hardships, Hairbreadth Escapes and Death Struggles of the Slaves in their Effort for Freedom.* 1883.

Taylor, Robert W. *Harriet Tubman: The Heroine in Ebony.* 1901.

Walls, William J. *The African Methodist Zion Church.* 1974.

Ida B. Wells

Bay, Mia. *To Tell the Truth Freely: The Life of Ida B. Wells.* 2007.

Davidson, James West. *"They Say": Ida B. Wells and the Reconstruction of Race.* 2007.

Giddings, Paula J. *Ida: A Sword Among Lions: Ida B. Wells and the Campaign Against Lynching.* 2009.

McMillen, Neil R. *Dark Journey: Black Mississippians in the Age of Jim Crow.* 1989.

McMurry, Linda O. *To Keep the Waters Troubled: The Life of Ida B. Wells.* 2000.

Royster, Jacqueline Jones, ed. *Southern Horrors and Other Writings: The Anti-Lynching Campaign of Ida B. Wells, 1892–1900.* 1997.

Schechter, Patricia A. *Ida B. Wells-Barnett & American Reform, 1880–1930.* 2001.

Wells-Barnett, Ida B. *Crusade for Justice: The Autobiography of Ida B. Wells.* Ed. by Alfreda M. Duster. 1970.

Wells-Barnett, Ida B. *The Reason Why the Colored American Is Not in the World's Columbian Exposition.* 1893.

Wells-Barnett, Ida B. *A Red Record: Tabulated Statistics and Alleged Causes of Lynchings in the United States, 1892–1893–1894.* 1895.

Wells-Barnett, Ida B. *Southern Horrors: Lynch Law in All Its Phases.* 1892.

Mary McLeod Bethune

Alexander, Florence. *Mary McLeod Bethune: Her Own Words of Inspiration*. 2003.

Collier-Thomas, Bettye. *N.C.N.W., 1935–1980*. 1981.

Fitzgerald, Tracey A. *The National Council of Negro Women and the Feminist Movement, 1935–1975*. 1985.

Flemming, Sheila. *Bethune-Cookman College, 1904–1994*. 1995.

Hanson, Joyce A. *Mary McLeod Bethune and Black Women's Political Activism*. 2003.

Hicks, Florence Johnson, ed. *Mary McLeod Bethune: Her Own Words of Inspiration*. 1975.

Holt, Rackham. *Mary McLeod Bethune: A Biography*. 1964.

Logan, Rayford, ed., *What the Negro Wants*. 1944.

McCluskey, Audrey Thomas, and Elaine M. Smith, eds., *Mary McLeod Bethune: Building a Better World, Essays and Selected Documents*. 1999.

Neverdon-Morton, Cynthia. *Afro-American Women of the South and the Advancement of the Race, 1895–1925*. 1989.

Peare, Catherine Owen. *Mary McLeod Bethune*. 1951.

Salem, Dorothy, *To Better Our World: Black Women in Organized Reform, 1890–1920*. 1990.

Sterne, Emma Gelders. *Mary McLeod Bethune*. 1957.

Weiss, Nancy J. *Farewell to the Party of Lincoln: Black Politics in the Age of FDR*. 1983.

Fannie Lou Hamer

Asch, Chris Myers. *The Senator and the Sharecropper: The Freedom Struggles of James O. Eastland and Fannie Lou Hamer*. 2008.

Hamer, Fannie Lou. *To Praise Our Bridges: An Autobiography*. 1967.

Lee, Chana Kai. *For Freedom's Sake: The Life of Fannie Lou Hamer*. 1999.

Marsh, Charles. *God's Long Summer: Stories of Faith and Civil Rights*. 1997.

Mills, Kay. *This Little Light of Mine: The Life of Fannie Lou Hamer*. 1993.

Payne, Charles M. *I've Got the Light of Freedom: The Organizing Tradition and the Mississippi Freedom Struggle*. 1995.

Watson, Bruce. *Freedom Summer: The Savage Season that Made Mississippi Burn and Made America a Democracy*. 2010.

Civil Rights Women

Brown, Cynthia Stokes, ed., *Ready from Within: Septima Clark and the Civil Rights Movement*. 1986.

Charron, Katherine Mellon. *Freedom's Teacher: The Life of Septima Clark*. 2009.

Chisholm, Shirley. *The Good Fight*. 1973.

Chisholm, Shirley. *Unbought and Unbossed*. 1970.

Clark, Septima Poinsette, with LeGette Blythe. *Echo in My Soul*. 1962.

Collier-Thomas, Bettye, and V. P. Franklin, eds. *Sisters in the Struggle: African American Women in the Civil Rights—Black Power Movement*. 2001.

Crawford, Vicki, et al., eds., *Women in the Civil Rights Movement: Trailblazers and Torchbearers, 1941–1965*. 1990.

Evers, Myrlie, with William Peters. *For Us, the Living*. 1967.

Fleming, Cynthia Griggs. *Soon We Will Not Cry: The Liberation of Ruby Doris Smith Robinson*. 1998.

Garrow, David J., ed. *The Montgomery Bus Boycott and the Women Who Started It: The Memoir of Jo Ann Gibson Robinson*. 1987.

Grant, Joanne. *Ella Baker: Freedom Bound*. 1998.

Height, Dorothy. *Open Wide the Gates: A Memoir*. 2003.

Holsaert, Faith S., et al. *Hands on the Freedom Plow: Personal Accounts by Women in SNCC*. 2010.

Hudson, Winson. *Mississippi Harmony: Memoirs of a Freedom Fighter*. 2004.

Jones, Beverly Washington. *Quest for Equality: The Life and Writings of Mary Eliza Church Terrell, 1863–1954*. 1990.

Jordan, Barbara, with James Haskins. *Barbara Jordan*. 1977.

Lanker, Brian. *I Dream a World: Portraits of Black Women Who Changed America*. 1989.

Ling, Peter J., and Sharon Monteith, eds. *Gender and the Civil Rights Movement*. 1999.

Martin, Waldo E., and Patricia Sullivan, *Civil Rights in the United States*, 2 vols. 2000.

McGuire, Danielle S. *At the Dark End of the Street: Black Women, Rape, and Resistance—A New History of the Civil Rights Movement from Rosa Parks to the Rise of Black Power*. 2010.

Moody, Anne. *Coming of Age in Mississippi*. 1968.

Olson, Lynne. *Freedom's Daughters: The Unsung Heroines of the Civil Rights Movement from 1830 to 1979*. 2001.

Ransby, Barbara. *Ella Baker and the Black Freedom Movement: A Radical Democratic Vision*. 2003.

Robnett, Belinda. *How Long? How Long? African-American Women in the Struggle for Civil Rights*. 1997.

Rogers, Mary Beth. *Barbara Jordan: American Hero*. 2000.

Rose, Phyllis. *Jazz Cleopatra: Josephine Baker in Her Time*. 1988.

Ross, Rosetta E. *Witnessing & Testifying: Black Women, Religion, and Civil Rights*. 2003.

Stockley, Grif. *Daisy Bates: Civil Rights Crusader from Arkansas*. 2005.

Terborg-Penn, Rosalyn. *African American Women in the Struggle for the Vote, 1850–1920*. 1998.

Terrell, Mary Church. *Confessions of a Colored Woman in a White World*. 1940.

Webb, Sheyann, and Rachel West Nelson, *Selma Lord, Selma: Childhood Memories of the Civil-Rights Days as told to Frank Sikora*. 1980.

White, Deborah Gray. *Too Heavy a Load: Black Women in Defense of Themselves, 1894–1995*. 1999.

Condoleezza Rice

Brown, Mary Beth. *Condi: The Life of a Steel Magnolia*. 2009.

Bumiller, Elisabeth. *Condoleezza Rice: An American Life, A Biography*. 2007.

Bush, George W. *Decision Points.* 2010.

Cheney, Dick. *In My Time: A Personal and Political Memoir.* 2011.

Dallin, Alexander, and Condoleezza Rice. *The Gorbachev Era.* 1986.

Felix, Antonia. *Condi: The Condoleezza Rice Story.* 2002.

Flanders, Laura. *Bushwomen: Tales of a Cynical Species.* 2004.

Kessler, Glenn. *The Confidante: Condoleezza Rice and the Creation of the Bush Legacy.* 2007.

Mabry, Marcus. *Twice as Good: Condoleezza Rice and Her Path to Power.* 2007.

Mann, James. *Rise of the Vulcans: The History of Bush's War Cabinet.* 2004.

Montgomery, Leslie. *The Faith of Condoleezza Rice.* 2007.

Rice, Condoleezza. *Extraordinary, Ordinary People: A Memoir of Family.* 2010.

Rice, Condoleezza. *Uncertain Allegiance: The Soviet Union and the Czechoslovak Army, 1948–1983.* 1984.

Rice, Condoleezza, with Philip Zelikow, *Germany Unified and Europe Transformed: A Study in Statecraft.* 1995.

Rice, Condoleezza, with Alexander Dallin, *The Gorbachev Era.* 1986.

Rice, Condoleezza. *No Higher Honor: A Memoir of My Years in Washington.* 2011.

Woodward, Bob. *State of Denial: Bush at War.* 2006.

Zelikow, Philip, and Condoleezza Rice. *Germany Unified and Europe Transformed: A Study in Statecraft.* 2002.

Oprah Winfrey

Abt, Vicki, and Leonard Mustazza, *Coming after Oprah: Cultural Fallout in the Age of the TV Talk Show.* 1997.

Brands, H.W. *Masters of Enterprise: Giants of American Business from John Jacob Astor and J.P. Morgan to Bill Gates and Oprah Winfrey.* 1999.

Cotten, Trystan T., and Kimberly Springer, eds. *Stories of Oprah: The Oprahfication of American Culture.* 2010.

Decker, Jeffrey Louis. *Made in America: Self-Styled Success from Horatio Alger to Oprah Winfrey.* 1997.

Farr, Cecilia Konchar. *Reading Oprah: How Oprah's Book Club Changed the Way America Reads.* 2005.

Gamson, Joshua. *Freaks Talk Back: Tabloid Talk Shows and Sexual Nonconformity.* 1999.

Garson, Helen S. *Oprah Winfrey: A Biography.* 2004.

Harris, Jennifer, and Elwood Watson , eds. *The Oprah Phenomenon.* 2007.

Illouz, Eva. *Oprah Winfrey and the Glamor of Misery: An Essay on Popular Culture.* 2003.

Kelley, Kitty. *Oprah: A Biography.* 2010.

King, Norman. *Everybody Loves Oprah! Her Remarkable Life Story.* 1988.

Lawrence, Ken. *The World According to Oprah: An Unauthorized Portrait in Her Own Words.* 2005.

Lowe, Janet. *Oprah Winfrey Speaks: Insights from the World's Most Influential Voice.* 2001.

Nelson, Marcia. *The Gospel According to Oprah.* 2005.

Peck, Janice. *The Age of Oprah: Cultural Icon for the Neoliberal Era.* 2008.

Rooney, Kathleen. *Reading with Oprah: The Book Club that Changed America.* 2005.

Timberg, Bernard M. *Television Talk: A History of the TV Talk Show.* 2002.

Winfrey, Oprah. *Live Your Best Life.* 2005.

Jesse Jackson

Barker, Lucius J., and Ronald W. Walters, eds. *Jesse Jackson's 1984 Presidential Campaign: Challenge and Change in American Politics.* 1989.

Bruns, Roger. *Jesse Jackson: A Biography.* 2005.

Collins, Sheila D. *From Melting Pot to Rainbow Coalition: The Future of Race in American Politics.* 1986.

Collins, Sheila D. *The Rainbow Challenge: The Jackson Campaign and the Future of U.S. Politics.* 1986.

Colton, Elizabeth O. *The Jackson Phenomenon: The Man, the Power, the Message.* 1989.

Farrakhan, Louis. *A Torchlight for America.* 1993.

Faw, Bob, and Nancy Skelton. *Thunder in America: The Improbable Presidential Campaign of Jesse Jackson.* 1986.

Frady, Marshall. *Jesse: The Life and Pilgrimage of Jesse Jackson.* 1996.

Gardell, Mattias. *In the Name of Elijah Muhammad: Louis Farrakhan and the Nation of Islam.* 1996.

Glasrud, Bruce, and Cary Wintz, eds. *African Americans and the Presidency: The Road to the White House.* 2010.

Haskins, James. *I Am Somebody! A Biography of Jesse Jackson.* 1992.

Hertzke, Allen D. *Echoes of Discontent: Jesse Jackson, Pat Robertson, and the Resurgence of Populism.* 1993.

House, Ernest R. *Jesse Jackson & the Politics of Charisma: The Rise and Fall of the PUSH/Excel Program.* 1988.

Jackson, Jesse L. *It's About the Money!: How You Can Get Out of Debt, Build Wealth, and Achieve Your Financial Dreams!* 1999.

Jackson, Jesse L. *Legal Lynching: Racism, Injustice, and the Death Penalty.* 1996.

Jackson, Jesse L. *Straight from the Heart.* 1987.

Landess, Thomas H., and Richard M. Quinn, *Jesse Jackson and the Politics of Race.* 1985.

Magida, Arthur J. *Prophet of Rage: A Life of Louis Farrakhan and His Nation.* 1996.

Marable, Manning. *Black American Politics: From Washington Marches to Jesse Jackson.* 1985.

Pinkney, Alphonso. *The Myth of Black Progress.* 1984.

Reed, Adolph L., Jr. *The Jesse Jackson Phenomenon: The Crisis of Purpose in Afro-American Politics.* 1986.

Reynolds, Barbara A. *Jesse Jackson: America's David.* 1985.

Stanford, Karin. *Beyond the Boundaries: Reverend Jesse Jackson in International Affairs.* 1997.

Stone, Eddie. *Jesse Jackson: A Biography*. 1988.

Timmerman, Ken. *Shakedown: Exposing the Real Jesse Jackson*. 2002.

Wills, Garry. *Under God: Religion and American Politics*. 1990.

Wilson, William Julius. *The Declining Significance of Race: Blacks and Changing American Institutions*. 1980.

Barack Obama

Race Rivals

Cottman, Michael H. *Million Man March*. 1995.

DeYoung, Karen. *Soldier: The Life of Colin Powell*. 2006.

Formicola, Jo Renee, and Hubert Morken, eds. *Religious Leaders and Faith-Based Politics: Ten Profiles*. 2001.

Harari, Oren. *The Leadership Secrets of Colin Powell*. 2003.

Levinsohn, Florence Hamlish. *Looking for Farrakhan*. 1997.

Madhubuti, Haki R., and Maulana Karenga, eds. *Million Man March/ Day of Absence: A Commemorative Anthology*. 1996.

Powell, Colin, with Joseph Persico, *My American Journey*. 1995.

Sharpton, Al, with Karen Hunger. *Al on America*. 2002.

Sharpton, Al, and Anthony Walton. *Go and Tell Pharaoh: The Autobiography of the Reverend Al Sharpton*. 1996.

Taylor, Clarence. *Black Religious Intellectuals: The Fight for Equality from Jim Crow to the 21st Century*. 2002.

Wright, Jeremiah A., Jr., and Colleen Birchett. *When Black Men Stand Up for God: Reflections on the Million Man March*. 1997.

Barack Obama

Alter, Jonathan. *The Promise: President Obama, Year One*. 2010.

Alterman, Eric. *Kabuki Democracy: The System vs. Barack Obama*. 2011.

Asim, Jabari. *What Obama Means*. 2009.

Balz, Dan, and Haynes Johnson. *The Battle for America 2008: The Story of an Extraordinary Election*. 2009.

Cobb, William Jelani. *The Substance of Hope: Barack Obama and the Paradox of Progress*. 2010.

Corsi, Jerome. *The Obama Nation: Leftist Politics and the Cult of Personality*. 2008.

D'Souza, Dinesh. *The Roots of Obama's Rage*. 2010.

Dunham, S. Ann. *Surviving Against the Odds: Village Industry in Indonesia*. 2009.

Dupuis, Martin, and Keith Boeckelman. *Barack Obama: The New Face of American Politics*. 2009.

Firstbrook, Peter. *The Obamas: The Untold Story of an African Family*. 2011.

Freddoso, David. *The Case Against Barack Obama: The Unlikely Rise and Unexamined Agenda of the Media's Favorite Candidate*. 2008.

Glaberman, Stu, and Jerry Burris. *The Dream Begins: How Hawaii Shaped Barack Obama*. 2009.

Glasrud, Bruce, and Cary Wintz, eds. *African Americans and the Presidency: The Road to the White House*. 2010.

Heilemann, John, and Mark Halperin, *Game Change: Obama and the Clintons, McCain and Palin, and the Race of a Lifetime*. 2010.

Hendon, Rickey. *Black Enough/White Enough: The Obama Dilemma*. 2009.

Ifill, Gwen. *The Breakthrough: Politics and Race in the Age of Obama*. 2009.

Jacobs, Ron. *Obamaland: Who Is Barack Obama?* 2009.

Jacobs, Sally. *The Other Barack: The Bold and Reckless Life of President Obama's Father*. 2011.

Kennedy, Randall. *Persistence of the Color Line: Racial Politics and the Obama Presidency*. 2011.

Kennedy, Randall. *Sellout: The Politics of Racial Betrayal*. 2008.

Kennedy-Shaffer, Alan. *The Obama Revolution*. 2009.

Kloppenberg, James T. *Reading Obama: Dreams, Hope, and the American Political Tradition*. 2011.

Logan, Enid. *"At This Defining Moment": Barack Obama's Presidential Candidacy and the New Politics of Race*. 2011.

McClelland, Edward. *Young Mr. Obama: Chicago and the Making of a Black President*. 2010.

Mendell, David. *Obama: From Promise to Power*. 2007.

Obama, Barack. *Dreams from My Father: A Story of Race and Inheritance*. 1995.

Obama, Barack. *The Audacity of Hope: Thoughts on Reclaiming the American Dream*. 2006.

Obama, Barack. *Change We Can Believe In: Barack Obama's Plan to Renew America*. 2008.

Plouffe, David. *The Audacity to Win: The Inside Story and Lessons of Barack Obama's Historic Victory*. 2009.

Presta, John. *Mr. and Mrs. Grassroots: How Barack Obama, Two Bookstore Owners, and 300 Volunteers Did It*. 2009.

Ramos, Constance. *Our Friend Barry: Classmates' Recollections of Barack Obama and Punahou School*. 2008.

Remnick, David. *The Bridge: The Life and Rise of Barack Obama*. 2010.

Scott, Janny. *A Singular Woman: The Untold Story of Barack Obama's Mother*. 2011.

Steele, Shelby. *A Bound Man: Why We Are Excited About Obama and Why He Can't Win*. 2008.

Street, Paul. *Barack Obama and the Future of American Politics*. 2009.

Sugrue, Thomas. *Not Even Past: Barack Obama and the Burden of Race*. 2010.

Suskind, Ron. *Confidence Men: Wall Street, Washington, and the Education of a President*. 2011

Thomas, Evan. *"A Long Time Coming": The Inspiring, Combative 2008 Campaign and the Historic Election of Barack Obama*. 2009.

Todd, Chuck, and Sheldon Gawiser. *How Barack Obama Won: A State-by-State Guide to the Historic 2008 Presidential Election*. 2009.

Walker, Clarence E., and Gregory D. Smithers. *The Preacher and the Politician: Jeremiah Wright, Barack Obama, and Race in America*. 2009.

White, John Kenneth. *Barack Obama's America: How New Conceptions of Race, Family, and Religion Ended the Reagan Era*. 2009.

Wingfield, Adia Harvey, and Joe R. Feagin. *Yes We Can? White Racial Framing and the 2008 Presidential Campaign*. 2010.

Wolffe, Richard. *Renegade: The Making of a President*. 2009.

Wolffe, Richard. *Revival: The Struggle for Survival inside the Obama White House*. 2010.

Woodward, Bob. *Obama's Wars*. 2010.

Index